W9-CVW-887

For All
White-Collar Workers

The Possibilities of Radicalism in New York City's
Department Store Unions, 1934–1953

Daniel J. Opler

The Ohio State University Press
Columbus

Copyright © 2007 by The Ohio State University.
All rights reserved.

Library of Congress Cataloging-in-Publication Data

Opler, Daniel J., 1975–
  For all white-collar workers : the possibilities of radicalism in New York City's
department store unions, 1934–1953 / Daniel J. Opler.
    p. cm.
  Includes bibliographical references and index.
    ISBN 978–0–8142–1063–5 (cloth : alk. paper) — ISBN 978–0–8142–9141–
2 (CD-ROM) 1. Clerks (Retail trade)—Labor unions—Organizing—New York
(State)—History. 2. Clerks (Retail trade)—Labor unions—New York (State)—
History. 3. Labor unions—New York (State)—History. 4. Communism—United
States—History. I. Title.
  HD6515.M39065 2007
  331.88'1138114109747109044—dc22
              2007003063

Cover design by James A. Baumann
Type set in Minion Pro
Printed by Thomson-Shore

The paper used in this publication meets the minimum requirements of the
American National Standard for Information Sciences—Permanence of Paper
for Printed Library Materials. ANSI Z39.48–1992.
9 8 7 6 5 4 3 2 1

Contents

Illustrations

Acknowledgments

I have had the great pleasure and the good luck to work with many talented people during the course of writing this study. My first thanks must go to the historical actors in this study, many of whom were kind enough to spend hours sharing their recollections of the department store unions with me. In this regard, I must especially thank Anne Haicken, Blanche Mendelssohn, Ruth Papa, Ruth Pinkson, Gertrude Reiss, Annette Rubinstein, and Jane Spadavecchio. It was my distinct pleasure to be able to record a few of their accomplishments in this book.

As always in a historical study, archivists played a key role in my work. At the Tamiment Library, I must thank the entire staff, every one of whom has contributed to this study in numerous ways. Especially appreciated was Erika Gottfried's assistance in tracking down illustrations. Archivists at the Museum of the City of New York, especially Marguerite Lavin, also provided assistance in my search for material on Union Square and 34th Street. I must also extend my deepest thanks to Joe Turrini for both informing me about and providing access to the Catholic University of America's excellent materials on the RWDSU, and to the late Debra Bernhardt, who not only created many of the oral history interviews that I use in this study, but also told me about the existence of the oral histories and the various collections that addressed the unions.

A number of scholars deserve thanks for their help. Joshua Freeman first recommended department store unions when I was an undergraduate seeking a subject for a research paper. Elaine Abelson at the New School was constantly encouraging and helpful during my stint as her research assistant. Lotte Larsen, Dan Bender, and Shannon Jackson all chaired panels where I presented material that made its way into this manuscript, and all three had important comments that eventually served to enrich this study. While I was at New York University, Tom Bender, Adam Green, Atina Grossman, Walter Johnson, and Ann Pellegrini all read and commented on material from the dissertation version of this study. Most importantly, Molly Nolan and Robin Kelley deserve extensive thanks for their advice and assistance throughout the dissertation process. Both of them contributed materially to this book. Finally, the two anonymous readers for The Ohio State University Press also offered important and valuable critiques.

While I was writing this study of American unions, it was my good luck that teaching and research assistants at NYU formed a union of their own, affording me a first-hand look at the practice and pitfalls of organized labor in America. I must thank all those who were and are involved with GSOC, many of whom—especially Derek Musgrove—had insights that enriched my own understanding of unionism.

While writing, I also taught at several schools, most recently at the College of Mount Saint Vincent. Colleagues at all the places I've taught have had plenty of encouraging words and helpful advice over the last few years, especially Heather Alumbaugh, David Gallo, Dave Kinkela, Claire Nolte, and Steve Tischler. I must also extend my very deepest thanks to my students, who repeatedly convinced me that the work that went into this project was balanced out by the joy of sharing a classroom with such extraordinary individuals.

My parents, Lewis and Annette, and my siblings, Mark, Michelle, and Douglas, all provided more support than I could have imagined or expected; thanks are due also to new family members Paul Grennan and Stacy Liechti. My grandmother, Charlotte Sagoff, read the early works that turned into this study, and patiently shared plenty of advice and criticism; her insights are greatly appreciated, as are her support and love.

Many grad students and recent Ph.D.'s also read and commented on parts of this manuscript. Special thanks on this account are due to Andrea Siegel, Laura Helton, and Donna Truglio Haverty-Stacke. In addition, Mark Noonan, Paul Naish, and my other fellow editors of the *Columbia Journal of American Studies* also provided important support and encouragement. Finally, Sandy Crooms and other editors at The Ohio State University Press were extremely helpful in transforming the dissertation into a publishable manuscript.

Four people contributed so much to this project that I have to single them out individually and at some length. As I was writing and becoming involved with GSOC, it was my great good fortune to become friends with Kimberly Quinn Johnson. A full-time union organizer for several years, Kimberly taught me by example of the complex tasks and contradictions that organizers confront.

Her experiences with the labor movement greatly enriched my understanding of the movement's history, and I thank her for sharing them.

Few people have contributed as much to the final shape of the manuscript as Jeannette Gabriel. Jeannette, whose important research on the Workers Alliance is gradually reshaping our understanding of the Depression, kindly read through the first few chapters of the manuscript, and her advice allowed me to restructure much of the material on the Depression, especially on chapter 3. Her advice and support in all things have been tremendous, and this publication likely would not exist without her help.

My dissertation advisor, Danny Walkowitz, has been at all times and in many different ways a role model. I cannot imagine that I would have gotten through graduate school, let alone the arduous process of job hunting, without his assistance and advice. Danny's sharp criticism and keen understanding of history; his ability to see exactly where my work was going off-course and suggest ways to correct it; his support in job searches; his advice on teaching style; his willingness to read and reread a seemingly endless stream of dissertation drafts; and his attention to detail, wording, and argument all contributed materially to this project as well as my development as a historian. I could not have wished for a finer advisor, and cannot thank him enough.

Finally, I must thank Tami J. Friedman, my friend, walking partner, fellow labor historian, sometime mentor, and sounding board for much of this study. Ever since she was my teaching assistant at Columbia all those years ago, Tami has been ready to read any passage that was giving me trouble, to give advice about research methods, to remind me of the need to be patient with all the pieces of the profession, and to provide at least as much advice about other aspects of my life. More than that, she always seemed so absolutely certain of me—certain that I would finish the dissertation, that I would transform it into a manuscript, that I would get a teaching job. That sort of faith is always welcome, and often necessary in working on a project that lasts as many years as this one did. It is, indeed, that sort of faith that allows projects of this magnitude to come to completion. And it is that sort of faith which I feel particularly honored, in having finished this project at long last, to have justified.

Introduction

1.

When the factories moved away from the industrial centers of the North, American labor unions became mere shadows of the mass organizations they had once been. Unionization rates in America in 2004 were at 12.5 percent, the lowest they have been since the 1920s. According to the U.S. government's Bureau of Labor Statistics, labor unions have been in decline for at least the past twenty years, and arguably for many years more.[1]

This decline was not an inevitable result of deindustrialization. Had the labor movement established a strong base in the retail and service industries, it is possible that labor unions would continue to play a central role in American public life. Yet in the retail and service sectors, unions have been noticeably ineffective. In the retail industry today, unionization rates hover around 3.6 percent, as opposed to approximately 12.9 percent in the remaining manufacturing jobs and 14 percent in the construction industry.[2]

This study seeks to explain the weakness of the American labor movement by explaining why labor failed to organize service-industry workers, particularly retail workers. As a way to better understand this failure, the study begins during the Great Depression, at the founding of the modern labor movement, when powerful and permanent retail workers' unions seemed a real possibility. In 1930s New York, organizers seemed to be realizing this possibility, and the managers of the largest and most famous stores in the country recognized the unions. The study then looks at the ways in which economic, social, cultural, and political developments of the 1940s and early 1950s forced retail workers' unions into decline, and permanently weakened the American labor movement.

In the mid 1930s, even as union organizers began to take seriously the possibilities of mass unions of unskilled workers in the great factory towns of the Midwest, they all but ignored the thousands of workers, skilled and unskilled

1

alike, in retail stores. There were several reasons for this oversight on the part
of 1930s union organizers: most important among them, the retail labor force
was largely made up of women, and they simply did not fit 1930s understandings of what a worker was. The very concept of a "white-collar worker," a
worker from outside manufacturing or construction, was a radical concept
at the time. Indeed, in New York City radical union organizers, associated
with the Communist party, were the ones to realize that white-collar workers
represented an important part of the working class and could form successful unions. As a result, union organizers affiliated with the Communist Trade
Union Unity League set up unions in the city's department stores in the mid-
1930s.[3]

There are many reasons that Communists made for such effective union
organizers in the retail industry, besides their insight that white-collar workers were, in fact, workers. Perhaps the most important advantage Communists
had was their link to a larger radical movement, one that included unemployed
people as well as workers in many industries besides retailing. This mass
movement was critical for workers in retail stores who wished to form unions.
A strike at a New York City department store, when led by Communists, could
gain support from Communists throughout the city. In the 1930s and early
1940s communism functioned as a remarkable network which allowed strikers to call upon a large and diverse group of allies in their battles against store
managers.

Additionally, Communists were successful partially because they had a
broader conception from the beginning of the rise of the retail workers' unions
of what a strike could be. To Communists, strikes could be ways to claim public space, and on more than one occasion in the unions' history, workers under
Communist leadership lay claim to the stores and the streets surrounding the
stores. In areas like Union Square, Brooklyn's Fulton Street, and Manhattan's
garment district, areas which were already difficult for managers to control,
Communists' willingness to challenge that control still further made them
formidable opponents indeed.

Finally, Communists were relatively supportive of working-class militancy.
By the late 1930s anti-Communist organizers frequently attempted to restrain
workers who were willing to strike, but, with the critical exception of the
World War II period, Communists were more willing to support workers'
strikes. As late as September of 1941, Communists in the department store
unions demonstrated their support for workers' militancy, despite less radical union leaders' emphasis on concession and compromise. And in the late
1940s, when Communists found themselves increasingly on the defensive,

they were still able to find support from the workers they led, by emphasizing their belief in workers' ability to lead the union at the precise moment when non-Communist union leaders were becoming less tolerant of workers taking initiative in their struggles against management.

These factors made Communists powerful leaders for retail workers in New York City. Communists were virtually unchallenged in their efforts to organize unions in New York City's department stores, and by the late 1930s most of the major stores in New York City had Communist-led unions: stores such as Gimbel's, Bloomingdale's, Stern's, Loeser's, and Hearn's all had unions led by Communists. At Macy's, Communists played a key but supporting role in a union led primarily by liberal non-Communists.

None of this is to say that Communists were ever ideal union leaders. As other historians have pointed out, communism was, in many respects, a top-down movement. Its leaders could be remarkably racist, sexist, and short sighted, and Communist union organizers made serious policy mistakes throughout the unions' history, most important among them their failure to adequately challenge racial hiring practices. But in the 1930s they were the only ones who recognized that these department store workers' unions needed to be formed. As a result, for all their faults, they played a critical role in these unions' successes.

This study also addresses anti-communism, one of the most important forces behind the failure of American unions in the retail sector. Anti-Communists in the late 1940s and early 1950s forced organizers in the department store unions to take a far more defensive position at the precise moment that store managers weakened the unions by restructuring the retail industry and cutting thousands of jobs. Eventually, union organizers capitulated entirely to the demands of anti-Communists, distancing themselves greatly from the militant labor movement of the 1930s and 1940s.

In the process of this examination, this study argues that some aspects of anti-communism have been underexplored by historians. In particular, it calls for a reexamination of the Taft-Hartley Act, which among other things required all union leaders to declare themselves non-Communists. I argue that this development not only made it impossible for Communists to lead unions; it also made it impossible for non-Communist and Communist union leaders to work together without acknowledging the political differences between them. In the CIO's retail union, the Retail Wholesale and Department Store Union (RWDSU), union leaders were virtually silent on the issue of communism between the union's founding in 1937 and its disintegration in 1948. This tacit agreement not to use the word "Communist" within the retail union was critical for the union's survival, since the national leaders of the union were anti-Communists and the leaders of some of the largest locals were Communists. However, when it was finally apparent that Taft-Hartley would not be overturned, RWDSU leaders could no longer ignore the issue of communism; their attempt to confront this issue split the RWDSU and led to disaster for the future of retail unionism in America.

As other historical studies have done in recent years, this study argues that the history of communism and anti-communism must be placed firmly within a local context. Communist organizers in the department store unions were far more affected by the Great Depression, working conditions in the stores, events in the streets surrounding the stores, the changing role of the federal government, and postwar suburbanization than they were by any policies coming out of the Soviet Union. To say otherwise—to treat American Communists, as some historians have, as mindless drones who took orders directly from the Comintern—is to dilute their politics and to fail to realize the possibilities inherent in the Communist-led union of department store workers.

Adopting a local context for communism requires historians to address the question of how and when Communist party (CP) policies affected activists within local struggles. These policies, I acknowledge, did affect Communists, but far more important than acknowledging the power of CP policies is understanding why Party members or fellow travelers followed these policies. In New York City's department stores, Communist union organizers sought alliances with non-Communists in the 1930s and early 1940s not because the Comintern called for such policies (at least at some points during these years), but instead because such a policy was a powerful organizing strategy. At the same time, in the late 1940s, as the CP retreated from any sort of united front with liberals, Communist union organizers in New York City's department stores found themselves isolated primarily because of anti-Communist attacks from the right, not simply because they chose to follow CP policy. Understanding why and how union organizers changed tactics requires far more attention to local conditions than to events or declarations taking place in the USSR.

Adopting a local context for the history of communism also requires historians to determine what constitutes a local context. Here, too, this study makes contributions in addressing the importance of the middle class, contests over public space, and the changing nature of consumption in the history of these unions. Anti-Communists began their most extensive attacks precisely in the years when suburbanization and the rise of the middle class were severely affecting retailing in general and upscale department stores in particular. As historians have long realized, these developments were closely linked to new patterns of consumption. In this study, I argue that these new patterns of consumption were visible not only in the consumer goods furnishing middle-class suburban homes, but also in a rapidly changing environment within the stores, in part created to better serve middle-class customers. Self-service shopping, which sprung up throughout New York City stores in the early 1950s, allowed managers to increase their control and cut their labor costs, permanently weakening the unions. And the closing of some stores whose managers were unable or unwilling to adjust quickly enough to the new retailing environment left the unions even more vulnerable to anti-Communist attacks.

By focusing on the role of communism in the history of these unions, this study addresses the history of department store workers in America in a very different way than scholars have previously done. Other studies, most importantly Susan Porter Benson's landmark *Counter Cultures*, describe in rich detail the history of worker-management relations in the department stores, although without addressing the unions formed within these stores. In this study, I move beyond the somewhat self-contained department stores that dominated Benson's excellent study, to place these stores within a much larger and more complicated historical framework. This study takes into account processes that affected the stores and unions directly, like suburbanization and the rise of anti-communism. It also looks at the changing nature of the streets outside the stores, streets that were dominated by radical protests and strikes in the 1930s, but rapidly became far less important sites of militant activism in the 1940s and 1950s. Finally, this study looks at larger historical events like the Great Depression and World War II from the vantage point of the stores and the unions.[4]

While this study moves away from previous studies of department store work and workers in placing greater emphasis on context, it retains the focus on women's history established by many of the scholars on the history of department stores. Women played a number of key roles in the history of New York City's department store unions. They represented, first of all, many of the workers organized within these unions. Second, especially in the early years of the unions' history, some of the most important union leaders were women, largely due to Communists' willingness to recruit women as union organizers. Finally, women played key roles in the unions' history as store customers. Unlike Benson, however, I argue that there was seldom if ever any consciousness of shared femininity between store customers and store workers, especially in the upscale stores where the unions were most successful. Instead, I argue that in the 1930s store workers found themselves in a highly antagonistic relationship with customers. Partially as a result of this antagonistic relationship between department store workers and their wealthy customers, department store workers got the chance to prove that they shared the negative assumptions about upper-class women that were widespread in this era. During their sit-down strikes at Woolworth's and, later, during their more conventional strike at Gimbel's, women working in the department stores proved that they were as hostile to upper-class women as were any of their male counterparts.[5]

Women played key roles in the department store unions throughout the unions' history, but these roles were less pronounced in the late 1940s and early 1950s. Even in these years, union members continued to hold discussions about gender equality and gender relations at union meetings and in the union newspaper. At the same time, by the late 1940s, union leaders openly began supporting the male breadwinner norm, something that had not been the case a decade earlier. By the 1950s, as the unions shifted towards a more conservative political stance, union leaders also supported a more conservative set of gendered assumptions, whether through cheesecake photographs in the union newspaper or fighting for the rights of "breadwinners and heads of families" to take the best-paying jobs.

Finally, this study uses the history of these unions as a way of addressing the history of white-collar workers in America. Particularly in the 1930s, as organizers in the department store unions made their most important gains, the term "white collar worker" had tremendous importance for the unions' history. During strikes in these years, department store workers actively employed a rhetoric that identified white-collar workers as members of the working class. This rhetoric allowed department store workers on strike to mobilize allies ranging from low-paid office workers to actors, writers, chemists, and doctors. By the late 1930s, however, as these unions entered the CIO, they ceased discussing the specialized nature of white-collar work and white-collar workers in favor of analyses that placed greater emphasis on the shared concerns of all working-class people. Within just a few years, people who had once called themselves "white-collar workers" began thinking of themselves as members of the middle class, and eschewed the sort of alliances with strikers that once gave the unions such power.

The connections between the history of white-collar workers and the history of the department store unions consists of far more than the history of the term "white collar worker" or the changing nature of the middle class. This study addresses the critical issue of when, how, and why white-collar workers became a minor part of the American labor movement. As already suggested, today such workers represent a tiny minority of union members. Statistics demonstrate that this weakness is rooted in the 1930s, 1940s, and 1950s. According to a study of American union membership between 1939 and 1953, the percentage of unionized workers in the service sector (including retailing) grew only slightly in these years, from 6 percent in 1939 to 9.5 percent in 1953. In the textile industry, the only sector of the manufacturing industry with similarly low rates of unionization in the late 1930s, unions grew tremendously in the same period, moving from 7 percent unionized workers in 1939 to 26.7 percent unionized workers in 1953. The numbers for the entire manufacturing industry are even more striking; in the same time period, from 1939 to 1953, the percentage of unionized workers in the manufacturing industries went from 22.8 percent in 1939 to 42.4 percent, a far larger growth both in actual numbers and in percentages.[6]

As these figures demonstrate, the growth in retail unions between 1939 and 1953 did not have anywhere near the success of the unionization drives in even the least unionized sectors of the manufacturing industries. By 1953, the year this study ends, the possibilities that had been so evident in New York City in the 1930s had disappeared. Divided around the issue of communism, facing managers' restructuring, suburbanization, and an extremely hostile government, department store union organizers in New York City were struggling to retain those unions that already existed. Fighting this struggle gave union organizers no chance to match the rapid expansion of retailing in post–World War II America.

2.

In recent decades, historians looking at blue-collar workers have discussed the concept of the radical possibilities of the 1930s at great length. In doing so, they have come to critical realizations about this decade. In particular, they have called for bottom-up histories of both American communism and American unions, trends this study seeks to continue.

In the early 1970s a group of labor historians made the changing nature of unions a central concern of American labor history. Using blue-collar workers and their unions as examples, these labor historians argued that unions began as powerful organizations created and controlled by the working class in the early and mid-1930s. During the mid- and late 1930s, these historians argued, paid CIO organizers and CIO leaders stepped in and took over the grassroots labor movement, and finally stamped out most workers' dissent in their enforcement of the no-strike pledge during World War II.[7]

At the very moment that labor historians were reshaping their field, other historians were also examining the history of American communism in a new light. By the 1970s and especially the 1980s many historians of communism argued that Communists had not been the sinister manipulators of the labor movement that consensus school historians had claimed. Instead, these new historians argued, Communists' role in the labor movement had been far more complex. Communists had served as among the most dedicated union organizers, who fought tirelessly for workers' rights, especially in the 1930s.[8]

Increasingly in the 1980s and early 1990s historians portrayed Communist union organizers as far more dictatorial and separated from the rank and file. By 1982, Nelson Lichtenstein was able to argue in *Labor's War at Home* that Communists' willingness to support the World War II no-strike pledge was tantamount to a betrayal of the working class, very similar to other labor leaders' betrayal in the same era. By the mid-1990s George Lipsitz, in *Rainbow at Midnight,* took this argument one step further, arguing that the very concept of the Communist party as the workers' vanguard was destined to separate them from those militant workers who were not willing to be led by Communists. These historians asserted that Communist union leaders, like non-Communist union leaders, benefited from workers' willingness to strike and resist in the 1930s, but then stamped out that militancy in the 1940s.[9]

This study seeks to address the issues raised by these historians, most importantly the subject of the missed opportunities of the 1930s. Staughton Lynd correctly called workers' successes in the 1930s a demonstration of the possibilities of radicalism, a phrase with echoes in nearly every study of the 1930s published since. This study points to one of these possibilities—the possibility for unions in the retail sector—that was even less realized than the possibilities of unionism in the factories that Lynd and his followers examined. To explain why these possibilities existed in the first place, I draw heavily upon the work of historians who have studied 1930s communism as, in part, a gender system. As these gender historians have argued, many Communists shared similar gendered assumptions: in particular, many strongly emphasized the masculine nature of working-class radicalism. While in the early 1930s, Communists did see important possibilities for women to play key roles in community-based organizing in particular, by the late 1930s, according to historians like Elizabeth Faue and Van Gosse, Communists argued that men were the fundamental agents of the working class.[10]

As these historians make clear, there was a great deal of complexity in Communists' understandings of gender. Communists did, as Faue especially has pointed out, associate bourgeois femininity with corruption and workers' oppression. At the same time, many Communists recognized the important role of working-class women in class struggle. Most importantly, in the early and mid-1930s Communists supported women workers' unions in ways that many more conservative union organizers did not. Unlike the far more conservative organizers in the American Federation of Labor (AFL), Communist union organizers were willing to go into department stores to aid women workers in their struggle to form unions.

This study also addresses some of the themes that Lichtenstein and Lipsitz address, namely, the relationship between Communist union organizers and workers. Unlike Lichtenstein and Lipsitz, however, both of whom focus on blue-collar workers, there is no evidence in the department store unions' history that Communists were at odds with the most militant workers in the unions. While in the late 1940s a few workers did form anti-Communist blocs within the unions, the anti-Communists represented a tiny and isolated minority within the department store unions in the 1940s. Most members, as demonstrated by the union elections of the late 1940s, continued to support union leaders' right to hold political beliefs contrary to the beliefs of most workers, and there is no record of any workers in these unions calling for wildcat strikes or rejecting the no-strike pledge.

Rank-and-file anti-communism in the department store unions was a result not of Communists' errors but of changing economic circumstances in the late 1940s and early 1950s. As suburbanization and restructuring continued, managers laid off workers; Communist union leaders could not prevent this. The end result was that by 1953 the rank and file was constantly criticizing union leaders' political views, demanding that union leaders recant their radical politics and concentrate more on the bread-and-butter issues workers had to confront. The union leaders, to their credit, followed suit, but this did nothing to help them combat managers' efforts to restructure the stores, efforts that eventually required fewer workers with fewer skills. The powerful coalitions that had formed around communism during the 1930s would never again reemerge, and the union leaders would find themselves and their membership increasingly isolated and unable to meet the challenge of the structural changes in retailing during the 1950s.

3.

Chapter 1 describes the first major strikes in the department stores of New York City, the Klein's-Ohrbach's strikes that took place in New York City's Union Square in 1934–35. Both Union Square and the stores were highly contested spaces at the time. Communists in the streets of Union Square repeatedly tried to make the square their own, while police and local business managers (including store managers) worked to contest Communists' efforts. While these parties struggled over the space in and around Union Square, a related struggle took place over the buildings on the square's southern border, the Klein's and Ohrbach's stores. Store managers found themselves constantly struggling to control working-class consumption, to prevent shoplifting and overcrowding. As these struggles raged, workers at the Klein's and Ohrbach's stores, many of them women, went on strike demanding union recognition. With support from Communist organizers in the Trade Union Unity League, the workers at Klein's and Ohrbach's were able to launch a dramatic and militant attack on the owners and managers of these stores in strikes that lasted for almost six months. At the end of these strikes, workers were able to declare a partial victory, after which department store workers throughout New York City began organizing unions within their stores.

Chapter 2 discusses the next three years of the unions' history, from 1935–37. In these years the Communists leading the department store unions sought greater legitimacy by uniting with the AFL's Retail Clerks International Protection Association (RCIPA). They also led two militant although not very successful strikes in 1935 and 1936. During these strikes Communists found themselves increasingly at odds with the corrupt anti-Communist leaders of the RCIPA, who shut down one of these strikes while condemning the settlement in another. In 1937 workers won their first major victories, in the sitdown strikes at Woolworth's and other five-and-dime stores. In these strikes, department store workers firmly established themselves as an integral part of the American labor movement. They adopted the same tactics and made many of the same demands as other workers in the fledgling industrial union movement that would result in the CIO. Late in 1937 the department stores' successful job actions forced CIO leaders to recognize the existence of retail workers, leading to the creation of the CIO's retail workers' union, the United Retail Employees of America.

Chapter 3 discusses the ways in which workers created unions at New York City's upscale 34th Street department stores in the later 1930s. Far more than in the downscale stores, workers' successes in these upscale establishments resulted in the creation of permanent union locals. Workers faced significant challenges in creating these unions. At stores like Macy's, Bloomingdale's, and Gimbel's, workers found themselves in a highly antagonistic relationship with customers, due largely to the system of consumption practiced at these stores. In part seeking protection from customers, workers joined the union, some of them even leaving the store to become permanent and full-time union organizers. By the late 1930s, 34th Street store managers, seeking a way to gain control of their increasingly restive workforce in a neighborhood constantly beset by street protests and strikes, accepted the union as one possible way to stabilize their situation. But the local leaders had other ideas, as the unions became an integral part of the anti-Fascist Popular Front formed in the late 1930s, gaining numerous powerful allies in the city's radical movement. By 1941, with these allies' support, workers at the 34th Street stores won the eight-hour day and the forty-hour week for retail workers throughout New York City.

Chapter 4 addresses the department stores and unions during World War II, when everything that had once guaranteed the union success began to disappear. The radical protests that had once dominated the streets around the stores now disappeared in favor of patriotic parades. Meanwhile, store managers began to use the stores in order to further the war effort, gaining the support of the government and the public in the process. National union leaders also found themselves increasingly in the government's good graces, winning support for their strike against Montgomery Ward after managers there refused to grant the closed shop. For the Communists in the department store unions, the newfound strength of managers and national union leaders was a constant and unanswerable threat. The threat was made all the more serious by managers' early efforts at restructuring the stores in an effort to deal with wartime labor shortages. Additionally, Communists' strong support for the no-strike pledge and their conflict with national leaders led to their condemnation of the government-approved Montgomery Ward strike, damaging their relationship with the national union leaders still further. By the end of World War II, the Communists in the department store unions found themselves isolated, with less power in the national union than ever before.

Chapter 5 addresses the immediate postwar era in the department store unions' history. In the critical period between 1946 and 1948, local and national union leaders came to an unstated agreement about what their respective roles would be within the union. The local department store union leaders gave up on any control over the national union's policies, while national union leaders allowed the local leaders greater autonomy in the running of the local unions. This compromise did little to meet the challenges department store workers faced in the postwar era. Managers, continuing their wartime efforts at restructuring the stores, now began laying off workers in record numbers and opening branch stores in the outer boroughs and in the suburbs to appeal to the increasing numbers of suburban residents. As the layoffs mounted, the U.S. government put the Taft-Hartley Act into effect, requiring all union

officials to declare themselves non-Communists, something the local leaders could not do. By 1948 local leaders' refusal to declare their opposition
to communism attracted national attention. The leaders of New York City's
department store unions were called to testify in a set of HUAC hearings
on communism in New York City's retail trade. Shortly after the hearings
concluded—and after several of the leaders of these unions pleaded the Fifth
Amendment and refused to answer questions about their political beliefs—the
national union leaders purged the department store locals from the CIO,
establishing dual unions to compete with the Communist-led department
store locals.

Chapter 6 looks at union organizers' efforts to continue to lead and even
expand the retail unions at the height of the McCarthy period, from 1948 to
1953. In these years Communist union organizers found themselves struggling with the simple tasks of retaining their leadership of the union while
staying out of jail. Meanwhile, in response to the rising numbers of middle-
class consumers as well as the rise of national brands and a desire to cut costs,
managers began even more radical reconstruction of the stores, instituting
self-service retailing, laying off still more workers, and closing some stores.
With organizers struggling to stay out of jail and workers losing their jobs by
the thousands, union members increasingly demanded that the union leaders move to the right politically. By the spring of 1953 the department store
unions had passed resolutions condemning communism as an anti-demo-
cratic movement. In condemning communism as a grave danger to American
democracy, the union leaders gained a degree of legitimacy, but they also lost
the ability to challenge decisions made by the anti-Communist state without
being accused of being Communists. This became critically important during
the Hearn's strike of 1953, when workers went on their first strike to challenge
managers' right to restructure the stores. When a court granted Hearn's managers an anti-strike injunction, strikers and union leaders, still determined to
prove their loyalty, strictly abided by the injunction. This decision effectively
deprived union organizers of the ability to challenge managers' restructuring
programs, bringing an end to the possibilities represented by the powerful
union of department store workers in New York City.

CHAPTER 1

Foundations, 1934–35

Introduction

Class determined where and how people shopped in New York City during the Great Depression. Wealthy consumers went to the upscale stores on Fifth Avenue, or to the great department stores on 34th Street, making their purchases amidst elegant surroundings. Working-class people had their own less elegant shopping districts, both in the city's outer boroughs and around Union Square, on Manhattan's 14th Street. 14th Street featured a number of working-class stores, and two of the most important, Klein's and Ohrbach's, were right on the square.

Union Square was a site of radical protest as well as working-class consumption throughout the 1930s. Both local business managers and Communists attempted to claim the square, putting up signs and staging dramatic pageants in order to attract the attention and support of working-class people within the square. These practices became extremely important when workers at Klein's and Ohrbach's declared themselves on strike, and set about creating a strike replete with signs and pageantry.

Like Union Square, the stores were contested spaces even before the strikes began. In downscale stores like Klein's and Ohrbach's, customers and managers found themselves at odds. Managers attempted to control customers' behavior very carefully, trying to force customers to behave in an orderly and legal way while making purchases. Customers fiercely resisted managerial control, crowding exits and shoplifting whenever they could. Although store managers tried to prevent this practice, they were unable to do so, and both businesses lost large sums of money to shoplifters each year.

Within these contested spaces, Klein's and Ohrbach's workers were highly exploited. Their salaries were some of the lowest offered in the city, and throughout the early years of the Depression, workers at these stores put in longer hours for less pay. Additionally, workers at these stores had no unions, largely because they were far removed from the concept of organizable workers as defined by the American Federation of Labor (AFL), the largest and most powerful union at the time. In 1934, however, these workers found that the Communists organizing protests in the streets outside the stores were willing to lead unions of white-collar women workers. As a result, workers at these stores joined the Communist-led Office Workers Union (OWU).

As part of this union, workers at Klein's and Ohrbach's were able to manipulate the rhetoric of class in order to take advantage of the contested public spaces in which they worked. In particular, workers and union organizers proclaimed the importance of their struggle for white-collar workers, and created a coalition of chemists, doctors, actors, writers, and office workers to support the strike. With the help of these white-collar workers, the strikers successfully challenged managers' control over both the stores and over Union Square, forcing managers to settle the strike and establishing Communists' role as leaders in the struggle to organize New York City's department store unions.

The Contested Square

The Great Depression was a nightmare for working-class people in New York City. "You can't possibly understand it if you didn't live through it," a working-class Bronx resident named Ruth Papa said in describing the city at the time. Papa's father—a self-educated worker in a shoe factory—had constantly searched for a job during the early years of the Depression, and attempted everything from running a push-cart to shoveling snow, with little success. Papa's mother and two older sisters, as well as Papa herself, took up housework to try to make ends meet, but the family was still barely surviving; eventually, both Papa and her older sister found jobs, and the family's financial crisis eased slightly. Papa remembered a near-constant fear of dispossession throughout the Depression, however, and remembered on more than one occasion having to use candles after not being able to pay the electric bill. Papa's family's experiences of poverty and unemployment were mirrored by many other New Yorkers during the Depression. Throughout New York City, working-class people, many of them immigrants or children of immigrants, struggled with unemployment and near-starvation during these years. Many lost their homes, moving into temporary shelters, but shelter managers had to turn away still more homeless men and women.[1]

The homeless victims of the Depression sometimes found shelter within the city parks, among them Union Square Park, an empty space of approximately three square blocks just north of Greenwich Village. One homeless man described sleeping in the park as a grueling experience: "Sleeping in the parks was much less satisfactory [than sleeping in subway cars]. Tired, hungry, and cold, stretched out on the bench . . . I was awakened by a patrolman who had swung his nightstick sharply against the soles of my feet, sending an indescribable electric pain through my hunger-racked body." Despite the misery this man associated with sleeping in the parks, homeless people continued to frequent Union Square Park throughout the early years of the Depression.[2]

While the rise in unemployment led homeless people to set up residence in Union Square, the related revitalization of the city's radical movement made the square a center of American radicalism. Communists and other radicals filled Union Square during the early years of the Depression, making Union Square what historian and journalist Matthew Josephson described as "New York's Red Square . . . the very vortex of revolutionary activities" in New York City. Josephson went on to describe his memories of a visit to Union Square in the early 1930s: "Soapboxers were going on in routine fashion: 'Garbage! That's what the bosses give the American workers,' one of them shouted suddenly. His small audience responded with a roar of laughter, some of them waving placards with slogans such as 'Jobs—Not Charity.'" While Josephson describes the audience as fairly passive, other observers disagreed. In the late 1930s, Federal Writers Project interviewers writing about these same soapbox speakers claimed that the audience frequently gathered not only to listen to the various speakers, but to argue with other listeners or even with the speakers themselves about the issues being discussed. One WPA worker, writing a few years after Josephson, described the square as the site of long debates, a "diminutive Hyde Park."[3]

The lengthy political debates extended to buildings around the square's border. A few small cafeterias lined Union Square, and one working-class woman who frequented them when she was young remembered that it was in those cafeterias that she had learned about literature and politics, primarily from other people her own age. Young people would sit in the cafeterias for hours, talking about unions, class struggle, and racism, among a variety of other subjects. Like the soapbox speakers in the square, working-class people used the cafeterias as spaces to debate and discuss a wide range of issues.[4]

Like the soapbox speakers and the cafeterias, political rallies in Union Square also allowed working-class people to express their opinions on political issues. Drawing on a century-long tradition of political protest in Union Square, Communists and other radicals staged rallies in the square nearly every week in the early 1930s, around issues ranging from the wrongful arrest

a.

b.

Figure 1 (a.–d.)
Protest in Union Square, probably in 1934. Outside the Klein's and Ohrbach's stores, the protests in the Square were large and militant and occasionally resulted in violence. Thus, any strike at those stores was a potentially serious situation for managers,

c.

d.

especially if, as happened in 1934 and 1935, the union was led by the Communist party, which also led many of the unemployed protests taking place in the Square. (Courtesy of Milstein Division of United States History, Local History & Genealogy, The New York Public Library, Astor, Lenox and Tilden Foundations) of the Scottsboro Boys to unemployment relief. Any of these protests could end in violence. Albert Halper, a novelist who lived just off Union Square at the time, later remembered that "there were weekly left-wing parades which frequently ended with clubbings by the police. On Saturday mornings, I could see the mounted cops in the side streets, bunched together, resting, healthy faced, chatting cheerfully before the afternoon's action."[5]

Other working-class people—particularly women—came to the square to shop in the numerous stores that lined its southern border. Here, too, the Depression affected people's presence within Union Square, as women in particular responded to the Depression by being more careful with their spending habits, and by bargain-hunting at the discount stores bordering on the square. As a result, Samuel Klein, the owner and manager of Klein's, one of the most important downscale stores in New York City at the time, was one of the few business owners who actually saw an increase in profits during the Depression. In addition to these indoor establishments, street peddlers selling food and other goods filled the southern end of the square. Combined with the easy access to the square by public transportation, these stores made Union Square "the place where we came to shop," as one working-class woman remembered it.[6]

People who owned buildings around Union Square were very aware of the crowd's presence, and many attempted to control the crowd's activities by putting up signs. On the southern side of the square, Samuel Klein put huge signs in his store's windows advising customers of the "tremendous values in fur coats" and reminding them that customers had a right to their "money back within five days." Even the water tank, standing up above the rest of the building, carried with it the name of the firm, "Klein's." On the northwest corner of the square stood another building, also covered in signs. These signs, however, called for viewers to "Fight Police Terror, Unemployment, and War Preparations!" They called "for Defense of the Soviet Union!" and for the struggle of "class against class!" This building was the headquarters of the *Daily Worker,* the official newspaper of the Communist party of the United States (CP). The signs on both buildings illustrate the building owners' determination to gain the support of the people who passed through Union Square Park.[7]

Both store owners and Communists used pageantry as well as signs to attract the attention of the crowds that filled Union Square. The Communists staged many of the weekly protests which took place in Union Square during this era, as well as what was probably the largest protest in New York City during the Great Depression, the International Unemployment Day protest of March 6, 1930. As a reporter for the *Daily Worker* described the proceedings, during this protest 100,000 people gathered in Union Square to hear speeches calling for "immediate relief for the jobless from the funds of the city treasury and from taxes on the wealthy exploiters, for unemployment insurance paid for by the employers and administered by committees of the workers and unemployed, and for the seven-hour day and the five-day week." The speakers—most of them CP officials—called on the huge crowd to elect a committee to take their demands to City Hall. The crowd roared back at the podium, apparently in agreement, and eventually a number of CP officials volunteered to serve as the Workers' Committee. However, when the protesters attempted to follow the committee to City Hall, the square became the site of a bloody battle. Police emerged, many with nightsticks, many on horseback. In order to prevent what they perceived as the beginnings of a riotous attack on City Hall, the police began beating those protesters who were attempting to march south. Most of the crowd fled in the confusion; police arrested those who did not escape quickly enough.[8]

International Unemployment Day and the smaller protests that frequently took place in Union Square served several functions. First, these protests allowed workers to express their political views; in this respect they were similar to the soapbox speakers and the cafeterias which lined the square. Second, Communist-led protests generally presented Communists as the leaders of the working class. At the International Unemployment Day protest, the Workers' Committee, made up of Communists, was supposed to represent the city's workers, although most workers in New York City would hardly have accepted this representation. Finally, protests in Union Square allowed the Communists an opportunity to lay claim to Union Square as their space, to force Josephson and other observers to acknowledge that it was a "Red Square."

Like the Communists, business owners and managers operating in the square also found political demonstrations useful tools with which to exert control over Union Square and to challenge Communists' control over the square. To this end, the city government and local business owners and managers cooperated to organize the Union Square Centennial Celebration on April 23, 1932. Local business owners and managers used this celebration as a lightly veiled challenge to the Communists' control over Union Square. The celebration began, for instance, with a large and very well-publicized "Americanization meeting," which featured former governor and Democratic presidential candidate Alfred E. Smith giving a speech on equality. Aware of the significance of Union Square for Communists and others who attacked ruling-class privilege, Smith opened his speech by stating that in America "there is no such thing as a ruling class, though that phrase is often used to arouse passion."[9]

The celebration organizers powerfully illustrated their claim to Union Square as a public space for anti-communism through the actions of the police on the day of the celebration. As the *New York Times* described their participation, the police presented an "exhibition drill by a company of the Police Rifle Regiment in riot drill and formation," which ended in "a bayonet charge into a mythical [rioting] crowd." This bayonet charge, taking place as it did at the site of so many actual confrontations between police and Communist-led protestors, could hardly be described as anything but a threat to the Communists, and a challenge to their continued presence in Union Square.[10]

Smith's casual denial of the existence of class in America and the Police Rifle Regiment's demonstration of crowd-control tactics did nothing to prevent the Communists from using Union Square for May Day only a week later. Despite heavy rain, the thousands of participants in the annual march gathered in the square that year for a brief rally before proceeding along their march to Columbus Circle. If the Centennial Celebration was intended as a threat, the Communists did not respond as the backers of the celebration hoped they would. Local business managers therefore resolved to continue their campaign against communism in their neighborhood. Only a few weeks after that 1932 May Day protest, local business owners and managers formed the Union Square Association, an organization intended to "advance the interest of Union Square as a patriotic center." Samuel Klein served on the new association's board of directors.[11]

Store owners and Communists shared two goals in the early 1930s. First, both attempted to control the environment in Union Square through signs and demonstrations, and to use that environment to communicate with working-class people—both potential consumers and potential Communists—in the square. Second, as part of this campaign, store owners and Communists attempted to win the allegiance of the working-class people who frequented Union Square. The Communists wanted working-class people to view them as the legitimate representatives of the working class, and used the dramatic International Unemployment Day protest, before it erupted into violence, to make some of their leaders just such representatives, through the Workers' Committee which the protestors chose. The store owners used this environment to encourage working-class people to shop in their stores, a task which was all the more important since store owners in Union Square seldom advertised in newspapers and therefore lacked one particularly powerful way to draw in customers.

It is difficult to determine the nature of department store workers' relationship to these struggles over Union Square. Anne Haicken, who worked in

Ohrbach's during these years, remembered that the protests seemed far away from her daily existence: "You had to go all the way across 14th Street to the Park" and to enter Union Square and to hear the protesters or soapbox speakers, she remembered. At the same time, Matthew Josephson believed that at least some people may have made the trek across 14th Street. During one visit to Union Square, he claimed that "knots of people who looked like workers from the nearby garment shops were standing about listening to some speakers mounted on little portable platforms." And, when they did go on strike, department store workers willingly worked alongside the Communists who had previously organized demonstrations in Union Square, often laying claim to the same space.[12]

Whether or not department store workers paid attention to these struggles, other observers around the state and the country were very aware of the Communists' presence in Union Square. During a parade sponsored by the right-wing Veterans of Foreign Wars in Union Square just a few weeks after International Unemployment Day, speaker after speaker called for an end to Communist control of Union Square. Later that year, an assistant adjutant general of the New York State National Guard called the square "the frontier of today, right in the heart of your greatest city . . . and it is our duty, as much today as in the early days, to encourage our conservators of the peace and guardians of the frontier" to make sure that the Communists did not gain control over the square.[13]

Despite the importance of Union Square to the struggles of the early 1930s, it is important to remember that the entire country was in turmoil, not just these three city blocks. The most important of the struggles that characterized this era—the famous Bonus March—ended with the United States Army chasing World War I veterans away from Washington, creating widespread fear that the nation really was crumbling. Meanwhile, unemployed workers attended regular protests in front of city halls in major cities across the country. Particularly in northern cities like New York and Chicago, nearly any eviction could result in a spontaneous rally. The mass unemployment and mass poverty which began in 1929 had, it seemed, stirred the working class into action, and many believed that the country was on the brink of revolution.[14]

With hindsight, we now know that, in the end, the Communist movement was soundly defeated. We know that American workers did not create a revolution in the 1930s; and that the election of Franklin Delano Roosevelt in 1932 meant that, instead of revolution, workers and their bosses would come to what Roosevelt quite accurately referred to as a "New Deal" over the splitting of profits. We know that Union Square was to become a center of commerce, not of communism, by century's end. But in the early and mid-1930s there seemed to be at least a possibility that no solution would be found, that American capitalism was truly doomed to failure. And Communist control of Union Square, at the very least, seemed to many observers a near certainty.[15]

The conflict in Union Square, a microcosm of these much larger struggles taking place in the country as a whole, set one of the two stages for the strikes at Klein's and Ohrbach's. Communists' active participation in the fierce battle that raged over the square in the years before the strikes was almost certainly one reason that the Communists were drawn into the strikes to begin with. Additionally, the conflict outside the stores gave the strikers one of their most powerful opportunities to challenge managers, by disrupting still further managers' efforts to control the stores' exterior environment.

The Contested Stores

As in Union Square, the pre-strike struggles and conflicts inside the stores were critical for the way in which the strikes and the unions developed. Working-class consumers fought to get as many high-quality goods as they could for as little money as possible, while store managers fought to encourage spending and control customers' often unruly competition over goods within the stores. Like customers, workers and managers struggled even before the Great Depression. Workers, who had no union at either store before the Depression, frequently left their jobs to protest the poor working conditions. In response, managers set up limited benefits programs at both stores, attempting to convince workers to stay longer. These programs, combined with the high unemployment rates of the early Depression, made workers more likely to remain working at Klein's and Ohrbach's, despite the low pay, long hours, and dismal working conditions.

Managers at both Klein's and Ohrbach's used the self-service method of retailing, a rarity among clothing stores at the time. Customers at both stores had direct access to goods, without necessarily going through a salesperson. A reporter doing a profile on Klein and his store in 1934 described the process as "a clothing cafeteria" where "customers pick garments from the racks and shelves and try them on in communal dressing rooms where green baize curtains are the only concession to privacy. Then they take their selections to cashiers, pay for them and have them wrapped." It was a process far more efficient, inexpensive, and impersonal than the sort managers offered customers in upscale stores. In both Klein's and Ohrbach's, managers relied for profits on low prices, extremely rapid stock turnover, and low overhead (including wages). In Klein's, the overhead, including both rents and salary, was low indeed, reportedly around 6 or 7 percent of the store's total profits.[16]

Due to the low overhead and consequent low prices, as well as the high quality of the merchandise, these stores were very popular place for workers to shop. Working-class people throughout New York City, especially from the immigrant communities of the outer boroughs, would frequently take the subway to Klein's and Ohrbach's to do their shopping. Additionally, during the Depression, some women who might ordinarily have spent more money at the upscale department stores instead chose to limit their spending and shop at Union Square. As a result, Samuel Klein was one of the few business owners in New York City to see an increase in profits during the Great Depression, making over a million dollars in profit every year.[17]

Although profitable, catering primarily to working-class consumers had some disadvantages. Store managers had tremendous difficulty controlling customers, especially during sales. During these sales, working-class consumers sought to stock up on as much clothing as possible. Halper described one sale as rowdy and chaotic. "Greater crowds of women were now storming all the entrances to Klein's . . . overturning tables stacked with handbags and blouses." Klein and Ohrbach both employed private security guards in part to deal with these sorts of unruly crowds.[18]

Customers also engaged in shoplifting, which cost the store owners as much as $100,000 a year. Since, unlike at many more expensive stores in New York City, customers had direct access to merchandise at Klein's and Ohrbach's, customers frequently practiced shoplifting there. Some customers even took shoplifting a step further, using the stores as a training ground to pass the practice on to the next generation. Anne Haicken, who worked at Ohrbach's for several years, remembered years later her surprise that she had once caught a mother teaching her children how to shoplift.[19]

Managers at both stores sought to control this practice as best they could, with little success. While the hundreds of employees at each store could have been extremely useful in helping to catch shoplifters, they were, in many ways, caught between the customers and the store managers. On the one hand, not only were department store workers members of the same class as most of the stores' customers, but they also shared ethnic and neighborhood ties to the customers. They, like the customers, were primarily Jewish-American and Italian-American women. Many of these workers also lived in the same immigrant communities as did the customers (most of the store workers, at least at Ohrbach's, were the children of immigrants rather than immigrants themselves). On the other hand, part of their job was to catch shoplifters, and the extensive network of informants and detectives at both stores ensured that any store workers who did take part in shoplifting, even to the point of allowing customers to get away with it, might well get caught themselves.[20]

Since most store workers were of limited help in preventing shoplifting, managers turned to other methods. For the most part, they relied heavily on the store security forces to prevent shoplifting. In addition, managers at the Klein's store hung huge posters on the interior walls of the store, warning that "Dishonesty Means Prison" and that prison meant "disgrace to your family" in five different languages. There is some disagreement, however, about how regularly these threats were carried out. Klein's supporters claimed that "the few who disregard these formalities and get caught [shoplifting] usually end up in the 'crying room,' . . . [where] he listens to their excuses," and often allowed them to go free. One dissatisfied employee at Klein's, however, wrote that "it is well known that Mr. Klein prosecutes [shoplifters] to the bitter end," unlike department store managers who catered to wealthier people.[21]

If workers were little help in preventing shoplifting, they were more helpful in other aspects of customer control. In particular, store workers reportedly made sure that the boundaries of race were preserved at these stores. Despite the lack of de jure segregation, Klein's and Ohrbach's catered strictly to white working-class people, and store workers were responsible for guarding this status quo. A worker at one of these stores told Communist party leader Benjamin Davis that managers at Klein's and Ohrbach's encouraged employees to "insult Negro patrons so that they won't come back again," and there is no record of workers resisting these instructions.[22]

Managers at these stores had to balance out these attempts to control customers with attempts to encourage customers (at least white customers) to make purchases in the stores. Here, too, workers played a key role. The profit margins at Klein's and Ohrbach's did not allow managers at either store to resort to the sorts of extravagant and ornate methods of creating desire which have dominated department store historiography. In fact, both Klein and Ohrbach expressed tremendous disdain for such tactics. Ohrbach dismissed the fancy displays of the upscale stores as "fanfare and circus methods" of stimulating customer interest, and Klein agreed, joking in one interview that "a customer can't take a window home with her." Neither offered extensive services or even advertised in newspapers, relying instead on word of mouth as well as the prominence of their location to attract potential customers. At downscale stores like Klein's and Ohrbach's, where low overhead was key to the businesses' survival, managers simply could not afford to use any more extravagant methods.[23]

Downscale store managers' refusal to resort to expensive methods of attracting customers made the workers employed in these stores—matrons and cashiers as well as sales workers—almost the sole means of communication between managers and customers. Their work required few skills, and almost no training, but impeccable appearance and behavior. As a result, in downscale stores, despite the informal and inexpensive settings, managers nonetheless had to carefully control their workforce. In order to do so, managers at these stores carefully selected workers of a particular age, race, ethnicity, and gender; workers were young, almost exclusively white, and mostly female. At both Klein's and Ohrbach's, managers also hired mostly Jewish workers, with a few Italian workers as well, perhaps to appeal to the communities they viewed as their most important customers. As in almost all other department stores in New York City at the time, African American workers in these stores held only highly subservient jobs: the only recorded case of an African American worker at either store is at Klein's, where a matron in the fitting room, Julia Jacobs, was African American.[24]

Managers also had strict rules about other aspects of workers' appearance. Managers at some stores refused to employ "stout girls," for instance. Ohrbach took into account such things as "the appearance of nails, neatness of clothing, [and] general good taste shown by grooming," as well as general physical fitness, when hiring store workers. Store managers also controlled workers' appearance by carefully regulating the clothing which they allowed workers to wear. A 1929 *Journal of Retailing* study of New York City metropolitan stores found that managers of 19 out of 22 stores allowed workers to wear only dark blue or black clothing, and found that "all stores take for granted that long sleeves must be worn" with only "moderate or inconspicuous" trimmings.[25]

Although managers found hiring practices helpful in regulating employee appearance and behavior, they supplemented these practices through heavy employer supervision. In Nathan Ohrbach's 1935 *Getting Ahead in Retailing*, he described his own system for personally supervising his workers, noting that he spent "a good part of my time walking through the store . . . to hear how our floor people talk to our customers and what they say. Is that salesgirl trying to convince a customer that an obviously poorly fitting dress 'is simply divine'? Is this salesgirl talking to a fellow worker while a customer is being neglected . . . Is still another salesgirl showing signs of becoming impatient and possibly discourteous?" With this level of supervision, store owners were keenly aware of what their employees were doing, making these stores intimidating and uncomfortable places to work.[26]

While close supervision had always been an unpleasant part of working in these stores, before the Depression began there were also important advantages to working in department stores. This was particularly true when these jobs were compared to the other jobs open to working-class women in New York City, such as those in the garment factories. The most obvious advantage of retail work was that the work was less physically strenuous and less dangerous. In addition, wages tended to vary less over the course of a year than did most factory jobs open to women, although workers often made less money in the stores than they would make in a factory. Workers also tended to have to work fewer hours in the stores than in factories; especially before the Depression, many retail workers throughout the country worked only eight hours a day, years before the eight-hour day became the standard working day in the rest of the country. And in the 1920s, at another 14th Street department store, Hearn's, managers found that opening the store a half-hour later and allowing workers to work fewer than eight hours a day actually benefited sales, in that the more contented workers were better at handling customers.[27]

Whatever advantages retailers offered potential employees in the 1920s, however, were severely curtailed by the Great Depression. The Depression meant a sharp decrease in wages. This was especially a problem at stores like Klein's and Ohrbach's, where managers had historically offered lower wages and required longer hours than in many of the more upscale stores. Stella Ormsby, a Klein's worker hired in 1932, wrote a letter to *The New Republic* in which she claimed that "the girls whom [Klein] had [recently] displaced were receiving ten dollars per week and they were all discharged in favor of the new group who were getting only eight." According to Ormsby, a still later group of workers made only seven dollars a week. The result of these sorts of cuts was that, in New York City over the course of the first half of the 1930s, most sales workers experienced a 50 percent drop in wages.[28]

Department store workers also worked longer hours during the Depression. While historian Susan Porter Benson suggests a somewhat mixed picture on a national scale, she also observes that, in response to the Depression, many downtown stores stayed open later, increasing working hours. These long hours were a major concern of workers at both Klein's and Ohrbach's. At Klein's, Ormsby wrote, she was expected to work a 57-hour week, from "nine-thirty in the morning until seven in the evening, including Saturday." While the Ohrbach's store did not open until 9:45 A.M., workers at both stores worked six days a week throughout the early 1930s, and one of the first strike demands at Ohrbach's was for the forty-hour week.[29]

In addition to complaints over wages and hours, many workers found the store environment cramped, loud, and unsanitary. Ormsby describes "the

basement," the heart of Klein's operation, as "a long, winding, angular affair
. . . low-ceilinged and without windows . . . I walk many miles a day in performing my job [adjusting customer's dresses] and what with . . . the milling
crowds, the foul [unventilated] air and the noise and the bawlings out from my
supervisors, I find myself at the end of the day in a state of utter exhaustion." A
photograph of Klein's from the early 1940s backs up at least part of Ormsby's
descriptions; the ceiling hung only a few feet above women's heads, and huge
metal pipes hung down below the ceiling.[30]

Even before they began forming unions, workers had at least one powerful
weapon at their disposal to fight these sorts of working conditions: they could
quit. Up until the Depression began, the most dissatisfied workers simply
left the store. Both Klein and Ohrbach—and, to a lesser extent, managers at
higher-priced stores as well—found that store workers had extremely high
turnover rates. One study done in 1929 discovered that the average annual
turnover rate in New York City retail stores was approximately 137 percent—
that is, more workers left the average New York City store in a single year than
the total number of store employees. Once the Depression began, however,
workers tended to stay longer at their jobs, sharply reducing the turnover
numbers; and by 1936 a second study indicated that the rate of turnover had
dropped to somewhere closer to 25–35 percent.[31] While this drop is significant, it probably tells us little about turnover at Klein's and Ohrbach's. Due to
the unusually low pay and poor working conditions at these stores, those few
workers at downscale stores who chose to make retailing a career did so primarily in upscale stores, where working conditions, wages, and hours were all
somewhat better.[32]

In response to the constant possibility of workers quitting in search of new
jobs, managers at Klein's and Ohrbach's set up modest benefit programs within
the stores. Klein's managers offered employees yearly bonuses at Christmas
time, and discounts on store merchandise, as well as bonuses for weddings
(perhaps hoping that workers would not leave the stores after getting married).
Managers at Ohrbach's provided employees with paid vacations, a store nurse's
office, and, beginning in the early 1930s, a profit-sharing program as well.[33]

Many workers later claimed that these perks were much more rhetoric than
reality. While on strike, a number of workers claimed that the services were
definitely not worth the "fifteen cents and twenty cents taken from their salaries" to pay for these bonuses. One described the nurse's office at Ohrbach's:
"if they got sick . . . they were given a pass and allowed to go up to a room
to lie down. At the end of a half hour the nurse would tell them acidly that
the half hour had passed and they should go back to their work." In addition,

these workers claimed that managers seldom let workers take advantage of Ohrbach's much-touted free vacations. A striker told a columnist for the *Daily Worker* that "the company, just before vacation time, would lay a girl off. They could then say she had not been working a full two years for them," and therefore not give her a free vacation.[34]

With managers struggling to control both workers and customers, Klein's and Ohrbach's were sites of constant struggle during the Great Depression. Dissatisfied workers continued to quit the store, and customers continued to shoplift, and there was little managers could do to prevent either. Like the struggles taking place in the streets outside the stores, the struggles within the stores set the stage for the strikes of 1934–35. In fact, store managers' attempts to control the actions of store workers led directly into the Klein's-Ohrbach's strikes of 1934–35.

The Strikes Begin

Like many of the strikes of 1934, the Klein's-Ohrbach's were in many ways a response to the New Deal. The explicit support the federal government gave unions under the first New Deal meant that workers increasingly turned to unions as the solution. The workers at Klein's and Ohrbach's had a particular challenge here. Besides the extremely corrupt Retail Clerks International Protection Association (RCIPA), no unions affiliated with the AFL had a charter to organize retail workers. And even the RCIPA had never made any serious headway into department stores, where the employees were mostly women; instead the RCIPA restricted its efforts to grocery stores. Those workers who wished to join a union had to settle for a union not affiliated with the AFL, one that would organize white-collar women workers. This led directly to the rise of Communists within the department store unions.

As managers at Klein's and Ohrbach's cut workers' salaries and extended the number of working hours, the federal government offered unionization as a way to solve workers' problems with minimum disruption. The groundbreaking National Industrial Recovery Act (NIRA) of 1933 was primarily intended to bolster the economy by allowing businesses to set up self-regulatory agencies and thereby limit competition and end price wars. At the same time, one of the requirements of these self-regulatory agencies was that they all include a rule that "employees shall have the right to organize and bargain collectively . . . and shall be free from the interference, restraint, or coercion of employers" in forming unions.[35]

Despite pro-union language like this, many retail executives enthusiastically supported the NIRA, and with good reason. As *Business Week* described it, the first year of the NIRA meant national "inflation . . . living minimum wages, and . . . trade practice rules," all of which suggested the possibility for higher prices. Even the possibility that store managers might raise prices as a result of the NIRA meant that customers began to buy more, trying to get their purchases in before prices went up. For store managers, therefore, "industrial recovery looked like a *fait accompli*" after the passage of the NIRA.[36]

Like these managers, union organizers greatly benefited from the NIRA. In 1933 and 1934, a national strike wave took place, the first major strike wave since 1919. In the last six months of 1933, in fact, there were more strikes than there had been in any full year since 1921. More amazing than the sheer numbers was the workers' militancy; many of the larger strikes often developed into violent battles. Throughout the country, from Minneapolis and Toledo to San Francisco and the textile factory towns in the southern states, workers engaged in bitter and often violent fights to demand the right to form unions.[37]

Despite this national strike wave, most union organizers refused to organize department store workers, many of whom were women. The AFL, which contained by far the largest and most powerful unions in the country, had several unions with women members, but AFL leaders saw organizing women workers primarily as a way to support men's wages. Labor historian Alice Kessler-Harris notes that "articles [in the AFL press] that began with pleas that women stay out of the work force concluded with equally impassioned pleas to organize those who were already in it." The key to labor's success, in the view of AFL organizers, was to maintain the family wage, a wage earned by the male breadwinner. The sole worker of any importance, in the view of AFL organizers, was therefore the head of household, who was invariably assumed to be a man. As a result, while the AFL did not generally oppose women joining unions, many AFL organizers viewed working women as supplemental to working men, rather than workers in their own right.[38]

For workers in Ohrbach's and Klein's the AFL's gender analysis collapsed on a number of different grounds. Most of these workers were young women, and therefore defined out of the scope of the AFL's primary interest. At the same time, due to the high unemployment levels of the early Depression, these workers were sometimes the sole wage earners for their families. Within the department stores, it was very often young women, not male patriarchs, who were the earners of the family's only wage, however inadequate that wage was.[39]

To a great extent, Communist-led unions shared the AFL's gender analysis in the early 1930s. In her masterful study *Community of Suffering and Struggle,* historian Elizabeth Faue argues that during the 1930s American Communists were united with other leftists and liberals around a gendered narrative in which this male working class struggled against the weak, fat, and—in Faue's analysis—less masculine ruling class. There is plenty of evidence for Faue's claims in the literature produced by the Communist-led Trade Union Unity League (TUUL), which strongly emphasized the masculinity of the targeted membership. Illustrations in TUUL pamphlets, for example, frequently featured large and muscular men as the sole representatives of the working class.[40]

Communists had a number of different ways available to discuss women's role in class struggle, many of them relatively conservative. Women served, for instance, as powerful symbols of workers' poverty and hardship in Communist literature. One contributor to *Working Woman* identified women as the true victims of the Great Depression. "The wife of the unemployed gets the worst of it. She is the one to answer her children's cry for bread. She has got to face the landlord. All the misery of the shortage, of keeping the family from starvation in time of unemployment falls heaviest on the housewife." Other contributors to *Working Woman* discussed women in a different light, as helpmates to radical working men. During the Klein's-Ohrbach's strikes, for instance, articles in *Working Woman,* the CP women's newspaper, addressed issues such as how a working woman could dress without spending much money, what sorts of foods would most efficiently feed her family, and the importance of women's auxiliaries during strikes of male workers. Even this understanding of working-class women as home-based revolutionary helpmates could allow women a degree of agency that the family wage did not. As part of this concept of the revolutionary helpmate, *Working Woman* devoted a number of articles to more overtly political issues centered on the home. The paper's editors printed a number of articles on the proper methods of birth control, for example. More importantly, the paper repeatedly addressed the food boycotts in New York City during the early 1930s, boycotts which were led by women.[41]

All of these discussions of women's role in class struggle were in some ways similar to the role of women in the AFL's notion of the family wage. All, for instance, depicted the primary duties of working-class women as being within the home, dealing with issues of consumption and reproduction, despite the key role labor played in women's lives in this era. As a result, many of these articles used women to reaffirm men's role as the head of Communist households.

The editors of *Working Woman* moved beyond these relatively conservative gender divisions by adding extensive coverage of women's own struggles within the workplace. Contributors constantly discussed women who were involved in the labor movement, and they portrayed women strikers not only as newsworthy and admirable, but also as militant fighters for workers' rights, much like male strikers were. *Working Woman* also included extensive coverage on women strikers, coverage that was mixed in among the recipes and fashion tips and the use of miserable women as symbols for the oppressed. The Communists may have considered women helpmates and victims, but unlike the AFL, Communists also made a point to identify women as fundamental agents in the class struggle. The editors of and contributors to *Working Woman*, and presumably many of the Communists who read it, never successfully resolved this tension. They seem instead to have accepted the contradiction, between victims and actors, symbols and agents, as a fundamental part of their understanding of women.[42]

Like other Communists, the TUUL emphasized the importance of men's activism while nonetheless recognizing the need to organize women workers. In the organization's mission statement, TUUL leaders reminded their readers that "women workers play an increasingly important role in American industry . . . [they] are subjected to the fierce speed-up of capitalist rationalization, and are super-exploited." In the same mission statement, the TUUL attacked "the trade union leaders [who] have typically failed to make a fight for the women workers, barring them from the unions and discriminating against them in industry" and promised that the TUUL would fight for the rights of these women workers.[43]

TUUL leaders therefore set up the Office Workers Union (OWU), the union which initially organized department store workers in New York City. This union was created primarily to organize office workers, another group of white-collar workers largely made up of women. Its commitment to women workers was further signified by the fact that the union included several women in leadership positions. Gertrude Lane, who was the highest-ranking union official, and Clarina Michelson, one of the two full-time OWU organizers, were both women, and both won a great deal of respect from the workers whom they organized. In part, this was because both Lane and Michelson were somewhat older than the other union members and leaders, many of whom were only in their teens. Ruth Pinkson, the nineteen-year-old National Organizer of the OWU at the time, later described Michelson as having a "motherly" relationship with the teenagers whom Michelson helped to organize. The seniority and competence of Michelson and Lane, at least according to

Pinkson, made both men and women in the OWU far more aware of women's important role in labor struggles.[44]

The OWU had a strong presence in Union Square in the early 1930s. OWU members often participated in the May Day parades and other protests which, as the OWU press described them, "choked Union Square and all the streets surrounding the Square." In addition, during these parades, the OWU newspaper claimed, "a continuous chant rose from the ranks, 'White collar workers join our ranks! White collar workers join our ranks!'"[45]

In 1934, due either to the OWU's presence in Union Square or simply to the absence of any alternative, workers at Klein's and Ohrbach's went to the OWU for assistance in creating a union. The OWU agreed to provide support, and Clarina Michelson was assigned full-time as an organizer of department store workers. Michelson, an openly Communist member of an upper-class family from Massachusetts, and the wife of fellow TUUL organizer Andrew Overgaard, was in some ways a surprising choice to lead a union of department store workers. Unlike the women working and shopping in Klein's and Ohrbach's, Michelson was not from an immigrant community, and—except for her work as a union organizer—she had apparently never held a job. Despite this very different background from the workers she organized, Michelson had some important strengths. She was a highly skilled and experienced organizer by 1934, having been involved in radical politics ever since the campaign to free Sacco and Vanzetti. She also had significant experience organizing unions, having had numerous successes in TUUL campaigns in the southern coal-mining industry. Finally, she had some important connections for the union, among them her participation as the Recording Secretary of the League of Struggle for Negro Rights (LSNR), a Communist group that helped lead the "Don't Buy Where You Can't Work" campaign, a movement to get African American workers jobs in stores where they made purchases. Over the next five years, during which she continued to lead New York City's department store unions, Michelson would prove herself a major asset for the unions.[46]

These workers' decision to join a union, especially one under Communist leadership, greatly upset their employers. Despite their avowed support for the NIRA, managers at both stores took a strong anti-union stance, and managers at Klein's went so far as to fire union workers in the winter of 1934, openly defying the NIRA. In an interview with *Newsweek* in December 1934, Samuel Klein professed his bewilderment that anyone would have the right to tell him whom to fire and whom not to fire: "'My store's business always falls off at Christmas time . . . About Dec. 1 each year I have to lay off a few employees. This year we let only 87 go, against 300 last year and 250 in 1932. Then the other day I got a "summons" from the NRA"' (National Recovery Administration, the agency which was responsible for seeing that the NIRA codes were followed).[47]

The "dimple-cheeked proprietor," as he is referred to in this article, failed to mention that nearly all of the 87 employees he laid off in 1934 were members of the newly formed Klein's branch of the Office Workers Union. He also failed to mention that during that same month, December 1934, workers under OWU leadership had already gone on strike against Ohrbach's, just a few doors away from Klein's. Ohrbach's workers, also encouraged by the NIRA's official support for the rights of labor, were demanding a pay raise, a forty-hour work week, and an end to discrimination for union activity. It did not take any more encouragement than the firings to get Klein's workers to join Ohrbach's workers on the picket line.[48]

The strike was a very small one—only 200 of the 2600 workers employed at the two stores joined picket lines in 1934–35. With workers struggling to support families on their already meager wages, it was a difficult decision to join the picket line, and to make matters even more discouraging, Ohrbach's managers obtained an anti-picketing injunction from the state supreme court, which meant that being on the picket line was breaking the law. But despite all the obstacles they faced, the tiny number of strikers were determined to lay claim to the stores and to Union Square, to create a broad coalition of support-ers, and to effectively demonstrate that retail workers could force managers to back down.[49]

Monkey Business

When Leane Zugsmith described a fictionalized version of the Klein's-Ohrbach's strikes in her 1936 novel *A Time to Remember*, she chose to have the initial call for a strike take place in a fictionalized setting. Aline, a young woman worker who had never been part of a union before, let alone a strike, is about to go onstage during a store-sponsored play performed by store employees. Nervous at performing and even more worried that she and her fellow workers had voted the night before to go on strike, Aline stops just before going onstage, returns to an empty dressing room, retrieves a handful or two of strike leaflets, and then returns to stage "half-smiling, her face feverish beneath a mask of grease paint . . . the leaflets pressed against her breast . . . like a shield." Aline then proceeds to toss the leaflets out over the audience and make a speech about the strike which will begin the next day. This section of *A Time to Remember* appears to be entirely fictional; no evidence exists that plays were even performed at either of these two stores.[50]

Zugsmith's hijacked theater works well as a metaphor to describe the strikers' use of a set of tactics that union leaders nicknamed "monkey business." Monkey business was an attempt to wrest control of the department store and its surroundings from the store managers. In many ways store employees continued performing as they had while working within the stores; they certainly continued to focus on communication with customers, a factor which had been so important to the stores' daily functioning. Only, as with Aline standing on the employer's stage while distributing strike leaflets, during monkey business actions the Klein's-Ohrbach's strikers no longer worked to communicate with customers for their employer's ends. During the strike, they instead worked to communicate with customers for their own ends, disrupting managerial control over both stores and square alike in the process.[51]

If they were to disrupt managers' control over the stores and the square, workers had to find ways to get support from people not directly involved in the strike. By far the most important group of allies the strikers recruited were the people they called upon as "white-collar workers." Again and again in the strike literature, one sees reference to the label of white-collar work and white-collar workers. Ruth Pinkson remembered these strikes as the "first big white-collar strikes in New York City," and suggested that the strikes were seen by many white-collar workers as a test case. In her novel Zugsmith referred to Aline's discovery "that a victory for them would be a victory for workers in all department stores, for all white-collar workers, for the labor movement as a whole." And Arnold Honig, a Klein's striker, suggested that the strikes proved that even white-collar workers could be "good, militant fighters who can dose a backward boss with a good assortment of hell-fire."[52]

The category of "white-collar workers," which these workers used so successfully to recruit allies, gave the strikers a broad base of support. Particularly during the 1930s, people who might have thought of themselves as members of the middle class instead defined themselves as white-collar workers. Edward Dahlberg, a writer who joined the Klein's-Ohrbach's picket line, suggested that this new consciousness was a direct result of the Depression:

> The college diploma was the exchange currency in the student's mind
> . . . for a ritzy law office and a motor car . . . Marriage for the department
> store girl, being another economic diploma, was thought of in terms of
> leisure and West End Avenue, and the Holy Grail for the writer was the

boulevards of Paris . . . but with vast unemployment, evictions, empty stomachs, [and] the wholesale slashing of wages these sleepy, moving picture wishes lost for the wisher[s] whatever little reality they once had.

The Depression, in Dahlberg's eyes, had destroyed the privileges which allowed certain workers to think of themselves as anything besides workers. As a result, many who had once thought of themselves as middle class found it "impossible and suicidal . . . to stand aloof," and instead decided to organize, to begin to think of themselves as part of the working class. By using the term "white collar worker" to describe themselves, department store workers implicitly called upon these workers to support them. In response, office workers, actors, chemists, doctors, and writers all joined the fight in support of the workers at Klein's and Ohrbach's. For a moment, at least, these people rejected the idea of the middle class, instead throwing in their lot with the strikers.[53]

These white-collar workers who emerged as strike supporters were critical to the tiny strikes on Union Square. Not only did they swell the numbers of strikers; they also played active roles in creating tactics, including monkey business. The monkey business committee, described in the strike records as a "very small, very secret committee to work out stunts," was not made up of only strikers. Other OWU members and organizers from outside the department store industry were also committee members, Clarina Michelson and Ruth Pinkson (at the time an office worker as well as an OWU organizer) among them.[54]

In addition, due to the OWU's close association with the Federation of Architects, Engineers, Chemists, and Technicians (FAECT), another TUUL affiliate, workers had access to technical knowledge and tools that rivaled store managers' own technical advisers. The strikers' technical abilities, however, were put to very different ends. At another point, for example, a chemist who was a member of the FAECT provided the employees with a box of white mice. The employees took the box into Klein's and let the mice run free, thus "frightening women shoppers who entered the store in ignorance of the fact that a strike is in progress there," as the *Daily Worker* put it. Other monkey business actions required more technical abilities. At one point, a strike supporter poured a substance into the elevator motor in the Ohrbach's store which caused an elevator to get stuck between floors. On these occasions, as Pinkson recalled, "people started to get afraid to go into the store, because they didn't know what [the screaming] was all about."[55]

While many monkey business actions were derived from technical abilities, very simple actions could also be extremely effective. Clarina Michelson recalled one incident when strikers at Ohrbach's gave children of shoppers entering the store balloons reading "Don't Buy At Ohrbach's!" "When the children would go into the store, the managers would have to run up and take the balloons away," Michelson remembered. The managers frequently caused the children to get upset, leading to loud and often disruptive arguments between store managers and the children's parents.[56]

Actions like these, which created disruption inside the store, were very powerful. First, of course, they slowed down purchases, and made customers uneasy about shopping in the stores. In addition, these actions also made the managers' job of controlling customers more difficult. As already suggested, this control was always somewhat tenuous. By adding mice, elevator malfunctions, and other disturbances, the workers were able to lessen this control still further, and thereby give managers an additional reason to settle the strike.

Strikers were also able to take advantage of the struggles outside the store, the struggles in Union Square. Since signs visible from Union Square were a central part of managers' efforts to attract customers, the strikers made Union Square an essential part of the strike, beginning with attacks on the exteriors of the store buildings, which were important tools for store owners to communicate with the public. Ruth Pinkson remembered one such incident, which, like many of the actions within the stores, required the aid of FAECT members to make it work:

> We cut out a sign from cardboard, saying "STRIKE—DON'T ENTER!" . . . We had a base, some kind of metal base, and we poured in a chemical and cut out the words, but we had to put that up against the window. . . . We had to work quickly . . . so one of the young men in the union and myself were standing by the window, and we were hugging and kissing, and I pressed it against the window. A cop walked by, but . . . he just saw a young couple kissing, so he didn't bother [us]. . . .
>
> It didn't cut through immediately. But the next morning . . . it was etched in, the chemical had etched [the slogan] into the window. [Store managers] were panicked. . . . A couple of us had gotten there early, to see what effect it would have, and [managers] didn't know what to do, so they got cardboard [and covered the sign], but it kept people out. People coming out of the subway were confronted with the sign.

If managers at Klein's and Ohrbach's could use signs to make the exterior of the building serve their purposes, so could the strikers. With the help of their white-collar allies, the strikers here transformed a store building itself into a strike weapon.[57]

Strikers also combated managers' billboards by literally going into the square. They did so first by staging weekly rallies. Every Saturday—the busiest shopping day at the stores—became an occasion for a mass strike rally in Union Square, and each rally had a particular theme. The strikers held Catholic Day, Jewish Day, Writers' Day, Theatrical Day, and a number of other different theme protests, when a different community was supposed to come to the square in support of the strikers. Radical novelists like James T. Farrell, the author of the Studs Lonigan trilogy, and Nathanael West, author of *Day of the Locust* and *Miss Lonelyhearts,* joined Leane Zugsmith and Edward Dahlberg on the picket line for Writer's Day, and all were arrested for breaking the anti-picketing injunction.[58]

The strikers also made use of the importance of Union Square to other protests. Participants in unemployment demonstrations, for instance, mixed freely with the strikers, often joining the picket line after their own demonstrations. As a result, Pinkson claimed that at least five young women on the picket line met their future husbands during the strike, because so many men came over to offer their support to the strikers. Picketers responded to this support by taking part in other left-wing activities centered on Union Square, at one point carrying signs in celebration of the eleventh anniversary of the *Daily Worker.*[59]

Store managers deployed police as a response to these sorts of rallies. Police frequently arrested strikers and their supporters, often forcefully. However, unlike in most strikes, here police violence had strong negative effects on employers' businesses. Zugsmith, who had been on the picket line on at least one day when police had made arrests, described the fighting which took place on the picket line: "The policemen had driven their horses into the swarm of pickets and passers-by on the sidewalk. Fanny's leg had been broken. But . . . patrons, sickened by the sight of blood, thrown into panic by the plunging horses and swinging nightsticks, had not made their purchases . . . that day." Police violence might terrify the strikers; it might make the strike into a bloody and very one-sided battle; but it also scared away customers. This violence was therefore a two-edged sword in the battle for control over Union Square and the potential customers within the square.[60]

Perhaps the most pointed attempt on the strikers' part to control Union Square was their use of the statues. At the time there were two major statues in Union Square, one of Lafayette and one of Washington. The statue of Washington stood near the stores, on horseback, with its arm outstretched.

Early one morning the strikers took one of their strike posters, reading "Don't Buy At Ohrbach's," and placed it on the Washington statue's outstretched arm. By doing so, the strikers made Washington, the symbol of freedom and of Americanism, a representative for the strike, at least until the sign was removed later that day.[61]

For the five months of the strike, from December 1934 through April 1935, the Klein's-Ohrbach's strikers became an intrinsic part of daily life in Union Square. The mass protests of the strike became so much a part of Union Square's atmosphere that at least one painter trying to capture the essence of life in Union Square included in the background picketers in front of the stores.[62]

The strikes also had effects far beyond Union Square and the stores; indeed, they were felt throughout New York City. For one thing, the numerous protests in Union Square—and the repeated and brutal reaction by police to the protests—resulted in the regular disruption of traffic throughout the area. The strikes also led to the temporary cancellation of the off-Broadway play, the *Shores of Cattaro*. Actors were also included in the strikers' call for support from white-collar workers, and the cast of *The Shores of Cattaro* was strongly supportive of the strikers. One day, the entire cast came down to the picket line, only to be immediately arrested for breaking the anti-picketing injunction. According to one source, when the announcement was made at the theater that night that the play was canceled because the entire cast was in jail for breaking the injunction, the audience burst into applause.[63]

Allies played a critical role in the strikers' campaign to make the strike a city-wide issue. At one meeting held at a high school near the stores, both playwright Lillian Hellman and strip-dancer Gypsy Rose Lee addressed the striking workers. The strikers rather optimistically believed that the more celebrities they could attract, the more press coverage they would receive. As it turned out, the press—hardly anxious to offend an advertising bloc as important as the retail industry—all but ignored these two strikes, and frequently belittled the strikers when it did cover their actions.[64]

The strikers also determined to win press coverage, disrupt managerial control, and make the strike a city-wide event by challenging Ohrbach and Klein directly when the store owners were away from the stores and the square. At one point, for example, "Mr. Ohrbach, escorting a young lady into the Astor Hotel at about 11:30 at night, was met by a parade of strikers and sympathizers over 200 strong that was marching down Broadway." Zugsmith also reports in her fictionalized account that picketers went to one of the retailers' homes, though there is no evidence to support this claim.[65]

The most powerful action taken during the strike, one of the few that did win extensive press coverage, was another attack against Nathan Ohrbach's non-business life, particularly against his charity activities. At the time of the strike, Ohrbach, who had given a great deal of money to Brooklyn Hospital, was on the hospital's board of trustees. As a trustee, he was required to attend certain charity events, including a large banquet in the Grand Ballroom of the Waldorf-Astoria Hotel, to which New York City Mayor Fiorello LaGuardia was also invited. Some of the senior doctors for whom the dinner was being thrown considered themselves white-collar workers and, as such, strongly sympathized with the strikers. These doctors offered to get tickets to the event for a number of strikers. The strikers, knowing both that the mayor would be there and that the entire event would be broadcast on live radio, gladly accepted the offer.[66]

In the strikers' decision to confront Ohrbach at the Waldorf-Astoria that night, we therefore have Zugsmith's theatrical metaphor played out for high stakes. Ohrbach had a forum with a large audience of radio listeners, and had helped to create a drama to demonstrate, among other things, his role as a great philanthropist in supporting the hospital. And strikers and their supporters were ready to steal the forum, to instead send their own message, that Ohrbach was an exploiter of workers.

On the night of the banquet, dressed in their finest evening clothes, strikers surreptitiously entered the Waldorf-Astoria ballroom. And, as LaGuardia began to speak of the important work done by Ohrbach and by the doctors themselves, one of the strikers spoke up from the balcony. "I want to introduce myself. I am an Ohrbach striker," she said.[67] By the time hotel security guards realized that she was chained to the balcony, another woman striker spoke up, also from the balcony: "Nathan Ohrbach may give thousands to charity, but he doesn't pay his workers a living wage." Security guards rushed over, only to find out that she, too, had chained herself to the balcony.[68] The security guards immediately sent for hacksaws. As the audience struggled to make sense of the disruption, another striker, also in the balcony, took handfuls of flyers about the strike and tossed them out over the audience, to the amazement of all concerned. According to the *Times*, LaGuardia continued to speak, although without much success in being heard, since both workers also continued speaking.[69]

In the Waldorf that night, the strikers made their message heard. They also successfully disrupted Ohrbach's drama on live radio. The action was a stunning success, in some ways an even greater success than workers had hoped. At the time, workers thought that the two strikers inside the hall would receive up to six months in jail for their actions; it was not until later that night that the rather bewildered hotel managers, apparently not knowing exactly what else to do with them, freed both strikers after giving them a warning never to return to the Waldorf-Astoria again. In a slightly ironic twist, the lawyer who had arranged for the anti-picketing injunction at Ohrbach's gave the two workers cab fare to get home, perhaps acting out of paternalistic motives.[70]

The end result of the actions at the Waldorf-Astoria was an outpouring of press coverage the next day. Not all or even most of the coverage was favorable; the *New York Times,* for example, described the workers as "hecklers" who had maliciously disrupted a charitable event. Perhaps not surprisingly, only the *Daily Worker* portrayed the strikers in a positive light, as "comely pickets" who had made their exploitation known to the entire city through radio.[71]

Despite its tone, the press coverage which resulted from this event turned the tide of the strike. Klein and Ohrbach, now acutely aware that their business and personal lives would be disrupted until they agreed to settle, finally backed down. Managers at both stores agreed to hire back the strikers in late February and early March 1935, much to the strikers' delight. As Zugsmith described strike headquarters on the day of the announcement, in noticeably gendered terms:

> The floor quakes under their stamping feet. The ear drums recoil at the roar of rejoicing. Peck Hirschberg rushes outside to tell the pickets and call them off. Duke prances like a bear on his hind legs, forcing May Lundstrom to curvet with him. Mrs. Bauer's stumpy frame is shaken by shuddering sobs and her little girl, hanging onto her skirt, looks up with a puckered face, ready to cry with her mother. With a kind of ferocity, Manny Lorch and Muriel Cline hug each other, their eyes glazed with joy.[72]

As some were quick to point out when Zugsmith's novel appeared in print, the workers' victory was far more limited than Zugsmith acknowledged in *A Time to Remember.* At Klein's, workers got back pay and reinstatement; at Ohrbach's, strikers did not receive the raise they had demanded, although they did receive a verbal contract guaranteeing a decrease in hours. Neither Klein nor Ohrbach agreed to recognize the Office Workers Union as the workers' bargaining agent.[73]

Store managers proved unwilling to live up to even those demands to which they had agreed. As early as April 1935, at a leaflet distribution in Klein's, union organizers encountered what they called "the old pre-strike difficulties." As organizers attempted to distribute leaflets outside the employees' exit, store executives positioned themselves in front of the exit, and, as the OWU paper described it, "suggestively 'eyed' the outgoing workers" to see if any of them accepted flyers. Policemen were also present, ostensibly to make sure that no littering took place. In addition, managers at both stores began steadily laying off workers who had participated in the strike. The workers at Klein's, without a strike fund, having survived for five months with no income during some of the worst years of the Great Depression, decided not to return to the picket line, instead choosing to look for work elsewhere. Most workers at Ohrbach's followed their example, except for about twenty workers, who returned to the picket line again in 1936. As discussed in the next chapter, they eventually achieved a controversial and somewhat unsatisfactory settlement.[74]

If in many respects the Klein's-Ohrbach's strikes were defeats for workers at both stores, the strikes were nonetheless important victories for the union. During these strikes, the strikers had forced two major retailers to submit to negotiations, even if managers in the end got the best of the negotiations. As a result of this victory, RCIPA organizers were finally forced to acknowledge that department store workers could be organized, and in 1935, just after the strikes, RCIPA and OWU organizers met for the first time. That year the OWU joined forces with the leaders of the RCIPA. By the end of 1935 the victories at Ohrbach's and Klein's, fleeting though they were for many strike participants, had made it possible for New York City's department store union, consisting primarily of workers at Klein's and Ohrbach's, with only a handful of members in other stores around the city, to become Local 1250 of the RCIPA.[75]

In merging with the RCIPA, the OWU leaders took a serious risk. The East Coast branch of the RCIPA was under the leadership of a man named Roy Denise, who had a long-standing practice of giving RCIPA charters to company unions. Perhaps not coincidentally, Denise was paid on a commission basis, receiving a bonus for every new member of the union as well as every charter.[76] With corrupt practices like these commonplace in the RCIPA, some OWU organizers were worried about the merger from the very beginning. "They were crooks. And we knew that they were," one OWU organizer said some years later. Still, at least for the moment, the OWU leaders agreed to the alliance. Michelson later stated that, at the very least, she believed that being affiliated with the AFL would bring them some sort of legitimacy within the labor movement and the city at large, and perhaps make department store managers more willing to sign contracts. In this belief, Michelson was gravely mistaken.[77]

Conclusion

The Klein's-Ohrbach's strikes demonstrate the role Communists played in American labor history. The Communist party never contained more than a tiny minority of the working-class people who presumably were its target membership. Yet Communist union organizers, who embraced a more complex notion of women's role in the labor movement than did the AFL, had a critical role to play during the Great Depression. Without them, the Klein's-Ohrbach's strikes would never have taken place, and the union never would have won its first victories, however negligible those victories were for the workers themselves. It is quite possible that the 1930s labor movement would not have so centrally included workers in the retail industry without the radical influence of the Communists in 1934–35.

This does not mean that Communists controlled these strikes, in the sense that some historians of communism argue that Communist party policy was the controlling factor in the unions in which Communists participated. What Communists did, as seen quite vividly during the strikes, was to provide tools for workers to struggle against managers. Communists no doubt played a role in giving the workers the ability to etch signs into the side of the store buildings, and getting workers tickets to the banquet at the Waldorf-Astoria Hotel. But the Communist party did not force workers to etch a sign into the store window, or control what workers said once they entered the banquet hall.

On the contrary, far from confirming the top-down analysis of Communists' role in the labor movement, these strikes demonstrate the necessity to examine both American radicalism and American labor in their local contexts. Neither the strikes nor the Communists who led them can be separated from the daily struggles taking place in Union Square, or in the stores. To attempt to perform this separation, to write about communism or the labor movement as though local developments did not play a critical role in the creation of these movements, is in the end an impossible task.

Besides complicating historians' understanding of communism, the strikers had also demonstrated something else—something more important for their immediate future. Not only could strikes, like those at Klein's and Ohrbach's, take advantage of larger movements; they could also become part of larger movements. On their own, the Klein's-Ohrbach's strikes were minuscule—two hundred workers are easily ignored amidst the far larger strikes of 1934. But the Klein's-Ohrbach's strikes did not exist in isolation. Instead, they were part of a larger campaign, led by Communists and their supporters, to reimagine class and reclaim public space. The Klein's-Ohrbach's strike became, for those few weeks in 1934 and 1935, an occasion for yet another challenge to Union Square, and an occasion for creating a vision of the working class that included white-collar workers, ranging from doctors and actors to the low-paid clerks at Klein's and Ohrbach's. As such, it was an important victory for the Communists in more ways than one.

At the same time as the Klein's-Ohrbach's strikes represented an important victory for the Communist leaders of New York City's department store unions, they also exposed a number of weaknesses that union organizers attempted to correct during the next few years. For all the creativity that the strikers had shown, only a small minority of the workers in the two stores had honored the picket lines. Additionally, managers, while they had finally agreed to negotiate, had nonetheless refused to recognize the union. In the end, as we have seen, the strikes were a defeat for the workers in the two stores, and resulted in mass firings in the strikes' aftermath. Organizers believed their weaknesses stemmed from a lack of legitimacy, which, they felt, allowed store managers, workers, and the press to dismiss the union as nothing more than a radical fringe group. Union leaders attempted to correct this weakness over the next few years, during their disastrous alliance with the RCIPA.

CHAPTER 2

Legitimacy, 1935–37

Introduction

Throughout their alliance with the more conservative leaders of the American Federation of Labor's RCIPA, the Communists leading the department store unions sought legitimacy. Now officially affiliated with the AFL, they had every reason to believe that affiliation with this legitimate and less radical organization would convince managers to sign union contracts, and thereby avoid the debacle in the aftermath of the Klein's-Ohrbach's strikes. Instead, the alliance with the RCIPA was marked by one crisis after another. Scandal, defeat, and internal conflict racked the department store unions, now RCIPA Local 1250, from 1935 to 1937. While Clarina Michelson and other leaders of Local 1250 maintained their close relationship with workers and continued to encourage workers to take leadership roles in the union, they found themselves increasingly at odds with the more authoritarian and conservative leaders of the RCIPA, who determinedly and sometimes destructively meddled in the local union's affairs. Throughout these years, national leaders and their allies unilaterally called off strikes and launched public campaigns attacking Michelson and Local 1250 alike.

Although union leaders' attempts to gain legitimacy in these years ended in disaster, workers proved themselves far more able to gain a prominent role in the burgeoning labor movement. In March 1937, with the full support of the Communist union leaders, workers began massive sit-down strikes at five-and-dime stores throughout New York City. In these successful sit-downs, workers captured national media attention. By the end of 1937, under pressure from Local 1250 and other RCIPA dissidents, the CIO set up the United Retail Employees of America, a union designed specifically to organize retail workers like those who had launched the five-and-dime sit-downs of 1937.

Developments in the department store unions exemplified much larger changes going on in American radicalism in these years. Beginning in 1935, communism became more and more a part of American cultural and social life. That year was the beginning of the United Front, when Communists began to form alliances with socialists and eventually with liberals as well. This development would play an important role as Communists in the department store unions searched for allies of their own. Despite the importance of shifting Communist party policies in the unions' history, however, workers' actions cannot and should not be reduced to Communist politics. Workers, like union leaders, sought a way to make their union more permanent and more powerful. As during the Klein's-Ohrbach's strikes, communism was to be a powerful tool in pursuit of this goal.

Disasters at May's and Ohrbach's, 1935–36

The period immediately following the Klein's-Ohrbach's strikes did not look promising for the union that had once been part of the OWU. Union organizers' attempts to find legitimacy within the AFL resulted in two brief strikes that brought defeat and scandal to the union. In the strikes at May's and Ohrbach's, as in most of what union organizers attempted in 1935–36, they found the alliance with the national RCIPA leaders to be a hindrance. By early 1937, the split between the Communist leaders of Local 1250 and the national RCIPA leaders had become very public, eventually leading Local 1250 to bolt from the RCIPA with other dissident RCIPA locals.

Like Union Square, Fulton Street in downtown Brooklyn was a busy working-class shopping district as well as the site of political protests. However, the protests in downtown Brooklyn never rivaled the size or importance of those that took place in Union Square. Protesters did occasionally emerge, particularly after the city's Emergency Relief Bureau opened a headquarters at Fulton Street. Labor disputes also occasionally disrupted life on Fulton Street: when workers at Dean's cafeteria announced that they were paid starvation wages, students from nearby Brooklyn College immediately set up a picket line in front of the cafeteria. But protest was always relatively rare on Fulton Street.[1]

Consumption was far more central to Fulton Street life than were strikes and protests. Fulton Street was a center for consumption, particularly (in the nine blocks between Flatbush Avenue and Court Street, where the May's store was located) working-class consumption. "An endless procession of shoppers," the WPA Guide to New York City reported, patronized large downscale department stores like A&S, Namm's, and Loeser's. Smaller stores selling clothes, eyeglasses, accessories, and numerous other goods also offered customers chances for consumption. Towards the Flatbush Avenue end of the area, "an amusement center," with a half-dozen movie theaters, burlesque houses, "legitimate" theaters, cafeterias, and an automat, allowed working-class people spaces to relax and eat. As a shopping district, Fulton Street presented one major drawback. Above all the bustling stores stood the elevated train, blocking out sunlight and creating what one observer described as a "constant din." Throughout the 1930s the elevated train stood above the stores, making shopping in these places a dark and noisy experience, and making the Fulton Street shopping district less prestigious than many shopping districts in Manhattan.[2]

Nestled beneath the elevated train and among the larger downscale stores stood the May's store. In the 1920s May's had been a relatively upscale store, built to serve the wealthy customers living in nearby Brooklyn Heights. But when the stock market crashed in 1929, May's manager Joseph Weinstein was among the first retailers to respond, instituting a new store policy: "small profits and large volume." The store began selling $1 dresses and coats, and tens of thousands of customers, most of them from immigrant neighborhoods, began flooding the store during sales. No longer would May's offer deliveries or charge accounts; now it would be strictly self-service, much like the stores on Union Square.[3]

There were many similarities between May's and the Union Square stores. Weinstein, for instance, made his profits by keeping overhead and labor costs down, and shoplifting was a constant—and expensive—problem at May's. There were also some important differences. Weinstein engaged in more physical intimidation than did the managers at the Union Square stores. By the time of the strike, workers had given Weinstein the nickname "King Kong" for his habit of stomping around the store and yelling at workers who were not performing to his satisfaction. Workers at May's were also worse off economically. Since most workers at the store were only part-time employees, they took home even less money than workers at Klein's and Ohrbach's, and their situation was even more precarious than that of the workers in Union Square.[4]

Working conditions in May's were also far worse than conditions in Klein's and Ohrbach's. Pearl Edison and Evelyn Cohen, who worked at May's and made affidavits concerning their work within the store, reported that there were only two toilets for all the store employees, which "were kept in a filthy condition." The bathrooms were also located in the store's basement, which was "infested with rats. . . . Occasionally, a rat will die, and the stench from its rotting body will be present in this unventilated [basement] for weeks." Edison and Cohen also complained of the lack of steam heat and the failure of May's managers to provide chairs for the workers. They also complained that the workers were used as human elevators, to lug dresses and other merchandise from the storage facilities in the basement up to the top floor, and remembered that when they "protested at the size of the load[s], the favorite crack [of managers] has been that 'We will shoot you and get another horse.'"[5]

The strike at May's grew out of the strikes at Ohrbach's and Klein's. It began, in October 1935, when a May's worker named Elsie Monokian began trying to organize a union in May's "after a friend of hers, who had worked in Ohrbach's Department Store in Manhattan [and had presumably been involved in the union's struggles there], had interested her in trade unionism." After Weinstein found her handing out union literature on multiple occasions, he called Monokian into his office and offered her a bribe to get the names of any workers meeting with the union. Monokian refused, and in response Weinstein promptly fired both Monokian and her best friend in the store, who presumably also helped to organize the union. Both workers left the store and formed a picket line outside. Their two-person picket line grew into a strike of between fifty and one hundred of the approximately 150 workers employed at May's.[6]

As with the Union Square strikes, workers' primary tactic throughout the strike was to prevent customers from crossing the picket line to shop at May's. Their tactics were therefore strongly reminiscent of those used during the Klein's-Ohrbach's strikes. For one thing, the strikers attempted to claim the same revolutionary heritage as they had claimed by dressing up the George Washington statue in Union Square. On Washington's Birthday workers gathered with signs announcing that "Exploitation Without Representation Is Tyranny," and that "The May's Strikers in '36 Have the Spirit of '76." And on Lincoln's Birthday one of the male strikers came dressed up as Abraham Lincoln, complete with beard and hat. The police immediately arrested the man dressed as Lincoln for disturbing the peace, to the great amusement of the strikers.[7]

Workers also drew other tactics from the monkey business of the earlier strikes, laying claim to Fulton Street as they had once laid claim to Union Square. On November 16, for example, workers reenacted part of the invasion of the Waldorf-Astoria Ballroom, by chaining themselves to the elevated train pillar in front of the store. "Within a short time," a police department memorandum claims, "Fulton Street became a seething mass of humanity," as crowds gathered to hear what the chained strikers had to say. At other times the elevated train platform became a speakers' podium for rallies, as it did at one point for members of the left-wing Artists' League, where they gathered "a vast crowd, which was more or less disorderly, interfering with the business of the merchants on either side for five or six doors down the street." Fulton Street, crowded and somewhat chaotic under the best of circumstances, was now also the site of a contest over public space, much as Union Square had been the year before.[8]

The major difference between the Klein's-Ohrbach's strikes and the strike at May's was political. Now within the AFL rather than the OWU, strikers were less openly radical in their tactics than they had been during the Klein's-Ohrbach's strikes. Certainly no workers during the May's strike carried banners honoring the *Daily Worker*, for example; and there is no record of any unemployed workers joining the picket lines in front of May's.

Possibly as a result of these less openly radical stances, the workers were able to attract far more prestigious allies, including some quite wealthy women who had become involved with the League of Women Shoppers (LWS). Clarina Michelson co-founded the LWS in June 1935, along with the wife of Arthur Garfield Hays, a leader of the American Civil Liberties Union at the time. After the Klein's-Ohrbach's strikes demonstrated to union organizers that they would need the support of customers to be successful during strikes at retail stores, Michelson set out to form a lasting organization which would provide customer support for striking workers, both in the retail industry and elsewhere. The LWS was the result, and it quickly attracted numerous prestigious women from around the country. LWS stationery listed a number of very well-known women as supporters, including Suzanne LaFollette, Stella Adler, Mary R. Beard, Dorothy Day, Mrs. Morris Ernst, Mrs. Ira Gershwin, Freda Kirchway, Fola LaFollette, Lucy Sprague Mitchell, Mrs. Elmer Rice, Mrs. Jacob Riis, Mrs. George Soule, Mrs. Leo Sulzberger, Mary Van Kleeck, and Leane Zugsmith, who played an active role in the May's strike while finishing *A Time to Remember*.[9]

There were important differences between elite women's involvement in the Klein's-Ohrbach's strikes and the LWS's support for the May's strike, in terms of the ways in which strikers and union leaders called upon wealthy allies for support. During the Klein's-Ohrbach's strikes, Michelson and others had called upon these people as white-collar workers. LWS members, however, supported the strike out of moral obligation, not out of class solidarity as white-collar workers. In one LWS leaflet, in fact, the organization's leaders boasted of this very lack of class affiliation, claiming that "we are outsiders and not part of either the labor groups or the employing groups."[10]

Michelson's actions in setting up the LWS, antithetical as it was to the concept of class struggle that was a guiding principle during the Klein's-Ohrbach's strikes, was fairly common for a Communist union organizer in 1936. In the era of the United Front, the Communist party actively encouraged cross-class coalitions like the LWS. In fact, Communist party officials criticized Michelson's work because she was not willing to participate in additional coalitions of this nature. This criticism sometimes bordered on outright attacks, as did a letter Communist party functionary Gussie Reed wrote to Michelson:

> It should not be necessary for us to point out how extremely important it is to begin doing work in the Women's Trade Union League . . . Unless you take an active interest in this important work we will not be able to work in an organization which gives us access to thousands of organized and unorganized women. The success or failure of this work depends upon you. I am sure you do not want to bear the responsibility of any possible failure.[11]

Reed's letter is, of course, a remarkable one for what it tells historians about the Communist party's problematic role in the activities of individual Communists. Michelson, over the course of a few short months, had led a remarkable strike and set up a new organization to support workers that did not rely on the sometimes tenuous support the Women's Trade Union League showed for women workers. Yet in this letter Reed ignores these achievements, instead issuing the rather cold warning that Michelson, should she continue in her present course of action, would "bear the responsibility of any possible failure." If Reed's letter illustrates the worst aspects of Communist activism, however, Michelson's response also is highly illustrative. There is no evidence that she got actively involved in the Women's Trade Union League as a result of Reed's order to do so; nor is there any record of any response Michelson wrote to Reed's letter. Michelson would remain a Communist, but that did not mean that she followed party orders without question—instead, she would interpret policies like the United Front in her own way, setting up the organizations and alliances that she believed worked best for her circumstances.

With the support of the LWS, the May's strikers represented a formidable challenge to store managers. Managers responded by launching a determined campaign against the strikers. Some of their tactics were extralegal if not illegal, such as (even according to lawyers in the employ of May's) planting listening devices in strike headquarters. But store managers acted through the law as well as outside it. The company that owned May's gave tremendous sums of money to local Tammany Hall officials, and as a result managers at the store had strong connections to the local justice system. Once again, police became strikers' most determined adversaries. According to one LWS petition, the police were "beating and clubbing men, women, and pedestrians," in their efforts to break up picket lines and rallies, and, as a result of their determination to end the strike, placing a number of fairly prestigious strike supporters under arrest. Both Mrs. Harry Ward and Socialist party leader Norman Thomas went to jail during the May's strike.[12]

Throughout the strike, police and local judges acted openly in the interest of store managers. According to a report by the League of Women Shoppers, store officials "would point out individual pickets and direct police officials to arrest them." On another occasion, after LWS members complained to a police captain that police were making arrests with no cause, the captain "said he would let them repass the store with their signs" with no further arrests if the strikers would then disperse immediately and go back to work. Local judges consistently set high bail for strikers and supporters arrested during the strike, and sentenced at least two strikers to thirty days in jail for extremely minor offenses. The district attorney's office even allowed Abraham Kartzman, a lawyer employed by May's, to act as the prosecuting attorney in several cases.[13]

Elite members of the LWS demanded that Mayor LaGuardia intervene to put an end to these questionable practices. Throughout late 1935 and early 1936 LaGuardia found himself confronted with petition after petition and letter after letter on the May's strike, some of them signed by very prominent citizens. In response, LaGuardia got involved in the strike. Demanding an explanation, he forwarded the LWS complaints about police misconduct to the local police department, who quickly denied the validity of the strikers' complaints. LaGuardia then appointed a committee of three local religious leaders to investigate the claims of police and managerial misconduct during the May's strike. The investigative committee LaGuardia appointed found heavily in favor of the strikers, finding store management guilty of everything from underpaying their workers to providing substandard working conditions and manipulating the local justice system. The committee ended its report to Mayor LaGuardia with a ringing endorsement of the strike, suggesting that "the shoppers of Brooklyn make their purchases where a sense of justice controls employment policies." Store managers, who challenged the validity of the entire report, were especially furious about this last statement, complaining that the committee had no right to "tell the people of Brooklyn where to shop."[14]

These events during the May's strike suggest that union organizers during this strike had found the sort of legitimacy they had sought through the alliance with the RCIPA. Suddenly, with the aid of the AFL and the LWS (many of whose members would no doubt have balked at supporting an openly Communist union like the OWU), the union organizers found moderate support from the mayor's office. Other signs of the union's new legitimacy were also forthcoming. Perhaps most important for the strike itself was the support of the AFL-affiliated Teamsters; as a result of the department store union's affiliation with the AFL, union truck drivers refused to cross the May's picket line, seriously disrupting deliveries to the May's store. Department store managers across the city found this perhaps the most worrisome prospect of all. "One of [store managers'] weak spots," industry expert Ruth Prince Mack asserted later in 1936, "is in the engineering and operating ends of the store. A strike here could, and would cripple any store."[15]

Important though this legitimacy was, it came at a huge price for the strikers at May's and for Local 1250 as a whole. The national RCIPA had assigned professional organizer Benjamin Goodman as an organizer of Local 1250 to replace the OWU organizers lost when the department store union became part of the RCIPA. Goodman was a poor replacement. Both the workers he was supposed to be organizing and Michelson found him aloof and undedicated, a hindrance rather than an ally. Goodman's actions during the May's strike, combined with the actions of the national AFL leaders, made the strike one of the greatest defeats the union suffered, despite the massive success in getting support from both Mayor LaGuardia and the Teamsters.[16]

Throughout late 1935 and 1936 Michelson and other local RCIPA leaders in New York City were involved in a series of conflicts with the national RCIPA leadership. The national RCIPA allowed local union leaders to have representation in policy decisions in proportion to the local's membership, but the proportions were based on the 1924 membership rolls. This meant that those locals which had grown since 1924, such as Local 1250 and the much larger Local 338 (the local which had the charter for organizing all the grocery clerks in New York City), had little say in the national union's policies. This practice, combined with East Coast leader Roy Denise's standing practice of issuing charters to company unions and taking a percentage of the per capita union dues as a bonus, infuriated a number of local leaders, Michelson and Samuel Wolchok, the leader of Local 338, among them. Though Denise was removed in response to their furor, the national RCIPA leaders refused to hear any of the local leaders' other complaints. In response, Michelson, Wolchok, and a few other New York City local leaders refused to pay dues to the national RCIPA throughout 1936.[17]

This degree of tension between the radical local leaders of Local 1250 and the national RCIPA leadership created an awkward situation for Benjamin

Goodman. Goodman had been assigned to the union solely due to his connections to the national RCIPA leaders, not to Michelson or the department store workers themselves. Rather than condemn Michelson outright, Goodman withdrew from the union, refusing to take any role at all in the May's strike after an initial promise to take charge of fundraising activities. Michelson and the strikers took on the task of fundraising, in addition to running the picket line and arranging bail for arrested strikers. With all these other responsibilities, strikers had little time for fundraising, and by early 1936, the strike fund was nearly empty.[18]

The combination of Goodman's inaction and Michelson's open defiance of the national RCIPA leaders led to a disaster at May's. In the spring of 1936, with the local union's strike fund nearly empty, national RCIPA leaders ordered that control of the strike be turned over to Local 1125, the Retail Women's Apparel Salespeople's Union, whose leaders were not withholding dues from the national union. The May's strikers immediately protested, since they had been working so closely and for so long with Michelson and other members of Local 1250. The national leaders of the RCIPA refused to reconsider, and they even took the fight a step further, warning workers and Local 1250 leaders that unless the strike was turned over to Local 1125, there would be no more strike benefits, since Local 1250 had no money with which to run the strike. The strikers, badly in need of these benefits, which represented their only source of income during the strike, agreed to switch unions.[19]

Local 1125 leaders immediately proved that the strikers' hesitancy about the switch in jurisdiction was justified. In the midst of the strike, the leaders of Local 1125 refused to issue union cards to any strikers. Since Weinstein had fired them, the strikers were technically not employed at any retail store, and, as one Local 1125 official stated, "[T]he international's constitution forbids membership to clerks who are unemployed." The leaders of Local 1125 then immediately took away the workers' picket signs and closed the strike headquarters, declaring the strike at an end.[20]

In contrast to the aftermath of the strikes at Klein's and Ohrbach's, the department store union could not claim even a symbolic victory at May's. While Michelson and her allies in Local 1250 could claim that their leadership of Local 1250 had not been responsible for this failure, even this claim was an empty one. It had been Michelson and other ex-OWU leaders who had chosen to follow the United Front policy by allying themselves with the corrupt and conservative RCIPA, hoping to gain greater legitimacy, and as a result the workers at May's lost their strike.

The scandal surrounding the second strike at Ohrbach's was just as devastating as the defeat at May's. Like the May's strike, this second strike at Ohrbach's was an outgrowth of the Klein's-Ohrbach's strike. Managers at Ohrbach's had fired practically every worker who had been involved in the 1934–35 strike, and a few of these fired workers still had the courage to return to the picket line in 1936. This time only around twenty workers went out on strike, most of whom had been involved in the earlier strike as well. Among those few who had not been involved with the earlier strike was a young Italian-American worker named Nicholas Carnes, who became Michelson's second-in-command during the strike and eventually became an important leader of the department store unions.[21]

Workers faced even more obstacles during this second Ohrbach's strike than during the Klein's-Ohrbach's strike. This was partially because of the smaller number of strikers, and partially because—once again—Benjamin Goodman promised to handle the fundraising activities and then proved either unable or unwilling to do so. Nonetheless, the workers—after close to two hundred arrests during a nine-month strike—created enough of a disturbance in Union Square to force Nathan Ohrbach to agree to meet personally with Michelson and a representative group of strikers by the fall of 1936. On October 2 Ohrbach and Michelson reached a settlement that became the cause of much controversy and eventually resulted in the split between Local 1250 and the national RCIPA. The terms of the settlement were fairly straightforward: the picket line would be withdrawn, and the strikers would get back pay of $5000, to be divided amongst themselves as they saw fit. Ohrbach, while he promised to stop discriminating against union employees and to rehire the strikers, again refused to recognize the union. Michelson and Ohrbach agreed to settle the strike on those terms, and the workers, some of whom had been on strike, on and off, for almost two years, voted to accept the settlement at a meeting the next day, on October 3.[22]

Only after workers accepted the contract and officially ended the Ohrbach's strike did Benjamin Goodman involve himself in the strike, to the great annoyance of Michelson and the Ohrbach's workers alike. Though Michelson and the strikers both insisted that they had invited him to attend the negotiations as well as the meeting where the workers ratified the agreement, Goodman chose not to attend either event. Instead, two days after the strike ended, on October 5, Goodman sent out a strongly worded statement to the press and to elected officials calling the agreement a "sell-out" and a "deal" rather than a true settlement. He also pointed out (correctly) that, in the end, much of the money from the agreement would go to fees for lawyers who had been present during the negotiations. That same day, as though to place the union under his control by sheer force, Goodman removed all the union's records from the union offices, as well as the union's petty cash and personal items which various strikers and organizers had left in the office. Whether Goodman was merely attempting to force Michelson to back down in her continuing fight with the national RCIPA leaders or whether he sincerely believed that she had betrayed the workers is impossible to determine with any certainty, but given his lack of involvement in the union up until that point, it seems unlikely that his concern over the agreement was genuine.[23]

Whatever Goodman's motives actually were, Michelson and the strikers quickly responded to his charges. On October 12, they began a union hearing on Goodman's actions. Participants from both the Ohrbach's and the May's strikes offered statements concerning Goodman's involvement—or lack of involvement—in the union. The Ohrbach's workers whom Goodman had ostensibly been trying to defend were bewildered by Goodman's actions. Some, like Anne Little and Anne Friedman (the two workers who had sat in at the Waldorf-Astoria the previous year), had participated in the earlier strike under Michelson's leadership and viewed Michelson as a friend and ally, whereas Goodman was a comparative stranger. They, like other Ohrbach's workers who attended Goodman's hearing, used the hearing as an opportunity to voice their trust in Michelson, stating for the trial record that Michelson had been "empowered . . . with full rights" to make any deal she could make to get them their jobs back. Other workers pointed out that it had been they, and not Michelson or the lawyers, who had decided on the distribution of funds. Not one member of the trial committee voiced any defense for Goodman, and not one striker ever came forward to publicly challenge the settlement. At the end of the proceedings, the trial board voted to dismiss Goodman from his post at Local 1250.[24]

By this time, of course, the damage had been done, and the failures at May's and Ohrbach's were only the most glaring among many. During these years, the union continued to hold chapters throughout New York City, at nearly every store where workers later won contracts, and even held some chapters where workers never won union recognition. Altman's, Abraham and Straus (A&S), Alexander's, Bloomingdale's, Gimbel's, Hearn's, Macy's, Namm's, Oppenheim Collins, Loeser's, Saks Fifth Avenue, Stern's, and Wanamaker's, among others, all had chapters of Local 1250. But the existence of the union seems to have had little effect on the lives of most workers within these stores.

To make matters worse, rather than expanding their network of allies, the formation of Local 1250 seems to have limited the number and types of allies that the union had. As we have seen, during the years in the OWU, the department store unions had been linked to the "Don't Buy Where You Can't Work" campaign through Michelson's activity in both struggles. Tenuous though this connection had been (the leaders of the "Don't Buy Where You Can't Work" campaign refused to support the Klein's-Ohrbach's strikers, for instance, unless the strikers took a stand on racial discrimination in hiring, something neither strikers nor strike leaders apparently ever considered), there had least been an attempt to find common ground. With the formation of Local 1250 and the transformation of the LSNR into the National Negro Congress (another result of the United Front strategy), however, these attempts ended, and for the remainder of the 1930s the unions would do little to agitate against racial discrimination in the department stores.[25]

The overall weakness of Local 1250 in these years was a direct result of the alliance with the RCIPA. Throughout 1935 and 1936, Local 1250 had virtually no money, receiving no money from the national union and collecting only small amounts for dues payments. The union was also desperately understaffed; thanks to Goodman's lack of involvement, Local 1250's support for workers basically consisted of one union organizer, Clarina Michelson. In addition, the union had few long-term members. Many workers, even at upscale stores where turnover was a less serious issue, moved through both union and stores very quickly, often within a matter of months. As a result, the union, lacking funds, staff, and a solid membership base, could be a factor in workers' lives only after large numbers of workers were on the verge of striking. The union's inability to win a solid victory during these early strikes meant that even at stores where workers did strike, the union had no future once the strike ended.[26]

By early 1937, after almost two years as a local of the RCIPA, Local 1250 leaders had determined that the benefits of RCIPA membership were negligible. The RCIPA affiliation had not won department store workers a single contract. Union leaders had lost one important strike they had organized, at May's, and even Michelson's strongest supporters admitted that the settlement at Ohrbach's, their only other major strike during these years, was a weak settlement at best. The union was underfunded, and had only a handful of members who stayed in the union for more than a few months. And, especially considering that the union leaders had agreed to join the RCIPA in search of greater legitimacy and respectability, Goodman's attack on Michelson and the union had created an unacceptable scandal.

Luckily for Michelson and Local 1250, at this time, early 1937, the leaders of other New York City RCIPA locals began to reject the national union's policies and leadership as ineffectual and corrupt. On February 18, 1937, the various dissident locals met at the Manhattan Opera House. Amidst some interruptions by Local 1125 leaders, who continued to support the national RCIPA leadership, the dissidents formally banded together as the "New Era Retail Committee" in an open revolt against the RCIPA's national leadership, choosing Local 338 President Samuel Wolchok as the New Era Committee's leader.[27]

The New Era Committee was a diverse but weak coalition of dissidents. Despite the important role played by Communists in Local 1250, most of the leaders of the New Era Committee were anti-Communists. Wolchok himself, for instance, was a liberal Democrat and a strong supporter of President Roosevelt and the New Deal. He was also a particularly strong anti-Communist, who sometimes went so far as to claim that he had confronted Communist aggression physically. One acquaintance of Wolchok's remembered that "Wolchok carried a . . . scar on his face, and always claimed that he got that scar from a knife wound that [a TUUL leader] had inflicted on him."[28]

Despite his anti-communism, Wolchok and the radical organizers of Local 1250, of whom Michelson was still by far the most important, joined together in the New Era Committee. They united largely around a common enemy, namely, the national RCIPA leadership. Of course, the United Front policy may have had a role to play in this alliance as well, but if the United Front called for alliances, as seen in Gussie Reed's letter to Michelson, it was Michelson and others in Local 1250 who would decide who those allies would be, not the party bureaucrats. Wolchok, at least at the moment, seemed like a logical choice. Organizers in the department store unions had attempted creating unions without AFL affiliation during the OWU years, and had met with little success. If anything, things had gotten worse during their merger with the RCIPA. Now Wolchok's offer of an alliance gave rise to what seemed like an explanation for why the RCIPA merger had failed that did not require condemnation of the Communist party policies: namely, that the national leaders of the RCIPA were themselves too corrupt to function as legitimate union officials. The New Era Committee therefore offered a United Front strategy which was more acceptable than alliance with the RCIPA: Local 1250 leaders could work with honest, if less radical, labor leaders, who were willing to take a stand against corruption.[29]

Wolchok, well aware that he was dealing with Communists, was extremely tactful when he addressed the issue of what this alliance would mean for the department store union's future. He emphasized to Michelson that, if nothing else, the department store union would have more autonomy under the New

Era Committee than they had under the RCIPA. To Wolchok's credit, he faithfully lived up to this promise, allowing Local 1250 to remain autonomous and intact throughout the existence of the New Era Committee.[30]

Wolchok agreed to work with Local 1250, and even agreed to grant them autonomy, because he badly needed the Communists' support. As the leader of a dissident union, Wolchok was singularly ill equipped, with neither the members nor the funds to present a serious challenge to the RCIPA. Immediately after forming the New Era Committee, he and the committee were so without options that they applied for membership in the AFL, as a separate union from the RCIPA. In order for this request to even be considered, he would need as many locals as he could possibly get to join the New Era Committee. And Local 1250, while hardly the most successful local in the RCIPA, at least had a leader who was willing to take a chance on Wolchok's committee. (Even with Local 1250, no record exists of a response from the national AFL on the request for a charter.)[31]

The New Era Committee's decision to apply for a new AFL charter is particularly significant since the committee apparently made no attempt to make an alliance with the newly formed Committee of Industrial Organizations (CIO). In general, most CIO leaders in these early years were men like Wolchok, who rejected the policies and practices of certain AFL leaders as corrupt and ineffectual. In addition, the CIO leaders often had political beliefs similar to Wolchok's; most of them, like Wolchok, were liberal Democrats. Finally, CIO leaders were strong supporters of industrial unionism, the practice of organizing all workers in a shop or a factory into a single union, regardless of either skill level or of particular job description. According to retail industry analysts, this policy was the best one for organizing within department stores and other retail establishments, where salespeople, cashiers, elevator operators, and stock people all worked within the same building.[32]

The CIO and the New Era Committee, both increasingly dissatisfied with AFL policies in these years, remained separate due largely to the types of workers each organized. The New Era Committee's decision to avoid the CIO, at least initially, is best explained by the CIO's strong connections to blue-collar workers; the CIO, after all, was centered in the mining, rubber, automobile, and garment industries. To lead a union of white-collar workers, Wolchok sought instead the support of the mainstream AFL, which had long supported organizing white-collar workers. For their part, CIO leaders apparently showed no interest whatsoever in early 1937 in using Wolchok's New Era Committee as the backbone of a CIO-affiliated retail union, something which would come to pass later that same year.

In February 1937, as they left the RCIPA to join the New Era Committee, the leaders of Local 1250 discovered that the legitimacy they had sought in joining the RCIPA remained illusive. To the extent that the RCIPA provided any sort of legitimacy at all—as seen by the actions of the Teamsters, the LWS, and Mayor LaGuardia—this legitimacy was offset by the corruption, scandal, and conflict rampant within the RCIPA. By early 1937 Local 1250 and the department store workers represented by this union had yet to demonstrate the legitimacy of their cause to the city and the country at large. Instead, the Communist leaders of Local 1250 were forced to take the rather slim chance that Wolchok and the other dissidents in the RCIPA would at least be more supportive of the department store unions than their former allies in the national RCIPA had been.

Counter Girls vs. the Countess, Spring 1937

The spring of 1937 found Local 1250 weakened and relatively isolated, with strong ties neither to the AFL nor to the emergent CIO. Their sole affiliation, the New Era Committee, was at best a weak alliance with a few other retail workers' unions around New York City. But it was at that moment of the union's weakness that department store workers won the legitimacy that union leaders had long sought. Three factors would play major roles in the workers' victory. The notoriety of Woolworth's heiress Barbara Hutton, the increasing controversy around chain stores, and the rising tide of unionization in blue-collar industries all contributed to the department store unions' first major successes in New York City, in the sit-down strikes of March 1937.

The mid-1930s were busy years in the life of Woolworth heiress Barbara Hutton. As the department store unions were still reeling from the struggle with Benjamin Goodman and the defeat at Ohrbach's, the twenty-four-year-old heiress had divorced her first husband, Prince Alexis Mdivani, and was entering her second marriage to impoverished European nobility, this time to the Count Haugwitz von Reventlow. Hutton was an infamous figure, described by one paper as "the sure-fire sensation of the tabloid, glamour girl of the roto-gravures, and American whom two foreign marriages have converted into a foreigner." Hutton made news both through her marriages and by spending immense sums of money on lavish parties.[33]

With many Americans unemployed and going hungry, wealthy women like Hutton were prominent negative symbols in American culture in the mid 1930s. In 1934, Dashiell Hammett's popular novel *The Thin Man* attacked the rich, particularly rich women like Hutton who bought and paid for their foreign husbands. Much of the social content was erased when the novel was transformed into a screwball comedy in 1935, but other film comedies were less subtle. In 1936, as newspapers reported that Hutton had spent $1,200,000 on gems once owned by Napoleon, William Powell, the star of *The Thin Man,* appeared in *My Man Godfrey,* perhaps one of the most negative portrayals of rich women in mid-1930s film. In *My Man Godfrey* heiresses like Hutton are portrayed as wasteful, foolish, and generally immoral, paying little if any attention to the needs and concerns of others while they spend their time and their parents' money finding all sorts of foolish amusements, all pointless and some cruel.[34]

These sorts of negative images of wealthy women as extravagant, wasteful, and unfeeling were especially prominent among leftists. Nowhere was Communist party member and novelist Mike Gold's work more brutal than when he described the wife of his father's boss. In "a large gaudy room glowing with red wallpaper, and stuffed like the show window of a furniture store with tables, chairs, sofas, dressers, bric-a-brac" the boss's wife "lay on a sofa. She glittered like an ice-cream parlor. Her tubby legs rested on a red pillow. Her bleached yellow head blazed with diamond combs and rested on a pillow of green." Fat, lazy, stupid, and constantly whining, the boss's wife was, in Gold's work and in much of Communist literature of the 1930s, the sheer embodiment of the bosses' wealth, barely distinguishable from the gems and rich furnishings surrounding them. As such, these women were the symbols of exploitation, and attacks on them could have tremendous rhetorical power.[35]

If Hutton and her ilk were powerful negative icons in the mid-1930s, so too were Woolworth stores themselves. Beginning in the early years of the Depression, with a 1931 Supreme Court decision legalizing prohibitive taxes on large chain stores, some politicians began to argue that large chains like Woolworth's were damaging to small retailers and therefore bad for the country's economy as a whole. Chain-store owners immediately launched counter-campaigns through the National Chain Store Association and the American Retail Federation to "give the public a clearer understanding of just what the chain store meant in terms of superior merchandise at lower cost," even going so far as to prepare a "comprehensive Debaters' Manual, covering every phase of the chain-store subject" for use in high school and college debates.[36]

This debate over chain stores reached its height in 1935, when Representative Wright Patman of Texas led a congressional committee to

> investigate the American Retail Federation, its capitalization, its membership, its objectives, the sources of its funds, its financial connections

and its officers and agents and to investigate the record of stock divi-
dends, officers' salaries, profits, interlocking directorates and banking
affiliations of all corporations directly affiliated with, or contributing to,
the said American Retail Federation.[37]

By 1937, when the committee's findings came out, anti–chain store activists
had assembled a long list of accusations against chain-store owners, including
"undercover organizations, expensive 'influence,' . . . state organizations mas-
querading under misleading names . . . Millions of dollars are being poured
into undercover propaganda to sell the American people the idea that the
chain store system is an economic blessing," for the benefit of "a few men in a
few little offices in New York," while small retailers paid the price. These activists had also succeeded in passing the Robinson-Patman Act, making it illegal
for manufacturers to sell at a discount to large retailers.[38]

Anti–chain store activists and department store union organizers always
remained separate. Anti–chain store spokespeople saw themselves primarily
as supporters of small retailers rather than workers at large retail establishments. Yet there was an attempt by at least some anti–chain store activists to
suggest links between the workers' struggles against the stores and what these
activists viewed as the overarching issue of "absentee ownership." In his anti–
chain store manifesto, *Wells of Discontent,* Charles Daughters, a close ally of
Patman's in the struggle against chain stores, claimed that "employees fall heirs
to one of the greatest evils of absentee ownership" in the lack of job stability,
low wages, and long hours which these employees had to work. Daughters's
claim, it should be noted, has little factual justification. Active owners like
Samuel Klein and Nathan Ohrbach, for instance, were often present within
the stores they owned, yet, if anything, their presence seems to have been an
additional burden for their employees, adding another level of supervision to
an already oppressive environment.[39]

Despite this division between the unions and the anti–chain store activists,
the presence of these activists played a major role in the workers' 1937 strikes
at five-and-dime chain stores. By calling these chains' legitimacy into question,
anti–chain store activists helped set the stage for workers' challenges to chain-
store managers' control in 1937.

The final factor which played a major role in the victories in 1937 was the
rising tide of strikes and unions in factories. The massive sit-down strikes
in Flint and Akron introduced a new tactic to the labor movement, and the
sit-down strike was an incredibly effective tactic, since it allowed workers to
seize control of the factories and prevented managers from using scabs. As a

result, this tactic quickly spread to other workers, including other assembly line workers, hospital workers, janitors, teachers, and even blind workers in pencil factories. Throughout the early months of 1937 sit-down strikes were becoming a new and extremely important facet of American life.

As sit-down strikes grew in importance, managers at Woolworth's and other five-and-dime chain stores continued to exploit their workers. Like the managers of other downscale stores, five-and-dime store managers relied on quick turnover, large numbers of customers, and low overhead and labor costs for their profits. As a result, managers forced all the labor possible out of their workers, forcing them to work "one girl to more than one overcrowded, busy counter," as one worker described it. Here, as at the other downscale stores, workers complained of the constant supervision, where "professional shoppers [are] paid to spy and antaganize [sic] . . . to see whether they answer politely." For working in these conditions, five-and-dime store workers drew only slightly higher pay than workers at other downscale stores, making around $10 to $11 a week as opposed to the $7 to $8 a week Klein's workers made, for instance.[40]

Workers at the five-and-dime stores had some problems not shared by workers at other downscale stores. For one thing, there were no employee lunchrooms at the small Woolworth's stores. Employees at these stores generally ate in the filthy storage rooms. Woolworth's managers also kept the workers long after the stores closed in order to give them pep talks to encourage morale. Finally, unlike in most stores, managers required Woolworth's workers to wear uniforms; workers not only had to buy their own uniforms, but they also had to pay to keep these uniforms clean and in good condition.[41]

In response to these conditions and the increasing popularity of sit-down strikes among workers throughout the city, five-and-dime store workers in Detroit went on a sit-down strike in March 1937. Woolworth's managers used what may have been their most powerful weapon in response. Woolworth's was a large national chain, and managers could therefore afford to have stores in any one area shut down, at least temporarily. They threatened to do so throughout Detroit if the workers did not end the sit-down strike immediately. Similar actions had worked in the past for chain-store owners. In 1934, for instance, managers at A&P grocery stores in Cleveland had closed all the stores in response to a strike there, and had forced workers to withdraw their picket lines.[42]

Closing all the stores in Detroit was a powerful threat, but if managers could draw on their regional and national presence to solve a local dispute, in 1937 workers could do the same. Woolworth's workers in other Detroit

stores walked out in sympathy with the sit-down strikers, defying the bosses'
threat, and in New York Clarina Michelson immediately called for a boycott
of all New York Woolworth's stores until the strike was settled. In addition,
this threat by Woolworth's management drew greater attention to the situation of Woolworth's workers in the rest of the country, including those in New
York. Local 1250 released a statement in response to this threat noting that,
in New York, "most workers received $10, $11, or $12 [a week], and no pay
for overtime," in conditions that caused the union to suggest that the situation of Woolworth's clerks in New York City were "as bad or worse than those
in Detroit." Like Woolworth's itself, the labor movement was increasingly a
national movement, capable of at least attempting to act on a national scale.[43]

Whether the threat of a New York boycott was a factor or not, by the time
Local 1250 began mobilizing to support the Detroit workers' sit-down, the
strike was already nearly over. By March 5, only two days after Local 1250
began calling for a New York boycott, Woolworth's managers gave in to the
strikers' demands, offering a contract like none of Woolworth's workers had
ever seen. Workers won 20 to 25 percent pay raises, time-and-a-half for overtime (after a 48-hour work week), half-pay for the time they'd been on their
sit-down strike, free uniforms, and the right to be hired through the union, not
the company.[44]

If Woolworth's managers settled in the hope of preventing the development
of other strikes, their gambit failed. By the time the strike was over, New York's
department store union organizers and union members alike were all thinking
about a sit-down strike of their own. Early in March 1937, Local 1250 released
a set of rules entitled "What To Do In Case Of a Sit Down," where the rules for
sitting-down were carefully laid out: "Upon receiving the signal, you will finish
whatever you may be doing at the moment. Then you will stay at your post,
fold your arms, and inform any customer who may want to be waited on that
you are on strike." A *Daily Worker* reporter who interviewed New York City
Woolworth's workers during the Detroit strike announced that "every one of
them knows about the happenings in Detroit. . . . One girl said, 'Just wait till
this thing breaks in New York, we'll even show Detroit how to sit down.'"[45]

Workers and union organizers in New York City got their chance. On March
14 workers at five different five-and-dime F&W Grand stores in different parts
of New York City began sit-down strikes. Workers at two Grand stores in Far
Rockaway, Queens, at stores in Park Slope and Bay Ridge, Brooklyn, and at
one store on Fourteenth Street in Manhattan, just off Union Square, went on
strike simultaneously. Later that day, workers sat down at a Grand store on the
Upper West Side of Manhattan, and strike supporters began to picket another

Grand store on West 14th Street, much to the delight of the sit-down strikers. The strike quickly spread to other five-and-dime stores. By March 17 workers at two Woolworth's stores—one in Brooklyn, and one on 14th Street—sat down as well, and their actions made the front page of the *New York Times*. The strike was now in full force.[46]

As it had been two years earlier during the Klein's-Ohrbach's strikes, 14th Street, the location of three of the struck five-and-dime stores, again became a battleground between police and strike supporters. Unlike during the Klein's-Ohrbach's strikes, here much of the support was initially on a personal level, as families and friends of the strikers set up picket lines outside the stores. Other supporters, however, quickly emerged. The picket lines greatly expanded, to include hundreds of other working-class New Yorkers, and prominent union leaders also sanctioned the sit-down strikes. William Green, the president of the American Federation of Labor, immediately announced his support for the strike, as did Wolchok and other New Era Committee members. Not everyone issued statements, however; the national leaders of the RCIPA remained conspicuously silent on the sit-down strikes.[47]

Wolchok in particular used the sit-down strikes as an opportunity to show his support for Local 1250. Knowing that Michelson and Nicholas Carnes, who was present in the Grand store on 14th Street during the sit-down strike, were already working very closely with the sit-down strikers and their supporters, Wolchok did not attempt to interfere with their efforts. Instead, he concentrated on setting up negotiations between store management, himself, workers, and Michelson. The Grand store managers agreed to negotiate within three days of the beginning of the strikes, and never attempted to use force against the sit-down strikers. They did, however, prove so intractable in negotiations that Michelson threatened to call for a strike in all Grand stores in New York City if negotiations did not improve. After Michelson's threat, Grand store managers began negotiating in earnest.[48]

Managers at Woolworth's responded in a far more confrontational and violent manner. On the very first night of the strike, Woolworth's managers hired agents of the Burns Detective Agency, which specialized in breaking strikes, to invade the store and ensure that nothing was touched. In addition, following the advice in an editorial in the *Dry Goods Economist,* one of the retail industry's trade publications, Woolworth's managers had city police stand in front of the store to make certain that the strikers received no food, cots, or blankets.[49]

The workers turned the ban on food into a tremendous opportunity for drama, by declaring themselves on a hunger strike. This decision was made entirely by the strikers. When the news came that no food would be allowed into the Woolworth's stores, Michelson suggested that the workers simply buy food from the store, which she felt was legal so long as the workers paid for anything they took. One of the women strikers, Michelson remembered, looked at her in disgust. "'Buy food from a store that's on strike?'" the striker asked her, apparently astonished that Michelson would suggest such a thing. The Woolworth's workers were determined to make this strike a memorable one, even if it meant some personal discomfort.[50]

Begun late on March 17, the hunger strike lasted only a few hours, due primarily to the actions of the supporters in the streets outside. By 1:30 A.M. on the morning of March 18, a large crowd gathered to form a picket line in the streets outside, since the strikers' families, friends, and other supporters had gotten word of the ban on food and the resulting hunger strike. Some of these picketers sneaked around to the back of the store and formed a human ladder, with strike supporters standing on top of one another's shoulders to reach the store's windows. Inside, workers—having been informed of this action in advance—climbed the shelves to open the windows. The supporters outside immediately began passing food, blankets, and even cots to the strikers. When the goods were received, the strikers officially declared the hunger strike over and began eating.[51]

The store managers' ploy of banning food had therefore failed twice. First, the ban had created the opportunity for the hunger strike. By declaring the hunger strike, workers used managers' own tactics to draw attention to their plight. Second, by allowing strike supporters to sneak food into the store regardless of the ban, managers had effectively created the necessity for strike supporters to be alert and present in front of the stores at all times.

The presence of supporters in the streets outside also greatly benefited the strikers when store managers adopted a new tactic. The night after the hunger strike, managers had police evict the sit-down strikers at both striking Woolworth's stores, charging them with disorderly conduct. While police refused to take this action in response to sit-down strikers in other cities, in New York police entered the stores and arrested the strikers. Doing so was no simple matter, however. By the time of the police raid, huge crowds had gathered around the Woolworth's stores, including representatives from the Communist-led International Workers Order, as well as the radical seamen's and bakery workers' unions. Upon hearing of the imminent eviction, these supporters gathered around the police wagons and the store entrances, trying to block the police from leaving the store with the strikers. The police fought their way through the crowd and headed back to the station with the prisoners, only to find another demonstration of several hundred people, yelling, "Woolworth's strikers must go free!" The sit-down strikers were released after a brief arraignment in night court. After they were released, the strikers immediately went back to the store and sat down again. The next day, again, Woolworth's management charged the strikers with disorderly conduct, resulting in another round of arrests, street protests by supporters, arraignments, and then the strikers' return to the store to sit down again.[52]

The Woolworth's strike was quickly becoming a cause for extensive Communist-led working-class protest, and there is no telling how long it might have continued or how the strike would have developed had Mayor La Guardia not intervened. This time La Guardia advised both the company and the union that "labor controversies in your stores have reached a point where the public is obviously involved," and he then offered his services as mediator in order to bring an end to the strike and the protests surrounding it.[53]

After La Guardia stepped in, the strikes ended quickly. Workers had gone into the strike demanding union recognition, paid vacations, and better working conditions. In both Woolworth's and the Grand stores, the workers received a 10 percent increase for all workers earning $20 or less, with a minimum weekly wage of $15.60, an end to any mandatory overtime, and paid vacations. Managers signed one-year contracts at all New York City Woolworth's stores. In short, the strike was, for the first time in the union's history, a stunning clear-cut victory.[54]

In addition, workers, union leaders, and supportive journalists all identified the five-and-dime strikes as part of a national labor movement. Communists in particular quickly identified the strikes as part of the United Front and therefore part of an international movement against capitalist exploitation and inequality. Harry Raymond's description of the sit-down strikers' St. Patrick's Day celebration in the *Daily Worker*, ostensibly a passage designed to demonstrate how happy the workers were, also shows the way in which Communist journalists linked the strike to the United Front:

> We were given a real St. Patrick's Day surprise. France Czechoshi, a Polish girl, did an Irish reel . . . Eddie Summers, Negro kitchen man . . . stepped off a fast tap dance. There was another hot dance by Honey Cohen and Dave Levitt . . . And we won't forget those three dark-eyed Italian girls for a long time . . . They sang "La Luna Mezza Mare" ("The Moon in the Middle of the Ocean").[55]

The wide variety of ethnic and racial forms of celebration was a clear reference to the Front, as workers of all races and ethnicities came together to struggle against the bosses. Other *Worker* articles also emphasized this interethnic and interracial aspect of the strike. For example, the *Worker* reported, "one of the songs most popular among the sit-down strikers . . . is the following . . . [version of a] familiar Negro song of protest . . . 'We Shall Not Be Moved:' 'Clarina is our leader/ we shall not be moved; / . . . Just like a tree, / standing by the water, / We shall not be moved." Workers actively accepted this link to the international movement, even including as one of their demands (one of the first that they negotiated away) that Woolworth's boycott all German-made goods.[56]

While only supporters invoked the narrative of the United Front, both opponents and supporters attempted to place the strike into familiar gender narratives. Observers who criticized the strike and strikers, such as *New York Times* reporters, identified the strike as a moment of "hysteria on the part of women workers." Later in the same article, the reporter also referred to "at least a half a dozen girls" who "gave way to hysteria during the first excitement," while noting that "one [girl], Julia Myers, fainted, and was taken to a first-aid room in the basement." The women were, in fact, mere "pawns" in the hands of unnamed union leaders, as a judge who presided at their arraignment (and who was quoted in the *Times*) described the situation. These sorts of descriptions in the *Times* represented a fundamental negation of the strikers' agency as well as a powerfully gendered narrative. The Woolworth's workers during the sit-downs were simply, in this analysis, women acting as women, that is, fainting and being hysterical. Union leaders, presumably men, were then able to take advantage of these hysterical women, at least in the imagination of the judge and of the *Times* reporters.[57]

The Communist press, on the other hand, addressed the strikes with typical confusion around gender, often recognizing the agency of the women strikers while belittling women's actions. *Daily Worker* reporter Harry Raymond, who stayed inside the Grand store on 14th Street during the sit-down, recognized the agency of the strikers, describing the sit-down as "a glorious strike [that] these 85 sales girls are conducting." Similarly, Esther Cantor, who wrote a series of *Daily Worker* articles about the sit-down strike in the Grand store on Pitkin Avenue in Brooklyn, similarly described the strikes as the act of militant workers: "The 36 girls who began a sit-down strike here . . . are now pushing cots . . . against the front door to keep out . . . store executives."[58]

Despite recognizing the agency and militancy of these women, however, the Communist press combined celebration with condescension. *Daily Worker* journalists did so in part through their constant use of the term "girls," a term which observers seem to have used universally when discussing these strikes conducted by women who were mostly in their twenties. In addition, many of the descriptions suggested that these sit-downs were rather light-hearted affairs in many ways. According to one sub-headline in Harry Raymond's article, the girls "Are Firm, Disciplined, and Merry in F.W. Grand Sit-Down."[59]

Strike supporters also had another gendered symbol at their disposal: the wealthy heiress, Barbara Hutton. Such a symbol not only allowed the workers at Woolworth's a chance to make clear that they shared nothing with the negative stereotypes of women that dominated the era; it also allowed them an easily identified and generally hated enemy. Michelson, as soon as the sit-down strikes broke out at Woolworth's, began using Hutton's name by making a speech to the strikers announcing that "their employer was cruising about the world amidst barbaric splendor while her employees were fighting for a $20 weekly wage." In response, strikers proposed to send Hutton a transatlantic cable, informing her that "hunger strikers in New York store ask your intervention for a living wage."[60]

Workers also used Hutton's "barbaric splendor" as a recurrent theme in their songs and chants. In both the Detroit and New York strikes, strikers adapted a popular song of the day, "Mademoiselle from Armentieres," as a strike song: "Barbara Hutton has the dough, parles vous, / Where she gets it, sure we know, parles vous." In addition, in New York, workers invoked Hutton's name in one of their more imaginative chants, making the contrast between their own economic status and Hutton's more explicit still: "Barbara Hutton, she gets mutton! Woolworth's workers, they get nothin'!"[61]

Daily Worker journalists placed even more emphasis on Hutton's role in the strike. The *Worker* ran Barbara Hutton's picture twice during the sit-down strikes, along with two separate articles, one of which was entitled "Counter Girls Vs. The Countess." One of the two photographs was captioned in terms which heavily stressed Hutton's wealth: "Countess Barbara sits down over champagne and looks on aghast." Al Richmond, who wrote "Counter Girls Vs. The Countess," was equally clear in the text: "Enough of those dimes [made by sales in the store] have gone to Babs Hutton for trading in worn-out Mdivanis for later model Haugwitz von Reventlows." And reporters claimed "the [Woolworth's] strikers were sarcastic yesterday when a news dispatch from Cairo, Egypt, where the multi-millionaire Woolworth's heiress is reveling in luxury, stated that she said she was 'powerless to take any action in the sit-down strikes.' "[62]

Even less radical journalists emphasized Hutton's connection to the strike. The liberal *New York Post,* for instance, printed a story about Hutton (ironically entitled "Babs Sits Down Also—After Swim, Sun Bath") right next to a story about the Woolworth's sit-downs: "41 More Arrested In Woolworth's 14th Street Sit-Down." Hutton, the *Post* reported, "lazes through the days here [in Cairo] at her hotel overlooking the desert." She "usually takes a long swim and sun bath in the morning . . . The afternoons are mostly devoted to long drives through the country with her husband and in the evening they dine quietly together at the hotel." The contrast was a remarkable one: the useless, lazy Hutton, the epitome of negative stereotypes about wealthy women, basked in luxury while Woolworth's workers took up the tactic of other workers, the sit-down strike, and fought for the rights other workers had demanded.[63]

On one level, the attacks on Hutton that accompanied the strikes were justified: Hutton's wealth was, as these workers charged, the result of exploitation; and the contrast between Hutton and the Woolworth's workers was a powerful one, to say the least. At the same time, Hutton was no longer the strikers' employer. As Hutton herself was quick to point out, even though her inheritance had originally come from Woolworth's, she had no real control over the way in which the stores were run, since her family had long since sold off much of her Woolworth's stock. The amount of emphasis placed on Hutton's wealth and title during the strike was therefore not an attack on management, but rather a way of allowing the women retail workers to recast the strikes as having a recognizable class- and gender-specific opponent: the wealthy woman.[64]

Through the five-and-dime sit-down strikes and the ways in which they were described, workers and their supporters made Local 1250 and the New Era Committee an integral part of the national labor movement. Like other workers of the day, retail workers had launched sit-down strikes, and they had done so against none other than the infamous Barbara Hutton, whom the rest of the labor movement could condemn with tremendous fervor. The strikers' success also made the unions a permanent factor in New York City's department stores. In the weeks and months after the sit-down strikes, both the unions' supporters and their detractors would recognize the unions' new permanence and legitimacy.

The fastest reactions to the strikes came not from supporters, but from the opponents of retail unionism. Store managers throughout the country found the events in Woolworth's troubling signs of things to come. In response to the Detroit sit-down strikes, the *Dry Goods Economist* published an editorial condemning sit-down strikes, offering a fierce defense of the employer's right to use industrial espionage against unions. "The employer is supposed to sit twiddling his thumbs while plans are being perfected to attack his interests," the *Dry Goods Economist* editors complained. "He may suspect, but he is not allowed to find out what special type of gehenna is being worked up against him. Utterly regardless of the things that are being said about labor espionage in committee chambers, any store owner who these days does not fix up for himself an underground for keeping track of what is going on is inviting the same sort of surprise" as the Woolworth's store managers.[65]

Other retail industry analysts found different lessons in the sit-down strikes. The editors of New York University's prestigious *Journal of Retailing* focused the April 1937 issue of the *Journal,* the first since the five-and-dime sit-down strikes, on personnel problems in retailing, specifically focusing on the issue of unionization. The journal's editors, not surprisingly considering that it was written primarily for an audience of store managers, deplored what they saw as the collapse of "the American concept of equality of opportunity," and its replacement by "the European concept of class consciousness" among store workers. Most deadly of all these European ideas, John Wingate and O. Preston Robinson suggested in a *Journal of Retailing* article on "Unionization in Retailing," was the sit-down strike: "This type of strike has provided workers with a powerful weapon that employers cannot help but heed. Strikers can be replaced . . . but it is proving much more difficult to oust sit-downers." If the editors of these publications were clearly opposed to the new atmosphere of unionism and strikes, they and their audience now had to acknowledge strikes and unions as major factors in running a retail store, something which no trade journal had been willing to admit before the spring of 1937. It was a strong indication of the permanence of retail workers' unions.[66]

More supportive reactions were also forthcoming. Late in 1937, the musical revue *Pins and Needles* opened on Broadway. Since it was the International Ladies' Garment Workers Union which produced this long-running hit, the revue was basically a combination of two different types of songs: songs about garment workers and songs about the news of the day (the rise of fascism in Europe, the split between the AFL and the CIO, and government attacks on labor, among other subjects). To this already eclectic mix, however, songwriter Harold Rome added a sketch about the plight of department store workers, "Chain-Store Daisy." This song, ostensibly about a college-educated woman who winds up working in Macy's, could also be seen as symbolic of the department store worker's new position as part of the working class: "I used to have the Honors Seat. / Now I sit down with pains in my feet / I used to be on the daisy chain / Now I'm a chain-store daisy." In Rome's eyes, if retail workers had once been relatively privileged members of the working class, they were now just as exploited as workers in other industries, and could justifiably share the same stage with factory workers. For Rome, who began rehearsals of *Pins and Needles* two years earlier, long before the Woolworth's sit-down strikes, these lyrics may have had almost nothing to do with the sit-down strikes or the department store unions, and the potential double meaning of "sit[ting] down with pains in my feet" may have been nothing more than a lucky coincidence. Yet the opening of *Pins and Needles* a few months after the sit-down strikes mirrored a new awareness of department store workers among labor activists.[67]

The most important indication of this new role of retail workers in the labor movement came from the leaders of the New Era Retail Committee. In May 1937, the committee sent a letter to John L. Lewis, formally requesting a CIO charter. The letter spent some time decrying the RCIPA leadership for their failure "to react to organizational opportunities" as well as the way in which the international leadership "has hindered and . . . virtually sabotaged the organizational efforts of its affiliated locals," including attacking locals "in the midst of important strike activities," an open reference to the debacle during the May's strike nearly a year earlier. The committee spent most of the letter discussing the New Era Committee's own successes, first among them the "agreements with the Woolworth's and Grand five-and-dime stores in New York City."[68]

John L. Lewis, in many ways the *de facto* leader of the sit-down strike wave, responded warmly to the New Era Committee's request. He granted the committee a CIO charter under the name of the United Retail Employees of America (UREA), and granted the new union jurisdiction over "all employees engaged in or about retail establishments." In the letter announcing the new charter, he also wrote that he was "certain that under the inspiration of your affiliation with [the] CIO, your efforts will ultimately result in the complete unionization of the industry."[69]

Lewis's optimism seemed well founded. The department store unions in New York City were now at the forefront of a national movement that might well be able to organize all workers in the retail industry. It was an amazing transformation from the unions that had been crumbling only months earlier, and it boded well for the unions' immediate future.

Conclusion

The failures of 1935 and 1936 and the tremendous victory of 1937 are highly telling about the role of retail workers in American labor history. The events of the spring of 1937 demonstrate that white-collar workers were an important part of the industrial union movement of the 1930s. Their entrance into the CIO that year indicates that despite the emphasis—both at the time and since—on the CIO as a movement of male blue-collar workers, it was actually a far more complex and diverse movement than such descriptions allow.

The unions' history in these years also demonstrates yet again the critical role played by Communists in American labor history. Unlike in other sit-down strikes, here the strikers had full support from their Communist union leaders, who coordinated and negotiated the strikes that the workers conducted. By both acknowledging—again—the critical role women workers could play in the labor movement and by supporting workers' determination to take the lead in the union, the Communist leaders of Local 1250 again demonstrated how important radicalism was to the labor movement of the 1930s. Without these Communist leaders' support, without their recognition that workers themselves would be the most important labor leaders, the strikes that won the CIO charter for the retail workers' union would almost certainly not have been as successful.

Finally, the unions' history in these years is telling about what legitimacy actually meant for the labor movement of the 1930s. Legitimacy was not, as Michelson and other Communist organizers initially believed, necessarily the same thing as becoming less radical. Certainly that was their way of following the Communist party's United Front policy, but in the sit-down strikes of 1937, workers demonstrated that finding legitimacy could mean just the opposite of such a policy. In these strikes, the most militant and aggressive challenges against store managers in the unions' entire history, workers found the legitimacy that organizers had sought to gain through moderation and compromise. The alliances that union leaders created in 1935–36 certainly played a role in the strike's conclusion, but it was the five-and-dime store workers themselves who won these strikes, and in the process forced the CIO to take notice of the existence of retail workers.

These years resulted in a great victory for New York City's department store unions, unions that had finally won the legitimacy that leaders had long sought. The sit-down strikers had won a groundbreaking one-year agreement with Woolworth's and Grand's. Clarina Michelson, Nicholas Carnes, and the other leaders of the department store unions had won a certain stature within the city's left-wing movement; Michelson in particular won extensive public praise for her leadership of these strikes from ex-IWW organizer and Communist party leader Elizabeth Gurley Flynn. And, in an event that had massive implications for the unions' future, Samuel Wolchok, the anti-Communist leader of the New Era Committee, won the presidency of the UREA. For the next decade the complicated relationship between anti-Communist national leaders like Wolchok and Communist local leaders would be a defining factor in the history of New York City's department store unions, as these unions expanded into New York City's famous upscale department stores.[70]

CHAPTER 3

Stability? 1937–41

Introduction

New York City's department store unions expanded rapidly throughout the late 1930s, primarily in upscale stores. Between the sit-down strikes of 1937 and the beginning of World War II, managers signed contracts at many of the city's largest and most famous stores, including both Macy's and Gimbel's. These upscale stores would continue to represent the union's strongest base throughout their history.

The upscale stores presented different challenges from any that union organizers had encountered in their earlier struggles. In the upscale stores on 34th Street, workers with highly diverse educational, racial, ethnic, and geographic backgrounds waited on wealthy white customers. The process of consumption forced workers and customers in these stores into very close and often antagonistic contact; unlike in the downscale stores where customers were at least sometimes quite supportive of unionization efforts, in the upscale stores the union would find customers to be outspoken critics of workers and their unions. Managers, meanwhile, offered workers substantial benefit packages, winning the loyalty of many workers and making organizing a union even more challenging.

If these stores were difficult places to organize, however, they were well worth the effort. The upscale stores were the logical step for a union that now, due to the 1937 sit-downs, had a certain amount of legitimacy. Unlike in the downscale stores where union organizers had been struggling for years against the rapid turnover, many workers in upscale stores viewed their jobs as permanent careers rather than brief stints. These workers tended to stay at their jobs longer, meaning that a union might have a far greater chance of lasting at the upscale stores than at the downscale stores. Additionally, these stores were far better known: managers of Macy's, for instance, proudly advertised that it was the world's largest store, and to win a union contract there would be a tremendous demonstration of the union's power. If the unions could win at these upscale stores, they would have a future.

Additionally, the late 1930s was an ideal time in which to attempt organizing unions in the upscale stores. In these years midtown Manhattan was a tremendously complicated neighborhood. The stores may have dominated a small section of 34th Street, but they were right in the middle of New York's chaotic garment district; unemployment demonstrations, May Day marches, and strikes all infringed upon the sanctity of the area in the later years of the Depression. These disruptions outside the store made managers' control over the stores more difficult to maintain, and made their jobs somewhat analogous to the jobs of the managers of the Union Square stores where the union had begun its history. Here, as in Union Square, managers did what they could to insulate the stores against the working-class crowds outside, but union activists were always ready to disrupt these efforts.

Communists again played a key role in the union drive at these stores, and became the leaders of most of the local unions that formed at the upscale department stores. As a result, these unions participated in the Popular Front, as members and organizers alike welcomed Communist authors as guests at union events, sang the spirituals and other folk songs that were sung throughout the Popular Front, and helped raise money for the Abraham Lincoln Brigade in the Spanish Civil War.

Non-Communists also took part in the creation of these unions. The local leadership of these unions, though Communists predominated, was politically quite diverse. Additionally, the non-Communists in the national union leadership were critical to the local unions' successes. Samuel Wolchok, in particular, earned tremendous respect from store managers and other business leaders for his moderate politics and his willingness to compromise with store managers. As war approached, however, this support emboldened Wolchok to seek more control over the affairs of the radical local unions.

Everything that union organizers dealt with between 1937 and 1941—the antagonism between customers and store workers, the cultural and political alliances formed during the Popular Front, and the role of non-Communists like Wolchok in the unions—exploded late in 1941 into a huge strike at Gimbel's. The largest strike that the unions had led up until this time, the Gimbel's strike grew out of the conflict between Wolchok and the Communist leaders of the Gimbel's local. Once the strike began, the Popular Front coalition that had come to be so important to the unions emerged to support them, and workers and customers attacked one another, sometimes literally, in and around the Gimbel's store.

As the unions extended their power and finally won permanent union contracts at these upscale stores, they demonstrated again the importance of these unions to American labor history. Again, Communists demonstrated a willingness to work closely with white-collar workers in the retail industry and to encourage these workers, men and women alike, to take the lead in their own struggle. And, again, local union leaders found their power within these unions challenged by store managers and national union leaders alike. The different groups were heading toward a collision, with investigations and charges flying between local leaders, national leaders, store managers, and the government. But before any final confrontation between these different groups could take place, the bombing of Pearl Harbor brought the Depression, and the height of the department store unions' power, to an end.

The Streets Outside

Union Square had long been a center of radicalism and working-class consumption, but midtown Manhattan, only a mile or so away, was a different neighborhood altogether, and generally a more chaotic and complex one. On West 34th Street, stores designed for wealthy shoppers nestled against garment factories and wholesale merchants, blocks away from the city's West Side docks. Store managers fought, aided by city officials, to gain some sort of control over the complicated neighborhood outside the stores, but unlike in Union Square, here the battle was not for a public park, but for the behavior of people on streets and sidewalks. Store managers were only a small part of the world of midtown Manhattan, and their control of the streets outside the stores was always tenuous at best. On 34th Street as in Union Square the Communists challenged managerial control of public space before the department store unions entered the picture, raising the constant possibility of a dangerous challenge to managers' tenuous control of the streets outside.

Along with Fifth Avenue, West 34th Street was one of the prime locations for upscale consumption in New York City. On this one street were Macy's, Gimbel's, Oppenheim Collins, McCreery's, and Saks-34th Street. The sheer size of these stores allowed them to dominate 34th Street to an extent. At the same time, the stores were never isolated. All around the 34th Street shopping district, stretching as far south as 12th Street and as far north as 40th Street, and covering more or less the entire West Side of midtown Manhattan, lay the garment district, where wholesale merchants gathered up both clothing made in the city's garment factories and clothing that was shipped into New York, and prepared it to be sold to stores all over the country.

Although there were obvious advantages in having wholesale businesses so

Figure 2
Shoppers on 34th Street, 1936. The chaos of 34th Street in the 1930s is brilliantly captured by Berenice Abbott in this photograph. Just outside stores that provided a refined and elegant upscale shopping experience were streets that were crowded, complex, and largely outside of managers' control. The chaos in the streets outside greatly aided workers in their efforts to create unions. (Berenice Abbott, Herald Square, West 34th Street and Broadway, August 16, 1936. Courtesy of the Museum of the City of New York, Federal Arts Project, "Changing New York")

close to the stores, there were equally important disadvantages. The garment district was a far less genteel area than store managers might have wished. Traffic clogged the streets as trucks stopped anywhere they could to load and unload goods. Streetcar peddlers, wandering through the neighborhood selling fruit and other goods, made matters even worse, and at least sometimes the sidewalks were packed from edge to edge, making movement difficult if not altogether impossible.[1]

Like congestion, labor strife contributed to the disorder that dominated the garment district in the 1930s. In November 1934, elevator operators and building service workers in the garment district staged a highly disruptive strike before forcing landlords there to back down. (The garment district's labor troubles reached new heights that year shortly after the elevator strike ended, when the guards hired to protect the warehouses during the strike did not get paid promptly and immediately staged a march through the garment district, demanding justice from the detective agency that employed them.) If anything, the labor problems in the garment district got worse in succeeding years. In 1935, during a strike of shipping clerks on 38th Street, a Western Union messenger simply going by the picket line was shot, and in 1936 and 1937 strikes of thousands of building service workers once again hit the garment district.[2]

Labor troubles and congestion in the garment district were complemented by industrial accidents and the activities of the Communist party. At least a few factories were located in the garment district, some of them on 34th Street. And like many factories in these years, safety standards here could be dismal. In a single week in early 1941 dozens of workers from two different garment factories had to go to the hospital for carbon monoxide poisoning. To make matters worse still, the May Day protests that began in Union Square went straight through the garment district. At least one day a year, therefore, the neighborhood streets were crowded not only by trucks and pushcarts, but by protestors actively calling for an end to capitalism.[3]

Perhaps most disruptive of all the factors around the 34th Street stores were the actions of unemployed workers. In the late 1930s Communists and other unemployed workers staged repeated protests in front of the Works Progress Administration (WPA) offices a few blocks south of the stores, on West 23rd Street. When the WPA began in 1935, workers initially met the program with great enthusiasm, and willingly stood on line for hours at the WPA's city offices trying to get jobs. By the spring of 1936 things had changed dramatically. Congress voted to cut much of the WPA funding, and workers met the news of the cutbacks with what historian Barbara Blumberg describes as "tremendous protest and resistance," with "almost daily picketing of WPA headquarters in the Port Authority Building," a few blocks south of the stores. In March 1936 the furor reached a boiling point when demonstrators staged a sit-down protest. After police attacked the protesters who were sitting down, and dragged them—through a hostile crowd—to waiting patrol cars, "the demonstrators reverted to mass picketing outside. On many days two thousand to three thousand persons congregated on the street below the central offices, shouting and chanting."[4] Unemployed workers staged even larger and more militant protests over a year later, in the aftermath of the 1937 sit-down strikes, when Congress announced a new round of cuts. Some workers set up mass picket lines; other workers again staged sit-ins in the WPA offices, only to be removed by police again. "Still other protesters attempted to seize and destroy personnel records so that the WPA could not tell how long anyone had been on work relief." Most dramatic of all, however, and most important for the history of the department store unions, were the protests of the Workers' Alliance, which led a symbolic "mass job hunt. Wearing white tags that read 'WPA dismissed worker looking for a job,' they visited firms" in the surrounding area. "At all the establishments they heard the same thing—no jobs available."[5]

There is no way to tell at this late date whether the workers conducting this mass job hunt stopped at the great 34th Street department stores. Certainly it is likely—there were many unemployed white-collar workers among unemployed New Yorkers in this era, and, as discussed further below, white-collar workers frequently viewed department store work as a way to tide them over between more prestigious jobs. But whether unemployed workers ever actually entered the stores or not, these actions in the streets outside certainly threatened the pristine and elegant world that department store managers worked so hard to create.

Managers did what they could to control the chaos outside, but they had little success. May Day was a particular concern for them, and store managers even went so far as to sit in on conferences between the police and May Day parade organizers to ask that the parade routes be moved further from the stores. But these negotiations, at which managers' requests were flatly denied, only served to demonstrate that managers lacked the ability to control the streets outside, and were forced instead to negotiate for control of these streets. On 34th Street managerial control was limited to the store buildings themselves. The palaces of consumption, as other historians have aptly named them, were supposed to be areas where the chaos of the streets was invisible, where class struggle held no sway. Unfortunately for managers, creating such an environment on 34th Street was all but impossible; to get to the stores, customers had to trek through the chaos outside, and managers could do little to change that. In this situation, where control of the stores was all managers had, workers' efforts to form unions, especially unions that were allied with the Communists who presented such troubles in the streets outside, were even more threatening. If workers began a serious union campaign, or went on strike, they would threaten managers' already tenuous control still further.[6]

Organizing in Upscale Stores

Upscale department store workers faced some, but not all, of the same challenges blue-collar workers faced when trying to form unions. The department stores, unlike the mass-production factories that have dominated the literature on union organizing in this era, were spaces designed for wealthy women's consumption, greatly complicating the question of control over the workplace that is so central to labor history. At the same time, workers in department stores faced many of the same challenges that blue-collar workers faced when creating unions. In the department stores, as in other fields, organizers had to contend with managers' efforts to control workers through both benefits packages and close supervision.

By far the biggest complication union organizers faced in the upscale stores was the role of customers. Upscale department store managers had always attempted to allow wealthy customers, particularly women, spaces for consumption which were protected from workers and from class unrest. From their very origins, department stores had therefore been spaces reserved for the bourgeoisie. The department stores' architecture marked these spaces accordingly. In the mid-nineteenth century, A. T. Stewart's store, generally considered the first department store in America, was sometimes referred to as the "marble palace" for its extraordinary architecture. Throughout the early twentieth century, store managers became ever more elaborate in their efforts to make the stores pleasant environments for wealthy women. Everything became more ornate and extravagant, as managers replaced wooden floors with marble or stone, and increasingly embellished the walls and floors with mirrors and elaborate ornamentation.[7]

These decorations not only stimulated customer interest in goods; many of them also worked to establish shopping as a form of leisure. Most important among the decorations that served both functions were the window displays. By the late 1930s department store windows had become highly dramatic, with some windows depicting actual events of the social season, like opera openings, flower shows, and Broadway plays. Windows by this era had become "so significant, so lively . . . that stores report regular 'window fans' who check each change of display." The windows were "like movie stars," *Women's Wear Daily* reported; each store window had its particular devotees, who kept track of the changing displays.[8]

Like the luxurious decorations and displays, many of managers' tactics not only made shopping convenient but also worked to emphasize the connections between shopping and leisure, by making the stores more pleasant places for potential customers to spend time. They also provided customers with a wide range of complementary services, including, in the words of historian Susan Porter Benson, "public telephones, parcel checkrooms, lost and found services, shopping assistance, free delivery, waiting rooms, gift suggestion departments, mail-order departments, telephone order departments, accommodation bureaus, barber shops, restaurants, post offices, hospitals, radio departments, bus service, and shoe-shining stands." Some store managers also set up lectures, live musical performances, and services for shoppers' children including nurseries, children's theater, and even miniature indoor zoos. All of these services created a space where shopping was accompanied by other pleasant pastimes, where opportunities both for consumption and for leisure were available at the same time, and in the same location.[9]

Advertisements made this combination of leisure and shopping even more explicit. As a Macy's advertisement from the 1930s boasted, "Lots of people come to Macy's [just] for the view. . . . They claim the sprightly tempo does their spirits good. . . . One matron we know of refuses all social engagements for Thursday evenings—says she has a better time seeing life at Macy's." Another Macy's advertisement featured a customer riding an escalator backwards, telling her companion, "I always go up backwards so as not to miss the view." In these advertisements managers encouraged customers to come to the store to sightsee as much as to make purchases: as with the display windows, advertisements meshed consumption and leisure.[10]

Perhaps most important of all the cultural programs provided by the store managers were those that were open to all people in New York City rather than just store customers, like the Macy's Thanksgiving Day parade. Beginning in 1924, the parade gave store managers a chance to entertain customers and noncustomers alike, with marching bands, circus performers of all sorts, caged wild animals, parade floats, and, in case any onlookers had forgotten about the holiday shopping season, Santa Claus. The planning and costs for the event were enormous, but the Macy's parade was an excellent opportunity for managers to encourage workers, customers, and community alike to have pride and admiration for the store that every year provided the joyous spectacle. Again, managers worked to connect consumption and leisure, making the two as interchangeable as possible.[11]

The buildings and free services were only two of many tools at managers' disposal in their quest to merge consumption and leisure. Store workers served a similar function. Workers' jobs in these stores were to see to customers' every need. To some extent, this was a racialized process: well-educated and well-trained white men and women waited on customers to help them make purchases, while in the elevators and the lavatories, uniformed African American workers waited to accede to white customers' requests. As in many other places in American society of the 1930s, African American workers functioned in part as a way to allow whites to experience yet again the privileges of whiteness and to make white customers feel pampered and at ease.[12]

The meshing of leisure and consumption, with its racial overtones, was only one important factor that defined upscale shopping; there were others. Most important, managers fostered a complex relationship between customers, store workers, and merchandise, one far different from the relationships between these factors in downscale stores. Kenneth Collins, who had been a vice-president at both Gimbel's and Macy's, described the process of upscale consumption in 1940: "The history of most stores in the past fifty years has included innumerable steps by which customers have been pushed farther and farther away from the temptation to buy freely." By the beginning of the Depression, Collins wrote, managers increasingly kept "gloves, hosiery, shoes, underwear, neckwear, and similar articles hidden behind fixtures or under counters, so that the customer cannot even see, much less feel, the merchandise."[13]

Upscale store managers denied customers direct access to goods for several reasons. For one thing, managers determined that this tactic would decrease customer shoplifting, a serious problem in upscale stores. Separating goods from customers also allowed the managers to surround customers with ornately decorated paneling rather than racks of goods, enhancing the creation of an upper-class environment. Most important, managers could create and control a relationship between customer and salesperson through arranging the stores in this manner. As Collins wrote, "the customer is better served when a clerk is available to meet her promptly, to analyze her needs, and to dig out from a hidden stock the goods the clerk thinks will satisfy." Through arranging the storage and presentation of goods so that the customer would have to deal directly with a salesperson, store managers at upscale stores forced customers and store workers into close contact.[14]

Managerial tactics therefore placed great emphasis on the abilities of the salespeople. Even more than in the downscale stores, sales clerks were essential actors in the upscale store managers' presentation to the customers. To ensure a favorable impression, managers required neat appearance and good manners from salespeople. They also required highly trained and competent salespeople: without the salespeople's knowledge of the stock on hand and their ability to provide customers with acceptable merchandise, the stores would immediately cease to operate, since customers could not gain access to goods without the intervention of a salesperson. Unlike those in the downscale stores, the workers in the upscale stores were skilled workers, whose expertise and training were highly valued.[15]

These practices left managers in a paradoxical position. In order to create what they viewed as an ideal environment for upscale consumption, an environment for leisure that was free from the chaos and class struggle that dominated the streets outside, upscale store managers had to employ thousands of workers and place them in close contact with wealthy customers. These workers included not only skilled salespeople, but also workers who were responsible for the stores' numerous other services, some of them far less skilled: elevator operators, gift wrappers, cafeteria workers, and, in the credit and billing departments, office workers. These department store workers, in a sense, were at once both the most vital agents in creating the stores' exclusive culture of service and refinement and also, throughout the stores' existence, the biggest potential threat to that environment should they become dissatisfied.[16]

The paradox was a dangerous one for managers, particularly due to the often antagonistic relationship between store workers and store customers. Some customers resorted to treating store workers as they would their servants, the only other workers with whom wealthy people might have come into close contact on a daily basis; but in an era when domestic servitude was considered the most degrading job possible, this sort of treatment could easily lead to informal protests on the part of department store workers. Benson found that saleswomen would allow particularly condescending customers to stand in the store for hours before waiting on them, or could escort the difficult customer to a dressing room and then simply abandon them.[17]

There is no record of this sort of conflict between customers and workers in the downscale stores. While it is possible that such conflicts simply went unrecorded, it is more likely that the peculiar situation of workers in upscale stores meant that there was greater potential for conflict between customers and workers. At Klein's, Ohrbach's, and May's, most customers shared class, neighborhood, and ethnic ties with store workers. At the upscale stores, however, while workers lived in a variety of different places, few if any lived in the expensive neighborhoods from where many of the stores' customers came.[18]

Workers in these upscale stores found customers to be a nuisance, an additional grievance for which they were not adequately rewarded, and this conflict drove at least some workers towards the union. When asked why he joined the union, for example, former salesperson and union organizer Irving Fajans launched into a lengthy speech about the various types of customers whom he had to serve. The types included, according to Fajans, "the kind who tells you she knows exactly what she wants, and then takes two hours to make up her mind . . . The 'match it' type [who will] come in with a smudge of lipstick on a piece of paper, for instance, and want you to match it exactly in the article," and "the customer who will place a C.O.D. order for a large amount, sometimes hundreds of dollars, to impress the clerk, and then the merchandise is returned the next day." While Fajans' comments on customers were not all gender-specific, most of his comments indicated that the customers whom he disliked the most were female. Other workers went even further in their gendered depictions of the hated customers, with one worker attacking customers in verse as those "ladies of leisure / who always dally, way after the closing bell," which of course meant extra work for the salespeople waiting on these customers.[19]

This antagonism between workers and customers greatly complicated the task of organizing unions. On the one hand, the workers who did find customers' behavior intolerable often found common ground with union organizers, particularly considering the strong rhetorical attacks on wealthy women that had proved such a powerful weapon during the 1937 sit-down strikes. At the same time, workers who dared attempt to organize a union at these stores would find that, at the upscale stores, they could not count on customer support during conflicts with management.

If customers were one factor that union organizers could count on to drive workers towards the union, there were others. The various forms of discrimination that existed within the stores drove some workers to support unionization. The workforce at the upscale stores was more heterogeneous than at stores like Klein's and Ohrbach's. While workers at the downscale stores almost universally lived in the city's immigrant communities, workers at the upscale stores tended to live in many different neighborhoods, ranging from these immigrant communities to the Upper West Side and Harlem. While at the downscale stores a large majority of the workers were Jewish, in the upscale stores only around half of the employees were Jewish; Irish, African American, Italian, and white Protestant workers also worked at these stores.[20]

Store managers had several means of controlling this complex workforce. First, they instituted a system of rigid ethnic and racial segregation. As Macy's worker and union organizer Charles E. Boyd later wrote,

> Hiring was controlled by department heads and some would hire no Jews while others would hire no Catholics or no Protestants. Some would hire only Irish; others would hire *no* Irish. Discrimination was practiced somewhere in the store . . . against almost any group, but one general rule was observed throughout the store. Except on passenger elevators, blacks were not visible.

Additionally, there was significant gender discrimination within the stores. Although stores made public their willingness to promote women from within the stores into managerial positions, women salespeople in the 1930s were generally restricted to relatively low-paying departments, such as women's garments and notions. The highest-paying jobs, such as those in the furniture department and the toy department (both of which were paid by commission, and considered very lucrative) were reserved for white men.[21]

Discrimination may have driven some workers towards the union, but it also served to complicate the task of organizers. The divisions among workers at upscale stores made it even more difficult to organize workers into a single entity, like a union. Certainly there is no evidence that large numbers of white workers objected to the discrimination against African American workers in the stores. And the union itself was hardly a paradigm of anti-racist activism; they continued to ignore the "Don't Buy Where You Can't Work" campaigns going on further uptown, and their actions against job discrimination were minor at best. Despite the unions' massive gains in the late 1930s and vocal commitment to racial equality, unionization did nothing to challenge the racist hiring practices that existed within the stores.

If many white workers accepted discrimination, they objected to other aspects of store work. In one early CIO publication, a Macy's worker described the feverish pace of store work: "the frantic rush from subway to store—the mad dash to put away your stock—the brusque appearance of the section manager." Workers spoke also of the overly short "half-hour lunch—the long wait in line at the cafeteria—[and] the attempt to swallow your food with one eye on the clock." Additionally, working in these stores could be incredibly dehumanizing. Fiction writer Shirley Jackson worked at Macy's for a short time during this era, and in a story for *The New Republic* she described Macy's as bureaucracy at its most bewildering, where people were essentially replaced by numbers:

> I enjoyed meeting the time clock, and spent a pleasant half-hour punching various cards . . . I went and found out my locker number, which was 1773, and my time-clock number, which was 712, and my cash-box number, which was 1336, and my cash-register number, which was 253, and my cash-register-drawer number, which was K, and my cash-register-drawer-key number, which was 872, and my department number, which was 13. And that was my first day.[22]

However, if working conditions could be strenuous and unpleasant, they were decidedly better than in the downscale stores. Managers at upscale stores placed great pride and emphasis on their training programs for sales workers, investing extensive time and money into training each worker. Managers at these stores therefore encouraged workers to remain with the store for as many years as possible, despite the various drawbacks of working in these stores. Upscale store managers had all sorts of ways to gain workers' loyalty: they paid workers well, with salaries for sales workers averaging around $15 a week rather than the $7 to $12 a week workers received in the downscale stores. In addition, upscale store managers offered workers numerous benefits and cultural programs. Macy's serves as an excellent example. Macy's workers later remembered that the store provided free turkeys at Thanksgiving, and even a house upstate where workers could go during their vacations. Macy's managers also provided limited health insurance, through the Macy's Mutual Aid Association (MMAA). Like many other department stores in New York City, Macy's participated in the Greater New York Department Store Baseball League, allowing workers to represent the store where they worked, and encouraging them to identify themselves as part of the store's team. And, while it does not appear to have been a factor at Macy's, other city department stores also offered workers opportunities to perform in plays, setting up dramatic clubs for their employees.[23]

These tactics worked to gain the loyalty of at least some employees, but caused others to resent the managers' interference in their lives. Jane Spadavecchio remembered the benefits packages (especially the free turkeys) very fondly, proudly stating years after working in the stores that she was still a "firm Macyite." Yet some of these practices were extremely intrusive. Managers took money for the MMAA, for example, directly out of workers' paychecks, even if workers never used the MMAA's services. In addition, the MMAA was responsible for sending the personnel office "a list of all the people employed . . . who have been rated 'poor risks' by the hospital," and managers often fired these people first during the much-feared post-Christmas round of layoffs. Union organizers raised this issue wherever possible, labeling the MMAA "Macy's Public Enemy Number 1," and issuing frequent demands for "information about the administration of the funds collected . . . for its maintenance" in order to remind workers that they were paying for this program. Union supporters also claimed that the funds were being spent "in planning artistic murals" and "in purchasing non-break swivel chairs for the doctors" at the MMAA infirmary rather than in improving workers' health.[24]

Besides keeping workers satisfied through high pay and good benefits, managers had other means of controlling their workers, most important among them an elaborate system of supervision. With an extremely wealthy group of customers without direct access to goods, managers at the upscale stores regarded workers rather than customers as the most significant group of potential shoplifters. As managers did at Klein's and Ohrbach's, upscale store managers hired large numbers of store detectives. In addition, managers at some of these stores, like Macy's, required workers to leave all their personal possessions in lockers throughout the day, so that if detectives did find any goods in a worker's possession, managers could then demonstrate that worker's guilt. Macy's managers also attempted to control their employees' shoplifting by resorting to searches of all workers, a practice which workers strongly disliked. In an OWU publication from the early 1930s, one Macy's worker wrote indignantly of the intense scrutiny: "Are we prisoners who have to be searched before we go to our departments?" the anonymous worker asked, complaining of the security department's demands "that we shake out newspapers, packages and books before the eyes of the guards and leave them under surveillance all day." The ironies of these sorts of security measures were inherent: one article in the union paper pointed out that the "head of the Protection Department at Macy's is paid $50,000 a year to see that $10,000 worth of merchandise isn't stolen."[25]

Despite their dislike of the store security procedures, union organizers did not endorse shoplifting as a legitimate way for workers to supplement their wages. If shoplifting was an important form of personal and informal protest, union organizers held, almost by definition, that formal protests like unionization would be a more powerful way to resist exploitation. On the other hand, contributors to the union papers also avoided condemning shoplifting. One anonymous contributor even offered a mild defense of the practice, suggesting that it was mere "petty theft," the elimination of which "does not depend upon a prison-like supervision, but on the establishment of a decent standard of wages." The message of this article was determinedly ambiguous: shoplifting might not be the best way to combat store managers' exploitation, but the author of this article clearly felt that for many workers shoplifting was a method of self-help, of informal resistance against low wages.[26]

At least some upscale store managers employed security measures that went far beyond simple searches. A detective at one unnamed upscale store in New York City, Alfred Gerrity, claimed that the store employed "'information employe[e]s' in almost every department [who] receive $2 a week extra for reporting anything unusual they observe," thus combining the jobs of preventing shoplifting and keeping an eye out for anyone prone to union organizing. Gerrity also described the way in which "at night, we turn the lights off in the elevators and run them from floor to floor, observing the actions of maintenance men, stock clerks, and porters [the lowest-paid workers in most stores] through the little windows." Store detectives would also attempt to trap employees by "plant[ing] merchandise to tempt employees to steal."[27]

These sorts of security practices were of special concern to union organizers, since pro-union workers were frequently targets of security sweeps. An anonymous department store worker and union organizer recalled in an interview with WPA interviewer May Swenson, "When I first started there, they were just beginning to try to organize, and everything pertaining to the union had to be on the q.t. If you were caught distributing leaflets, or other union literature around the job you were instantly fired."[28]

But workers in the upscale stores persisted in organizing unions, despite the efforts of managers to quash such activities. This was especially true of non-sales workers, who were in a decidedly worse position than the salespeople. Since nonsales workers did not have to undergo as lengthy a training process, managers were much less concerned about turnover. As a result, nonsales workers worked for much lower salaries and often worked longer hours. Cashiers at Macy's, for example, made only $8 a week during the 1930s, comparable to what workers made in downscale stores. Managers also required many of these nonsales workers to work seven days a week, and to do so even on some holidays.[29]

Managers, as already noted, strongly and successfully opposed workers' efforts to form unions throughout the early 1930s. Despite their need for trained sales workers, managers at the upscale stores fired both nonsales workers and highly skilled sales workers who attempted to join the union in the early 1930s; several of the first leaders of the local unions became full-time organizers after being fired by managers for union organizing.[30]

As a result of this scrutiny, union organizers in the upscale stores, Communists and non-Communists alike, resorted to extremely inventive tactics in order to recruit other workers to the union. Many of these tactics made the perpetrators almost wholly undetectable, no matter how many spies store managers employed. The worker Swenson interviewed remembered,

> Sometimes we'd insert the leaflets into the sales ledgers after closing time . . . In the morning every clerk would find a pink sheet saying: "Good Morning, how's everything . . . and how about coming to Union meeting tonight . . ." . . . we [also] swiped the key to the toilet paper dispensers [in] the washroom, took out the paper and substituted printed slips of just the right [size]! . . . We also used . . . store chutes,

and when sending down a load of merchandise, would toll [*sic*] down a bunch of leaflets with it, while the super had his back turned. They'd all scatter out on the receiving end, and the clerks would pick them up when they handled the stock. The floorwalker might be coming along and see those pink sheets all over the place—he'd get sore as hell—but what could he do?

The workers involved in these sorts of anonymous organizing activities were able to spread the word about union actions, without making themselves vulnerable to managers' counterattacks. [31]

Anonymous or not, the organizing was eventually successful. With Communists and other activists laying claim to the streets outside, and with a growing number of their employees lobbying for the right to join the union that had led the Woolworth sit-down strikes only months before, the managers of the 34th Street department stores found themselves in desperate need of greater stability. In the late 1930s Samuel Wolchok and the other national leaders of the CIO's retail workers union, the UREA, offered those employers who were willing to sign union contracts the stability that managers so anxiously sought.

Stability with the CIO, 1937–39

Samuel Wolchok's greatest achievement in the UREA's early years was to create a situation where upscale store managers came to view him as a stable, responsible, and relatively conservative alternative to the increasingly powerful radicals who took over most of the local unions in New York City's department stores. In order to secure Wolchok's support in their struggle against local leaders and gain the stability that he promised, at least some store managers signed contracts with the UREA.

When the CIO officially granted the UREA a charter in May 1937, no one could have imagined that the union would grow as quickly as it actually did. When it was created, the UREA was an extremely small union of just under 15,000 members, and it was almost entirely confined to ex-RCIPA locals from New York City. By the end of 1937 the union, now with 40,000 members, represented a beachhead for the possibility of a labor stronghold in the retail industry.[32]

This numerical growth greatly strengthened the union's left wing. The largest new sector where the union organized was in wholesale firms, firms which sold to retailers rather than to the general public. In particular, the UREA recruited a large number of left-wing union leaders in the New York City wholesale trade when these locals joined the union as UREA Local 65. After this, the name of the union was immediately changed to the United Retail and Wholesale Employees Association (URWEA).[33]

Another major change also took place between the sit-down strikes and the December 1937 convention: the CIO set up a special organization, the Department Store Organizing Committee (DSOC), to organize department store workers. Wolchok had played a key role in DSOC's creation, and in so doing had further cemented his place as the leader of the new organizing drive in the retail industry. In September 1937, months before the convention, Wolchok again wrote to John L. Lewis, asking Lewis for help with a new organizing drive. As Wolchok envisioned it, the new drive would be

> a uniform drive throughout the various states, in organizing the Department Store workers. I am firmly convinced that if we could have such a unified drive, placing a given number of organizers in this field, that remarkable progress could be made. . . . Place at our disposal fifty organizers for the next four months—to concentrate a drive in the Department Stores."[34]

Wolchok might have known, even while writing this letter, that no amount of statistics on nonunionized department store workers was likely to convince Lewis to grant his request. The four months' of organizing that Wolchok proposed would have cost the CIO $40,000 at a time when Lewis had just loaned the UREA $5000 at Wolchok's request. In addition, Lewis had already assigned twenty CIO organizers to help Wolchok and the UREA. Whatever Wolchok thought would happen as a result of his letter, Lewis provided neither additional funds nor the organizers whom Wolchok had requested.[35]

If it was therefore unlikely that Lewis would grant Wolchok's request, it was nonetheless possible. The two union leaders had apparently been close allies from the beginning of their acquaintance, in the summer of 1937. One of Wolchok's strongest supporters in the UREA, Vice-President John Cooney, reported that during the first actual meeting between Lewis and Wolchok, "Lewis clearly indicated that he recognized in Brother Wolchok a leader, a man of courage, a man of executive ability." While Cooney is hardly an objective observer, Lewis himself indicated his strong personal admiration for Wolchok. At one point during the early years of the URWEA, Lewis sent Wolchok a telegram announcing that Wolchok was "personally entitled to great credit" for the "splendid achievement[s]" of the UREA, and Lewis gave particular reference to Wolchok's "able handling of negotiations."[36]

Perhaps because of their mutual respect, Lewis agreed to bring the subject of DSOC up at the national CIO meeting in October 1937, and suggested that Wolchok attend. Wolchok immediately began work on a report of the UREA's accomplishments, calling their work (quite accurately) "a spring-board for further progress" despite the "meagre funds at our disposal and the limited number of organizers available," and ending with an appeal to Lewis and the CIO Executive Board to reconsider his request. Wolchok also insisted, at the end of the report, that the retail clerk was actually

> the most effective medium of CIO propaganda, contacting as he does thousands of persons in his establishment, his store ... The SALESMAN of America is the most ARTICULATE type of worker and a CIO button on his lapel means a standing, ever-present symbol of labor unionism to untold populations.

This report illustrates more than Wolchok's abilities as an organizer, which would later be called into serious question. It also suggests the continuing importance of gender within the CIO leadership. Many of the department store workers whom Wolchok spoke of organizing in this drive were women; yet these workers were conveniently unmentioned in Wolchok's strongly gendered description of the articulate salesman wearing a CIO button "on his lapel." Wolchok's immediate assumption of workers as men was one way in which he reaffirmed his commonalties with Lewis and other CIO leaders. As Elizabeth Faue has demonstrated, gendered assumptions like these bound labor leaders together in the 1930s, giving them even more common ideological ground than they already had.[37]

Wolchok got almost exactly what he requested at the October meeting where he presented his report. On October 17 the CIO Executive Board approved both funding and organizers for DSOC. The Executive Board agreed that Wolchok would serve on the board of DSOC, as would John Cooney. Neither Wolchok nor Cooney, however, was placed in charge of DSOC. That responsibility went to CIO co-founder and Amalgamated Clothing Workers of America President Sidney Hillman. For a few days at least it looked as though Hillman, and not Wolchok, would take charge of organizing the nation's department store workers. Circumstances intervened, however; Hillman became severely ill almost as soon as DSOC was formed, and Wolchok stepped in to take control of DSOC. By November 1937, barely a month after the Executive Board had created the organizing committee, Wolchok, not Hillman, was leading the drive to unionize department store workers in America.[38]

By the URWEA's first convention, in December 1937, the union was therefore in a very favorable situation for a massive and successful organizing drive. They had a new vehicle for organizing in DSOC, one with additional funding and organizers. They also had a readily identifiable and notorious enemy, since the issues raised by the anti–chain store activists were still fresh in the national imagination. In one reference to the discussions surrounding chain stores, an ally of Wolchok's named Henry Fruchter reminded the delegates to the 1937 convention that "the corporations in ownership of department and chain stores are the most ruthless in the world. They command tremendous financial resources, they control the reactionary press, they are in league with corrupt politicians, they will stop at nothing to check the onward stride of labor."[39]

Perhaps most important, in Samuel Wolchok, the URWEA also had a leader with a growing national reputation among business leaders as a moderate and responsible union organizer. Wolchok's rise to national prominence in many ways mirrored the URWEA's own rise. As a result of the successful sit-down strikes and the union's earliest contracts signed by store managers in New York City and throughout the country, Wolchok became a figure of some importance in the CIO in the late 1930s. In 1938, for instance, Wolchok became the vice-president of the New York State Industrial Union Council, the CIO's New York State governing organization; he also was invited to speak at an international labor congress that same year.[40]

Like CIO leaders, business leaders also had a high opinion of Wolchok's abilities. Louis Broido, the vice-president in charge of personnel relations at Gimbel's, held Wolchok in such high regard as a union leader (and held such little respect for local leaders) that Broido insisted on negotiating exclusively with Wolchok, much to the annoyance of the local leaders. In addition, an article on retail unionism in *Business Week* showered praise upon Wolchok, suggesting that Wolchok "had jumped into the Class A rating of union leaders," and going on to claim that Wolchok was "no longer in the shadow of Lewis and Hillman, but was instead rising to power in his own right."[41]

While to employers Wolchok emphasized his willingness to compromise and negotiate, at the union's convention Wolchok and his allies portrayed the union's president as a picture of rugged masculinity. As Henry Fruchter put it: "Our leader [Wolchok] is a simple man, with a background of vast labor experience. . . . He is much more at home in a world of strife,—strikes, pickets, organization. The limelight and glory of a few hours do not go to his head, nor do they arouse an exaggerated sense of superiority. . . . a man of character, of rugged strength, of vast human experience in the battle for labor."[42]

In the late 1930s Wolchok had at least two contradictory reputations: among managers, he had a reputation as someone willing to compromise, while, among his supporters in the union, he had a reputation as a militant fighter for workers' rights. Faced with this combination, department store union delegates to the 1937 convention supported Wolchok's bid for the presidency, declining the right to put up any more-radical candidate for the office. At the same time, the Communist leaders of the department store unions retained some reservations about their own lack of representation in the national leadership. One Local 1250 delegate, for example, sponsored a resolution during the convention calling for a "Vice-President, who shall be drawn from the ranks of those actively organizing in the department store field, and who shall be designated to the task of directing and coordinating the organization of the department store field." This position was not created, but the resolution itself, particularly with its qualification of someone "drawn from the ranks of those actively organizing," was enough to suggest that department store union leaders were concerned about how much control they would have over the new organization.[43]

Wolchok's leadership attracted the support of many retail managers besides Louis Broido. By February 1938 some industry experts in fact were beginning to suggest that capitulation to unionism might be the retailer's best option. That month, in an article in the *Journal of Retailing*, M. D. Mosessohn and A. Furman Greene wrote that "the most [employers] can hope for is peace in the ranks of organized labor with the elimination of jurisdictional conflicts." To secure this peace, the wise employer "dare not, by word or act, intimidate, coerce, or discourage" workers from joining the union, since, due in part to the new labor laws, the employer "must proceed with collective bargaining and must continue to bargain" in order to keep the store running with any semblance of order. Not coincidentally, "peace in the ranks" and "the elimination of jurisdictional conflicts" were goals which Samuel Wolchok offered as his own, so long as store managers signed union contracts.[44]

With local organizers willing—for the moment—to follow Wolchok's lead, many store managers did sign contracts. The managers at the Hearn's store, a large downscale store on 14th Street, became the first in New York City to sign a collective bargaining agreement when they signed an open-shop contract with the New Era Committee in April 1937, only a few weeks after the Woolworth-Grand strikes. Local 1250, still led by Clarina Michelson, with former Ohrbach's worker Nicholas Carnes as her second-in-command, came to represent the union at Hearn's as well as several other stores, most important among them Loeser's, one of the large downscale stores on Fulton Street.[45]

Shortly after Wolchok's emergence as the leader of the URWEA and DSOC, other store managers began to sign contracts as well. In February 1938 Macy's managers signed a contract with Local 1-S, the local covering all Macy's workers who worked within the Herald Square store. (Locals 1 and 1-A covered the warehouse and delivery workers respectively.) Local 1-S was extremely unusual among department store unions, in that the local leadership was politically diverse from the union's very beginnings. The single most important leader of Local 1-S was Samuel Kovenetsky, who began leading the local union as the business manager in the late 1930s, and continued to do so throughout much of the union's history. Kovenetsky himself, though he worked closely with Communists, was a liberal Democrat rather than a Communist. Among his fellow leaders of Local 1-S, however, were several Communists. Most important among these was Marcella Loring, a white woman from the Midwest who served, on and off, as the union's vice-president and sometimes even president over the next decade.[46]

In March 1938 DSOC won another important success: Gimbel's Local 2 finally won a contract, after fourteen weeks of negotiating and years of organizing at Gimbel's. As at Macy's and Hearn's, the union's contract at Gimbel's guaranteed workers at that store significant wage increases and somewhat shorter hours. Like most of the other locals, Communists led Local 2, most important among them an ex-furniture salesman named William Michelson, who, like Loring, Carnes, and Clarina Michelson, was probably a member of the Communist party, and was at the very least a strong supporter of CP policies. William Michelson, who eventually married Marcella Loring, would, like Samuel Kovenetsky and Nicholas Carnes, remain a major figure in New York City's department store unions for the next several decades.[47]

Many store managers, however, held out somewhat longer. At Bloomingdale's, at the time a somewhat less upscale store that sat under the Third Avenue elevated train, store managers adamantly refused to negotiate, despite having a majority of their employees support unionization. On October 27, 1938, Bloomingdale's employees voted to give management a choice: negotiate with the union or face a strike. The workers gave management two days to make up their mind, and the store managers, faced with more than 1500 workers threatening to strike, quickly capitulated. By December 12 not only was the union victorious, but Bloomingdale's managers had agreed to a closed shop and wage increases which totaled $150,000 a year among the 3000 employees at Bloomingdale's.[48]

Besides the huge success that this contract represented for the union, the Bloomingdale's negotiations represented a crucial moment in the unions' history. It was during these negotiations that union leaders first made use of the Labor Relations Board formed by the 1935 Wagner Act. Legislators had originally intended the Wagner Act as a substitute for the NIRA, which the Supreme Court had declared unconstitutional in 1935. The Wagner Act was somewhat more complicated than the NIRA, since it called for the creation of a permanent and extremely powerful National Labor Relations Board (NLRB), which would be responsible for handling negotiations between workers and employers. Unlike the NIRA, the Wagner Act was strongly and explicitly pro-union, and offered no real benefits to employers beyond a faint hope that it would stabilize the labor movement. In order to achieve this stability, the Wagner Act established the right of workers to hold fair and federally mediated union elections, once the union received NLRB certification. While the Wagner Act was a tremendous victory for labor, the events at Bloomingdale's illustrate that the NLRB's intervention was the beginning, not the end, of workers' struggles to get a union. Despite the NLRB's decision in the union's favor at Bloomingdale's, it was the workers' decision to strike, not federal intervention, which forced the Bloomingdale's management to capitulate.[49]

Both the Bloomingdale's local and the local at the 42nd Street Stern's store, where managers succumbed to unionization in 1939, became additional strongholds of radicalism within the URWEA. The Bloomingdale's local, Local 3, was led by Lowell Morris, a former cafeteria worker. Morris was at least close to the Communist party, though it is not clear if he was ever actually a member. Radical ex-saleswoman Sadka Brown became the leader of Stern's Local 5.[50]

These leaders of the new department store unions—Clarina Michelson and Nicholas Carnes at Local 1250, representing Hearn's and a few other downscale stores, William Michelson at Gimbel's Local 2, Samuel Kovenetsky and Marcella Loring at Macy's Local 1-S, Lowell Morris at Bloomingdale's Local 3, and Sadka Brown at Stern's Local 5—quickly formed a solid bloc within the URWEA. While they united primarily around their shared Communist politics (except for Kovenetsky), other factors also served to unite them. The leaders' youth served as a strong bond between these leaders; except for Clarina Michelson, these men and women were all still in their twenties when the union formed. All of the younger leaders also had learned much of what they knew about organizing from their participation in RCIPA Local 1250 under Clarina Michelson, who was still a major influence within all of the department store union locals. In addition, they had all worked in department stores themselves, although several of them had been fired from their jobs for union organizing before managers capitulated. Finally, all seem to have been personally very popular with union members, despite the fact that few members shared their leaders' radical politics.[51]

Wolchok devised several responses to these local leaders' presence as an oppositional bloc within his organization, trying both to control and to appease the new coalition of Communists who now led the URWEA's largest locals. Wolchok's attempts to control these leaders took several forms. First, he established a rule, similar to that which had driven the unions from the RCIPA, that every local would have one vote on issues of national union policy, regardless of the size of the local. As a result of this rule, the large radical department store unions got the same number of votes as the other locals, many of which were much smaller and much less radical. In addition, Wolchok's decision to break up the department store union into a separate local at each store, the new leaders of department store union organizers believed, was an attempt to divide and therefore to more easily control their unions.[52]

Wolchok's attempt to appease the New York City local leaders eventually created even more trouble for the URWEA's future. After local union organizers came to the conclusion that the creation of the separate locals was an attempt to control them, they demanded some sort of structure binding the separate locals together. Their most common demand in the late 1930s and early 1940s was the right to form a Joint Board, a formally recognized, united group of locals within the union. This board would allow the local unions a certain amount of autonomy from the national union, and—more importantly perhaps—would allow them to remain formally linked. The establishment of a Joint Board, however, required the national union leaders' consent, and, while Wolchok repeatedly promised the New York City local leaders that they would receive their Joint Board at some point, he was unwilling to make it a priority, focusing instead on organizing more locals outside of New York City.[53]

Department store union organizers responded to this delay by soundly criticizing Wolchok among themselves and at local union meetings. Particularly, by the late 1930s these leaders complained that Wolchok's conciliatory attitude towards management was a poor strategy to win workers the best contract they could win. William Atkinson, an African American union member at Macy's who would become a leader of Local 1-S in the 1940s, remembered years later that Wolchok's attitude when dealing with management "was a begging attitude." To Atkinson, Wolchok's efforts simply were not as powerful as the far more confrontational bargaining tactics, including strike threats, which were increasingly favored by the local leaders in these unions.[54]

The two sides nonetheless maintained an uneasy unity through the rest of the decade, a unity that had extremely positive effects for the union. Wolchok's so-called "begging attitude" beautifully complemented the local union organizers' more confrontational style. Where Wolchok could not convince managers to sign a contract through negotiations, as at Bloomingdale's, the workers, with the support of the local leaders, could scare managers into signing by threatening to strike.

Despite their powerfully complementary strategies, there were certain stores where neither local nor national department store union leaders seemed able to win. Two areas in particular eluded union organizers in the 1930s. First, union organizers made no headway against the upscale stores on Fifth Avenue. Facing none of the disruptions and chaos in the streets with which 34th Street store managers had to contend, the promised stability of unionization was not a particularly pressing issue for Fifth Avenue store managers. Additionally, the unions had relatively few successes in the downscale stores. Most important among their failures in the downscale stores was Alexander's, the large downscale chain, where union organizers continually tried, and failed, to create unions. While Local 1250 did lead a two-week strike at Alexander's, they lost an NLRB election there after an extensive anti-union propaganda campaign by store managers. Somewhat ironically, the union also never gained a real foothold at Ohrbach's and Klein's, having never gained a written contract at either store. Despite their tremendous successes in the late 1930s, the department store unions were not gaining ground where managers were at their most exploitative, and where the union had initially had its strongest roots. The only downscale stores where the union was able to win—Hearn's, Loeser's, and Bloomingdale's—were the stores where managers gave up before the workers had to go on strike.[55]

There were several reasons for the URWEA's weakness in downscale stores. First, the anti-customer rhetoric that worked so well as an organizing tool in the upscale stores had little relevance in the downscale stores. As already noted, customers and workers at downscale stores had much more in common than at upscale stores. Perhaps more importantly, downscale store managers' employment practices doomed most unionization campaigns to failure at these stores. As we have seen, downscale store managers employed large numbers of unskilled workers for relatively short periods of time. If turnover was a factor in upscale stores, there were people working there who viewed selling as their career; indeed, most of the people who wound up leading local unions at these stores had been working in the upscale stores for several years before they began organizing, a situation which would have been highly unusual at the downscale stores. At Alexander's, Klein's, Ohrbach's, May's, and other downscale stores throughout the city, only a small minority of workers had any intention of making their job in the store a lifelong commitment. Working in these stores was a job to be taken for only a short time before moving on, either to a better job or, for some of the women workers, to marriage. For those workers in downscale stores who were looking for a more permanent position in retailing, there were jobs which offered better wages, with or without unions, in upscale stores. Career salesperson and union activist Irving Fajans, for example, worked in Ohrbach's, May's, and several five-and-dime stores before getting a job at Macy's, where he stayed to help organize the union. Similarly, Jane Spadavecchio, who worked at Macy's from the age of 19 until she was 35, had already worked in a five-and-dime store before getting her job at Macy's.[56]

Despite their inability to establish permanent union locals at most downscale stores and on Fifth Avenue, the years 1937–39 were years of success for union organizers within New York City's department stores. In these years the uneasy unity between national and local leaders, workers' willingness to strike if provoked, and the federal government's support for unions forced managers at New York City's upscale department stores to sign union contracts. By doing so, they established these stores as centers for the growing white-collar segment of the CIO. But they also realized that if they were to continue winning struggles, they would need to establish alliances. If the struggles at Klein's, Ohrbach's, May's, and the five-and-dime stores had taught these organizers anything, it was that powerful alliances could easily be deciding factors in conflicts with management. In the late 1930s store workers and union organizers turned to the growing network of activists around the Communist party's Popular Front for support.

Creating the Popular Front

Within the upscale stores, organizers faced two major obstacles to powerful unions. First, many store workers still regarded managers with tremendous respect, due to the extensive benefits programs in place in these stores. Second, without the promised Joint Board, department store union leaders found themselves divided into separate union locals. In the late 1930s department store union leaders attempted to solve both these problems and gain a broad-based coalition of support by establishing a wide-ranging set of cultural programs, many closely connected to the Communist-led Popular Front.

Like store managers, union organizers used sports as a central part of the unions' cultural programs. Organizers created a number of different sports programs, including a Swim/Gym program, which began as a swimming and basketball program at a local high school. Organizers expanded the basketball activities from the Swim/Gym, originally a Local 1250 program, into part of a city-wide women's basketball league, with teams from each store's union competing with one another and with other local teams once a week. These events were critical in forming the sorts of attitudes that the union needed if it was to thrive. If store managers could allow workers a chance to play in a store-sponsored baseball team, the unions now offered similar opportunities. In addition, workers who took part in the union sports program would spend their leisure time not only with union members in their own local, but also with workers from other local unions around the city, hopefully forging bonds of class solidarity in the process.[57]

Organizers put equal effort into other cultural and social activities. Within Gimbel's Local 2, for example, workers not only set up a local union library but also launched a forum and lecture series where union members were encouraged to engage in what the union newspaper described as "a sparkling exchange of opinion" between various union members. Furniture salesmen at Gimbel's, who were the highest-paid employees in the store, also set up parties at their homes, to allow workers to temporarily escape to larger and presumably more comfortable homes. Other union organizers followed their examples, setting up "beach parties, boat parties, house parties, and boat rides." Union organizers were very explicit in their belief that these sorts of activities were designed to do more than offer workers a chance to socialize. To organizers in the department store unions, these activities were "valuable organizing tools," ways not only to unite workers, but to unite them as union members.[58]

In addition to fostering alliances between workers employed within the same store, these social and cultural activities served to unite members of different department store union locals. Many of these activities, such as the sports league, were established by the department store unions' Joint Activities Committee, which was in charge of the social and cultural aspects of the various union locals. If the union leaders wished to continue emphasizing the unity of the now-separate locals, the Joint Activities Committee was an excellent way to accomplish this. It was also a way to make sure that workers understood the shared nature of their struggle.

Perhaps even more importantly, these social activities allowed the members of the various department store locals to create alliances outside the stores.

Many of these activities drew upon the culture of the Popular Front, the broad anti-fascist coalition which the Communist party called into creation in the late 1930s. Union members who joined Local 1250's "Song Shop," for example, printed booklets of Popular Front standards like "Solidarity Forever" and "We Shall Not Be Moved," songs which were sung both by department store workers and by participants in other Popular Front struggles around the country. By placing these songs in the union's songbook, the Song Shop members emphasized the unity between the department store unions and the other struggles going on throughout the country.[59]

Like the songs in the union songbooks, parties and dances also served to emphasize the unity between department store union members and others involved in left-wing causes. Particularly in the late 1930s union organizers frequently sought to connect dances to the Spanish Civil War, one of the issues attracting the most attention and admiration to the Communist party. For the Allies in the Spanish Civil War, at least according to the Communists, the Popular Front was real: in Spain, leftists of all stripes literally fought against the Fascist threat. And the department store unions worked the Spanish Civil War into many of their activities, by using union parties and dances as fund-raisers for the war effort or for American veterans of the Abraham Lincoln Brigade. While there is no record of how large these parties got, organizers did manage to attract some quite famous entertainers, including bandleader and radio star Rudy Vallee.[60]

Similarly, the union's Counter Carnival, which took place in April 1939, both brought union members together in a social setting and provided links with important supporters. In addition to fortune tellers, balloons, masks and confetti, and a skit featuring a "mock marriage between capital and labor," several "Guests of Honor" attended the carnival, among them Popular Front figures like Leane Zugsmith, Ruth McKenney, and Mike Quill. Zugsmith, of course, had long been involved with the department store unions, and by 1939 that involvement had gained her and her work national recognition, including favorable reviews of *A Time to Remember* in the *New York Times,* the *New Republic,* and other major publications around the country. While earlier Zugsmith had supported department store workers as a fellow white-collar worker and, later, as a member of the League of Women Shoppers, now her role changed yet again: she would now be a fellow supporter of the Popular Front.[61]

For Zugsmith these changes may well have been merely rhetorical, but the other supporters who attended the carnival were new supporters of the unions, and demonstrated in some ways the value of the Popular Front.

Zugsmith's fellow guest of honor, Ruth McKenney, was an excellent example of this. By the time of the carnival McKenney's work on the contemporary labor movement was already very popular in left-wing circles. In 1938 and 1939, for instance, the left-wing American Writers Congress awarded McKenney its annual prize for nonfiction. Like Zugsmith, McKenney was probably a member of the Communist party in the late 1930s, and was a regular contributor to the Communist literary magazine *The New Masses*. But unlike Zugsmith, McKenney had never before associated herself with the department store unions. Now she was part of their coalition. Perhaps most important of all the carnival guests was Mike Quill. Like McKenney, Quill had shown no interest in the department store unions before the establishment of the Popular Front. One of the most prominent figures in the city's labor movement, Quill served on the city council and was a leader of the large, militant, and very progressive Transport Workers Union of America (TWUA), one of the largest left-wing unions in New York City at the time. Like in many such cases, it is not known for sure whether Quill was ever a member of the Communist party, but in the late 1930s he certainly supported many of the CP's policies, the Popular Front among them.[62]

The Counter Carnival, with these guests of honor, in some ways exemplified the department store unions' cultural programs of the late 1930s. Like other cultural programs in these years, the carnival brought workers from all the different stores together as union members in a recreational setting. In addition, particularly with the guests of honor whom the union chose to invite, the carnival allowed union members and leaders to reinforce the alliances to the city's radical movement that had proved so valuable in their earlier struggles.

In creating these cultural programs, union leaders were more than mere participants in the Popular Front; they were the creators of one small segment of the Popular Front. The Popular Front, after all, was essentially a network between different American radicals, precisely the sort of network that formed around the unions in these years. As some historians of communism have always claimed, Russian policy actively called for and supported the sorts of alliances which department store union leaders formed in the late 1930s. On the other hand, the decision to abide by this policy or not to abide by it was not made in a vacuum, but was instead made by activists on the ground. The unions' Popular Front policies reflected Communist party policies, but Communist organizers in the department store unions adopted the Popular Front not simply to follow CP policy. They adopted the Popular Front as a valuable tool for making this union an integral part of workers' lives, one that further solidified union leaders' connections to the rank and file and that further solidified the unions' connections to the city's radical movement. And, even as the Popular Front policy disintegrated in 1939 with the Hitler-Stalin Pact, the alliances formed through the Front would continue, with important results for New York City's department store workers.

Making the World of Tomorrow: Managers on the Attack, 1939–41

If workers were forging alliances in the late 1930s, managers had their own tactics with which to respond to workers' efforts. In 1939 store managers participated in a massive effort by American businesses to reestablish a favorable public image at the New York World's Fair. At the same time, the new Parkchester housing development in the Bronx presented an alternative plan for public space, one that eliminated the sort of contests over that space that dominated 34th Street. Both developments would set the conditions for the unions' future decline.

As early as 1935 New York City businessmen, including Macy's manager Percy Straus, and local government officials began plans for a massive World's Fair in New York. In keeping with the vision of its organizers, when it opened in 1939 the fair was largely a paean to American business. Ford, General Motors, AT&T, RCA, and the Metropolitan Life Insurance Company all set up exhibits at the 1939 World's Fair, reminding visitors of the tremendous and productive role big business played in American life, and implicitly responding to the massive rhetorical attacks on big business that were so much a part of Popular Front culture. Each exhibit was planned separately, and extolled the virtues of its particular sponsor. Thus the RCA building, built in the shape of a radio tube, educated the public about the glories of broadcasting and electronics, including one of the first public exhibits of television broadcasting. In another of the exhibits, gas corporations joined forces to set up the Gas Exhibit Building, where visitors could learn of the important roles gas power played in modern life.[63]

Store managers played a particularly central role in the fair's development, and were featured prominently at the fair. Macy's managers opened up Macy's Toyland in the amusement area, a building full of toys for young people to go and observe in wonder. Toy manufacturers paid a hefty sum to lease exhibits within Toyland in order to inform parents of the latest product. Not to be outdone, Gimbel's opened a building in the amusements area as well, where children could take a ride and see models of attractions from around the world. And many store managers (especially the managers of the large department stores) cooperated in setting up the Consumers' Building, designed both to display the latest fashions and to encourage customers to visit the various stores supporting the fair's exhibits.[64]

Managers also proclaimed their connections to the fair at the stores themselves, further emphasizing the connections between shopping and leisure in the process. In Macy's windows fair visitors could find examples of appropriate outfits for the city's numerous attractions, and managers also opened a fair visitor's bureau within the store. Over at Gimbel's managers erected scale models of World's Fair attractions in the display windows, reminding customers not to forget the Gimbel's exhibits. Even Klein's, down on Union Square, expected and prepared for greater crowds due to the fair, suggesting that visitors "have heard a great deal about the store" and might wish to "satisfy a curiosity to visit this unique establishment." In typical downscale fashion, however, Klein refused to put up any special display windows, instead joking with reporters that he might take down all the windows and put up doors instead in preparation for the greater crowds.[65]

In addition to its links to the city's retail and business communities, the 1939 World's Fair held two alternative visions of cities of the future. The first, and the one which attracted the most attention, was Democracity, a huge diorama of a future city. As one observer described it, the "strange, inspiring vision of Democracity" was that of an ordered paradise where people had "triumphed over chaos," and were free from any struggles to control public space. It was

> a mighty metropolis, done in model scale. Factories stand in special areas, and around the city itself are rows of garden apartments. The daylight wanes and thousands of lights appear in the city . . . Men of all degrees stride forward in those legions of tomorrow. Miners with lamps, engineers with blueprints, teachers with books, farmers, businessmen—all looking forward to the city waiting to receive them. With arms upraised, faces shining in the blaze of color, the paraders sing the hymn of tomorrow. In matchless precision this great throng advances until at last a circle of heroic figures is formed under the vault of heaven . . .[66]

It was a far cry from areas like the garment district, dominated as they so often were by conflict and struggle.

The second vision of the future was in some ways more important, because it was based not on a vision of the distant future but rather on a plan already in motion. Metropolitan Life's building at the fair came complete with a model of a new housing development, Parkchester. When planning began on Parkchester in 1938, Met Life officials envisioned the new development as a "self-contained city of perhaps 40,000 people." The largest private housing project ever built, it would have not only 51 apartment buildings, but also a theater, churches, a fire house, a police station, public schools, a post office, parks and playgrounds, and retail stores.[67]

Its self-contained nature made the Parkchester development relatively unique in the city's history; so too did the amount of control that Met Life would exercise in Parkchester. Like Democracity, Parkchester would represent a public space where no conflict was allowed. The company would exercise tremendous control over tenants' behavior: a private security force issued warnings and fines for everything from walking on the grass to climbing the trees in the community's courtyard. The company would make sure that the families who would move into Parkchester would have control only inside their apartments; all the public space would be under the corporation's domain.[68]

Even more important than the control Met Life exerted at Parkchester was the class and racial identity attached to living in the new development. Observers constantly remarked upon the middle-class nature of the apartment complex. As the development finally opened in 1941, *New York Times* reporter John Stanton hailed this as one of the most wonderful aspects of the project in his Sunday magazine feature on Parkchester: "there are no extremely rich people in Parkchester to be lived up to, nor extremely poor people to be tucked out of sight . . . In Parkchester . . . they have taken to nodding and saying hello to one another in the elevators, to playing badminton with one another in the parks, to organizing clubs and teams and even symphony orchestras." It was a description that could have been made a decade later about the postwar suburbs: class conflict (and indeed class itself) was all but invisible, and everyone was expected to be friendly and pleasant with one another. Like the postwar suburbs Parkchester was to be, at least in concept, a conflict-free haven, where values of community and civility served as a bulwark against a bewildering and troubled world. And while few observers remarked on it at the time, Parkchester's new community had racial limits as well. Like the department stores themselves, Met Life managers set up Parkchester, as they did some of their later housing developments, for white tenants only.[69]

The vision of the future offered by Parkchester was extremely important to the unions' future, for at Parkchester, department store managers would find themselves a new market. In 1939, as the Fair opened, Macy's managers announced a planned branch store to service the middle-class residents of Parkchester, and in October 1941 the Parkchester branch store opened to great fanfare. Met Life President Frederick Ecker, Bronx Borough President James J. Lyons, and Macy's President Jack Straus all assembled at the ribbon cutting ceremony. As with Parkchester itself, the new Macy's branch store was a sign of things to come; Macy's Parkchester branch, a success virtually from its beginnings, was a forerunner of the explosion of suburban branch stores that would follow World War II, a store within a middle-class community designed to service the residents of that community.[70]

If Parkchester and the World's Fair had the unintentional result of weakening the unions' position against store managers (there is no evidence to demonstrate that either was an intentional challenge to the unions), Macy's managers' other great project in the early months of the 1940s was a far more obvious attack on the power of workers at the upscale stores. Late in 1940 Macy's managers announced the opening of a branch store in Syracuse, in upstate New York. By expanding into this new market, managers accomplished two goals. First, they created an alternative source for profits, one that they could draw upon in case of strikes at the New York City stores. Far more important, however, managers at Macy's sought to change the operations of the Syracuse branch store to require fewer workers, changing the store to what they called a "semi-self-service" store. By this, store managers meant that salespeople would be available to assist customers, but only if customers specifically requested assistance. Not only did this mean the elimination of many of the sorts of services which store managers had come to offer their customers over the years, but it meant that the number of workers could be significantly reduced, and that a strike would quite possibly have less serious effects on the store's day-to-day operations. Managers at Macy's, in short, envisioned their new branch as something similar to a downscale store, with few services and as few employees as possible. Later, managers would call the store "a laboratory to test the possibilities of limited service units operated in connection with our New York store." In other words, if self-service could work in Syracuse, it just might work in New York City.[71]

The Syracuse experiment was a disaster for Macy's managers from its very beginnings. Customers simply didn't seem interested in a downscale version of Macy's in 1940. With no intention of continuing to fund a losing venture, Macy's managers wrote the Syracuse experiment off as a failure by the end of 1941, but left the possibility of self-service retailing on the table, insisting in public statements that the store "is being closed without prejudice," and announced that "it is possible that with the return of favorable times further experimentation with limited service units will continue."[72]

Between 1939 and the end of 1941 managers gained the tools to retake control over the city's streets and the stores alike. The celebration and creation of communities free from class conflict at Parkchester and the World's Fair, as well as the Syracuse branch store, with its tentative leanings towards self-service at upscale stores, would prove critical in managers' efforts to destroy unions in the late 1940s and early 1950s. But in the later years of the Depression, these efforts still seemed relatively minor. Not until the late 1940s would workers and union organizers face the new social order that these developments signaled. As managers moved to strengthen their position, in fact, union organizers faced a series of rapidly changing circumstances that would culminate in a massive struggle for the eight-hour day.

A Matter of Respect:
The Struggle for the Eight-Hour Day

Nothing demonstrated the newfound power of the leaders of New York City's department store unions as did the Gimbel's strike of 1941. In this strike the unions once again assembled a large number of supporters to lay claim not only to 34th Street, but to the store buildings themselves, and forced department store managers and Wolchok alike to recognize the strength in the local unions.

The relationship between local and national leaders got progressively worse between 1939 and 1941. In January 1939 the differences between local and national union leaders became far clearer as the union contract at Macy's came up for renewal. Wolchok quickly moved to renew the contract, to ensure the stability of the union. Kovenetsky and other Local 1-S organizers opposed renewal, hoping to renegotiate and thereby get more workers into the contract, as well as to gain more favorable agreements concerning wages and hours. Workers voted to authorize a strike and, on March 30, 1939, they formally rejected Wolchok's proposed settlement. Under pressure from Mike Quill, Mayor LaGuardia stepped in to negotiate a new settlement, and, with LaGuardia now present at negotiations, store managers made a better offer, making concessions on union membership, wages, and hours. Local leaders and workers accepted the new settlement. By making this better offer to the local leaders, Macy's managers gave local leaders a much stronger position within the union, since it had been the Local 1-S leaders and not Wolchok or the national leaders who had pressed the issue, and had won important concessions on all fronts: union membership, wages, and hours.[73]

Macy's was not the only example of the local unions' new and more strident tactics. At Hearn's, despite the fact that the store operated at a loss of $265,000 in 1938, the union demanded raises and reduced hours for 1939. Here, too, managers backed down, agreeing to arbitration and eventually giving the union most of what negotiators had demanded. Here, too, the union had scored a tremendous success, and here, too, negotiations were carried on by local leaders, not by the national union. The lesson for local leaders was clear: ignore national leaders' conciliatory tactics, and they could win far better contracts.[74]

As the union gradually descended into conflict, national events also worked to shift the balance of power between the unions and store managers. By February 1939 AFL leaders, judges on the Supreme Court, and congressional conservatives (both Democrats and Republicans) launched a full-scale attack on the NLRB and the CIO. Roosevelt quickly retreated to what he thought was a safer position, assigning William Leiserson, a professional mediator with no strong pro-labor sympathies, to head the NLRB. Leiserson's appointment meant that the board moved to the right, and the critics, feeling strengthened, renewed their attacks, behaving, in the words of historian Melvyn Dubofsky, "like a herd of rogue elephants off on a destructive rampage." By the summer of 1939 Congress created a committee to investigate the NLRB, and Roosevelt, apparently willing to let it slip away, made no move to defend the board. Without the NLRB's support for unions, Wolchok's "begging attitude" would simply not be effective; only strident demands, like those the local leaders were willing to present, would be able to force managers to back down.[75]

One more event in 1939 worked to worsen the relationship between local and national union leaders. In October of that year Clarina Michelson retired as the Organizer of Local 1250. While her reasons for leaving are not entirely clear, her departure deprived the other department store union organizers of their longtime mutual mentor and ally, and created an even greater need for a formal structure binding the unions together.[76]

It was a dramatic series of events in a relatively short time: Wolchok had now demonstrated he was not strident enough in his demands on management, the department store unions found themselves without a recognized leader, and the government could no longer be relied upon to support workers. More disturbing still, news came from Russia of the Hitler-Stalin Pact. American Communists, having long denied any rumors of an alliance between Hitler and Stalin, now suffered their worst embarrassment ever, losing face with many of their former Popular Front allies and abandoning the struggle against fascism that had been the centerpiece of the Popular Front.

For whichever of these reasons, or indeed for all of them, the younger local leaders of the department store unions decided they needed a stronger alliance. Losing all patience with Wolchok's repeated promises, these younger leaders created their own Joint Council without Wolchok's permission. Though it was never officially recognized by the national union, the local leaders regarded the Joint Council as a permanent organization, and even created a newspaper for the new council, the *Department Store Employee*. The *Department Store Employee,* which was written by and distributed to members of New York City's department store unions, quickly became a major thorn in Wolchok's side, as contributors to the paper attacked his policies and practices, and called for a more vigorous defense of workers' rights than Wolchok was willing to present.[77]

At least initially, Wolchok was unaware of how serious a challenge the Joint Council actually was. Far from being alarmed, in fact, he seemed to be at least somewhat supportive of the organization's existence. In a 1939 letter Wolchok not only acknowledged the council's existence but also stated that he and other URWEA leaders had "sat in on their meetings on various occasions." If the Joint Council was critical of Wolchok's leadership, he did not seem to respond to this criticism until the end of 1939.[78]

Wolchok was far more hostile toward the local leaders at the union's December 1939 convention, the first of many conventions racked by conflict and struggle between the radicals and liberals within the union. At the 1939 convention Wolchok devoted part of his opening statement to a warning to all of his political opponents that "those who have political axes to grind will be compelled to grind them outside of our ranks." At times during the convention it seemed as if Wolchok was attempting to bait the local leaders into a fight. At one point Wolchok declared that "the big industrialists who own and run the department stores have come to respect our union and to consider it a responsible organization . . . [due to] a great deal of my time and energy," since local leaders were, in his words, too "immature or inexperienced" to gain this sort of respect. At another point Wolchok found occasion to mention that "although in 1937, Local No. 1250 secured a contract with the F.W. Woolworth Company, when recently the Five and Dime Organizing Committee took over this division, we found that we did not have a single member," attributing the union's few successes in the five-and-dime stores solely to his own willingness to work on these issues rather than to the effort put in by Local 1250 organizers or the sit-down strikers.[79]

Despite Wolchok's barbed comments, the delegates from the Communist-led department store unions simply refused to respond during the convention. Their reasons for remaining silent are somewhat unclear; they may have been attempting to forestall any future attacks, or perhaps felt they were not yet strong enough to challenge Wolchok. For whatever reason, however, the delegates from the left-wing New York City locals, the department store unions as well as Local 65, seem to have limited their participation in the convention to issues which were relatively free from controversy, including resolutions for national health care, expanded old age insurance, and federal funding for housing.[80]

Left-wing delegates did raise at least one new issue during the convention, by sponsoring a resolution against the growing war in Europe. As other historians of communism have repeatedly suggested, Communists in the department store unions probably favored peace in 1939 due to the signing of the Hitler-Stalin Pact and the Communist party's subsequent opposition to American war preparations. Even here, however, they were outdone by Wolchok's supporters. Sidney Hillman, for instance, whom Wolchok invited to speak at the convention, called for peace in far stronger terms than the department store union delegates:

> What is happening abroad is the tragic culmination of lack of leadership, of failure to find a real solution for the things that troubled mankind over there. . . . we propose to keep out because there is no good that we can possibly do, neither [sic] to ourselves nor to the suffering peoples abroad, by participating in war.[81]

At the December 1939 convention, despite all the increasingly apparent divisions, department store union organizers still made an effort to avoid outright conflict within the URWEA. In 1940 department store union leaders went so far as to join Wolchok in his request to the CIO Executive Board to disband DSOC and officially place the department store unions back in the URWEA under Wolchok's leadership. Department store union leaders sent several telegrams to the CIO Executive Board in pursuit of this cause, as did Wolchok; and in 1940 the CIO Executive Board voted to disband DSOC and reunite the department store unions into the URWEA, renamed yet again, this time as the United Retail, Wholesale and Department Store Employees of America (URWDSEA).[82]

The cooperation which brought about this jurisdictional change was not to survive the merger. In fact, less than a year later, the internal disagreements which had been brewing for the previous two years finally came out into the open, and the union fell into utter disarray. The Gimbel's strike of 1941, one of the URWDSEA's greatest successes, marked the end, at least temporarily, of the alliance between the local leaders of the department store unions and the national URWDSEA leadership.

The Gimbel's strike was in many ways a surprise to all concerned. The union at Gimbel's was not particularly strong. Bea Schwartz, a union organizer and office worker at Gimbel's, remembered that at the time of the strike the union was so weak that it was still just beginning to make inroads into the office division. In addition, the Gimbel's management was unusually union-friendly. As already mentioned, Louis Broido, vice-president in charge of personnel at Gimbel's, was one of the strongest supporters of the union among store managers, and he repeatedly emphasized that unionization would bring greater stability to the retail industry. In his search for unionization accompanied by stability, Broido had found a strong ally in Samuel Wolchok. Because of this, Wolchok and Broido had gotten into the habit of negotiating the union's contract on a one-on-one basis, without rank-and-file participation and, at least in 1941, without direct input from any of the local leaders.[83]

In some ways the pro-union sympathies of Louis Broido were a key cause of the strike. On August 8, 1941, Samuel Wolchok went into negotiations with Broido to demand a $2/day wage increase and a 40-hour workweek. While the wage increase was important, it was the 40-hour workweek that department store workers and union leaders regarded as key in 1941. Many American workers had already won the long-demanded 40-hour week in 1938, as a result of the passage of the federal Fair Labor Standards Act (FLSA). The FLSA did not, however, guarantee the 40-hour workweek to all workers. The FLSA specifically exempted, among others, "any employee engaged in any retail or service establishment the greater part of whose selling or servicing is in intrastate commerce." Legislators, in other words, specifically exempted many retail workers from the rights which other workers had already won. Because of this clause and its exemptions, both department store workers and retail labor leaders had to fight to make the 40-hour workweek a standard in the retail industry. Workers viewed the 40-hour workweek as a matter of "respect," strike supporter Annette Rubinstein later remembered, since it meant achieving conditions equal to those that other workers had. Even Wolchok, far removed as he was from working in the stores, was aware of the importance of this cause. As late as July 1941, only weeks before entering into negotiations with Broido, Wolchok told a reporter that he was "anxious to extend [the 40-hour, 5-day week] to all eastern department stores."[84]

Despite Wolchok's official support for the 40-hour week, he immediately accepted Broido's offer of a 42-hour workweek accompanied by a raise of $1.50 a day, taking the contract directly back to the workers for their approval. Considering Wolchok's already tenuous relationship with the local union leaders, it was a mistake on his part to give in so easily, and a second mistake not to at least consult with local union organizers before doing so. William Michelson, the leader of Gimbel's Local 2, refused to accept the settlement without the 40-hour week, and instead called for a strike. The workers agreed with Michelson, and on August 25, Local 2 officially voted to strike.[85]

Despite the fact that the workers had rejected his settlement and declared a strike against his express wishes, Wolchok nonetheless officially moved to support the strike. Broido was astonished, both at Wolchok's support and at the strike itself; to Broido, the strike was evidence that he had miscalculated, that the local leaders could destroy Wolchok's promised stability any time they chose to do so. Broido and the other Gimbel's managers chose the rather dangerous tactic of keeping the store open despite the strike, having managers double as salespeople and using what few scabs there were to try to service any customers brave enough to cross the picket line.[86]

During the Gimbel's strike, the department store workers found themselves in an unusually favorable position, one far different from the earlier strikes at large stores, such as the Klein's-Ohrbach's, May's, and Ohrbach's strikes. Unlike in these early strikes at downscale stores, during the Gimbel's strike the overwhelming majority of workers were active participants in the strike. Out of the 2100 workers employed in the store, the union had 1500 workers on strike, making it by far the largest single strike in the union's history up to that time.[87]

There were also new obstacles which the strikers had to face, most important among them the dreaded customers. During the Gimbel's strike, for the first time in the unions' history, there was nearly as much animosity between customers and workers as there was between workers and store management. Out of the thousands of charge customers at Gimbel's, for instance, fewer than 200 were even willing to attend a customer tea hosted by the strike committee. Although several of those who came were supportive (one even gave the strikers enough money to pay for the tea), it was a far different situation from the strike at May's, for example, when members of the League of Women Shoppers became the strikers' strongest allies.[88]

Gimbel's customers bitterly attacked the strikers in letters to Mayor Fiorello LaGuardia. One Gimbel's customer named R. T. Harnie who described herself as "a gray-haired woman of seventy" wrote to LaGuardia complaining vaguely of the "disgraceful treatment" at the hands of the picketers. Another Gimbel's customer, Miss E. T. Newell, had a more constructive suggestion for the mayor; Newell complained that the picketers "march with a constant roar all day. Could not this come under nuisances—city noises—which you have done so much to eliminate?" Still another customer, Miss M. Dun, wrote of her annoyance at the amount of traffic the picketers caused, complaining that "at times it is impossible . . . to walk on the sidewalks along the entrances" to Gimbel's. In the most direct reversal of the role played by the League of Women Shoppers during the May's strike, Dun even went so far as to suggest that because it was an election year, the police—under LaGuardia's orders—were being too lenient when dealing with the strikers.[89]

The customers had several reasons for their opposition to the Gimbel's strike. In addition to the adversarial relationship between workers and customers, the strikers directly challenged the customers' understanding of what upscale department stores were meant to be. Managers had designed upscale department stores as spaces reserved for the bourgeoisie, spaces for leisure and relaxation free from the chaos of the streets outside. During the strike, store workers showed no hesitation about invading these spaces, often betraying their own animosity towards customers in the process. On one occasion, striker Helen Jacobson splashed a customer's clothing with bright red ink, and was immediately arrested for assault. Other strikers were more circumspect in their attacks on customers. As in the Klein's-Ohrbach's strikes, workers again resorted to setting a box of white mice free in the store. In addition, to the great frustration of Gimbel's managers and customers alike, the strikers somehow managed to smuggle a flock of pigeons into the store. And in what was almost certainly the most dangerous moment of the strike, someone even released a swarm of bees into the store, though this seems more likely to have been the act of an *agent provocateur* rather than a striker, and no union member was ever arrested for it.[90]

As they had done in earlier strikes, workers also assembled a number of powerful allies, many as a result of the union's participation in the Popular Front. Annette Rubinstein, at the time a high school principal and local political activist, was greatly intrigued at the news of the strike, because she had recently read Leane Zugsmith's *A Time to Remember* and viewed this strike as a chance to see the activists Zugsmith wrote about in action. It was Rubinstein's suggestion to call together the charge customers who supported the strike. Other contacts organizers made in the 1930s played equally important roles during the strike. Representatives from Mike Quill's Transportation Workers Union came and marched with the strikers, and along with the strikers, they took the picket line inside Gimbel's, completely shutting down the store's business for a day. In another throwback to the Klein's-Ohrbach's strike, actors also supported the strike at Gimbel's; they helped to pay for the strike's soup kitchen, which was literally the only way some strikers had to get food, since the local union had no money for a strike fund.[91]

The combination of this wide range of allies and the workers' willingness to use militant strike tactics resulted in a terrifying situation for Broido and other department store managers. The carefully ordered world inside the store was now under attack, and instead of the promised order, unionization had brought, in Broido's eyes, nothing less than class warfare. As he later described the Gimbel's strike before a state legislative committee, the strikers "did everything possible . . . to make the employer understand that they expected to use the forces of . . . mass movement to gain their end. . . . The line between that mass demonstration . . . and civil commotion, the line between that mass demonstration and revolutionary mass action, is so fine that nobody can say where one starts and the other stops." Broido no doubt exaggerated his own fears of working-class revolution somewhat for the committee's benefit. At the same time, his comments indicate that the workers were causing enough disruption in and around Gimbel's to throw Broido and the other Gimbel's managers into a panic.[92]

As a result of the amount of disruption they caused, the strikers emerged victorious. Broido, aware now of the strength of the vast array of forces brought to bear against him, re-opened negotiations only a month after the strike had begun. With local representatives now present at the negotiations, Broido granted the workers the 40-hour week and a small salary increase for nearly all full-time employees.[93]

Department store workers throughout New York City shared the benefits of the victory. Within days of the end of the strike, managers of the nonunionized A&S store announced that workers there would work the 40-hour week. Managers at Lord and Taylor's and at McCreery's, a nonunionized 34th Street store, also instituted the 40-hour week in the strike's aftermath. Those stores which did not immediately offer workers the 40-hour week in the aftermath of the strike announced that they would do so within a few months. None of these managers acknowledged the importance of the Gimbel's strike in making the eight-hour day standard, but there can be little doubt, considering the timing of managers' decisions to institute the 40-hour week, that these changes were results of managers' desire to avoid a repeat of the Gimbel's strike.[94]

The strike was also a major victory for the department store union leaders. It showed that the local unions were strong enough to win a strike called against the advice of the international leaders. The strike also demonstrated that the allies with whom the local union leaders had joined forces during the Popular Front era were strong enough to gain the workers a victory even against store managers as powerful as those at Gimbel's. Finally, the strike demonstrated that militant and disruptive tactics were in some ways even more effective against upscale stores than they had been against the downscale stores.

Samuel Wolchok took a different lesson from the strikes: the local leaders were too powerful. Early in October 1941, in union hearings, he charged William Michelson with "conduct unbecoming a union leader." In particular, Wolchok charged that Michelson was associated with an unauthorized subdivision of the union, the Joint Council. Wolchok's decision to attack Michelson as a representative of the Joint Council rather than for picketers' actions during the Gimbel's strike is in some ways difficult to explain. Certainly, considering Wolchok's earlier favorable statements on the Joint Council, he could hardly have been shocked at the organization's existence in late 1941. And, equally certainly, the timing of the charges and the decision to use Michelson as the target for these attacks both indicate that Wolchok's attack on Michelson was a response to the Gimbel's strike. Yet there are at least two key reasons that Wolchok would have found it difficult to attack Michelson for the strikers' often-illegal actions at Gimbel's. First, Wolchok had no evidence that Michelson was involved in or even aware of the strike tactics. Second, these tactics had led the Gimbel's workers to a victory which had eluded Wolchok: the 40-hour work week at Gimbel's. It was a victory that Wolchok saw no need to publicize further. [95]

Wolchok used more devious means of attack against the department store union leaders as well. When the Local 1-S contract with Macy's came up for negotiation again in October 1941, Wolchok offered the Local 1-S Executive Board a bargain. He would put his support behind a contract covering the entire store rather than just the portions of the store that Local 1-S had already organized, on two conditions. "The price for his aid in securing such a contract would be the expulsion of Miss Loring as organizer" as well as the payment of union dues directly to the international. Loring, upon hearing of Wolchok's condition, willingly offered her resignation, but, instead of accepting it, the Executive Board created a committee "to go and see Mr. Wolchok to show him that Ms. Loring is a valuable asset to the organization and to discuss his specific reasons for not desiring Miss Loring to remain in our employ." Wolchok, the committee reported upon returning from their meeting, was unable to give any "other reason for wishing us to discharge Miss Loring except 'her connections,'" namely (though no one said so outright), her connections to the Communist leaders of New York City's other department store unions.[96]

As Wolchok staged careful and somewhat veiled attacks on the Communist-led department store unions, Broido and other store managers launched a more strident campaign against these same unions. On December 5, at the urging of store managers, conservative New York State Assemblyman Irving Ives began hearings on picketing tactics in New York City. Though the hearings were ostensibly focused on cross-picketing (one union's picketing of a business in order to oppose another union, a common and much-criticized result of dual unionism), the hearings quickly turned into a discussion on the tactics employed by department store union members and leaders in New York City. Broido, as well as speakers from Macy's management and even a representative from the Downtown Brooklyn Association who spoke on behalf of the management of May's, all attended to give testimony.

Together, these managers complained of the tactics employed by the department store union leaders. Broido, the star witness, went into great detail on the various tactics used during the Gimbel's strike, declaring not only that the department store unions practiced cross-picketing (a charge for which he offered no evidence), but also that these unions practiced "other kinds of picketing and activities hitherto unknown in New York."[97]

Despite the vague relationship between Broido's testimony and the ostensible subject of the hearings, Ives responded to Broido's complaints with great enthusiasm. By the time the hearings ended, Ives openly voiced his opposition to the sort of tactics that the union leaders allowed. Ives concluded the hearings by suggesting that this was the sort of disruptive activity that led Fascists to demand state power:

> We are seeing something today which we might expect to see in Nazi Germany, or might have seen in Germany before it was Nazified, in the late 20's, in the very early 30's, before Hitler took power in 1933. You have something here which perhaps might have taken place in Russia at one time or other. . . . I would like to know a little bit more definitely how much of this business originated from sources outside the United States. . . . If you want to bring about the kind of conditions you have in Europe, the kind you have in Nazi Germany, for instance, at the present time, that is the way to do it.

With these brief but incredibly prescient comments, Ives captured many of the most common themes of anti-communism of the 1940s and 1950s. Not only did he emphasize (without even suggesting that any evidence for the claim existed) the supposedly foreign origins of the unions' policy and tactics, but he also brought Nazi Germany and Russia together as being in some sense equivalent.[98]

All of these attacks, the ones by Wolchok as well as those by Broido and Ives, came to a sudden halt, primarily due to the rapidly changing international situation. The cross-picketing hearing took place on December 5, 1941. Japanese pilots bombed Pearl Harbor two days later, on December 7. As a result, the disciplinary hearings scheduled for William Michelson, along with any plans Ives had for the department store unions' future, were immediately canceled. America's entrance into World War II delayed, for a time at least, the attacks on the department store unions.[99]

Conclusion

In May 1941, only a few weeks before the Gimbel's strike, Republic Studios released *The Devil and Miss Jones,* a film about a labor dispute in a New York City department store. Based in part on the labor struggles at the five-and-dime stores years earlier, *The Devil and Miss Jones* is a remarkable treatment of these department store workers. The tale of a store owner who goes undercover as a store worker to spy on labor agitators, it portrays the department store unions as a noble enterprise, one that even the store owner comes to support. In the process, it allows glimpses of many relatively realistic aspects of both the stores and the unions (including one scene where a worker chains himself to a pole and makes a speech). One of only a small handful of mainstream films to celebrate industrial unionism, *The Devil and Miss Jones* is a remarkable historical document, one that suggests just how successful the department store unions seemed in the late 1930s. Today, setting a film about labor unions in a department store would be an odd choice at best, but at the end of the Great Depression, with the Woolworth sit-downs still in recent memory and retail workers' unions still on the ascendant, it seemed as though the entire country would be able to understand and sympathize with the plight of the department store workers.[100]

Of course, *The Devil and Miss Jones* is a Hollywood film, and not a particularly accurate one. In particular, communism goes entirely unmentioned in this film. The labor organizers in the department stores are fine upstanding young men and women, who are radicalized purely by their experiences in the stores. There is no hint that the radicalism within the stores was in any way connected to any larger movement, nor any suggestion that the streets outside the stores were a factor in the unions' formation.

These flaws are important. Without understanding the struggles going on outside the stores, and without understanding particularly the role of communism as a way to link the union to these conflicts over public space, we get only a very partial picture of the development of New York City's department store unions. The department store unions would not have been anywhere near as successful as they were had it not been for the remarkable struggles going on in the streets outside, or had it not been for the allies they were able to recruit through the Popular Front. The result of the Gimbel's strike—the eight-hour day for retail workers in New York City—is directly attributable to these causes.

Despite their incredible successes, in some ways *The Devil and Miss Jones* was quite an accurate depiction of the unions. Like the film, the unions avoided race whenever possible; and, like the film, the unions increasingly avoided the subject of women's rights or the need for women leaders. Despite their tremendous power during the later years of the Depression, in fact, there is no evidence that the unions considered launching a sustained struggle against racial hiring practices in the stores. As happened in other unions in this era, department store union leaders and members alike seem to have ignored the racial hiring practices, focusing instead on issues that affected workers already employed, like pay raises and the eight-hour day. Additionally, with Clarina Michelson's departure, the period where the unions were led by women came to an end, at least for a time. But Michelson's achievements—her emphasis on recruiting workers into leadership, her ability to forge alliances, and her willingness to resort to imaginative and dramatic tactics—were nonetheless important legacies that came to fruition during the Gimbel's strike.[101]

The last years of the Great Depression were remarkable ones for American labor. Finally having established a foothold both in the retail industry and in the great assembly-line factories of the Midwest, the labor movement was on the rise, and seemed nearly unstoppable on the eve of World War II. As the nation entered the war, the Communist leaders of the department store unions had reason for hope, but there was also reason for caution. The anti-Communist alliance between national union leaders, the government, and store managers that had emerged in the aftermath of the Gimbel's strike would reemerge with a vengeance after the war. And managers' attempts to restructure the stores and expand their markets would continue throughout World War II, making these years some of the most challenging in the unions' history.

CHAPTER 4

Realignment, 1941–45

Introduction

"Through the war years nothing had fundamentally changed in Manhattan
. . . in many respects the 1930s had lingered on," popular historian Jan
Morris wrote in 1975. Morris's contention is not strictly accurate either for
Manhattan or for New York City: the city and its people had played numerous
roles in the war effort, some of them extremely important to the conflict's
outcome. New York functioned as a leisure center for soldiers and sailors on
leave; many of the great ships used in the war were made in the Brooklyn
Navy Yard; even the experiments which led to the atomic bomb began at
Columbia University in Manhattan. And, as in many other cities throughout the country, a riot took place in New York in the riot-torn year of 1943,
when Harlem residents lost patience with the absurdly high rents they were
expected to pay for limited and segregated housing.[1]

Despite its inaccuracy, Morris's observation has some truth buried in it. The
war years certainly were less dynamic than other periods in the city's history
had been. Many of the most striking images of wartime New York are not of
the riots or even the bustling Navy Yards, but rather the dimout, where residents turned off all unnecessary lights, leaving the city virtually in darkness.
As John Von Hartz observed, the dimout left New York "a somber ghost of
its former nighttime self." And, as though to accompany the darkened city, the
political radicalism which had once been such a central part of New York City
life, and which had given such vibrancy to the department store unions, had all
but vanished with the arrival of the war. Morris wrote that since "the war had
brought new prosperity to nearly everyone . . . the edge was off radicalism."[2]

If political radicalism had faded from the forefront of city life, this had little
to do with prosperity. In fact, due to wartime rations, increased rents, and
price gouging by resourceful retailers, many New Yorkers faced some form
of economic distress during the war. But the Communist party, which had

previously led so much of the city's radicalism, now held that all radical protests should be suspended to support the war effort. The Socialists had a somewhat more complicated attitude towards the war, but due to Socialist party leader Norman Thomas's attempt to combine pacifism with support for the war, the Socialists had less than a thousand members nationwide by mid-1942. After the bombing of Pearl Harbor, it seemed as though radicals in New York had abandoned any effort at social change in order to fight the war.[3]

Like the rest of the city, New York's department store unions at least seemed relatively stable during the war. There were no wildcat strikes in New York City's department stores, and there was plenty of evidence that workers and union leaders alike strongly supported the war. It was a far cry from the dramatic struggles exploding in the midwestern factory centers, where workers increasingly felt alienated by their conciliatory union leaders and launched massive wildcat strikes in protest. Instead, in New York, the shared support for the war seemed to minimize if not eliminate the sorts of conflicts going on elsewhere in the country. In fact, as Governor Dewey proudly pointed out, in 1944 New York State lost only 15 man-days of work for every 100,000 such days, whereas the national average was approximately 73 lost days of work per 100,000. New York workers were determined to make "a great contribution toward the winning of the war," and most gave up the right to strike for that end.[4]

The apparent stability masked tremendous structural and political changes taking place in and around New York City's department store unions. The stores and the unions were both changing very rapidly, and the changes that took place during the war years would define the course of the unions' history in the postwar years. The stores themselves were the site of some of the most dramatic changes. The end of the Depression meant an end to the easy vilification of store managers that had so benefited retail workers' unions during the Depression. The war led to new patterns of consumption, and store managers were in the best position to encourage proper wartime consumption. They took up this cause with great dedication, and during the war the department stores became patriotic centers as well as centers of leisure and consumption. Store managers also took advantage of the wartime labor shortage to change the costly labor practices that they had used during the Depression. They found self-service, in particular, to be a more attractive possibility now that labor was in short supply.

Like store managers, national union leaders also took up the patriotic cause. During the war, Samuel Wolchok became a figure of great national importance, not only to the labor movement, but to the war effort as a whole. He met with government officials on both national and state levels and worked with them to map out plans to ensure workers' support for the war. And he did so while vocally supporting liberal reform, calling for a strong Fair Employment Practices Commission and even offering mild support (though no milder than most of the local leaders' support) for women's rights. Additionally, Wolchok's favorite tactics, those of conciliation and compromise, were now the only acceptable tactics for organizing unions, thanks to the government's active role in settling labor disputes through negotiation rather than strikes.

In short, the two most visible enemies of the leaders of New York City's department store unions were now no longer acceptable targets. National union leaders and store managers alike were virtually beyond reproach, and attacks on either would gain the local unions extreme unpopularity. Indeed, during the war, local union leaders seemed to retreat from their earlier criticisms of Wolchok in particular. Wolchok, on the other hand, used his newfound power to staunchly criticize the left-wing opposition that had been such a thorn in his side only months earlier.

The only major issue around which the union divided found the left-wing leaders within the department stores decidedly in the minority. Arthur Osman, the leader of Local 65 and the unofficial leader of the URWDSEA's left wing, severely criticized Wolchok's willingness to allow workers to strike against Montgomery Ward, despite the fact that the government had approved this particular strike. Although no department store union or department store union leader publicly took a stand on the Montgomery Ward strike, the effect of Osman's criticism of the strike and Wolchok were to make Osman a pariah within the union, and increase the power of conservatives. As the war drew to a close, everyone connected with the unions would be left scrambling, trying to ensure that their particular base of power—the left wing, the department store unions, the warehouse division, the national union leaders, or the stores themselves—would be preserved or even strengthened after the war ended.

Consuming War

Among the most remarkable of the changes which took place in New York following the attacks of September 11, 2001 were signs of new consumption patterns. As if by magic, American flags appeared everywhere. Goods with patriotic themes—ranging from still more flags to bumper stickers and coffee mugs—were available at city stores within a few days of the attacks, and commemorative items with images of the World Trade Center buildings on them could be found in almost any neighborhood of the city. Consumption was a way—arguably the primary way—many people in New York and throughout the country confronted the day's tragedies.

It was not the first time that residents of the city had used consumption as a way of confronting a national crisis. Consumption changed dramatically in the aftermath of Pearl Harbor. Although overall business initially fell off due to the war, there was a rush for blackout materials; candles, flashlights, and dark fabrics sold in December 1941 at a pace unmatched in the stores' history. Emergency goods were now a priority, and store managers hurried to make the appropriate adjustments, making sure that store clerks were educated as to where in the store customers should go to purchase materials to prepare for a blackout.[5]

Consumption was central to the war effort in many different respects, and store managers became "the interpreters of a national and local policy" of proper wartime consumption, according to a professor of retailing at the University of Tennessee. Managers had good reasons to support proper wartime consumption. For one thing, it was the wisest course: at a time when the public was expected to make massive sacrifices, if retailers refused to cooperate, they might well increase the public animosity towards big retail establishments. On the other hand, if retailers supported the war effort and demonstrated their patriotism, they could go a long way to winning back the public approval of big retailing that the government investigations and union activities of the late 1930s had destroyed. Additionally, their support for the war might convince some retail workers that their jobs were important enough not to leave the stores for factories that often offered higher pay and an opportunity to make a more direct contribution to the war effort.[6]

If public opinion was one force driving retailers to support the war, the government was another. Government officials openly advocated an active role for retailers during the war. R. R. Guthrie, an official of the Office of Production Management, attended the 1942 annual meeting of the National Retail Dry Goods Association, the department store's trade association. Retailers, Guthrie informed his audience, had a central role to play in the war effort: "We need, right now, a Victory Budget for the [average] family, a budget of essential wartime needs, a budget which will enable the family to reach top efficiency as a group of war workers, but stripped of everything else. Upon retailers depends the responsibility . . . of securing acceptance of such a budget, hearty, willing acceptance of it, by American families."[7]

Store managers, with all this pressure to support the war effort, rose to the occasion. One of the primary ways they had of supporting the war was by selling products made of appropriate materials. Gimbel's managers, for instance, heavily advertised curtains and carpets made of bomber cloth, which they described as "a sturdy, non-priority fabric." Gimbel's also hosted a Civilian Defense Fashion Show, where customers could "learn to be comfortable while they work." Several department store managers took part in the 1942 *New York Times* fashion show, which, as Mayor LaGuardia described it, would "show that even with substitute materials because of the emergency, it is still possible to have useful, attractive, and pretty clothes."[8]

While buying nonpriority materials and other practical goods was one important part of wartime consumption, managers also lauded purchases of patriotic items as a way to support the war. American flags, for instance, were sold at several stores. So were other patriotic goods. Macy's managers—who were particularly adept at advertising their contributions to the war—offered customers a chance to purchase a film of the Japanese attack on Pearl Harbor: "Now, on your own home screen, you can view the actual bombing, the heroic American defense! Here is grim history, on film. Don't wait to own this great movie of the beginning of our nation's most tremendous fight for liberty!" Macy's also sold films of Douglas MacArthur and the bombing of Manila.[9]

Some patriotic goods had more practical applications. Macy's and other stores offered customers a chance to buy food boxes for soldiers, pointing out that "he's training for the fight of his life (and yours). Besides, it gives him terrific prestige among his buddies, when that food box comes through regularly." Gimbel's managers followed suit, offering customers a chance to buy "patriotic envelopes" and stamped envelopes "mailed from 17 American [military] bases." Gimbel's advertisements also encouraged customers who were "knitting like mad for that man of yours in the service" to buy yarn "in regulation colors," conveniently available at Gimbel's.[10]

Many of the stores also offered customers a chance to buy war bonds and stamps. At Macy's, for instance, managers set up a Victory Booth near the store's main entrance, where customers could purchase war stamps. One 1942 Macy's advertisement reminded customers that "it takes only 75 twenty-five cent Stamps to become an 18.75 bond, which in ten years will net you $25." Customers could purchase the stamps at the Victory Booth, or if they desired, take them in lieu of change after making purchases. The strategies for selling bonds were extremely effective. By December 1942 Macy's proudly announced to potential customers that the store had sold "over $3,000,000 worth of war bonds and stamps."[11]

Even items that had only indirect connections to the war effort were advertised in terms of the war. Customers, one Macy's advertisement told the readers of the *New York Times,* were buying their shirts "in double-quick time," and

Macy's furniture would be "as much at home in an army post in Vermont, as in a one-room apartment in Washington." Gimbel's offered customers a chance to purchase "Red Cross Nylon Stockings," connected to the Red Cross, apparently, only in that they were comfortable for women who were on their feet a lot. Stern's sold women's slacks by calling out to "air raid wardens" and "Red Cross" workers to buy them. And a Macy's advertisement for women's shoes described them as "sleek as an officer's dress parade boot." The same advertisement went on to inform women workers that these shoes "mean comfort even if your war work means being on your feet a lot." Many other advertisements throughout the war carried with them a small note encouraging customers to "buy United States savings bonds and stamps" or asked customers to give to the Red Cross.[12]

Sales were one part of wartime consumption, but there were other aspects as well. Customers had to be taught not only to buy, but to avoid over-buying, to conserve goods and labor wherever possible. Twelve New York department stores participated in a joint advertisement condemning hoarding goods, reminding customers and employees alike that hoarding could lead to "great dissatisfaction among the millions of people who cannot afford to build up reserves of merchandise and who would be content to endure mild deprivations if everyone were in the same boat." Store managers also offered any number of suggestions as to how customers could avoid consuming too much. Bloomingdale's devoted a display window to the cause in the spring of 1942, informing customers that "spring house cleaning" could "aid war production." In store advertisements Macy's encouraged customers to "carry home their purchases," and save not only money, but also "rubber, gas, [and] paper." Or, as another Macy's advertisement reminded readers, "Your government wants you to buy only what you need—take care of what you own!" Likewise, Gimbel's informed customers in one advertisement that "To Save Is To Serve," and asked them not to throw away paper, rubber, scrap metal, or rags. Gimbel's also emphasized the store's accessibility by mass transit, reminding customers that "it's easy to get to Gimbels [sic] without a spoonful of gas," thus saving gasoline for the war effort. Other advertisements took advantage of the war to advertise lower prices. "We know it isn't easy," one Macy's ad assured readers, "to be a breadwinner these days, and provide for both the family and Uncle Sam's defense efforts. We know it takes budgeting, no matter how large one's income. . . . Let Macy's be YOUR Cash Conservation Corps." Or, in a similar vein, a *Wall Street Journal* advertisement for Macy's assured customers that "the world's largest store is especially helpful in times like these, when the rising cost of living and mounting war taxes make everyone feel the need to save."[13]

The most direct educational role managers played during the war was in Macy's regular advertisement feature, "News On The Home Front," a special column run in Macy's ads which taught customers about the new rules of consumption. The first of these columns explained the advice column's presence in an advertisement: "running your home efficiently and economically today is a bigger job than ever before. You're trying to make everything you own give extra service and last longer . . . Here at Macy's Home Centre . . . we'll show you how to prepare easy, economical menus that add up to a lot in good taste and good health." The feature became more formalized later on; by April 1942 it had become "The Home Front News," and informed customers of sewing classes available at the store at a cost of $0.74 for two hours. Besides allowing customers a chance to save money by sewing their own clothes, the feature encouraged women to carry their own packages, and save their scraps. Some of the suggestions in "The Home Front News" are in retrospect almost comical: shoppers were offered detailed instructions in how to shine their own shoes, for instance, and later that year, another column taught customers how to "keep your curtains fresh and lovely longer!" But at the time, of course, all these suggestions were deadly serious. The April column concluded with a reminder: "Learning how to do for oneself is all part of this countrywide and patriotic determination to conserve the things needed by our Armed Forces."[14]

Store managers also found ways to use their control of the store spaces—large public spaces in high-traffic areas—for the war effort. In 1943, store managers throughout the city set up collection boxes in all their stores, asking customers to donate used books to be sent to soldiers overseas. Individual store managers also came up with many different additional ways to use store space to promote the war. Managers at Macy's, for example, allowed the Red Cross to open a blood donation center within the store, where customers could also apply for free courses in "first aid, home nursing, water safety, accident prevention, and nutrition." They also set up a Kids' Day at their War Bond Center, allowing customers and their children to come in and watch a team of experts assemble a jeep, watch exclusive war films, and see an exhibit of war photography. Gimbel's managers allowed the Navy to set up a counter where customers could donate binoculars, and eventually set up a demonstration Victory Garden "to prove that two persons can grow all the vegetables they need for three months in a tiny plot." Managers at Gimbel's also set up a "Women's Spring Offensive" lecture series, where they invited women customers to come and see "lectures, demonstrations, and programs designed to acquaint the women of New York with the essential points of home defense." Perhaps most ambitious of all, managers at Hearn's set up a "Win-The-War Show," where customers could go and see displays about the war, including "a new dive bomber trap, . . . ammunition, gas masks, and other [war-related] material," with the strong support of Mayor LaGuardia, who presided over the show's opening ceremony. Upon seeing the success of the Hearn's show, Macy's immediately announced their own industrial exhibit to "create a better understanding and acceptance of the many amazing substitutes and improvements for civilian use."[15]

Similarly, during Labor Day weekend of 1942, when car trips were discouraged due to the gasoline shortage, store managers, with the full support of Mayor LaGuardia, threw a sale. LaGuardia himself praised the sale in a half-page advertisement in the *New York Times*, telling potential customers that the Saturday of Labor Day weekend would be "one of the greatest bargain days in the history of the retail trade in New York City. Now is the time to prepare the children for school; to replace utensils and household articles that have been given to the Government in one drive or another, curtains, rugs, furniture, and better put in the supply for the Autumn and Winter clothing now!"[16]

And, beginning in March 1943, store managers throughout the city gave up one of their display windows to advertise the Red Cross's wartime achievements. Each store took a different aspect of the Red Cross's functions: Gimbel's displayed Red Cross workers "building morale" in Alaska; Hearn's window had the Red Cross "aiding our allies" in China; and in Bloomingdale's window the Red Cross was "providing aid to service men's families" in Hawaii.[17]

Managers also worked to make sure that their employees supported the war effort. At Hearn's, managers set up a storewide "national defense corps" to prepare for a civil emergency, with both managers and workers as members. Managers took out huge display advertisements for the defense corps, one featuring a saleswoman standing helpfully behind a counter with the words, "Yes, Madam . . . We Sell Guns, Tanks, Planes!" The advertisement went on to preach a set of values that fundamentally expressed the challenges that the wartime ethos offered to unions:

> We're salesmen and saleswomen, porters and electricians, executives and stock clerks, shippers, carpenters, and cashiers . . . but we're all ONE for national defense. . . . We're ready, eager, and anxious to do our bit . . . we've trained ourselves in fire fighting and first aid. We're Blood donors, we're Air Raid wardens, we have our own knitting groups which supply wool and instructions. We're bond sellers and stamp sellers to the tune of $100,000 already . . . *and we've just begun to sell!* We're like YOU! We love liberty and we love our country!

The advertisement is remarkable in just how far it takes the concept of war-time unity. Not only are all workers to be united, but they are united with executives and even, towards the end of the advertisement, with customers. Everyone, at least as far as managers were concerned, would indeed be united as "one for national defense." Store managers throughout the city encouraged similar attitudes, sponsoring rallies and parades for their employees to encourage them to take their pay in war bonds. Other managers went even further; at Macy's, managers set up a United Service Organization branch to encourage women working at Macy's to become hostesses for soldiers on leave. Actions like these both demonstrated management's support for the war effort and served in some ways as extensions of certain tactics that managers had engaged in before the war. Like the prewar bonus programs in upscale stores, these programs also served to emphasize the common interests of managers and workers, weakening workers' ties to their unions in the process.[18]

Managers' support for the war was only one way that the war affected upscale department stores. The war also brought the loss of most of the male workers within the stores. Unlike many blue-collar jobs, the federal government classified department store work as nonessential, and male workers were therefore eligible for the draft. The loss of nearly all the men working in the stores created a labor shortage; and the fact that many women were now leaving department stores to go to work in other jobs (the Brooklyn Navy Yard offered particularly tempting employment for women working in the New York City stores; banks also began employing women tellers at this time, drawing still more workers from the stores) made the labor shortage even more acute. Managers therefore began searching for a replacement labor pool. Suddenly, all sorts of people became eligible to work in department stores. Managers began searching for "extras, contingents, and part-time store employees . . . older men and women . . . [and] recent graduate of high schools," as well as a few high school students. Their search was at least partially successful. In New York City, store managers found many older men and women—some as old as sixty. These workers were a far cry from the people in their late teens and twenties who had taken sales jobs before the war. Store managers also began recruiting straight out of high schools. Bloomingdale's worker John O'Neill began working in the store in 1944, when, as a junior in high school, he saw a list of jobs for students, including several stockroom positions at Bloomingdale's.[19]

Store managers also used other measures to take the place of the lost labor, some of which broke with prewar practices of discrimination. By 1942 women began working in the stockrooms of some department stores, and by 1943 some store managers allowed women to take jobs as delivery truck helpers. Despite these changes, managers continued emphasizing the importance of gendered divisions of labor throughout the war. Even as they began hiring women to make deliveries, managers assured the newspaper reporters covering the story that women would not be "required to tussle with heavy pieces of furniture and equipment," but instead only to "deliver parcels light enough for the women to handle alone." Perhaps more importantly, there is no evidence that women ever entered the highest-paying department store jobs, such as the coveted sales jobs in furniture departments.[20]

Like white women, African American workers in the stores made a few gains during the war, as managers compromised their discriminatory hiring practices to cope with the labor shortage. In this sense, the war economy accomplished what years of efforts by the "Don't Buy Where You Can't Work" campaign (and, in their almost nonexistent campaign, the unions as well) had failed to do: it won African American workers their first sales and office jobs in the upscale stores. During the war, African American women began to make some inroads in sales positions at Gimbel's and office positions at Macy's. Like advances made by white women, managers allowed only limited changes to their prewar system of job segregation. African American sales and office workers remained rare exceptions throughout the war era. In addition, African American workers typically received lower salaries than whites in the same jobs.[21]

Just as African American workers began winning better jobs in these stores, the jobs themselves began to change. In perhaps their most historically important effort to meet the wartime labor shortage, store managers began experimenting with self-service forms of retailing, often eliminating jobs in the process. Managers had of course begun experimenting with self-service even before the war, with the opening of Macy's Syracuse branch store. However, considering the failure of the Syracuse experiment, New York store managers were very uneasy with the possibilities that self-service offered, and with some reason. If full-service shopping allowed managers tremendous control over customers' activities in the stores, managers had less direct control over a self-service operation, where customers interacted with salespeople only if customers approached salespeople or vice versa. Nonetheless, with labor shortages threatening the industry, managers increasingly found self-service a necessity. Early in 1943, the NRDGA began sponsoring talks on how self-service would affect the stores. At one such talk Franklin Lamb, the president of a company that manufactured store shelving fixtures, reminded store managers that they had no real choice in the matter of self-service, at least for the duration of the war. "To meet present conditions," Lamb informed his audience, "it becomes necessary to deliberately break up the practice of forcing assistance on customers . . . The fewer salespeople on the floor simply do not have the time for anything but stock-keeping and giving asked-for help to customers."[22]

Despite the shortages, upscale store managers moved hesitantly towards the self-service system, often employing a full staff of salespeople while attempting to initiate the transition. Viola Sylbert, an industry analyst who wrote about the self-service experiments during the war, argued that the very hesitancy with which managers approached the new system doomed some of these early experiments to failure. Sylbert describes one such experiment in a shoe department at an unnamed upscale store in New York City: "All styles of shoes were piled on tables with the size and width clearly marked on large placards," but "a complete selling staff [all paid by commission] was maintained on the floor" anyway. As a result, "shoe salesmen . . . very naturally disregarded instructions and approached customers whenever possible," trying to make sales and increase their commissions.[23]

Department store managers did eventually hit upon a more successful intermediate method of store organization by creating what Sylbert called "open-merchandise displays." In these types of sales operations, sample goods were laid out for customers to examine without the intervention of sales workers. However, in order to purchase anything, customers still had to find a salesperson to get the item they wished to purchase from the stockroom. With this tactic managers continued to require salespeople and customers to interact, but at the same time they no longer needed quite as many salespeople to deal with customers. Salespeople in the stores now only had to carry goods back and forth from the stockroom, a practice that required both fewer sales workers and far less training for these workers.[24]

All of these changes inside the stores strengthened the store managers' position in relation to their workers, and the changes in the streets outside reinforced managers' strength still further. The May Day parades which had once been a major challenge to store managers' domination of the streets of the garment district were now suspended for the duration of the war. Communists tried to argue that there was a basic continuity between the prewar marches and the wartime cancellation of the marches: *Daily Worker* contributor Art Shields, for instance, argued that "again May Day this year is a day of international solidarity, though the workers will demonstrate against fascism in the workshops instead of the streets. They will demonstrate against their main enemies by producing the weapons to destroy them." To the Communist party, arguably the central organization of the city's radical movement, the war effort was a radical cause, one that directly benefited workers, and interfering with the war, or attacking those who supported it, would be a betrayal of the working class.[25]

With the Communists ceasing their disruption of the streets outside the stores, the struggles over public space that had been a central cause of the unions' victories before the war were now over, replaced by pro-war demonstrations that often denied class conflict. In June 1942, for instance, only weeks after the Communists canceled their first wartime May Day parade, the city held a "New York at War" parade, where soldiers, their commanders, and—in the ultimate irony considering the open and sometimes violent class struggle that had been declared in those same streets only months before—"George L. Harrison, president of the New York Life Insurance Company, heading off-duty production workers from the ranks of industry and labor." Class struggle, the parade organizers attempted to argue by allowing Harrison to lead the workers in their support for the war, had been called off for the duration of the war. It was a message similar in many ways to the message of the 1932 Union Square centennial celebration, but during the war, with the Communists' new policy, there was no attempt to answer this enacted call for an end to class struggle.[26]

Similar changes in the tenor of the neighborhood took place throughout the war. As the Allied victory looked more and more certain in 1944 and 1945, union leaders throughout the garment district co-sponsored rallies with business owners, in order to encourage workers to continue their support for the war effort. "The surging crowds," *Women's Wear Daily* reported, "cheered trade leaders, union representatives, and stage and radio celebrities in the most enthusiastic trade rally since the beginning of the war." And this was nothing compared to the rallies in the aftermath of V-E day, when everything south of 40th Street became "a beehive of activity" as "swatches, paper, and whatever else was handy flew through the air." So far was the neighborhood's atmosphere from the former struggles that had dominated it that now dignitaries visiting the city paraded through the area. General Eisenhower, for instance, marched through the streets of the garment district upon his visit to New York in the summer of 1945, and was greeted by throngs of workers from garment factories and stores alike celebrating his victory against Germany.[27]

If the changes in the garment district weakened any threat of disorder that the unions might once have used to their advantage, other developments in the city that took place during the war would more permanently affect the unions' situation. Perhaps the most important was an act of tremendous foresight by

Met Life, the same company that had opened Parkchester shortly before the war. During the war, with encouragement from both Mayor LaGuardia and Robert Moses, Met Life executives began work on a huge housing project on the East Side of Manhattan, just a few blocks east of Union Square. Stuyvesant Town, as the new development was called, would play a central role in the city's postwar development. So began what newspapers heralded as "the greatest and most significant mass movement of families in New York City's history," as the working-class residents of the area east of Union Square began to move away from the site soon to be cleared for the new development. It would take several years before the effects of Stuyvesant Town would be felt on the department stores, but when they were felt, the effects would be devastating for the unions' future.[28]

If the effects of Stuyvesant Town were not immediate, the effects of many of the other changes taking place in the city were, as these transformations generally strengthened managers' efforts to control their employees. As strong and visible supporters of the war, managers now ended the stigma attached to large retail firms that had been so powerful during the Depression. Thanks to self-service, managers also could now eliminate many of the workers who had once been so integral to the functioning of both the stores and the unions. While workers in other industries did go out on highly controversial wildcat strikes to protest factory managers' wartime actions, there is no evidence that workers in New York City's department stores considered this option. Far from it: workers and union organizers alike actively participated in management-sponsored activities like war bond rallies and USO parties, demonstrating their own support for the war.[29]

If there was no conflict between workers and union leaders during the war, there was plenty of wartime conflict within the unions. During the war, Samuel Wolchok found the support within the URWDSEA that had somewhat eluded him in the late 1930s. He would now set about solidifying his own base as a national union leader.

Unions at War, 1941–45

While store managers found themselves in a stronger position due to the war, New York City's local unions were greatly weakened by changes within the retailing industry during the war. Changes in personnel and tactics seriously threatened the local union leaders who had once been so powerful within the URWDSEA. Local leaders' strong support for the no-strike pledge, due in some cases to their support for the Soviet Union, forced them to abandon the confrontational tactics that had served them so well during the Depression. As they shifted tactics, Communist and non-Communist local union leaders alike endorsed a double-V campaign, voicing their support for the war as they simultaneously called for campaigns against racism, sexism, and economic injustice on the home front. In doing so, these local leaders found themselves in close political agreement with Samuel Wolchok and other national URWDSEA leaders, even as national and local union leaders struggled for control of the union with even greater determination.

The most immediate effects of the war upon the department store unions were the changes in union personnel. Several of the most respected leaders of the local unions, Bill Michelson and Lowell Morris (the leader of Bloomingdale's Local 3) among them, left the unions for the army. Morris subsequently died in combat, to be replaced in leadership by Bloomingdale's sales worker Carl Andren. In addition, at some stores, a number of workers who had previously been union organizers were recruited for management positions, and thus were out of the union for the duration of the war.[30]

This vacuum in leadership represented both a challenge to those local leaders who remained and an opportunity for those workers who had not been part of the union leadership before World War II. It was in part as a result of these changes in union personnel that women and African American workers advanced into important roles in union leadership during the war. Gimbel's worker Anna Blanck, for example, became an important figure in the leadership of Local 2 partially because of William Michelson's absence, while William Atkinson, a non-Communist African American elevator operator at Macy's, advanced in the union ranks to become the vice-president of Local 1-S before Atkinson was himself drafted. Both Atkinson and Blanck would continue to play important roles in the union leadership after the war ended.[31]

As African Americans and women advanced into union leadership, local union leaders became even more vocal about the need to combat gender discrimination. In a speech before the general membership of Local 1-S, for instance, Samuel Kovenetsky went on record in favor of women becoming "more active in the union and that gaps in the [local] leadership be filled by women in the event of the drafting of our male leaders." Union organizers also became a little more outspoken in demanding rights for African American workers within the stores. Since retailing was not a defense industry, Roosevelt's Executive Order 8802 did not apply, and the Fair Employment Practices Commission had no power to regulate the department store industry. Union organizers nonetheless set up local anti-discrimination committees in their first serious effort to end discrimination within the stores. In the same speech where he called for increasing the numbers of women workers in the union leadership, Samuel Kovenetsky declared that African American workers, now "in categories of work besides elevators and kitchens . . . have a right to be able to do the same work for the same salaries as their white brethren." Whether the anti-discrimination committees had any effect on African American workers' winning jobs in sales and office work is less clear; as has already been mentioned, due to the labor shortage, African American workers likely would have won these jobs regardless of the unions' support.[32]

Organizers also made additional efforts to struggle against racism outside of the stores. The Executive Board of Local 1-S, for example, issued a formal protest against segregated baseball leagues in 1942. In addition, the local unions' newspaper, the *Department Store Employee,* published a number of articles against discrimination, particularly in the American South. According to the *Department Store Employee,* union leaders wrote multiple letters to their congressional delegates protesting African American citizens' mistreatment throughout the South.[33]

As these efforts to fight racism indicate, organizers increasingly worked around a wide range of issues, some quite removed from the day-to-day lives of department store workers. The Local 1-S Executive Board passed a resolution calling for the opening of the Second Front in Europe, a popular cause among those who wished to take some pressure off Stalin's Red Army. Other issues around which the unions organized were closer to home. One article in the *Department Store Employee,* for instance, indicates that union members focused on organizing campaigns to support the wartime price controls, designed to curb inflation and to thereby ensure that the wage freeze did not result in workers' impoverishment. When Congress voted to allow even limited price increases, local leaders called on all union members to participate in a massive letter-writing campaign to protest this action.[34]

Local leaders repeatedly attempted to connect these wartime struggles to the history of the unions before the war. They did so first by continuing many of the demands and practices that had begun before the war. The Local 1-S Executive Board, for instance, issued a resolution in 1942 calling for "one department store local" in New York, rather than the multiple locals which then existed, a continuation of the union organizers' prewar demands for the Joint Board. In addition, union organizers continued to use cultural programs as well as the unions' newspaper as a way to bind the different locals together. By the end of the war not only did members of the department store union locals all share the same newspaper, but all participated in activities like those begun under the Joint Activities Committee before the war began. Shop stewards in all the department store locals also participated in a single set of union leadership classes, since—as one article put it—the leaders of all "our local unions realized the necessity for training [stewards] in the problems that confront labor, in order to strengthen the internal structure of our locals."[35]

The local leaders also emphasized the connections between their wartime struggles and the pre-war history of the union by explicitly celebrating the local unions' history. Nicholas Carnes, whose long presence in the union made him a *de facto* expert on the subject, published several articles on the department store unions' history in the *Department Store Employee* during the war. While at least one of these articles has been lost, in the articles that survived, Carnes recounted the union's history as a grassroots movement, by reminding his readers that it was "a few department store workers" who had "met together in the office of the Office Workers Union, independent" and thus created "the parent body of our present union." In Carnes's history, these workers had led the strikes against Klein's and Ohrbach's, the five-and-dime stores, and Gimbel's. And these workers had chosen to remain unified despite attempts on the part of the national URWDSEA leaders to divide them. Carnes's history is interesting both for what he omitted and for what he included. For one thing, his strong celebration of workers' grassroots militancy suggests that, contrary to the assertions of many historians, local union leaders during World War II did not in principle oppose workers' militancy. To the contrary, Carnes celebrated the unions' militant history, but nonetheless supported the no-strike pledge, apparently seeing no contradiction in this attitude. Additionally, in an act that had increasing importance for the unions' future, Carnes omitted any mention of the Communist politics that had played such a key role in the unions' history. While this was not unusual (within the department store unions, as elsewhere, the word "Communist" was generally used only by anti-Communists, as a form of attack), it is nonetheless important for the way it allowed Carnes to construct the union's history. In order to avoid any anti-Communist attacks, Carnes created a history that gave communism no credit for the union's achievements, and deprived the workers who had created these unions of their radical political beliefs.[36]

Local union organizers celebrated their past militancy and continued campaigning for various causes, while espousing a far less militant set of tactics during the war. Like the Communist party's support for workers' going to work on May Day, there may have been some political justification for not disrupting the war effort, but it nonetheless made the unions less radical, less militant, and ultimately less powerful. In response to both rising prices and segregation, union leaders responded by issuing written complaints to federal officials and asking members to do the same. It was a far cry from the Depression, when they had called for a more confrontational approach to winning workers better contracts. And it was a tactic that simply would not result in as many victories as did their earlier, more confrontational efforts.

For the Communists within the local leadership of New York City's department store unions, this tactical shift had a special significance, since Samuel Wolchok and other national URWDSEA leaders substantially altered their own political program. To do so, the national URWDSEA leaders embraced liberalism and vocally opposed racism and gender discrimination. At the same time, unlike the local leaders, national union leaders endorsed militant strikes during the war (so long as the government approved them), while repeatedly and vocally endorsing the liberal agenda of equal opportunity for all. By war's end, therefore, the Communist-led local unions and the non-Communist national union had shifted their respective positions: the Communists were now the ones calling for restrained tactics, while the liberals were suddenly the more militant of the two factions within the union.

The national URWDSEA leaders illustrated their support for liberalism by supporting many different issues. At the 1942 convention the national leaders addressed women's role within the union for the first time. At that convention, the first since the country's entrance into World War II, delegates set up an official Women's Auxiliary, although there are no records indicating what, if anything, the auxiliary actually did. The national union leaders also went "on record for increasing the participation of women in the leadership in the International and its affiliated locals." Like Kovenetsky, they probably did so due to the entrance of large numbers of male union members and male union leaders into the armed forces.[37]

During the next year, 1943, Wolchok went even further in his pursuit of justice for working women. Among other things, Wolchok set up a meeting with New York State Governor Dewey to discuss women's wages, and received personal assurance from the governor "that $250,000 would be allotted out of the State Budget to set up facilities for establishing and supervising minimum hour and wage regulations for women in New York State retail stores." Although Dewey's promise does not seem to have resulted in any recorded change in women's status within retail stores, Wolchok's meeting with Dewey was still significant for the history of the URWDSEA. Wolchok, unlike the local union leaders, had the ability to set up meetings with the governor to make these demands for women's rights, and thereby take some credit for Dewey's statement, as he publicly did in the union newspaper.[38]

At the same time as he became more supportive of equal rights for working women, Wolchok also emerged as one of the foremost advocates for racial equality within the union. At the 1942 convention Wolchok announced that, in the postwar world, "there must be social and economic and political equality, not merely for the white man, but also for the black man, for the yellow man, for every man." In order to achieve this, Wolchok and other national leaders strongly supported the establishment of a permanent and more powerful Fair Employment Practices Commission (FEPC), one that would have the right to regulate all industries, not just defense industries.[39]

Despite these stronger stands against discrimination, the leaders of the national union, unlike the local leadership, remained exclusively white and almost exclusively male throughout the war. By the end of the war only one woman, Betty Weiner, sat on the national Executive Board, and none of the vice-presidencies or other major leadership positions were filled by women or nonwhites during the 1940s. Essentially, within the union's national leadership, white men were leading a struggle for women's rights and racial equality in the workplace.

The national union's newspaper during the war further demonstrates this lack of diversity. Throughout the war the editors of the union's national newspaper consistently reflected the national union leaders' stance on political and social issues. And, in the 1940s, despite the numerous articles opposing racial and gender discrimination, the editors continued to portray the URWDSEA as a union of white men. Cartoons, for example, depicted the union as a large and muscular white man, frequently in the same social-realist style that dominated CIO and other union propaganda in the 1930s. Women appeared in only one picture representing the union during the war: in a cartoon reflecting the delegates to the union's convention, the cartoonist added some women to the convention floor. Other than that, artists always represented the union as male.[40]

Like the local leaders, the national leaders used a presentation of the union's history to illustrate their vision of the union. The national leaders' history of the union, likewise presented in their union newspaper, gave the New Era Committee, led by Wolchok and URWDSEA Vice-President John V. Cooney, responsibility for attracting the CIO's attention. These brave, white, male leaders, a report presented in the national union's newspaper asserted, were "denounced as trouble-makers, their characters assassinated. . . . With no semblance of reason, with star chamber proceedings and not an iota of justification," they had been expelled from the AFL and had joined the CIO. Gone were the women workers at the five-and-dime stores whose strikes had been central to the union's reputation when the New Era Committee had applied for a CIO charter; gone, too, were Clarina Michelson and her followers, who had played such a large role in the union's history. And, as in Carnes's history, gone was any role communism had played in founding the unions. Just like Carnes's history, this history was an interpretation designed to emphasize the one faction's important role in the union's history. According to the national union's history, however, it was the national leaders, entirely white and male, personified by Wolchok and Cooney, who had established the URWDSEA. These officials, this account suggested, could best lead the struggle for social justice for the workers they represented, as well as for other marginalized groups.[41]

With their different understandings of the union's history, it was perhaps not surprising that local leaders of the department store unions and the national leaders of the URWDSEA were in a near-constant state of struggle throughout the war. At the 1942 convention, for instance, the first convention after the Gimbel's strike, when it came time for Wolchok to be re-elected (without any opposition) as president of the URWDSEA, the delegates from the department store unions as well as some other left-wing union delegates (Benjamin Gudes, the president of Drug Clerks' Local 1199, and Arthur Osman), abstained from voting in a protest of Wolchok's leadership. They also requested the right to address the convention floor to explain their abstention in detail. Wolchok found this demand absurd, and he made a speech to that effect, addressing himself to Osman, who had asked to make the speech:

> Brother Osman, if the majority of the delegates and the members they represent here do not want me, or did not want me to be reelected, why didn't you place somebody else in nomination? I think that would have been the proper thing to do. . . . I think that this Convention has heard enough to know that not you alone built Local 65, and that no Halperin [*sic*] alone built Local 1250. . . . [It was] the International's money, the Internationals' strength together with the efforts of local unions that did it.

Wolchok spoke for a long time after making these remarks, pointing out that Osman, Gudes, and others had had the opportunity to take the presidency away from Wolchok at earlier conventions in 1937 and 1939. They had instead chosen to support Wolchok, and in his view, their complaints ever since were tantamount to betrayal, considering all the money and time which Wolchok had put into helping to build union membership.[42]

John Cooney, who rose in support of Wolchok, was even more outspoken on the subject of Wolchok's immense contributions to the union. Cooney was also far more open about his contempt for the department store union leaders and their left-wing allies. As Cooney himself put it, "It is pretty difficult to stand here for a week's time, and listen to a campaign of vilification and insinuations, against a man whom those who really know, have grown to love, a man whose principal fault is that he happens to be a very decent human being, something some people in this hall know nothing about—decency."[43]

These discussions during the convention indicate that the war had only inflamed the conflict between liberals and Communists within the department store unions. During the war, however, the two sides were substantially in agreement about most political issues, endorsing negotiations rather than strikes and giving at least rhetorical support for women's rights and racial equality. As a result, their struggle was essentially over power, over whether Wolchok or the left-wing local leaders would gain the support of the delegates within the convention. And it was Wolchok, not the local leaders, who repeatedly won that struggle during the war.

As has already been indicated, one reason for Wolchok's success was the tactical shifts that took place during the war. Wolchok's favored strategy—which had always been far less confrontational than the local leaders'—was suddenly extremely effective in both intraunion politics and as an organizing tool. Success "in the conference room" was now equally important as success "on the picket line," as Wolchok proudly noted in a speech to the 1942 URWDSEA convention. The numbers bore out Wolchok's claim. Between 1939 and 1942 the union increased its membership by 50 percent, and by June 1942, the URWDSEA was a truly national organization, the seventh largest CIO union in the country.[44]

Wolchok's actions during the Montgomery Ward strike of 1944 enhanced his national power still further. Montgomery Ward Vice-President Sewell Avery and Wolchok clashed repeatedly throughout the early 1940s. Avery proved extremely reluctant to allow the union to set any conditions for his business, and found the notion of the closed shop, which forbade the hiring of workers who were not union members, particularly objectionable. Despite the fact that this demand was a government-sanctioned practice during the war, Avery refused to accede to Wolchok's repeated demand for the closed shop at Montgomery Ward. At one point before the strike, in response to Wolchok's repeated demands for the closed shop, Avery lost his temper and informed Wolchok that under no circumstances would Avery give way on labor issues, since, as Avery repeatedly put it, "no outsider is going to run my business."[45]

Avery was equally unyielding when dealing with the federal government's War Labor Board (WLB). Members of the WLB, which was empowered during the war to resolve differences between labor and management in order to prevent strikes, slowdowns, and lockouts in war industries, found negotiations with Avery to be particularly difficult. In fact, William H. Davis, the chairman of the WLB, remembered his dealings with Avery as "a rather amazing experience," since, no matter what Davis and other WLB members did, they could not convince Avery to compromise on any labor issues.[46]

Avery's determination to retain complete control over his employees eventually forced Wolchok into the strike. On December 8, 1943, the union's contract with Montgomery Ward expired. Although Wolchok quickly attempted to set up a meeting with Avery in order to negotiate the next contract, Avery refused to meet with him. Avery backed up his refusal by a dubious claim that the union no longer represented a majority of the store's workers and that the union was therefore no longer the workers' legal bargaining unit. Unable to convince Avery to compromise, Davis reluctantly asked Wolchok to agree to new elections. In keeping with his desire to avoid industrial conflict during the war, Wolchok agreed to Davis's request, and ordered that the local union hold a new election, at the time an almost unheard-of practice for a union which had already won recognition.[47]

Despite this victory, Avery continued to defy both the union and the WLB alike. The WLB issued an order to the company, demanding that they extend the previous contract until the elections. Avery refused to follow this order, claiming that since his industry was classified as nonessential, he was not required to follow the WLB directives. On April 12 workers at Montgomery Ward went on strike. They did so with the full support both of the War Labor Board and of Samuel Wolchok, who had finally given up on peaceful negotiations with Sewell Avery. As Davis later described the Montgomery Ward strike, "this is the first strike that has occurred in America since the no-strike plan started in which the War Labor Board was helpless to act. We just could not order these men back to work for an employer who was defying our order . . . and had refused to maintain the status [quo] long enough to give them a chance to vote."[48]

The strike lasted thirteen days, and sympathy strikes broke out at five other Ward stores in Detroit and Albany. On April 25 President Roosevelt issued an order that the workers return to their jobs and Ward's comply with the WLB order. The strike, Roosevelt informed workers and management alike, was a condition "which cannot be permitted to continue in a nation at war." It ended only after the United States Army took over the offices of Montgomery

Ward and the attorney general issued an order requiring Avery to negotiate. Despite the Army's possession of the building and the attorney general's order, Avery still refused to compromise on a single demand. United States soldiers in full uniform removed Avery from the store building, much to the delight of Montgomery Ward employees and the news photographers waiting outside.[49]

With the army in possession of the store, the War Labor Board again issued its order to negotiate. Company managers, now with no control over their store, agreed to comply and extended the old contract. After the army left the store, however, Avery quickly reverted to his earlier behavior. He unilaterally decided to pay only around 30 percent of the back pay awarded to the strikers. Montgomery Ward workers prepared again to return to the picket line, this time planning in advance to launch strikes at all Ward stores throughout the Midwest. Once again, the army intervened. On December 28, 1944, the U.S. Army again took over Montgomery Ward, this time seizing the company's properties in seven different cities across the Midwest and instituting the closed shop and back pay rulings of the WLB. The army continued holding onto the Montgomery Ward properties and running the stores until October 1945, when the army finally left and the closed shop at Ward's ended.[50]

Samuel Wolchok found these strikes at Montgomery Ward wonderful opportunities to recoup whatever damages his conciliatory strategy had caused him before the war. Unlike during the Gimbel's strike of 1941, here it was Wolchok who refused to compromise and emerged victorious after a strike. At the same time, he had demonstrated his determination without running any risk of losing his reputation as a responsible and conservative union leader. The president, the attorney general, the War Labor Board, and the overwhelming majority of the URWDSEA endorsed these strikes. The success of the strikes proved, to almost all concerned, that, as a responsible but still militant labor leader, Wolchok was doing a wonderful job as president of the URWDSEA.

Communist representatives of New York City local unions were the only people within the union who seemed to oppose Wolchok's leadership in 1944. In part due to the Communists' unyielding endorsement of the no-strike pledge, and in part because of the numerous earlier disagreements between Wolchok and the union's left wing, Arthur Osman bitterly attacked Wolchok's actions during the Montgomery Ward strike. He released a joint statement with Local 65 shop stewards condemning the strike as an unnecessary violation of the no-strike pledge. As the Local 65 resolution put it:

The Montgomery Ward Company and its president, Sewell Avery, have scored another victory in their campaign to sabotage America's war effort and to incite strikes and other interruptions of the workers' contributions to victory. This is the tragic significance of the strike at the Montgomery Ward Co . . . The union, by falling for the Company's provocations, is in effect helping Sewell Avery's treasonous activities.[51]

Wolchok responded by launching an all-out attack on Osman, whom he dubbed a traitor to the workers at Montgomery Ward as well as the URWDSEA. In this response, Wolchok particularly emphasized Osman's inconsistency in both politics and tactics. "Osman," Wolchok wrote in the union newspaper, "is always out in front, fist clenched, teeth set, tongue lashing out in all directions. He issues protests, conducts parades, demonstrates in parks, threatens with dire punishment anyone daring to disagree with him." Wolchok went on to point out that Osman had, only a few years earlier, been a firm supporter of the peace movement. This was only one example of what Wolchok suggested was Osman's larger pattern of hypocrisy. "It is extraordinary," Wolchok delighted in informing his readers, "that [Osman] who but recently strutted to the slogan, 'What is Good for the Bosses Is No Good for Labor' now looks to employers for support against the action of Detroit workers. About this I shall say nothing for the present, leaving it for [your] further consideration."[52]

In attacking Osman, Wolchok found yet another issue to unite almost the entire URWDSEA. Osman's actions met with condemnation from virtually all local union leaders outside of Local 65, Local 1199, and the department store unions. Representatives from these left-wing unions were noticeably silent on the issue. But that did not protect them from attacks from the right wing. A particularly conservative Joint Board in St. Louis, for instance, sent the national union a letter, reading, in part: "It is time that our International Union be purged of Arthur Osman and his kind . . . [who have] defied our International's policy and CIO policy in order to gain the objectives of the Communist party . . . We therefore request that you as International President suspend and remove Arthur Osman as President of Local 65 and as a member of our international." Dozens of other local leaders also moved to show their support for Wolchok as well, several of them also joining the call for Osman's resignation. Even leaders of unions that were not affiliated with the URWDSEA, such as E. E. Benedict of the Woodworkers of America, called on Wolchok to continue his attacks on Osman.[53]

Perhaps the most surprising aspect of the struggles around the Montgomery Ward strike was the fact that Wolchok made no effort to have Osman removed from the union. After Wolchok's accusation of treachery and the letters written in response to this charge, Wolchok apparently let the matter drop; no more mention was made of the event in the union newspapers or at union conventions. Several reasons exist for Wolchok's restraint in this matter. First, Osman's District 65 was by far the most powerful wholesale workers' union in the URWDSEA, and kicking Osman out of the union might well have meant losing District 65 in the process, thus severely weakening the union's presence in the wholesale industry. Even more important, however, these conflicts took place at a time when both Osman and Wolchok shared support for the need for a national alliance against fascism. Within this alliance all anti-Fascists (Wolchok and Osman included) had to unite until the threat of fascism had been defeated. Wolchok was among the most eloquent supporters of this alliance. In his first monthly column for the *Retail Wholesale and Department Store Employee,* for instance, Wolchok devoted the entire column to this united front:

> The past few years have given overwhelming evidence of the barbarism, cynicism, and ruthlessness of the Nazi-Fascist hordes. . . . Under [Roosevelt's and Churchill's] leadership, and with the inspiration of our Russian and Chinese allies, we are destined to win a glorious victory. We must prove ourselves worthy of the noble task in which we are engaged. . . . By every means at our disposal, as soldiers and civilians, as workers in production and distribution, as American citizens, we must render the utmost service and sacrifice. The war represents for all of us the paramount issue, the noblest cause.

But the struggle needed to extend beyond international issues, Wolchok reminded his readers:

> We must [also] give a thought to our domestic problems, those inner social questions affecting "life, liberty, and the pursuit of happiness." We must give thought to those freedoms which our forefathers struggled so hard to establish . . . There are certain things in life that the worker cannot sacrifice . . . decent standards of living, health and education of children, adequate housing for the family . . . the questions of the cost of living, social security, education, race discrimination, and many others, which call for intelligent solution.[54]

This endorsement of liberal reform, combined with total support for the war, matched Osman's wartime politics exactly. In some ways, in fact, labor leaders' dispute around the Montgomery Ward strike was more about who was the better anti-Fascist than it was about anything else. Osman and the Local 65 shop stewards who released the statement accused Wolchok of placing short-term concerns (the rights of Montgomery Ward workers) over the struggle against fascism. Likewise, in his attack on Osman, Wolchok accused Osman of being less committed and more vacillating on the need to fight fascism than was Wolchok himself. Yet both Osman and Wolchok restricted themselves to verbal sparring, stopping short of the upheaval and disruption that more substantive attacks would probably have caused.

If the actions of Wolchok and Osman were in many ways similar, the implications of these actions were far different. Osman, like many of the Communist leaders of the local unions, had taken pride in his confrontational and combative organizing style before the war began. Osman's willingness to shift his support—as the *Daily Worker* suggested that workers should—from street protests to ensuring continual production and distribution made him appear to be a hypocrite. Other historians have suggested that the shift was really one of method rather than priorities—that Osman and other Communists who supported the no-strike pledge sincerely believed that defeating Hitler was the workers' most important concern. It is possible this is true in some cases, but critics of the left-wing local leaders now had at least apparent evidence for their claim that Communists union organizers placed Communist party policy over workers' interests and had no genuine concern for workers' causes. While there is no evidence that the workers in Local 65 (or in the department store unions, for that matter) believed that Osman was a hypocrite, many other union leaders and members did believe these charges, and sided openly with Wolchok.[55]

New York City's department store unions were not directly involved in the Montgomery Ward strike. Perhaps in an effort to maintain some sort of peace with Wolchok, the union representatives apparently made no public statements either for or against Osman's position. At the same time, they continued working closely with Osman for the duration of the war as well as in the postwar era, and they would be subject to the same attacks as Osman in the postwar era.[56]

Ironically, the successful Montgomery Ward strike indirectly weakened the department store unions. Department store union organizers, like Osman, had previously been able to dismiss Samuel Wolchok as a compromising and weak leader who backed down to management's every whim. Their successful actions during prewar struggles like the Gimbel's strike allowed them to provide evidence that they were both more militant and, at least sometimes, better at winning concessions from management. In the Montgomery Ward strike, however, Wolchok had taken a widely popular stand and eventually forced management to back down. It was a reversal of their prewar positions, one that gave Wolchok a decided edge over his once-mighty opponents. Within the URWDSEA, the liberal national leaders, not the radical local leaders, were the ones in control by war's end.

Conclusion

Far from being a time when "nothing changed," the war was a period of realignment for New York City's department store unions. Store managers found far greater power as a result of the war, winning public and government support and experimenting with new retailing techniques. National union leaders similarly found themselves in the government's good graces as a result of their enforcement of the no-strike pledge, and found themselves in a position to demonstrate their defense of workers' rights during the Montgomery Ward strike. Local union leaders, however, department store union leaders among them, found themselves in a far less favorable position than they had held earlier. Rather than remaining the national union's sometimes-loyal opposition, who could successfully mobilize workers to fight against management, the war years left Communists in the department store unions severely weakened, without the confrontational tactics or reputation that had forced managers to submit to unionization during the Depression. And, equally important, the conflicts over public space that had given the union strength in the 1930s had disappeared during the war.

These new wartime relationships had critical legacies for the role of retail workers in the American labor movement. The postwar years would bring severe challenges to the Communists who had led the department store unions throughout these unions' history. A stronger national union leadership and managerial restructuring, both of which took place during the war, continued into the postwar era. Over the next few years these two wartime developments would bring the department store unions and the URWDSEA alike to the point of collapse.

CHAPTER 5

Collapse, 1945–48

Introduction

If the war was a time of shifting power relations, the postwar era was a time of rapid and catastrophic change for retail workers' unions in America. Store managers responded to postwar economic changes in ways that weakened retail workers' unions to the point of collapse. Rather than going back to the prewar methods of upscale retailing, store managers continued restructuring the stores within the city and began laying off workers in an effort to increase profits. Managers also opened branch stores in the city's outer boroughs and in a growing number of suburban shopping centers. Union organizers attempted to meet these challenges, but they were able to get satisfactory employment for only a few of the laid-off workers, and the unions at the branch stores would never be as strong as the unions at the main city stores.

While these changes weakened the unions, Communists and non-Communists within the CIO's retail union, now renamed the Retail Wholesale and Department Store Union (RWDSU), continued to work together despite their differences. (The change of the union's name took place primarily because of the addition of several Canadian union locals into the URWDSEA.) Throughout 1946 and 1947, to their credit, national RWDSU leaders like Samuel Wolchok refused to resort to anti-Communist attacks against the local union leaders. To the contrary, the postwar years seemed to be far more conducive to a productive working relationship than had wartimes. National and local leaders alike launched a massive campaign around what they agreed were the most important social reforms, like national health care, full employment, and a permanent federal agency to combat discrimination. And, as though to signify a true easing of tensions between the national union leaders and the department store union leaders, Wolchok finally created the Joint Board which department store union leaders had long demanded.

The Communists within the department store unions and other left-wing RWDSU locals were overjoyed with this new relationship. They took

advantage of the newfound autonomy that Wolchok allowed to return to some
of their prewar practices, particularly trying once more to create a vibrant
cultural dimension to the unions. Also in these years, department store union
leaders embraced as never before their connections to radical politics, proudly
featuring pictures of the unions' participation in the city's May Day parade in
their newspaper.

The productive relationship between national and local union leaders was
short-lived. Not long after the 1946 convention, where Wolchok made his
decision to continue working with the Communists in the RWDSU, Congress
passed the Taft-Hartley Act. This law forced liberal union leaders like
Wolchok to abandon the alliances that they had formed with Communists.
With the passage of the Taft-Hartley Act, the government made it impossible
to remain silent on the issue of communism, as Wolchok and other national
RWDSU leaders had attempted to do. In the summer and fall of 1948, the
federal government launched an investigation of Communist participation in
the RWDSU. Wolchok, facing increasing pressure from all sides, announced
his staunch support for anti-communism, and expelled the department store
unions from the RWDSU. Shortly afterwards, he himself resigned as president.
The RWDSU was devastated, and as a result, the role of retail workers in the
American labor movement was all but eliminated.

"Is Stern's Really Union?"
The Department Store Joint Board, 1946–48

August 14, 1945, was VJ Day, a day of tremendous celebrations in New York
City. The war that had once seemed endless had now been won, and workers
in the garment district turned out to celebrate, clogging the streets so badly
that photographers had difficulty getting through the throngs of revelers to
take pictures. In the garment factories, "employees dangled their legs out of the
windows . . . and shouted words to those on the street." And in the department
stores many workers simply did not show up, as managers rushed to redeco-
rate the store windows themselves with appropriately celebratory posters and
signs. (In perhaps the ultimate irony in the history of American retailing, managers at the upscale Saks Fifth Avenue store decorated the store windows with
heroic portraits of Allied leaders, including a huge picture of Joseph Stalin.)[1]

The elation at the war's end was not to last. Indeed, the end of the war itself
became the subject for the city's first postwar strikes, as elevator and dock
workers went on strike to demand pay for V-J Day. September of that year was

to be a month of seemingly endless strikes in the city: 8,000 painters struck when managers refused to guarantee an end to discriminatory firing practices, and only days later, 11,000 elevator operators in buildings throughout the city went on strike, shutting down some of the city's tallest buildings. Office workers lined up at pay phones all over midtown Manhattan, calling in to work to find out if they were really expected to climb dozens of flights of stairs in order to reach their workplace. Perhaps most important of all, in October 1945, in the largest of the New York City postwar strikes, dock workers returned to the picket line, as a strike of 35,000 workers shut down the New York City area's shipping industry against union leaders' orders, in a militant and often violent confrontation.[2]

As labor relations became increasingly unsettled in New York, so did residential patterns. People were on the move in postwar America, many of them moving into the suburbs in very large numbers. Suburbs were growing nationwide, at a rate of approximately 2,500,000 people a year. The trend was particularly pronounced in the New York area, where many residents moved to the city's outer boroughs, especially into Queens, which grew by more than 200,000 people between 1941 and 1947. Many others seeking to get out of Manhattan left the city limits altogether. During 1947–48, well over half a million people moved into the suburbs of Connecticut, New Jersey, and New York State.[3]

At least some store managers viewed the increasing suburbanization and the increasing consumption that accompanied it as a boon for the industry. Managers at Bloomingdale's even went so far as to set up an architectural contest for the "best suburban home for New York," complete with "life-size model rooms appropriately and imaginatively furnished to correspond to the architecture." At the same time, suburbanization also presented new challenges, since a large number of potential customers now lived further away and therefore would be less likely to make their purchases in the city. In response, store managers increased their efforts to set up branch stores in the suburbs and the outer boroughs. Shopping centers sprung up throughout the outer boroughs, like the Jamaica section of Queens, and suburban areas like Westchester and Long Island. Many of these shopping centers contained a department store branch. Managers at Hearn's, Bloomingdale's, and Macy's all set up branch stores in the late 1940s, and by the early 1950s such branch stores were everywhere. Retail sales were now a central factor of the suburban economy, with gross sales increasing over 300 percent in some parts of Queens, and over 100 percent in other suburban areas. By the early 1950s Regional Plan Association President Frederick Clark could claim with some justification that "practically everyone in the suburban area is now within reach of several branch stores."[4]

Managers ran the branch stores very differently than they did the main city stores. As branch store expert John Guernsey reported in a series of articles for the *Department Store Economist* in 1951, managers could operate branch stores at 70 percent of the expense of the main stores, in part by paying lower salaries to workers. As Guernsey demonstrated, based on a national survey of branch store managers, the lower salaries offered to salespeople reflected the different requirements managers had of branch store workers. Sales workers at the branch stores were less specialized and less highly trained, and therefore they could not demand the high salaries of the city-based upscale store workers. In branch stores, managers did not expect workers to be experts in an individual department or line of merchandise; managers certainly did not expect workers to know all the stock on hand, as had been the case for sales workers in the main city stores. Instead, managers expected branch store sales workers to follow customers through different departments. The real skill here, Guernsey wrote, was for workers to remain "folksy and interested," to keep branch store customers satisfied with their shopping experience.[5]

By emphasizing branch store workers' personality and manners rather than sales training, department store managers redefined the ideal salesperson. No longer was the ideal salesperson a highly trained worker who would remain at his or her job for many years. As had been the case in some downscale stores like May's, branch store managers sought part-time workers, especially women with "other incomes." These women would be required to create an atmosphere much like the one they were expected to create in the postwar suburban home: within the stores, as within the home, value was placed on politeness, friendliness, and companionship, as they traveled around with their customers from one department to the next.[6]

Union organizers generally responded quite effectively to the increasing decentralization of department stores, forming unions at many of the earliest branch stores. By 1944 Local 1-S had already organized at the Macy's branch store in Parkchester, and by 1948, only months after Macy's Jamaica branch opened, they had won union certification in the branch store there as well. Although organizers had more difficulty at some of the other branches (in the 1950s they were still working to establish unions within the branch stores at Bloomingdale's, for instance), the opening of branch stores did not immediately or automatically weaken the unions.[7]

Other changes taking place in this era were more difficult for organizers to meet. Most of the changes which took place within department stores during the late 1940s were a result of management's constant efforts to meet with what some managers perceived as decreasing profits in the department store industry, rather than demographic changes. Store managers had an easy scapegoat for their shrinking profits: the Office of Price Administration (OPA), the wartime price control administration which had been allowed to continue in the immediate postwar era. In an industry analysis published in the *Department Store Economist,* William Gorman, the Controller of Gimbel Brothers, Inc., argued that the OPA's function within the postwar economy was damaging to retailers. Gorman noted that a 0.3 percent reduction in the stores' markup "has been caused by the squeeze that OPA has put on retailers by granting increases to manufacturers without permitting retailers their historic markup on these increases." Gorman was even more worried by an even smaller increase of one tenth of one percent in the ratio of salespeople's salaries to sales. "This results from a combination of higher rates paid to employees, the development of shorter working hours, and a lowered efficiency. This latter may just be conjecture—perhaps it may be attributed to the fact that somewhere a saturation point is reached beyond which an employee cannot go. However, the net sales per employee in 1945 were $12,268 against $11,709[,] an increase of only 4.8%[,] the lowest increase in productivity since 1940."[8]

Gorman claimed that his figures demonstrated store owners' shrinking profits, but conveniently, he neglected to mention in the text that the ratio of salespeople's salaries to the store's total sales had dramatically decreased throughout the war, going from 6.8 percent in 1938 to 5.7 percent in 1945, despite a 0.1 percent increase between 1944 and 1945. In addition, Gorman offered a rather skewed interpretation of lowered efficiency. As his own data indicated, the net sales per employee did increase between 1944 and 1945, although the increase was less than had been seen the year before and may have been still smaller in real dollars (see table 5.1).

Other store managers cited different reasons for their reduced profits, pointing particularly to rising manufacturers' prices. In congressional hearings in Boston, store managers complained incessantly about manufacturers' prices, arguing that "the public benefits immediately from any price reductions which manufacturers and suppliers are able to give" to retailers, the result being that the profits of the retail stores themselves were diminishing. Needless to say, these retailers also felt that Congress itself was in part to blame, by its earlier passage of the Robinson-Patman Act, which tended, according to retailers, to "limit competition and raise prices."[9]

Because of their belief that it was in part responsible for their woes, department store managers attacked the OPA throughout 1945–46. The *Department Store Economist* reprinted the text of a radio address by J. Howard Pew, the

Table 5.1

Salaries and Sales in Large Department Stores, 1935–45

Year	Salespeople's Salaries (Percentage of Sales)	Net Sales per Sales Employee ($)
1935	6.5	6,062
1936	6.4	6,537
1937	6.5	6,579
1938	6.8	6,403
1939	6.6	7,208
1940	6.3	7,449
1941	6.2	8,193
1942	6.1	8,951
1943	5.9	10,641
1944	5.6	11,709
1945	5.7	12,268

Source: Data taken from William B. Gorman, "Looking through the Figures—1945," *Department Store Economist* (July 1946), pp. 18–19.

President of the Sun Oil Company, in full, arguing that the OPA was, if anything, adding to the problem of inflation:

> Price increases no more cause inflation than wet streets cause rain. Wet streets are the result of rain and rising prices are one of many disastrous results that follow in the wake of inflation. We have an inflationary condition today primarily as the result of 15 years of government spending in excess of income and the issuance of bonds and printing press greenbacks to pay the debt. On top of this we have war-accumulated shortages in certain consumer goods, aggravated by OPA controls. . . . Price controls in peacetime cannot be made to work without increasingly severe, additional restrictions, thus eventually destroying competitive enterprise and individual freedom.[10]

With the war's end, the department store industry's trade organization, the National Retail Dry Goods Administration (NRDGA), and the much larger National Association of Manufacturers, began a concerted effort to end price controls. With typical theatrical flair, NRDGA representatives set up a "chamber of horrors" show in Washington, giving senators and congresspeople an opportunity to see low-quality goods being sold at high prices, which they claimed was the natural result of price controls. Late in 1946 they emerged victorious; the OPA came to an end.[11]

Managers also sought other ways to cut costs and increase efficiency. One of store managers' first actions after the end of the war was to band together in the Retail Labor Standards Association (RLSA). Formed late in 1945, the RLSA was designed to coordinate the efforts of department store managers at Macy's, Stern's, Gimbel's, and Bloomingdale's to control their often unpredictable employees during contract negotiations. In future strikes and labor negotiations, store managers would be ready to work together, and would freely borrow anti-union tactics from each other.[12]

Managers also turned to new technologies to increase efficiency. It was in the immediate postwar period that store managers began making use of IBM's "billing machine," for instance, which automatically kept track of how much a customer owed. Managers also turned to other technological innovations to improve their filing and billing systems, introducing electric typewriters and machines that would speed up credit checks.[13]

Other cost-cutting methods were geared more directly towards cutting labor costs. In particular, store managers began programs of "work simplification," a practice of scientific management, in the nonselling jobs, which were, in the words of one industrial consultant, "particularly wide open for streamlining and improvement." As Frederick Winslow Taylor had done decades earlier, store managers now began to "break down the jobs" of non-sales employees into the smallest possible steps, and then began to examine every step of the work to consider how it could be made more efficient. As they instituted these practices, store managers began to lay off workers, often in very large numbers. In 1947, for example, managers laid off approximately 50 of the 1000 full-time employees at Stern's, or 5 percent of the stores' total full-time workforce. Other store managers followed suit in later years. Albert M. Greenfield, a former textile plant manager who took over managing the Hearn's store in 1949, began his career at Hearn's by laying off 200 of the 2100 union workers there. Shortsightedly, the union organizers at Hearn's accepted Greenfield's actions since the layoffs were accompanied by a threat that Greenfield would close the entire store if the union opposed the layoffs. Managers at Bloomingdale's and Macy's also laid off large numbers of workers in the period 1947–49, although it is not known how many. Managers often combined the layoffs with speedups, as they attempted to force remaining workers to perform additional duties to make up for the reduced staff.

Sometimes even low-level store executives faced additional responsibilities; at Macy's in 1947, for instance, Marcella Loring reported that supervisors were "selling, packing, and doing staff work in offices."[14]

These cuts almost all affected nonselling areas, in the back rooms of the stores. Managers determinedly avoided cutting back on customer services or on sales workers. In fact, many store managers seemed to be increasing services, preparing themselves for the end of the shortages that resulted from the end of the war. And the self-service experiments during the war rapidly came to an end once the war had ended. Store managers and customers alike apparently looked forward to the return of doormen, checkrooms, gift wrapping, and full-service shopping that customers had grown accustomed to in the prewar era. Many store managers restored these services by the summer of 1946, despite their cries of limited profits. Still others reported in an August 1946 *Women's Wear Daily* poll that they hoped to restore many prewar services as quickly as possible. And, in the clearest signal of a return to the prewar opulence, Macy's renewed its Thanksgiving parade in 1946. If the store managers had to make cuts, they were determined to do so without sacrificing the extravagance and luxury for which the stores were so famous.[15]

The cuts behind the scenes nonetheless represented an important challenge to the unions. Nowhere was this clearer than at Macy's, where managers attempted to cut delivery costs by turning their delivery system over to the United Parcel Service (UPS). Unlike Macy's delivery workers, who were members of RWDSU Local 1, UPS had a closed-shop contract with the AFL-affiliated Teamsters. The delivery workers, furious that their union had been changed without their consent, declared themselves on strike, and many workers in Local 1-S adamantly refused to cross the picket lines at both the main 34th Street store and the Parkchester branch. The strike quickly became a bitter and violent one, with frequent battles outside Macy's warehouses as police tried to escort UPS trucks past picket lines. On at least one occasion the UPS truck drivers got to the Macy's warehouse by ramming through a line of picketers, landing two strikers in the hospital. On other occasions mounted police rode into the crowds outside the store with horses, scattering strikers so that the UPS trucks could get through the line. Bitter though it was, the strike was also brief. Within two weeks Macy's managers backed down and agreed to pay the delivery workers any difference between what the workers had made working for Macy's and what UPS paid its employees.[16]

The strike was the cause of even more controversy after its conclusion, primarily due to the actions of Jack Straus, the president of Macy's. During the strike, Straus had promised to pay salespeople who had crossed the picket line two days extra pay for every day they worked; when the strike ended, Straus made good his promise, and those workers who had crossed the picket line received large bonuses for doing so. This policy, which the union quickly contested as an unfair labor practice, was eventually allowed, since the court declared that rewarding scabs was not legally the same as penalizing strikers.[17]

The Macy's strike never led to the sort of outcry that the earlier Gimbel's strike had, and certainly mice and pigeons were not introduced into Macy's during the strike. There are several reasons for this, of course, but perhaps the most important is that, unlike during the Gimbel's strike, workers and union leaders seem to have been at least under the impression that most customers were in fact in favor of the strike. As one contributor to the *Department Store Employee* described it, customers seem to have respected the picket line:

> A cab pulled over to the curb, and two ladies got out. "Please help us win our strike. Don't pass our picket line," [strikers said.] The ladies looked at one another, hesitated and one spoke: "I'm not going in—not me." They walked towards Saks-34th street . . . "Please don't patronize Macy's. You won't get waited on anyway. The salespeople are all out!" Two old dowagers made a neat about face from Macy's door.

Whether or not customers actually refused to cross the line, accounts like this indicate that pro-union observers took a far more sympathetic attitude towards customers during the postwar Macy's strike than they had towards customers during the prewar Gimbel's strike. The old stereotypes of customers as socially irresponsible and insensitive to workers' concerns had all but disappeared during the war, replaced in the public imagination by noble consumers who had made almost endless sacrifices for the sake of their country.[18]

Short of striking, workers lacked an effective response to the various challenges which shook the stores and the unions in the late 1940s. Many turned to the union for support. Anne Limitone, one of the fifty Stern's workers laid off in 1947, wrote a pleading letter to Sadka Brown: "I have been waiting patient[ly], for this letter saying when I can return to Stern's Dept Store. It would make no difference at all what department I be put in." This letter, and dozens of others like it in the union records, has on it a small notation in pencil, presumably made by someone at the union offices, stating simply "5–27–47—Unable to place." Union organizers did what they could, winning back a few jobs, and trying to make certain that layoffs took place in order of seniority, but their failures greatly outnumbered their successes.[19]

At least a few workers were shocked and upset that the union would or could not do more to resolve the various problems which workers faced. Another union member at Stern's, who identified herself only as Miss E. Goldstein, wrote Brown a note asking, "Is Stern's really union, and if they are why do they offer you the small sum of $30 per week? Is that union wages? . . . I was working for the lowest wage possible for Christmas and now I am out again. What about all this temporary work? I am a full-time worker. I have always worked steady until last February."[20]

To their credit, throughout the late 1940s, union organizers made serious efforts to raise workers' salaries to meet the rapidly rising cost of living, demanding and achieving wage increases with each successive contract. The $30 a week which made E. Goldstein wonder whether or not Stern's really had a union was, after all, approximately three times the weekly salary of many department store workers at the time workers had first formed unions, only a little over a decade earlier. But no matter how rapidly union leaders negotiated new contracts with wage increases, they could scarcely match the cost of living increases. In fact, as Bill Michelson argued in one article for *Union Voice*, $16 a week in 1941 was a better wage than $26 a week in 1945. The end of rent control and the higher subway fares, combined with national inflation, presented union organizers with a serious challenge, one they never adequately met.[21]

As workers began to question the value of their unions, local and national leaders of the RWDSU attempted to come to some sort of agreement as to how they would work together now that the war was over. National and local delegates began preparations for another convention in May 1946, this one to take place in Akron, Ohio. Local organizers and national leaders were at odds on a number of key issues at the 1946 convention. Most of these were questions of process and union structure. The left-wing delegates, from Local 65 and Local 1199 as well as from the department store union locals, challenged many initiatives of the national union leaders: whether the national undertook to collect dues directly from workers, to increase the proportion of dues going to the national union, to set voting procedure on union policy, or to appoint (rather than hold an election for) vice-presidents for organizing warehouse and department store workers, the left-wing union leaders were among the first to resist. Only weeks before the convention's opening, local leaders openly condemned Wolchok as a red-baiter and a tool of store management.[22]

With so many areas of fierce disagreement, it is important to note that both national and local union leaders continued to support many of the same political causes. In fact, most of the reformist platforms which the national leaders supported at the convention had the full support of the left-wing unions. Both the national and the local leaders called for "a real Full Employment bill [and] a people's tax program that will outlaw discrimination in employment and in the social and political life of our country," as well as "a Health Bill that will . . . protect our citizens in time of sickness," and support for the United Nations combined with a commitment to a more genuine world government, all of which were fairly standard parts of the liberal agenda in the postwar era. As during the war, the struggles between local and national union leaders were about power, not politics.[23]

Both the agreements and the conflicts between national and local union leaders were evident during the 1946 Akron convention. The convention was mired in procedural controversy from the outset. Local 65 delegate David Livingston demanded the right to have votes called at the request of the representatives of one-fourth of the members rather than the representatives of one-fourth of the locals. Had it gone through, this proposal would have given the left wing, whose locals had significantly more members than most locals represented at the convention, a strong advantage in calling such votes. Wolchok and the other national leaders strenuously objected, and Wolchok quickly tried to silence the opposition by promising that "Brother Osman and his delegates can depend upon the democratic way of our living and the democratic way of my ruling this chair." After Wolchok's statement, Livingston's proposal was dismissed.[24]

Wolchok was slightly more yielding when he raised the issue of establishing executive vice-presidents for the Department Store and the Warehouse Divisions. Wolchok insisted that these positions be filled by appointees of his own choosing. Delegates from the New York City department store unions opposed this move, demanding the right to elect their own leader. If this procedure was not followed, the department store union delegates warned, "[S]omeone who does not know anything about department stores might necessarily be elected to represent department store workers." Still trying to preserve some sort of unity, Wolchok put together a compromise. He promised Arthur Osman that if Wolchok was allowed to appoint vice-presidents of the Department Store Division and the Warehouse Division, Wolchok would then immediately appoint Osman as the head of the RWDSU's warehouse division. Osman accepted, but also warned Wolchok from the convention floor that "if I am to be the Director of the Warehouse Department . . . let him appoint me . . . [but] not because I will refrain from making an honest presentation of my views." Instead, Osman urged, he should be the vice-president of the Warehouse Department because, as leader of the largest warehouse local within the union, Osman was uniquely qualified for this position. The overwhelming

majority of convention delegates eventually sided with Wolchok on the issue
of the appointed vice-presidencies, with the department store union leaders
and their allies in Local 65 and Local 1199 almost alone in their opposition to
the plan. Wolchok closed the issue by appointing Arthur Osman as the head
of the Warehouse Division as promised, and making one of his fellow national
leaders, a strongly anti-Communist union organizer named Jack Altman, the
vice-president of the Department Store Division, over the objections of the
delegates from New York City's department store unions.[25]

The left-wing delegates found their greatest success when they challenged
Wolchok on the question of union finances. Wolchok raised the issue of
union finances by asking for an increase in the percentage of dues paid to
the national union in order to devote more funds to Operation Dixie, the
CIO's campaign to unionize the southern states. In response to this request,
a long line of speakers, many of them not connected with the New York City
department store unions, immediately rose to contest the increase. Martin
Kyne, who was chairing the meeting, tried to limit the number of speakers in
a vain effort to quell the protest, and the move backfired as the convention
broke down into shouts and arguments. Wolchok eventually lost his temper
and made an accusatory and impassioned speech, asking the delegates if they
wanted to "keep the International poor." Wolchok then accused the delegates
of a lack of true commitment to Operation Dixie: "Everybody speaks about
this drive, but wants to do nothing," he complained, before calling for a vote
on the motion. By turning the debate on dues into a referendum on Operation
Dixie, Wolchok managed to win, but only by a small margin, especially since
the left-wing delegates universally voted against the proposal. Of the 75,000
members represented by the convention delegates, the difference of opinion
on this subject was less than 15,000, a margin of less than 20 percent.[26]

During the 1946 convention, Wolchok refused to resort to attacking his
opponents' political beliefs, despite their opposition to his leadership. He
could easily have forced a showdown with the left-wing delegates by calling,
for instance, for a resolution against communism. Doing so would have won
him support from many local leaders outside of New York City. More than
six months before the Akron convention, the leaders of the RWDSU's Joint
Council in St. Louis issued a pamphlet that, among other things, argued that
all honest union members and leaders should cooperate to drive Communists
out of the labor movement. Honest union leaders, the pamphlet's author suggested, "should eliminate the Communists from any political influence. They
are not a legitimate section of the American labor movement and their tactics
give us a black eye. In all cases they put their devotion to the Russian dictator-

ship first, and are willing to sell out and disgrace the labor movement any time it suits Russia's foreign policy."[27] At the convention Wolchok refused to adopt this sort of anti-Communist rhetoric, opting instead to continue calling for liberal reform without condemning communism, or, indeed, even mentioning communism. By doing so, Wolchok created an alliance between Communists and liberals in the RWDSU around the reforms that both sought, and around their mutual (although never stated) willingness to avoid the word "communism." By not naming the real issue that divided them, both sides managed to allow room for compromise.

Samuel Wolchok's refusal to adopt anti-Communist language during the convention was only one piece of evidence demonstrating his renewed support for cooperation between local and national leaders. This attitude was also reflected in his new stance on the New York City department store unions' Joint Board. While before the convention Wolchok had offered to support the Joint Board only if the New York local leaders "agree to the Joint Board henceforth without [a] vote" on national policies, in November 1946 Wolchok reversed his earlier decision and voiced his public support for the formation of an official New York City Department Store Joint Board. The New York City leaders hailed Wolchok's decision as "one of historic significance for department store workers of New York City." And, despite the appointment of Jack Altman as the new director of department store organization, both Wolchok and Altman maintained a more hands-off policy with regard to local negotiation, refusing to participate in contract negotiations until after local negotiators met with store management.[28]

With the compromises at the Akron convention, national RWDSU leaders and local department store union leaders resolved at least some of their differences. For the moment, the left-wing local leaders and organizers, with no alternative, were willing to concede any real control over national union policy. At the same time, through allowing the department store unions to form a Joint Board, Wolchok effectively allowed the local unions more autonomy than they had seen since the New Era Committee. Formally united after nearly a decade of formal divisions, the department store union leaders set about creating a strong union movement within the New York City retail trade, and they allowed more-conservative union leaders like Wolchok, Cooney, Kyne, and Altman control over the national union.

Local union organizers, more autonomous than they had been for years, re-created their local unions as central parts of what must have seemed like a revitalized radical movement within the city. Now that the war was over, the Communists renewed their annual tradition of marching on May Day. On

May 1, 1946, as they had done so many times before the war, Communists descended upon the garment district, gathering between 36th and 39th Streets, and then marching down Eighth Avenue, a block or two west of the stores, before crossing east to gather once again in Union Square. At the head of the massive parade, which spanned several blocks, marched war veterans in full uniform, with a banner reading "Veterans March for Peace." Behind them, between 21,000 and 60,000 people marched, with thousands more lining the streets to watch the parade. Thousands of representatives from the city's garment workers' unions joined, despite the garment unions' official repudiation of the march. Joining them were representatives from other unions: the United Office and Professional Workers of America, the National Maritime Union, the Furriers Union, and the United Electrical Workers all took part. So, too, did the leaders and some members of the department store unions. They marched together in the parade, carrying signs announcing that they were the "Department Store Union, CIO, for Full Employment," calling on the huge crowd to "Make Gimbel's Pay a Living Wage!" The department store unions, for the first time since 1941, were renewing their connections to a broad-based and militant radical movement.[29]

If radicalism now seemed resurgent, so too did the department store unions. With the truce established at the convention, the next step seemed obvious: a united drive against the stores that had thus far eluded unionization, like the upscale stores on Fifth Avenue. Beginning with a campaign that Jack Altman was to lead against the McCreery store just off of Fifth Avenue, the local and international unions alike readied themselves to participate in a joint campaign to set up unions all the way up the avenue. And this, in the eyes of many observers, might well be just the beginning. Retail labor analyst George Kirstein wrote in the summer of 1946 that "the retail industry will see in the next year or so an effort to bring its employees under the union banner such as it has not witnessed before."[30]

As part of this renewed commitment to a larger and more dynamic movement, union organizers waged a campaign against one of the city's leading and most conservative newspapers, the *New York Daily News.* Since the department store managers advertised extensively within the *Daily News,* the main focus of organizers' campaign against the *Daily News* was set around forcing store managers to withdraw their advertisements from the paper. The campaign was a disaster. Not only did the campaign show the unions wholly unable to force managers to withdraw the advertisements; it also helped win the unions the focused enmity of the *Daily News* editors, who became some of the unions' most outspoken critics over the next years.[31]

Local leaders were more successful in their efforts to strengthen the union's cultural and social programs, to revitalize other aspects of the prewar union. To do so, they established close institutional ties between Local 65 and the department store union locals. In 1947 they adopted the Local 65 newspaper, the *Union Voice,* as the official department store union newspaper, replacing the *Department Store Employee.* At the same time, the department store union members, at the local leaders' suggestion, voted to join the Tom Mooney Hall Association (TMHA), Local 65's cultural society, centered on the Tom Mooney Hall, at 65 Astor Place. Among other things, the Hall featured a bar and food counter, a bookshop, frequent Saturday night parties, and Club 65, a party hall available for use by union members and individual shops within Local 65. Under the Joint Board and the TMHA, union organizers established local glee clubs, frequent dances and parties, and an annual boat ride. They also renewed their commitment to the unions' sports league. All of these activities had precedents in the late 1930s, but the scope of the unions' social activities in the late 1940s was both more ambitious and, especially with the existence of a permanent social center in the Tom Mooney Hall Association, a more established part of the unions' existence.[32]

By far the most ambitious cultural project attempted by the department store union organizers in the early postwar era was *Thursdays Till Nine. Thursdays Till Nine* was a union-funded musical comedy about workers at the fictional R.H. Maybe Department Store. As with *Pins and Needles,* the cast of *Thursdays Till Nine* was entirely composed of union members, and although the people who wrote *Thursdays Till Nine* were not department store workers, some evidence indicates that workers nonetheless had input into the musical: nearly every complaint workers had about working in the stores appeared in *Thursdays Till Nine,* often in an exaggerated format. At R.H. Maybe's, for instance, workers labor under such heavy scrutiny that the accounting department notices even a single lightbulb that is left on at night. The workers are allowed only twenty-minute breaks, although it takes them ten minutes to get to the front entrance of the store and another ten minutes to get back. The store owner, R.H. Maybe, has so much leisure time that he plays golf in the store when he has nothing else to do. Even the title of the play is a reference to the long hours store workers had to put in, since many store managers kept the store open until nine o'clock on Thursday nights.[33]

Like these details, the main story line of *Thursdays Till Nine* also demonstrated issues which department store workers had to confront. Perhaps drawing on Charlie Chaplin's famous department store scene in *Modern Times* (1936), *Thursdays Till Nine* described the department store as a paradise of consumption to which workers have only very limited access. In *Thursdays Till Nine,* Jess, the male lead, is a veteran who works in the store for a salary so low that he cannot afford an apartment. Like Chaplin in *Modern Times,* Jess therefore starts spending his nights in the store, and each night tries to pretend that the store is his own home. As Jess declared in his opening song, "I dream this is . . . a place where love could live and firelight shine. / . . . Five thousand toothbrushes stand in the rack / None may I legally use / Six hundred beds / And at none of their heads / May I legally line up my shoes." While *Thursdays Till Nine* therefore portrayed department stores as a sort of consumer's paradise, the authors took pains to demonstrate that the paradise was an illusion. Jess, after all, does not really own the endless rows of beds and toothbrushes; he can only use them illegally.[34]

The influence of workers on *Thursdays Till Nine* can also be seen in the criticisms of films and songs that portrayed department stores without attention to the class struggles that take place in such stores. When R. H. Maybe announces a contest with a grand prize of a fully furnished house for the best song written about working in the store, Jess jumps at the chance to win a house of his own. Jeannie, the female lead (a fellow worker as well as Jess's love interest), is shocked at Jess's willingness to participate in the contest, since only those songs which glorify department store work have a chance of winning the contest. The song will be used to "knife everyone in the store . . . The workers love it at Maybe's. Look, they write songs about it! No problems, no firings, no speedup—they say it here on paper—they're gonna say it in every screen in the country." This critique echoes and may have even been inspired by department store workers' complaints against some mainstream films of the day. Macy's worker Arthur Adler, for example, who reviewed *Miracle on 34th Street* for the *Union Voice,* wrote satirically: "What else but a fantasy could depict Macy's without a speed-up and low wages. . . . Perhaps the foreword should have mentioned something about any resemblance to actual persons or events being coincidental . . . Mrs. Walker is very materialistic. She doesn't believe in Santa Claus. (Would you if you had to fire 600 regular employees right after Christmas?)." Workers, and the writers of *Thursdays Till Nine,* had a very different view of the department stores than did the writers of *Miracle on 34th Street:* to workers and their allies, these stores were sites where workers struggled against managers on a daily basis.[35]

Although workers and union leaders enjoyed the production immensely, *Thursdays Till Nine* ran only from November 24 to November 27, far from the long-running success that *Pins and Needles* had become ten years earlier. Any number of reasons might explain why the show was never picked up by commercial producers. For one thing, as wonderful as much of *Thursdays Till Nine* was, it never attained the speed or cleverness of *Pins and Needles*. Additionally, the show's straight narrative structure, as opposed to the musical revue used in *Pins and Needles,* may have weakened *Thursdays Till Nine's* broader appeal. Using a musical revue for *Pins and Needles* allowed the producers of that show to draw together many workers' struggles that would have been difficult to compress into a single narrative. The creators of *Thursdays Till Nine* made no major effort to connect the struggles of department store workers to the struggles of other workers, focusing instead exclusively on the department stores.

Perhaps the greatest factor in the failure of *Thursdays Till Nine* was a new crisis which union organizers had to face, brought on by the Taft-Hartley Act. This act forced union organizers to turn their attention away from the cultural projects they had begun setting up under the Joint Board and begin a frantic campaign in their own defense. The Taft-Hartley Act, passed over President Truman's veto while *Thursdays Till Nine* was in rehearsal in June 1947, placed severe limits on the powers given to unions during the New Deal, particularly by the Wagner Act. If the Wagner Act had created the NLRB elections, the Taft-Hartley Act set up new rules regarding which unions could participate in NLRB elections. Union officials wishing to participate in these elections now had to abandon certain militant tactics, sympathy strikes and secondary boycotts most important among them. And, most devastating for the department store unions' immediate future, union officials wishing to use the NLRB had to sign affidavits stating that they were not members of the Communist party.[36]

This groundbreaking legislation was in many respects a mark of the beginning of the McCarthy era. It was by no means the first postwar appearance of anti-communism; nor was it the first anti-Communist legislation, since the Smith Act (which made it illegal to advocate the violent overthrow of the government) preceded it by eight years. But the Taft-Hartley Act, unlike the Smith Act, effectively demolished unity between liberals and Communists in the labor movement. By making it requisite for union leaders to declare whether or not they were Communists, the Taft-Hartley Act forced union leaders like Samuel Wolchok to abandon their alliances with Communists around specific reforms. Now, any support for reform that Wolchok wished to provide would have to be accompanied by his affidavit stating that he was not a member of the Communist party. And while Wolchok could sign such an affidavit and continue as an official of the union, his Communist allies in the local unions could not.

Local leaders had to be extremely careful about their opposition to the act.

While some workers were unquestionably well aware of the leftist tendencies of their union leaders, other members had only begun working in the store during or after the war, and many were unaware of the political views of their union leaders. Local organizers therefore avoided any discussion of leaders' politics while explaining leaders' refusal to sign the affidavits demanded by the act. At one point, Sadka Brown delivered a report to the shop stewards in Local 5 in which she declared that "the issue of signing the affidavits is not a matter of the political tendencies of the leadership of the union," but simply a result of the leaders' realization that "nothing good can come from" signing. In fact, she argued, signing the affidavits (and thereby endorsing the validity of the Taft-Hartley Act) was dangerous to the union's future in the department stores, with the complex anti-union security systems that many stores had in place. As Brown's report described the situation, "the Taft-Hartley Law will protect an individual from being thrown out of the union even though he admits it is his intention to destroy the union. Into every union, at the request of management . . . will come these paid agents. And whether you sign the affidavits or not the law says that these lice must be protected. . . . Under our current contract, . . . our membership has the right to throw out of our organization anyone convicted by the membership of anti-union activity." If Brown's report is any indication, the Communists within the unions decided that the way to fight Taft-Hartley was to fight it on grounds other than the affidavits: to focus on the fact that Taft-Hartley, as many labor leaders believed at the time, would likely make useless the NLRB certification that had earlier been one of the most important achievements for a union. The unions, she argued, would be better off abandoning the NLRB altogether.[37]

Beyond simple refusal to sign the affidavits and a willingness to give up the NLRB, one of the most important achievements of the New Deal era, union organizers lacked a systematic program for fighting Taft-Hartley. In September 1947 organizers were so desperate for a means to fight this act that they attempted to get support from store managers, testing the waters for managers' response if the unions lost the support of the federal government. In negotiations for the 1948 contract at Stern's, for instance, union negotiators attempted to get management to offer "some positive indication that management [is] not seeking to utilize the Taft-Hartley Act to weaken or destroy [the] Union." Surprisingly, some store managers did offer some vague rhetorical support for the unions. During a 1948 bargaining session at Hearn's, for example, managers publicly announced that "we have lived with Local 1250 peacefully for over eleven years. We say that it is our intention to continue to live under harmonious labor relations." Of course there was no guarantee that store managers would not take advantage should the unions lose in an NLRB election, but managers had little interest in fighting the unions so long as the unions retained members' support. "Harmonious labor relations," essentially meaning a lack of strikes, were worth the occasional aggravation of dealing with the Communists leading the department store unions.[38]

Even as store managers signaled their willingness to work around Taft-Hartley, a small group of union members indicated their refusal to compromise on the issue of communism. Among the most dangerous challenges to the Joint Board in the aftermath of the Taft-Hartley Act was the emergence of the Rank and File Committees, an organized anti-Communist coalition within the department store unions. In the late 1940s several right-wing groups of workers, many of them connected to the anti-Communist Association of Catholic Trade Unionists, emerged in different department store locals under the name of the Rank and File Committees. While these committees campaigned in union elections on several occasions, the Communists and their allies consistently defeated them. Even at Macy's, one of the strongholds of the Rank and File Committee, the committee never captured more than 954 of the 4600 total votes in union elections before 1948, and in most unions the percentage of Rank and File supporters was far smaller. Rank and File meetings were similarly ill attended; in a meeting of the united Rank and File Committee of all the department store unions, a *Union Voice* reporter gleefully announced, only around 600 workers came to the meeting. While a reporter for the *Union Voice* might have purposefully underestimated the number of Rank and File supporters, other evidence exists that the number of dissidents was extremely small. Even leaders of the Rank and File Committees, for example, acknowledged before a congressional committee that the largest individual Rank and File meetings had had only "as many as 100 people" in attendance.[39]

If the Rank and File Committees did not emerge as a serious challenge to the Communist leaders before 1948, there were still many reasons for concern. The attacks on domestic communism were swift and devastating and by no means limited to the department store unions. At the national level, the House Un-American Activities Committee (HUAC) began labeling all Communists as spies and traitors as early as 1946. HUAC and studio executives also moved to quash the few Communists who had established a base in the film industry, calling in dozens of writers and film executives to testify, and eventually black-listing any artists working in the industry who refused to state their opposition to communism. HUAC also began investigating CIO unions that were linked to the Communist party, calling in representatives from the Food, Tobacco and Agricultural Workers Union after a congressman from North Carolina claimed that the union's activities were "threatening to turn into race riots." Perhaps most terrifying of all the national attacks on communism in the late 1940s was the Mundt Bill, which would have made the Communist party an official foreign organization, and required the Communists to turn over the names of all members to the FBI.[40]

The Communist party also faced local opposition in New York City. By 1948 the May Day parade in Manhattan was countered by a Loyalty Day parade in Brooklyn. Attorney General Tom Clark, who attended the Loyalty parade, proudly proclaimed that "by this magnificent demonstration you are answering the challenge hurled by Communism, answering it in a peaceful lawful forceful American manner." If the May Day parade that year was large— around 20,000 people, according to most estimates—the Loyalty Day parade was even larger. May Day, the day when Communists claimed the streets and truly showed their strength, had now become a symbol of the weakness of communism and the strength of anti-communism.[41]

The Communist party had one final hope, or so it seemed. The 1948 election campaign of Henry Wallace was to be their last stand. Wallace, though no Communist, was nonetheless the most prominent opponent of the new anti-Communist hysteria that was increasingly gripping the nation. If Wallace could win the election, perhaps the conservative fervor would be stemmed, and perhaps the left could re-emerge. Within the department store unions as elsewhere, Communists began to campaign for Wallace, and as a result they likely doomed Wallace's presidential run, since newspapers snatched up the story of Communists' support for Wallace and used it to discredit his campaign.

The years 1946–48 had tremendous importance for the collapse of the RWDSU. Although no single event in these years automatically signaled the unions' coming crises, these were the years when everything began to turn against the unions, even as liberals and Communists in the unions attempted to resume a productive working relationship. In these years, managers continued to restructure the stores, laying off thousands of workers and weakening the union in the process. Meanwhile, local department store union organizers and national RWDSU leaders continued to push for widespread liberal reform like a permanent Fair Employment Practices Commission, national health care, and a full-employment bill without ever making explicit their political differences. Because of this, the RWDSU faced little internal upheaval. Disagreements, when they occurred, could be resolved in a relatively orderly manner, as they indeed were during the 1946 Akron convention. But the truce was only temporary. With the 1947 passage of the Taft-Hartley Act, Congress effectively demolished their unity. A commitment to liberal reform was no longer enough. Through the Taft-Hartley Act, the federal government now required that union leaders also declare where they stood on communism. By doing so, the government divided liberal union leaders from their former Communist allies. On the national level, the local level, and within the unions, the stage was now set for a massive national confrontation around communism.

The Fall of the RWDSU, June–September 1948

At the end of the tumultuous summer of 1948, Samuel Wolchok claimed that there was "just one issue" involved in the conflict between the department store union leaders and the national union leaders. Wolchok consistently claimed that the issue was whether local union leaders, considering the passage of the Taft-Hartley Act, could successfully represent department store workers in their struggles with management. Despite Wolchok's claim, however, the conflict was an exceedingly complex one that would have lasting importance for the American labor movement.

The national RWDSU leaders initially opposed the Taft-Hartley Act, and they refused to sign any of the required affidavits throughout 1947. In March 1948, the national leaders—like many other non-Communist union leaders—reversed their earlier stand on Taft-Hartley. Wolchok, his vice-president, John Cooney, and the union's treasurer, Martin Kyne, signed the required affidavits stating that they were not Communists. The only remaining obstacle to the union becoming certified by the NLRB was that many of the union's local leaders had not yet signed similar statements. As far as the international officers were concerned, it was extremely desirable that the local leaders also sign the affidavits. It would end any question of the union leaders' commitment to anti-communism, and would end the threat of active state repression of the RWDSU. Cooney wrote a letter "to all locals affiliated with the RWDSU, CIO," informing them that all "local unions desiring to use the services of the NLRB must . . . file the required affidavits" as soon as possible.[42]

While most local leaders followed Cooney's order and signed the affidavits, New York City's department store union leaders stalled for time. Under the Taft-Hartley Act, the unions had to comply with the new regulations by August 21, 1948; consequently, the department store union organizers attempted to gain themselves a few more weeks by extending their contracts to that date. Store managers, still anxious to avoid disruptive strikes, agreed to the contract extensions.[43]

Most department store union members supported leaders in their refusal to sign the required affidavits. This support was evident regardless of the ability of union leaders to sign the affidavits without committing perjury. Members of Local 1-S, for instance, voted against their officers—including both non-Communists like Kovenetsky and Communists like Marcella Loring—signing the petitions. To his credit, Kovenetsky followed their lead and refused to sign an affidavit. Later, Kovenetsky proudly remembered that he "would sign . . . not at the request of Wolchok, but [only] at the request and demand on the part of our membership."[44]

As the local union leaders delayed turning in their affidavits, the Rank and File Committees forced the issue. In an attempt to wrest control of the union away from the Communists, the Rank and File Committee in Local 1-S and Local 3 circulated petitions demanding that the union leaders sign the Taft-Hartley affidavits. The department store union leaders, attempting to steel themselves against attacks from the state and trying to work out a systematic way of resisting the Taft-Hartley Act, responded fiercely to the Rank and File Committees' attacks. In April 1948, with the full support of the union leaders, the members expelled three members of the Rank and File Committee of Local 3 for disrupting the function of the union. While these expulsions did not destroy the Rank and File Committees, they at least served as a powerful demonstration to Rank and File Committee members at the other stores where the support of most of the union members lay. Unfortunately, the expulsions also attracted the attention of the *Daily News,* which dedicated two editorials to the expulsions in June 1948. In response to the *News* editorials, New York State governor Thomas Dewey ordered an investigation of the firings. "If it is true," Dewey wrote in his call for an investigation, "that working men will lose their jobs because of anti-Communist activities, it is a condition that cannot be tolerated." The federal government also stepped in, as Congress announced its intention to hold hearings on the role of Communists in New York City's distributive trades. Before the hearings began, Wolchok ordered the expulsions of the three rank-and-file members reversed.[45]

Even as the Rank and File Committees were temporarily silenced, a new challenge emerged. Before the passage of the Taft-Hartley Act, Local 1250 had begun organizing at the Oppenheim Collins store in New York City. In August 1946, after lengthy and occasionally bitter negotiations, Local 1250 had won the contract at Oppenheim Collins. But in 1948, two years after the initial pact had been signed, organizers from the Retail Clerks International Protection

Figure 3
Workers on the picket line in front of the Oppenheim Collins store, 1948. The picket signs claim that store managers are trying to use Communism to distract the public from the real issue at hand. Meanwhile, the banner on the store window, barely visible through the crowd of picketers, informs the public, "The issue is Communism." (Courtesy of Robert F. Wagner Labor Archives, New York University, United Automobile Workers of America, District 65 Photographs Collection)

Association (RCIPA) entered the store to contest Local 1250's leadership. To add insult to injury, the store managers and the RCIPA organizers called for an immediate NLRB election, one in which Local 1250 could not participate since they had not yet filed the necessary affidavits. Store managers provided privately chartered buses to take workers to the election, which was won—with no other unions on the ballot—by the RCIPA on August 2, 1948.[46]

Immediately following the RCIPA's victory, the strongest Local 1250 supporters at Oppenheim Collins set up a picket line against both store management and the RCIPA. Organizers throughout the department store unions began support work for the strike, viewing it as perhaps the most important strike the union had conducted in its entire history. If they could win this one strike, then they could demonstrate to all concerned that the Taft-Hartley Act had not destroyed Communists' ability to successfully lead unions. "A victory at OC is the best guarantee that you will not have to go through a similar experience when your contract expires," one Local 1250 flyer advised members of the other department store unions. "Should this union-busting strategy succeed at OC, it will be the signal for the other managements to embark on this same course. You can help avoid a strike in your store by helping us NOW!" Oppenheim Collins managers also viewed the struggle as a test case, complaining that the managers were "being used as guinea pigs by the union [because] our contract ends before that of several other major department stores."[47]

If the union viewed this test case as management's fault, managers insisted that they were completely innocent in the issue. Publicly at least, managers insisted that there was no strike at Oppenheim Collins, but rather an act of pointless vengeance against managers whose hands were tied. As their lawyer put it, Oppenheim Collins "could not recognize this union local whether it wanted to or not" until the local complied with the Taft-Hartley Act. "The mass demonstrations are not related to this dispute. We have no dispute with the union, for we cannot under the law recognize it." Store managers also hired counter-pickets to stand in the window of the store bearing posters reading: "One hundred percent of our employees are at work ready to serve you . . . The demonstrators you have seen are hired by a Communist-led union in an attempt to force us to deal with Communists . . . Fifteen times the various courts of the land have directed that these demonstrations cease."[48]

These claims were extremely effective in winning the support of the mainstream press. During the Oppenheim Collins strike, the *Daily News* again emerged as the primary voice against the unions. Among other things, the *Daily News* reporters labeled the picketers at Oppenheim Collins as "sidewalk vendors" who were "try[ing] to sell the idea that the store's employees are on strike" despite the federally mediated election.[49]

Nor was the *Daily News* alone; a local judge issued an injunction against mass picketing at Oppenheim Collins, and even when state supreme court judge Samuel Dickstein ruled that the injunction was not acceptable, he made it clear where the sympathy of the court lay: the union's actions, Dickstein publicly announced, "clearly overstep the bounds of legal, peaceful picketing. Coercion of the type evidently practiced here violates all American standards of fair play." With sentiments like this, it could have been no surprise that the injunction was reissued only a few hours after it was struck down.[50]

Most insidious of all, however, were the actions of the federal government.

In July 1948, as the elections at Oppenheim Collins were getting underway, the congressional hearings began on communism in the RWDSU. As during the 1941 New York State hearings, Louis Broido was again the government's star witness. Broido, the first witness called to testify, informed the subcommittee that the Communist leaders in the department stores were a serious danger to national security. As Broido put it, within these unions there were "thousands of people, dominated and controlled by left-wing groups, which in case of trouble between this country and Russia . . . could cause this country very great trouble." Broido also made a much-quoted claim that he and other store managers who had contracts with these unions were constantly forced to deal with a "fellow with a red beard that we can't see." Demanding an apology and retraction for this bizarre and absurd statement, workers threw up picket lines around Gimbel's in a day-long protest.[51]

National RWDSU leaders also testified at the hearings, including Samuel Wolchok and Jack Altman. When he was asked why Communists had been so successful in the department store unions, Wolchok made the obligatory statement condemning communism, but he then used the question as an opportunity to express his continuing support for liberal reform:

> I am very much afraid there are many things that this Congress is responsible for. Take . . . housing. What did Congress do? Nothing, as far as workers are concerned. . . . You have excluded the retail industry from the 40 cents minimum . . . we don't ever get a promise of being treated fair[ly] in that direction.

After suggesting that the Congress itself was responsible for the growth of communism, Wolchok went on to add that, despite these facts, "99 percent out of 100 [union members] are not Communists," despite the press's determination to smear the international "with a red brush."[52]

Wolchok was in a difficult position at these hearings. As he was testifying, his union was slipping away from him. His leadership had always rested on the support of the Communists, however much he had fought with them over the years. Without them, nearly a fifth of the RWDSU's total membership would not exist, and arguably the union itself would not have existed had it not been for their contributions. These were people he could ill afford to lose. At the same time, Wolchok had no particular interest in protecting his Communist opponents, whose support for his leadership was fleeting at best. His testimony during the government hearings reflected this balance to some extent, as he focused whenever possible on larger issues, neglecting to discuss the specific

roles that Communists had played within the RWDSU. Other RWDSU leaders followed Wolchok's lead, combining condemnations of communism (in
its vaguest sense, with no mention of any actual individuals) with support for
liberal reform. Jack Altman, for example, condemned the Communist party as
"an international conspiracy" during his testimony, but then went on to suggest, as had Wolchok, that if Congress had gotten rid of unemployment, poll
taxes, the housing shortage, and anti-labor legislation, "then Congress could
make a great contribution to fighting Communism."[53]

Rank and File Committee members took a different tack, focusing not on
the larger question of why communism existed in America, but rather specifically naming names, and testifying that Communists in union leadership
made the unions undemocratic. Rather ironically, the committee members'
primary evidence of the lack of democracy in the union was the committees' failure in challenging the local leaders, with regard to everything from
their multiple defeats in union elections to their failure in getting workers to
support the Marshall Plan. Alice Bartoli, the main Rank and File Committee
witness from Local 1-S, even went so far as to testify that when she got up at
a union meeting to make a speech on the dangers of Communist leadership,
the Communists had outwitted her: "They have the same routine . . . whereby
Communists form sort of a diamond shape throughout the audience so that
they can have this claque start . . . booing and shouting derogatory remarks" so
that it would sound as though large sections of the audience opposed her. (Later
developments suggest that the derogatory remarks Bartoli heard were representative of many workers' attitudes towards the Rank and File Committees.)
Partially due to the unusual strength of the Rank and File Committee in Local
1-S, Marcella Loring became a particular target. According to Bartoli, it was
Loring who brought the agenda for the Executive Board meetings, after getting
it from what Bartoli suggested was a mysterious and unknown source. Bartoli's
claims were absurd in many respects; as already suggested, the Rank and File
Committee was always a small minority at Macy's, and neither Kovenetsky nor
any other non-Communist Local 1-S leaders ever claimed that Loring or other
Communists forced the union into any action; indeed, since the Communists
represented only a small part of the leadership of Local 1-S it seems somewhat
doubtful that Loring could have forced the union into any particular direction
even had she seriously intended to do so.[54]

Like Wolchok's testimony, the testimony of Bartoli and the other Rank and
File Committee members illustrated a very particular political argument. But
unlike Wolchok's argument that liberal reform would weaken communism,
the congressional representatives leading the investigation found Bartoli's

statements very much the ones they were hoping to hear. According to Bartoli, communism in the retail workers' unions was an undemocratic, sinister, and ultimately un-American philosophy. Communists had no interest, the committee now had evidence, in improving workers' lives; all they were interested in was serving Russian policy. The results of the hearings were unmistakable: the Communists had no interest in functioning as legitimate union leaders, and therefore no right to lead unions, regardless of workers' repeated willingness to vote for these sinister characters.

Despite their importance, the congressional hearings had no direct effects on the leaders of New York City's department store unions. This was partially because Communists in the department store unions never publicly declared themselves as such. Besides their participation in May Day marches—something that never came up during the hearings—there was no public record of these union leaders embracing communism. However, many people who did not openly declare themselves Communists went to jail in the late 1940s and early 1950s, primarily for avoiding questions by pleading the Fifth Amendment, something that union leaders did several times during their testimony. The government's inaction probably had more to do with the existence of the Taft-Hartley Act: the Communists within the union might plead the Fifth Amendment during their testimony, but they would either declare themselves opposed to communism in their Taft-Hartley affidavits or lose control over the union, and sending them to jail would be pointless.

The lack of direct prosecution allowed some non-Communists within the local union leadership to defend their alliance with Communists. Samuel Kovenetsky, for instance, insisted that the government's failure to convict or even charge any of the union leaders was proof against any claims of Communist insurgency. Years later, when he was asked directly whether any of the union leaders had been Communists, Kovenetsky's avoided the question, saying instead that "none of the people that [Wolchok] claimed were Communists were ever indicted for any Communist activity."[55]

The congressional hearings did have significant indirect effects on the RWDSU. On August 9, 1948, Samuel Wolchok called an emergency meeting of the RWDSU General Executive Board, which issued a resolution "to make compliance with the Taft-Hartley Law compulsory" for membership in the international union. Perhaps not surprisingly, the department store union leaders still refused compliance. Wolchok, well aware of his opponents' position, reissued his order, sending them letters ordering them to "take immediate steps to file the . . . non-Communist affidavits to be signed by all your officers" or be removed by the national leaders.[56]

Still, the local leaders did not sign the affidavits, instead taking steps to make certain that as many workers and other union organizers supported their position as possible. In Local 5, Sadka Brown again began lining up the Local's Executive Board behind the local leaders' position against signing, warning them that it would be the responsibility of all the local organizers to "maintain [the] support of membership on the REAL issues and make them understand the smoke-screen so that [even if] the International sends in administrators . . . the membership [will] support elected leaders." Brown also moved to line up individual union members behind their leaders' position, often by stressing the importance of worker agency and the dangers of consorting with state bureaucracies. "Will compliance with law—going to NLRB—win [our] program?" Brown rhetorically asked at one meeting with Local 5 members. The answer, she asserted, was an emphatic *no*. "Only unity and fight of [the] membership will!"[57]

After it became clear that the local leaders were not going to sign the Taft-Hartley affidavits, national union leaders officially took over the local unions. In September 1948, Jack Altman filed internal disciplinary charges against the local leaders, accusing them of refusing to comply with Wolchok's order. Wolchok immediately suspended the officers of the New York Joint Board, banning them from the international union. Wolchok then appointed John Cooney, Jack Altman, and other anti-Communist members of the national union leadership the official administrators of the RWDSU's New York City department store unions.

It was one thing to remove the local leaders on paper, but quite another to do so in practice. Local leaders offered members a chance to weigh in, calling for members of the local unions to decide whether to remain within the RWDSU and split with their local leaders, or disaffiliate from the RWDSU and remain within their local unions. Despite the anti-Communist propaganda being hurled at the local leaders by the federal government, store managers, and even national union leaders, in every department store union with Communists in leadership positions—Local 1-S, Local 2, Local 3, Local 5, and Local 1250—the members voted to support their local leaders, to disaffiliate from the RWDSU and become independent. The members of Local 65 did the same.

Union members had many reasons for siding so overwhelmingly with the local leaders, a surprising decision considering that some workers had been questioning the value of the unions, and that others had been strong critics of local leaders' radical politics. Certainly few department store union members shared the Communist beliefs of the local leaders, although many union members were evidently opposed to the sort of anti-Communist fanaticism represented by the Rank and File Committees. But workers had many reasons besides politics to support these leaders. Many of these union leaders had been officials of their unions, in some way or another, for as long as the unions had existed. Additionally, they had substantially improved working conditions with each successive contract.

Perhaps the deciding factor in the workers' decision was leaders' emphasis on union autonomy. The resolution on disaffiliation adopted by the members of Local 5, for example, accused Wolchok and other RWDSU leaders of entering "into a conspiracy to seize and maintain control over the International Union, its locals and its members and their affairs for the purposes, among others, of perpetuating themselves in office and destroying local autonomy and depriving the workers of material benefits and working conditions." The resolution went on to claim that the national leaders had attacked the local leaders because these local leaders "have acted in accordance with the desires and instructions of their membership." The language of such resolutions illustrated the power of the local leaders' position: members voting for disaffiliation would be voting for their right to choose their own leaders, and striking a blow against those who would deprive them of this right. The fact that a majority of the members of Local 5 (one of the unions which did have an active Rank and File Committee) voted in favor of such a resolution suggests that a large number of workers believed that Wolchok's actions were, in fact, attempts to limit workers' control over their unions. And, while no numbers are available for how many members voted against such resolutions, there is no evidence of a significant pro-Wolchok or pro-RWDSU movement within the local unions after disaffiliation.[58]

Samuel Wolchok's position was now a desperate one, and still he did not budge from his principles. He would not resort to accusations that the Communist local leaders were in maniacal and single-minded service to Russia, no matter how commonplace such accusations had become by 1948. Instead Wolchok tried to present a rational, reasoned argument why the local leaders simply could not provide adequate leadership for the union. In the aftermath of the union's defeat at Oppenheim Collins, Wolchok insisted, NLRB certification was a central factor in any effort to organize. "The only question involved," Wolchok wrote, "is how to protect you. . . . There are elements who will try to becloud this issue. They will yelp about 'autonomy.' They will scream about 'democracy' and the 'rights of locals.' . . . Don't fall for false issues. There is just one issue! You can't get a union shop without an NLRB election, and you can't get on the ballot for such an election if you fail to comply [with the

Taft-Hartley Act]." Wolchok's letter failed to convince workers to change their minds.[59]

Wolchok and the other national leaders continued in their efforts to retake the locals even after workers' votes for independence in September 1948. Wolchok's appointed administrators of Local 1-S attempted to take control of the union's funds in August, and throughout the remainder of the year these administrators continued to try to wrest control of the unions away from the elected leaders. Local 1-S leaders like Atkinson and Kovenetsky took direct action to prevent this, withdrawing all the union's funds from the bank before the national leaders could do so. Altman responded by showing up at a Local 1-S Executive Board meeting and demanding the money. Atkinson had considered this possibility in advance, and he asked two friends "that happened to be detectives" to attend the meeting as well. As he remembered, "When Altman got up and says, 'I'll take the bank-books,' the boys jumped up and pulled out their pistols, and said, 'You're not going to take anything.'"[60]

The national leaders simply could not retake control over the local unions, a tremendous blow to the prestige of the RWDSU. Wolchok personally bore the brunt of the national union's failure, and he consequently found himself under fierce attacks from all sides following the purge of the department store unions. Having at long last eliminated his most outspoken critics within the union, Wolchok immediately faced a new series of attacks from other local leaders, this time from the right. Conservative local leaders centered on the St. Louis Joint Council complained that Wolchok had been too slow to endorse anti-communism and drive the department store union leaders out of the RWDSU. As this new group of oppositional local leaders emerged, the mainstream press quickly turned on the once-revered Wolchok, publishing articles on his leadership of the RWDSU with titles like "The Sin of Sloth" and "The Penalty of Failure." *Business Week,* which before the war had gone so far as to compare Wolchok's leadership to that of John L. Lewis and Sidney Hillman, now castigated Wolchok as a failure among labor leaders. *Newsweek* magazine published an article observing that "Sam Wolchok [had always] plodded the well-worn rut of a trade-union wheelhorse," but also noting that Wolchok had now lost even that dubious distinction. *Women's Wear Daily* columnist George Kirstein wrote a scathing column declaring that Wolchok had paid "lip service to anti-Communism while at the same time harboring and supporting the leftist-led locals and urging employers to do likewise." And, although *Time* magazine's article was somewhat more sympathetic, even it agreed that Wolchok had appeared "hapless" in the face of the Communists' desertion. In addition, national CIO officials, once among Wolchok's strongest supporters, joined the attacks on the once-revered Wolchok. CIO President Philip Murray, for instance, described the RWDSU leadership as "sitting on their charter and running paper organizations," and called for the Amalgamated Clothing Workers to begin organizing retail workers. An anonymous CIO official, supporting Murray's stance, accused Wolchok of having allowed the RWDSU to "wither away on the vine."[61]

Facing attacks from the right wing within the RWDSU, from the CIO leadership, and from the national press, in January 1949 Samuel Wolchok took action. His career and his union in shambles, Wolchok went on what was politely termed an "indefinite leave of absence" from his presidency of the RWDSU. He never returned.[62]

Conclusion

The years between 1945 and 1948 marked the destruction of the RWDSU as a major force within the CIO. While the Taft-Hartley Act and the beginnings of the McCarthy era damaged many unions, few lost both their most recognized national leader and their largest locals within just a few months. It was not accidental that the CIO's retail union was the hardest hit by the early McCarthy period. The same Communists that helped create the union by recognizing that white-collar women working in department stores were able to form unions were now costly liabilities to the union.

Even as the events of these years led to the department store unions' expulsion from the CIO, they also set the stage for these unions' survival without the CIO's support. Due to Wolchok's willingness to allow the local unions so much autonomy following the 1946 convention, organizers during these years were able to create an administrative body in the Joint Board, to join the Tom Mooney Hall Association, to produce *Thursdays Till Nine,* and to establish the *Union Voice* as their local union newspaper. In doing so, they created the cultural and administrative backbones of what would become an independent retail workers' union in New York City. If the CIO would cease to be an important factor in organizing retail workers after 1948, perhaps this independent union would be able to take up that task.

As local union leaders took their first steps towards independence, and as anti-Communist fervor gripped the nation, store managers' actions would become just as devastating to the unions' future as were the government investigations. Managers' continued experiments with different retailing methods, as well as the increasing suburbanization and massive layoffs, would have severe effects on the department store unions in the years to come. Yet, perhaps understandably, in 1948 union organizers were so focused on the government investigations and the Taft-Hartley Act that they seem to have all but ignored the effects of managerial restructuring, at least temporarily. In the late 1940s and early 1950s, the decline of American retail unionism would continue, as managerial restructuring and anti-communism would come together to force union leaders to sever their ties to communism.

CHAPTER 6

Defeat, 1948–53

Introduction

In the late 1940s and early 1950s, the importance of retail workers to the American labor movement was increasingly evident. Manufacturing was now beginning its long decline in the heavily unionized North, as factory owners relocated to southern states where unions were less of a threat. If retail workers' unions could again emerge as a major part of the labor movement, perhaps the labor movement need not follow the manufacturing industry into its decline. The result was that the fate of the labor movement was to be decided during this period, at the height of the McCarthy era, and in the midst of the postwar explosion of middle-class suburbanization. The union leaders who had won disputes against some of the most powerful retailers in the country were ready to attempt a massive expansion, as New York City's department store unions once again would become the center for a national drive to organize retail workers.[1]

The drive to expand the department store unions barely ever began, despite declarations to the contrary. Instead of organizing the nation's growing pool of retail workers, the radicals leading New York City department stores spent most of their time trying to figure out how to retain control over the unions they had created. Anti-communism, as well as changes in the city and in the stores, all worked to threaten Communists' ability to expand the unions' power. The old coalitions had dissolved, with many who might once have thought of themselves as workers now thinking of themselves as members of the middle class, moving into the suburbs or the new housing at Stuyvesant Town. And, with their control over the exterior environment restored by the rise of anti-communism, managers were rapidly restructuring the stores' interior environments, allowing customers direct access to goods and eliminating skilled sales jobs in the process.[2]

In the midst of an increasingly more difficult situation for organizing, union leaders turned to workers for support, adopting first a policy of "union democracy" and then, finally, embracing anti-communism, turning on their former allies in the Communist party in the process. But no amount of anti-Communist rhetoric would protect workers from the effects of restructuring, or would protect union leaders from anti-Communist attacks. This they learned at Hearn's. At this store, workers—with the encouragement and support of union leaders—voted to make concession after concession after the closing of the Loeser's store, to allow managers at Hearn's to more successfully compete with the nonunionized 14th Street stores like Klein's and Ohrbach's. But the concessions did workers little good: in 1953, Hearn's managers announced that they were laying off thousands of workers in the store in an effort to restructure the store. Workers went out on strike in protest.

The Hearn's strike was a test for the newly anti-Communist union in two important ways. It was the first strike that took place after the union condemned communism, and the first strike where department store workers challenged managers' postwar attempts at restructuring of the stores. The union amassed powerful allies in this strike, winning the support of AFL and CIO leaders alike; but these allies were unable to force Hearn's to settle. Additionally, the union's official condemnation of communism did nothing to prevent Hearn's managers from referring to the union leaders' radical past in advertisements during the strike, insisting that the unions were radical political entities and keeping the union leaders on the defensive throughout the strike. Anti-communism, the workers would discover, in no way guaranteed victory. The Hearn's strike ended in defeat, and with it ended any chance workers had of preventing managers from restructuring New York City's department stores, and any possibility of a powerful retail workers' union in America.

The World of Tomorrow: Stores and City Transformed, 1948–53

By 1953 New York City had forever changed from the prewar era. Met Life's Stuyvesant Town project was open and accepting tenants by 1947, and by 1948 it had so dominated real estate in lower Manhattan that area landlords advertised to potential tenants that their apartments were "near Stuyvesant Town." Like Parkchester before it, Stuyvesant Town was an experiment in a new sort of city life, one that was friendly and serene. One resident quoted in the *Times* described Stuyvesant Town in terms that could have been used to describe the postwar suburban ideal:

Where I used to live, nobody said anything to anybody. Here, when we meet a neighbor in the elevator, we say 'Good morning.' or something like that. And when we come out of the building, do you know what we look at first? The grass, and that tree over there—it's a maple, they tell me. Sometimes we see a bird sitting on a branch. I say that's a good way to start the day—with neighbors, trees, and a little wildlife.

Pleasant neighbors, grass, wildlife, and nondescript trees, with no sign of strife or class struggle: that was what Stuyvesant Town, like the suburbs, promised residents in the postwar era.[3]

The reality was far more complicated than the pastoral images that Met Life and some tenants presented. In particular, Met Life's policies on choosing tenants came under fierce attack. "Negroes and whites," Met Life President Frederick Ecker openly announced, "don't mix." Like Parkchester before it, Stuyvesant Town reflected Ecker's beliefs, and no African American tenants were allowed in the new housing development. In response to critics, Met Life did construct a separate housing development in Harlem, the Riverton houses. But if this silenced some critics, others continued to protest against the segregation. The most important protests came from Stuyvesant Town tenants themselves, some of whom set up a Tenants' Committee to End Discrimination in Stuyvesant Town. Jesse Kessler, a Local 65 organizer and Stuyvesant Town resident, allowed Hardine and Raphael Hendrix, an African American couple, to move into his apartment in Stuyvesant Town for a month while Kessler was away. The month passed without major incidents, although there were plenty of minor ones: historian Arthur Simon noted that the couple's son "needed constant accompaniment because occasionally someone made a hostile remark . . . or anonymous shouts would come from some window. A few threatening phone calls meant that he had to be kept away from the telephone, too." When Kessler returned in September, the Hendrixes moved into the apartment of Lee Lorch, a mathematics instructor at City College, who was going to be teaching at Pennsylvania State College for an academic year. Met Life officials, although they made some efforts at continued resistance, backed down after the city council passed a bill making the continued de jure segregation of Stuyvesant Town and other Met Life properties illegal.[4]

The controversy around segregation illustrated not only the complexity of the Stuyvesant Town project; it also illustrated just how powerful anti-communism had become, even in a city that had once been a center of communism in America. The proponents of discrimination in Stuyvesant Town raised the issue of communism to attack their opposition. To conservative papers like the *Daily News,* the campaign for the integration of Stuyvesant Town was a Communist conspiracy, a way to stir up trouble where none actually existed. "Some of our Councilmen," the *News* proclaimed, "have allowed themselves to become so intimidated by Commie pressure that they're actually contemplating voting for . . . a bill with a most peculiar look and odor . . . aimed directly and viciously at Stuyvesant Town." Met Life executives agreed, claiming that the bill desegregating Stuyvesant Town "stems right out of the Communist line" and would "open the gates to race hatred" rather than integration.[5]

The rise of the middle class, both at Stuyvesant Town and in the postwar suburbs, would have profound effects on New York's department store unions. For one thing, the postwar middle class would openly reject the sort of radical politics that, during the Depression, had allowed doctors and writers to envision themselves as white-collar workers and to throw their support behind strikes at the city's department stores. Radicalism of any sort was taboo in Stuyvesant Town; Met Life evicted both Lorch and Kessler soon after the City Council passed the bill eliminating segregation in the private housing development. In the suburbs, the process of eliminating radicalism was, to be sure, more complicated, but equally important to community leaders. One of the many arguments for the prefabricated houses of Levittown, for instance, was that the homeowners there would never become Communists, since working on their homes would occupy all their spare time. Not until a new generation came of age would radicalism again become a central part of city life; by the 1960s, of course, the New Left—the children both of African American and Puerto Rican working-class migrants to the city and of the middle-class residents of Stuyvesant Town and the suburbs—would create powerful radical movements of their own; but throughout the 1950s the idea of a large-scale radical movement was highly unlikely.[6]

There were other ways in which the rise of the middle class would affect New York City's department stores, particularly in the branch stores. Workers at the branch stores (nearly all of whom seem to have been women) were teachers working on weekends, students who worked nights, and women over 40, at least some of whom were married. Much like the residents of Stuyvesant Town, these workers thought of themselves as members of the middle class, and part of being middle class was proving that husbands and fathers could support their families. The result was that workers in these stores now insisted that they didn't really need their jobs, that they worked mostly to get out of the house and earn a little "pin money . . . even though," as one union organizer later told historian Minna Ziskind, "many of these women worked when their husbands were laid off or ended up disabled or ended up with lousy-paying jobs." Attempting to prove to one another as well as to any observers that they did not need their jobs, workers in the branch stores, Ziskind suggests, had little interest in striking for higher pay or the right to form unions, making the unions at these branch stores weak at best.[7]

Finally, and perhaps most importantly, the emergence of the middle class would be a justification, if not the main one, for the rise of what one retail executive called a "new era in retailing." Throughout the city, managers would restructure their stores to meet the demands of the large numbers of potential middle-class consumers. This was warranted to a degree; at least some Stuyvesant Town residents decided where to shop due to the shopping experiences that different stores offered, even more than the merchandise carried by different stores. Corinne Demas, who lived in Stuyvesant Town as a child from 1948 through the 1960s, remembered her mother and other women living in Stuyvesant Town making these comparisons. Despite their proximity, Demas remembered, the downscale stores on 14th Street held little appeal for Stuyvesant Town residents. Klein's, for instance, still catering to the same market it had catered to in the early 1930s, was dingy and unpleasant: "Clothing that was not hung up on great long metal pipes was dumped out on palatial wooden tables with edges like animal troughs . . . Everything about Klein's had an aura of poverty: the dim lighting, the low ceilings, the dull linoleum on the floors. In the communal try-on room women . . . squinted at themselves in the narrow, cloudy mirrors. Everyone pretended not to be looking at each other," so heavy a stigma was attached to shopping in this sort of establishment. If they associated Klein's with forbidding and depressing poverty, residents of Stuyvesant Town also found stores that catered to the upper class unsuitable for their shopping needs. Demas remembered that, in stores that continued catering to wealthier customers, store clerks made middle-class people feel unwelcome. "I always felt," Demas wrote, "as if we didn't quite belong in these stores . . . The saleswomen always seemed like temporarily impoverished countesses, who treated us with polite disdain. Their 'May I help you?' sounded accusatory."[8]

As Demas's remarks suggest, with the opening of Stuyvesant Town and the expansion of the suburbs, there emerged a group of customers who fit neither in the rough-and-tumble world of Klein's and Ohrbach's nor in the exclusive and refined world of the upscale stores. Some managers, especially those at Hearn's, explicitly responded to Stuyvesant Town by restructuring the stores. At Hearn's, only a few blocks west of Stuyvesant Town, the store could now potentially come to serve a very different (and far more affluent) group of customers than the former working-class customer base. Hearn's managers met the challenge with enthusiasm, even opening a Stuyvesant Town "model apartment" so that Stuyvesant Town residents could come to the store and see how to most effectively furnish their new residences. The store also began carrying a "Stuyvesant Towner" collection of furniture, designed to save space in the relatively small apartments but still look attractive. Hearn's also hired many more salespeople, in an effort to offer a more upscale experience to the new Stuyvesant Town residents who, they were sure, would soon be crowding the store's aisles.[9]

If Hearn's was the earliest transformation, it was also an exceptional one. As Hearn's managers began to implement full-service shopping on 14th Street, everywhere else in the city store managers worked to replace full-service shopping with more efficient means of consumption. It was an era of tremendous experimentation: some store managers—most of them in cities besides New York—even went so far as to open vending machine branches, where customers inserted coins to purchase goods like hosiery, underwear, accessories, stationery, and toys. These machines, although they attracted a great deal of attention, were generally considered novelties, fascinating but ultimately not a particularly realistic substitute for the more traditional stores. At the same time, stores throughout the country did begin including a few of these machines inside nonautomated stores, particularly to sell candies and cold drinks.[10]

Unlike vending machines, nonmechanized self-service was an increasingly realistic and popular method for increasing efficiency. What had begun during World War II as a method to save labor now became a method to save money. Developments at Gimbel's illustrate the expansion of self-service retailing during the late 1940s and early 1950s. At Gimbel's in 1949 managers began their cost-cutting efforts by eliminating the entire gift-wrapping unit immediately after Christmas. Over the next year, store managers redesigned most of the departments in the store with open merchandise display cases, the World War II technique that allowed customers direct access to samples of merchandise without going through salespeople. By January 1951 they had completed this modernization program in many of the departments, and store managers were already announcing the plan's success. As Gimbel's manager Nat Cohen announced approvingly, "open fixtures almost amount to self-service for the shopper." Other managers seconded Cohen's opinion: the open displays, another manager claimed, "give the merchandise a chance to sell itself." Now customers could inspect and select their purchases *before* the intervention of a salesperson. But managers were not finished; at Gimbel's in 1950 they also initiated fully self-service shopping in select departments. In the notions department, for instance, customers could now enter, select an item from the shelves, and take it to the cashier without the intervention of a salesperson.[11]

Other store managers followed Gimbel's managers' lead in establishing self-service departments. At Bloomingdale's, managers transformed their housewares department into a fully self-service department in August of 1952, and top managers at Bloomingdale's also called for all departments in the store "to focus on merchandise assortments and encourage self-selection" from then on. Managers at Macy's also increasingly experimented with self-service, establishing a self-service counter for Maidenform® brassieres early in 1952 and then launching a one-day self-service dress sale in October of that year. By 1953 Macy's managers had also instituted a self-service toy department.[12]

There were numerous reasons that department store managers began to institute self-service. Certainly customer preference for self-service was a factor managers frequently cited, but there were many other reasons why self-service became so prominent in the early 1950s. First among them was increasing competition from supermarkets. For years before managers had introduced self-service into department stores, supermarkets in America had offered consumers an opportunity to try self-service when shopping for groceries, and they were so efficient that by the early 1950s these supermarkets had begun to branch out, carrying socks, nylon hosiery, toys, records, underwear, and sometimes even electrical appliances. These lines were extremely successful, offering customers cheaper and faster alternatives to the full-service department stores, and spurring department store managers to revamp their own operations to resemble the supermarket managers' success.[13]

In addition to the new competition from these self-service establishments was the increase in nationally advertised brands which accompanied the rise of television. By the early 1950s clothing and dry goods manufacturers were advertising their particular brands directly to customers, and the result was that customers entered stores already knowing what they wanted to purchase. By 1953 some store managers estimated that 60 percent of customers asked for children's merchandise by brand name, and between 25 and 30 percent of customers for other items asked for merchandise by brand name. Combined with television advertising, the result was that "nowadays . . . the average woman entering the store knows exactly what she wants," as one salesperson put it. For the first time, complete self-service was a real option, since customers did not need salespeople's help to make their selections. As in the branch stores, the salesperson's job was now primarily to show "courtesy [and] interest in the customer's needs" and only secondarily "to have some knowledge of merchandise."[14]

But the most important factor behind the rise of self-service was the cost efficiency of the practice. Initially, there was some question of whether or not self-service would be economically more efficient than full-service shopping. Store managers seemed particularly worried that they would be expected to reduce prices if they instituted self-service. As one manager put it, services were "business building activities" that were supposed to cost a lot of money. But as they experimented, store managers discovered that self-service was an extremely effective way to make more sales, and that the increase in volume more than made up for any loss in profits per sale. One study found that in a self-service department, an average employee totaled 20,250 sales each year, while in a full-service store, the same employee would make only 12,300 sales each year.[15]

As managers sacrificed the control that full-service shopping had allowed them, they began using new technologies to regain some control over the process of consumption. If self-service meant that customer shoplifting would now be a much bigger concern, television allowed store managers to keep an eye on customers, through the installation of store security cameras. Other new technologies had even more important implications for retailing in America, among them the electronic price tag. As Richard Neumaier wrote in the *Department Store Economist*, the introduction of the electronic price tag signaled that "a new era in retailing has arrived!" Now, rather than relying upon salespeople and cashiers to know the prices of goods,

> an electronic eye will read the punched hole information in the merchandise ticket and translate these electronic impulses into electromagnetic fields on a magnetic tape. . . . The only judgment required in this entire process is in the production of the original merchandise tag and in the punching of a tabulating card of the merchandise received which can be a by-product of the accounts payable operation. For all other phases the human element has practically been removed.[16]

Other store managers agreed with Neumaier on the importance of removing the "human element," namely, the large numbers of highly trained workers employed in the stores. As a Detroit store manager told a reporter for the *Department Store Economist*, "Every operation must be studied to make it easier and faster, so that there is greater efficiency and economy in operation. One of the necessities of the future is for stores to control expenses through greater and greater productivity per employee. The scientific layout of merchandise and service departments is one of the most important ways of accomplishing it."[17]

The introduction of self-service forced union organizers to pay close attention to the changes taking place in the industry. By late 1952 Local 1250 organizer Peter Montanaro declared at a union meeting that "the department store[s] as we now know them will no longer be—. . . They are all going to have some self-service departments, due to overhead and competition from non-service stores." But if union organizers were aware of the changes by 1952, they were not aware that these changes posed a threat. Montanaro assured his listeners, "members' jobs . . . would probably not be touched, except for changes in classification." The union seemed similarly unconcerned at Gimbel's, where Louis Broido was able to reassure the union that store managers would give the workers a raise if managers "were able to improve the efficiency of this business by the rationalization of our procedures, and the more effective use of manpower . . . all consistent with fair dealing with our employees." In return, union officials assured Broido that employees would support this practice, so long as the "fair dealing" with employees continued.[18]

Other labor leaders were even slower to realize the possible effects of self-service retailing on attempts to organize in the retail industry. As late as November of 1953, after New York City's department store unions had launched their first challenges to managerial restructuring, delegates to the national CIO convention in Cleveland nonetheless declared that "self-service must be accepted as means of cutting costs and of increasing sales" and that it "presented no great threat to organized labor and might even be a beneficial force for the workers in that particular industry." On this point, the CIO delegates were entirely incorrect. Managers' decisions to institute self-service retailing would, in fact, lead to some of the most devastating challenges which union organizers and workers faced in the first twenty years of the department store unions' history. And these challenges would arise at a time when New York City's department store union leaders were struggling just to retain the unions they had helped create over the previous decades.[19]

Unions Transformed, 1948–51

In the late 1940s and early 1950s, the left-wing leaders of New York City's department store unions increasingly emphasized the "democratic" nature of the unions in order to gain workers' support. They badly needed this support: the unions faced numerous challenges throughout these years, and serious internal divisions could have destroyed the unions. In order to prevent these divisions from forming, radical union organizers emphasized the unions as an arena for workers to express their political views, whatever those views might be. It was a particularly good tactic against the strongly conformist anti-communism that was becoming more powerful throughout the country in this era.

The split with the RWDSU left the department store unions in an extremely precarious position. Since union officials had refused to sign the required non-Communist affidavits, the unions were not certified, and could not participate in any NLRB elections should store managers call for any such elections. Meanwhile, the contracts which the unions had signed with the stores in 1948 were coming up for renewal in 1949, and the managers of at least some stores now began to announce in their training programs "that under [the] Taft-Hartley Act [the employees] do not have to join [the] Union." Managers at Macy's took a slightly different tack; in order to encourage dissension within the unions' ranks, managers there began publishing articles in the store newspaper, the Macy's *Star,* encouraging workers to "take an active personal interest in how their union is run," suggesting that "we hope you will attend its meetings regularly, stay all the way through, participate in debate and vote on the issues that come before you." On top of this, managers at all the stores continued to lay off large numbers of workers, weakening the unions still further.[20]

As managers continued to challenge the legitimacy of the newly independent unions, other labor organizers also launched attacks against the department store unions. The RWDSU and the Amalgamated Clothing Workers both began to attempt raids on the department store unions, launching repeated efforts to secure the "liberation" of the workers within the fugitive locals, who were "trapped behind the iron curtain," as one CIO leader described them. Even former allies had turned on the unions. By 1951 Mike Quill, once a staunch supporter and the guest of honor at the unions' Counter Carnival, threatened to picket the department stores during the Christmas rush "in order to compel management to sign with [the] CIO."[21]

Somewhat surprisingly, department store union leaders were able to find some common ground with store managers around the actions of AFL and CIO organizers. While store managers did oppose the unions on many issues, they also opposed the sort of jurisdictional fighting which Quill and other AFL and CIO organizers waged within the industry. And they had no intention of actively taking a side in the various intraunion struggles: the last thing store managers wanted was to have to contend with more cross-picketing. As a result, even while trying to undermine the unions, managers took pains to demonstrate their neutrality in the intraunion struggles. While control over

Local 1-S and the other department store union locals was still tied up in court between the national RWDSU and the local leaders, for instance, Macy's managers announced to employees that they would ask both local and national leaders to attend negotiations until the jurisdictional dispute was settled. Similarly, Bloomingdale's managers announced to employees that their biggest concern was not who won the bargaining rights, but rather that "the needs of the employees are met" by making sure grievances were handled as quickly as possible. Stern's managers went even further, barring international RWDSU officers from contract negotiations, since those negotiations had always been carried on by local leaders in the past.[22]

With store managers at least attempting the appearance of neutrality, department store union leaders quickly moved to meet the challenges posed by the state and the other unions. In late October 1948, only weeks after splitting with Wolchok over their refusal to file with the NLRB, the department store union leaders began submitting the required forms to the NLRB, including the much-hated affidavits asserting that they were not members of the Communist party. All the leaders except for William Michelson signed these affidavits in 1948 and 1949.[23]

As late as 1950, several union leaders had serious doubts about their decision to sign the non-Communist affidavits. When William Michelson finally decided to sign, in the spring of 1950, Arthur Osman strongly opposed Michelson's decision. As Osman put it, the point was to win workers' loyalty, not to get NLRB recognition:

> Now, two years after we made the stupid blunder of filing, two years in the course of which the dirt from our eyes was washed out by tears . . . let's not commit the same blunder . . . our leaders should no longer file affidavits wherever they can afford not to file . . . Without filing, you can't get a union shop. What does it matter if you have a union shop? Do you think that if we were certified at Stern's and all the people in Stern's who hate our guts were compelled to pay dues that this would make them good defenders of our union? We don't need their lousy few pennies. We're hoping to salvage their hearts and souls.[24]

The anxiety about NLRB certification, Osman said in this remarkably insightful and impassioned speech, was spurred by a fear of workers. If workers opposed the union, the NLRB might help convince them that the union was legitimate. But, as Osman here pointed out, if workers opposed the union, then they had already been defeated. Moreover, as Osman recognized, with

Communist-led unions under attack from all sides, their defense could not rest on the government, which was all that signing the Taft-Hartley affidavit could accomplish. The government, in Osman's view, was eventually going to attack the unions in any case. Only workers' support could give Communist organizers in the department store unions the ability to continue to resist the growing movement of anti-communism. Without that support, the unions could not survive, whether they had a union shop or not.[25]

As Osman predicted, the unions remained subject to anti-Communist attacks despite union leaders' decisions (Michelson included) to sign the required affidavits. In particular, raiders from the AFL and the CIO repeatedly reminded department store union members of the Communist politics of the unions' current leaders. One RWDSU flyer, for example, attacked Sam Kovenetsky by noting that the Russian-sounding "Ykstenevok . . . spelled backwards is Kovenetsky," and stating that "you'd be a 100% nobody today, Sam, except for [the] CIO." The RCIPA was even less subtle in their anti-Communist attacks on Local 1-S. One RCIPA flyer warned Kovenetsky "that workers have a right to expect . . . that their union will be administered without being torn internally by factional strife promoted by alien political groups." Faced with these attacks, the non-Communist Kovenetsky decided that the benefits of unity with the other department store union leaders were simply not worth the price of being dubbed a Communist. In 1949, only months after leaving the RWDSU, Local 1-S rejoined the CIO as a union independent from the RWDSU.[26]

With the attacks continuing, with their unity dwindling, and with jail as a near-certainty, organizers in the other department store unions made two defensive moves. First, they moved to consolidate the unions as much as possible. Throughout the late 1940s and early 1950s they experimented with various types of consolidation, first creating the Distributive Workers Union, which encompassed the department store unions and Osman's Local 65. Late in 1950, they joined the DWU with other left-wing unions which had been purged from the CIO as the Distributive Processing and Office Workers Union (DPOWU). Through the merger which created the DPOWU, the New York City locals of this union, primarily encompassing office, wholesale, and retail workers, became District 65, which its leaders proudly heralded as "New York's largest union!"[27]

As they moved to consolidate their unions, organizers also attempted to revive what they called "the fighting spirit" of the 1930s, to win, as Osman had so eloquently put it, the "hearts and souls" of the workers. Union organizers therefore set their sights on reviving and expanding the union's recreational program still further, to remind workers of the vibrant role the union could play in their lives. A union calendar from the fall of 1951 illustrates the unions' greater commitment to social and cultural activities. On September 10 the union sponsored a "founding festival," a party to celebrate the creation (nearly a year earlier) of the DPOWU and District 65. On the 15th, the Tom Mooney Hall Association night club reopened after renovations, and the union held a second party to celebrate. On the 17th, the District 65 photography club opened an exhibit of photographs at the Tom Mooney Hall. The 21st of September marked the beginning of a "festival of dance featuring square dances, international folk dances, etc." On October 1 began the union's art exhibit. On October 8 the union held a "Festival of Song." On October 15 the union began "Health Week," and on October 22 they rented Madison Square Garden, "the only hall [in New York] that can accommodate us," for a mass meeting. Other events, such as boat rides up the Hudson River, also gave union members a chance to socialize and make connections, some of them extremely important. (Stuyvesant Town resident Jesse Kessler first met the Hendrixes, the African American couple who would move into his apartment, on a union boat trip.)[28]

Other programs also contributed to make the union a more central part of workers' lives. In particular, District 65's cooperative buying service allowed store workers to buy all sorts of goods, ranging from hosiery to appliances to children's clothes, at prices below even employees' discount prices at the stores. And, in the early 1950s, the union also took over workers' pension funds from the company, partially in order to discourage raiding by AFL and CIO competitors.[29]

These programs, though they may have made the union far more important to workers' daily lives, were very different from the cultural programs of the late 1930s. In the 1930s, as already suggested, these programs had served to win workers' support, but they had also served to create coalitions between union members and the larger left-wing movement. Between 1948 and 1953, however, there scarcely remained a left-wing movement to unite with. In this era, the largest left-wing gathering in Union Square, once the center of a radical movement so powerful it threatened to wrest control of the city streets from store managers, was the vigil on the eve of the execution of Julius and Ethel Rosenberg. The somber mourning was a far cry from the dynamic and determined movement to bring about a new social and political order in the early 1930s.[30]

Yet if the cultural programs could no longer function as a way to create a broad-based coalition, the union organizers were successful in another of their key goals. They were able to retain the support of most workers within the store. At every union where the radicals had been in control they won the NLRB elections of 1948 and 1949. The victories were sometimes by very slim margins. While at Bloomingdale's the union's returns were overwhelmingly in favor of the local leadership, with 1886 of the 2600 workers voting for Local 3, at Stern's Local 3 won by a far less impressive margin of 763 to 612.[31]

The reelected union leaders responded to their narrow victories by attempting to solidify workers' support wherever possible by giving workers more power over the union, a practice they called union democracy. "Democracy" became an oft-repeated concept within the unions in these years. When the unions became part of the Distributive Workers Union, for instance, Nicholas Carnes announced that the DWU constitution guaranteed "real democracy," unlike within the RWDSU. "The right to secede [which was guaranteed under the new union constitution] would guarantee respect for each other's problems, and that eliminates the need to secede," Carnes announced at a union meeting. Additionally, Carnes emphasized that the formation of the DWU required "respect for diverse opinions and the right of all members to express them." Local 65 leader David Livingston agreed on this point, arguing that democracy meant the right of union members to hold many different opinions on political issues.[32]

Union democracy was accompanied by a greater emphasis on answering workers' complaints within the stores. The union leaders proudly announced to the readers of *Union Voice* that the unions repeatedly met managers' continual threats to cut jobs and wages either by ensuring that workers were laid off in terms of seniority, or, sometimes, by preventing layoffs and wage cuts altogether. As Sadka Brown instructed the Local 5 Executive Board, they had to take all actions on grievances on a "daily [basis] if need be," because "in this way, we can and will win over more and more Stern workers—until only [a] small group of disruptors will remain outside our ranks."[33]

Organizers' formal protests against management's actions were strongest when backed by the threat of a strike, and managers, engaged in restructuring the stores, resisted everything except strikes. At nearly every store during this period, even in places like Stern's where nearly half the employees did not support the radical union leaders, union members issued strike threats nearly every time there was a contract up for negotiation. Rather than face a strike, store managers backed down on nearly every issue, allowing the unions to expand their contract to include storewide seniority clauses, union-sponsored health insurance plans, and cost of living adjustments.[34]

Some of the unions' victories in these years went far beyond the standard subject matter for bargaining. Before Local 1-S split from the other unions, for example, union organizers in that local staged a protest against a window display at Macy's, which had a "doll representing a baby born on the 'Amos and Andy' radio program. Dominating the window display was a caricature of a Negro man in the style used by those who spread race hatred. . . . Macy workers who noticed the window immediately called management to ask for removal of the display." After some delay and numerous protests by union members, managers took the display down.[35]

With managers suddenly on the defensive against strike threats, union organizers pressed their advantage, making their first major efforts to fight discrimination within the stores. Their particular goal was the expanded hiring of African American workers in office and sales jobs. Five of the eighteen African American workers hired at Gimbel's and Saks between October 1952 and February 1953 received office jobs, once reserved for white workers. At some stores, the union was also beginning to demand desegregation even of the coveted sales jobs, long held exclusively by whites. By late 1951 *Union Voice* was able to report that, due to members' interracial struggles against discrimination, twelve African American workers had obtained sales jobs in Bloomingdale's over the course of the year.[36]

Union leaders also took measures to ensure that individual workers supported their struggle against discrimination. In May 1951, for instance, the union brought up charges against Rose Amos, an office worker at Gimbel's, after Amos reportedly used "slanderous remarks, vile language, and discrimination against other members in the department," including racial slurs against her African American and Jewish coworkers. The department store unions' joint General Council eventually expelled Amos from the union.[37]

While they took a stronger stand against racial discrimination than they had done in previous years, most union organizers were more hesitant than ever about demanding rights for women. In fact, some union leaders during the late 1940s and early 1950s even called for preferential treatment for male breadwinners, apparently without complaints from members or other organizers. At one report to a Local 5 general membership meeting, Sadka Brown assured the members that during negotiations the union "certainly want[s] to be sure that those jobs which, in the main, are filled by bread winners and heads of families, provide rates of pay which will enable families to maintain their self-respect and dignity."[38]

Although union organizers were actively celebrating the male breadwinner norm for the first time in the union's history, they nonetheless allowed workers themselves to discuss and debate gender issues within the union press and at union meetings. They often did so, however, in ways that limited workers' agency even as they allowed workers an opportunity to voice their opinions. A Local 65 member named Harold Pearlman, for instance, wrote a letter to the *Union Voice* demanding an apology for the editors' decision to print a "cheesecake" photograph of a young woman in a bathing suit with the caption "Looks inviting—the water we mean." Pearlman's letter unleashed a small and brief storm of controversy which illustrates the complex and in some ways limited nature of union democracy within the department store unions. Other union members quickly wrote in, with arguments on both sides. "Cheesecake" proponents adopted a wide range of arguments, arguing, among other things, that

> nature tricks out her products with all sorts of engaging curves and bumps and dimples . . . The cigarette people come along and say 'If nature can get continuity with these bumps and things why can't we use them to sell cigarettes?' They print a picture of a pretty girl in their advertising and the sales mount. . . . 'Why not [do the same in] UNION VOICE?'[39]

Women supporters of the validity of cheesecake photographs offered quite different arguments. Elizabeth Fallone, one of the few department store workers who got involved in the debate (most of the participants who gave their local union affiliation were members of Local 65), wrote in claiming that she was "ashamed of some of my fellow Union members who are jealous of a gal for being beautiful. Why shouldn't our union paper have a beauty, amateur golf, swimming or bowling contest? . . . One girl is beautiful, one is talented, another brilliant[,] so let each benefit in her own right." To Fallone, the editors' decision to print cheesecake photographs was the union's way to allow women to be recognized. Some other women in the union apparently agreed about the importance of these photos for women, one calling them (in verse) "beauties . . . selected from the brood / Of UNION chicks, who work and organize / To get out from the nasty solitude / Produced by what they call 'free enterprise.'"[40]

At least one additional opponent also spoke up, arguing that such photographs were politically dangerous:

> Is it not white chauvinism to characterize the Negro as only a good entertainer and only a good cook? Then it is equally supremacist to characterize the women as capable of only bearing children and only cooking. . . . Both attitudes help fascism, which grows stronger in the

soil of confusion and disunity. . . . To be consistent in the struggle against fascism, one must root out all attitudes which stifle the full contributions which all people can make.[41]

This debate over cheesecake photographs strongly suggests that Communists' support for women's importance within the union, limited as it had always been, was rapidly eroding. The editors' continual support for the right to print cheesecake photographs in the union paper was hardly the sort of attitude encouraged in the 1930s, when—as we have seen—men in the department store unions were reportedly more respectful of the role women played in unions. While some women in the late 1940s, Elizabeth Fallone among them, may have seen these photographs as opportunities for women to be recognized within the union, this suggests just how limited such opportunities were: exploitation of this sort was as close as these women came to feeling as if they did play an important role in the unions' daily existence.

The debate over cheesecake photographs also speaks volumes about the role of workers in affecting union policy during the late 1940s and early 1950s. The union newspaper in these years became something that it had never before been: a space for workers to address and discuss political issues. The editors' willingness to print the multiple views on the subject of these photographs illustrates their support for union members' participation in debate and discussion. At the same time, while printing the various sides of the debate, the editors continued to publish the photographs at the center of the debate, often with blurbs referring to the ongoing "cheesecake controversy," and asking the readers for their opinion on the suitability of the photographs in the union paper. In addition, in the end, the proposal to ban cheesecake (whose supporters wrote only two of the nine letters printed during the debate) was soundly rejected when the editors said that while they had "listened carefully to the arguments of both sides, and having a few ideas on the subject themselves, . . . will continue publishing, from time to time, photos of beautiful, shapely and alluring women . . . who by good fortune happen to come within our view." In the same editorial that announced this decision, the editors reminded their readers "that neither women nor anyone else should be judged by appearance alone, and that women play an essential and dignified role in our mutual fight for a better life for working people." In a decision fraught with irony, the editors printed this statement next to a photograph of a woman in a bathing suit holding a volleyball.[42]

Like *Union Voice,* union meetings also became spaces where workers could debate and explore political issues, even issues like women's rights to which union leaders paid little attention. By 1951 women workers were themselves raising issues of women's treatment in the union. Bloomingdale's worker Florence Holt, for instance, gave reports at several membership meetings at Bloomingdale's on the "Special Problems of Women Members," pointing out that while "women constitute a clear majority of the membership, yet this fact is hardly reflected in posts of leadership," and she called for a "thorough examination of job rates, job opportunities, and problems of women members . . . Such a committee might find, for example, that the double job of women members as homemakers and wage earners supplies the basis of a future struggle for the 35-hour week."[43]

Again, the fact that Holt was able to lead a discussion on gender discrimination within both the stores and the union demonstrates the extent to which union leaders allowed workers to play an expanded role in the union. At the same time, the fact that Holt's report, insightful though it was, had few if any actual effects on the roles of women in the union illustrates the limits as well as the possibilities for workers to take leadership during this era of union democracy.

Two major political issues became testing grounds for the fragile democracy that existed in District 65 in the early 1950s: the Korean War and the May Day parade. Union leaders voiced strong opposition to the Korean War at union meetings, pointing out that the wartime inflation (price increases which were not accompanied by proportional wage increases) made the war an issue which workers absolutely had to confront. As Local 1250 organizer Bernard Tolkow put it, "the National Emergency proclaimed by the President means that our members and all the rest of the workers who do the fighting and dying in the war will pay the costs in increased taxes, higher prices for food, clothing and rent, and at the same time suffer the wage freeze." In addition, Tolkow argued, the war was responsible for some of the layoffs workers faced. The war created "shortage[s] in certain materials, such as are used for major appliances, with resultant lay-offs in these departments."[44]

Union members were more supportive of the war than their leaders. In one vote that took place in Local 3 on a resolution supporting a cease-fire, 297 workers abstained, 86 voted for the cease-fire, and 450 voted against any resolution for a cease-fire. While these figures demonstrate that the overwhelming majority of Bloomingdale's workers supported the war, they also illustrate that Communists still wielded considerable, albeit minority, influence within their unions. Not only could they raise the issue of the war; they could also convince approximately one-sixth of the voting members to oppose it.

The discussion around the Korean War again illustrates the limits as well as the extent of union democracy in New York City's department store unions in the early 1950s. As had occurred in the late 1940s, union organizers allowed and even encouraged discussion and debate on the issue of the cease-fire. Even more importantly, the local department store unions took no official stand on the Korean War, despite union leaders' and many organizers' strong opposition to the war. However, District 65 did take an official stand opposing the war, much to the anger of many department store union members. It was a compromise, but one that allowed union leaders to continue to support the Communist party's line on the war.[45]

Similar debates and compromises occurred around the unions' role in the Communist party's annual May Day Parade. In a report from a 1951 union meeting, one pro–May Day worker voiced firm support for marching on May Day, calling the annual parade a "commemoration of the struggle for the 8-hour day," and loudly denying that supporting the parade would necessarily mean supporting communism, something which almost none of the workers favored. The discussion surrounding May Day engulfed the union in such controversy that even District 65, one of the largest Communist-led unions in the country, did not endorse the parade. As one report put it, "In keeping with the harmonizing policy of the District, the officers propose that our District not endorse the parade, though individual Locals could do so." The individual department store union locals did not endorse the parade; any members or leaders from these locals who wished to march in the May Day parade were welcome to do so, but they would not be allowed to carry banners giving the union's name.[46]

Union organizers' continual efforts to radicalize their members earned them the enmity of more-conservative union members. As early as February 1951, Local 1250 Executive Board members informed Nicholas Carnes that "1250 members believed that the union was no longer theirs and we must find a way to bring the Union back to the people" and that some felt that he was "losing touch and interest in 1250" since the formation of District 65. William Michelson reported similar complaints that year, the year when the debates on the Korean War and the May Day march reached their height, the most common being that there was "too much politics in the Union," and that "District 65 is a subversive organization."[47]

In response to these sorts of charges, for the first time since the late 1930s union leaders recruited store workers to become additional full-time organizers. Florence Holt, the activist who had raised the issue of women's role in the union, became a full-time organizer of Local 3. Local 1250 recruited three department store workers to help work full-time for the union: Peter

Montanaro, Peter Stein, and Bernie Tolkow. Similar influxes of male workers into leadership roles occurred in Locals 2 and 3, where John Meegan and
Murray Silverstein became full-time organizers as well. At the same time as
it represented a continued shift towards male dominance of the local unions,
this shift helped solidify the unions' commitment to their version of democracy in several ways. First, by recruiting workers as organizers, the union leadership became significantly closer in age to the workers in the stores. Second,
adding more organizers meant that there were more people to deal with workers' complaints and questions. Third, at least some of these new organizers
did not share the leaders' radical politics: Peter Montanaro and Peter Stein in
particular were some of the unions' most outspoken opponents of Communist
politics.

In the aftermath of their purge from the RWDSU, New York City's department store union organizers therefore adopted union democracy both as a
rhetorical tool and as a limited political practice. Whether in Osman's rejec-
tion of the NLRB, Livingston and Carnes's emphatic verbal support for union
democracy, Brown's instructions to stewards to concern themselves more with
workers' grievances, the new role of the union newspaper and union meetings
as vehicles for workers' discussions, the compromises around May Day or the
Korean War, or the recruitment of workers as additional full-time organizers,
union leaders took every opportunity to demonstrate the existence of democracy within the union. To some extent, this tactic was successful; it allowed
organizers, for a time at least, to convince workers that the local unions were
worth the fight against opposing unions and a federal government that might
at any moment resume its attacks on the department store unions. At the same
time, the union leaders' particular version of union democracy meant, among
other things, a strong emphasis on men as the critical actors in the union, as
editors began printing cheesecake photographs in the union newspaper, and
men emerged both as the primary subjects of collective bargaining and as
the overwhelming majority of the new full-time organizers recruited in this
period.

It is also important to remember that, despite the successes in keeping the
union at the stores where it already existed, the union was utterly unsuccessful
in expanding to new stores. In fact, the union signed not one new contract
after its defection from the CIO. Instead, most of the union organizers' efforts
in these years were devoted to fighting off raids by the CIO and the AFL. In
the late 1940s and early 1950s, when retailing was becoming a more and more
important part of the national economy, New York City's department store
unions were struggling simply to keep unions where they already existed. To

make matters even more tragic, at least at times they were unable to accomplish even this limited goal.[48]

Closings

Their efforts at union democracy bought the union leaders little time. By the early 1950s managerial restructuring had become an even more serious threat to union members' jobs. The closing of the Loeser's store in 1952 was the most serious sign of the new threat, and the result was that union leaders now sought to break their connections with American radicalism, renouncing communism as an undemocratic and anti-American movement and attempting a reconciliation of sorts with the AFL and CIO leaders whom they had so recently come to condemn.

The closing of stores was the most devastating of the effects of managerial restructuring. Those store managers who could not restructure their stores as quickly as their competition lost customers, and their businesses were in serious danger. Stores on Fulton Street in Brooklyn were in particular danger, since the managers of the Fulton Street Abraham & Straus (A&S) store were by far the most successful at exploiting the new sales environment. Even A&S's main Fulton Street store was easily accessible to new residents of the Long Island suburbs. In addition, the store had two successful branches, both on Long Island. Finally, A&S managers, who had never signed a union contract, established self-service retailing in A&S branch stores immediately after the war and cut costs accordingly, long before most other managers were able to follow suit. In addition, A&S used extensive television advertising, one of the first New York City stores to begin regular use of the new medium. In November 1951, A&S managers, having already cut operating costs and established themselves as the leaders in the new retailing environment, had passed Gimbel's to become the second largest retail establishment in New York City. They had also begun to take over other store branches, including a Loeser branch on Long Island.[49]

By the late spring of 1951, A&S was already in a very strong position. And in May of that year, when the Supreme Court struck down state "fair trade" laws—laws which allowed manufacturers input into the retail prices store managers charged customers—managers at Macy's launched a price war, cutting their prices across the board. Other store managers declared their indignation at Macy's tactics, but they quickly followed suit as best they could. A&S was among the most successful in the price war, promising that Macy's might be offering a 6 percent discount, but A&S would offer "immediate savings of up to 10 percent and even more." For most of June 1951, shoppers crowded into stores throughout the city, especially at Macy's and A&S.[50]

The workers represented by Local 1250 at the Loeser's store, always one of A&S's major competitors, were the first casualties of the 1951 price war. In January 1952 Loeser's owners declared that they were no longer making sufficient profits to make the store worth running, and announced that they would either sell the store or simply close it. In any case, the workers who were employed there were going to lose their jobs, although workers could apply for jobs with the new management if someone else was willing to buy the store.[51]

At first, union leaders expressed confidence that, if necessary, they could virtually prevent the closing of Loeser's by picketing managers' all-important going-out-of-business sales. As William Michelson said in a speech before a District 65 General Council meeting:

> The Loeser management is playing with the idea of selling all of the present stock of merchandise to some other department store in New York for the purpose of a gigantic liquidation sale. We have informed them that if they sell the goods to any of our stores, our people won't handle a stick of the merchandise and if they sell it to another store, not in our union, no customer will be able to pass the picket lines that we intend to establish.

In order to secure workers' support, Michelson promised, store managers would have to offer a significant severance package. In addition, Nicholas Carnes, the leader of Local 1250 and therefore the head of the Loeser's union, called for an intensive letter-writing campaign asking community, government, and religious leaders to do something to protect the workers at Loeser's.[52]

Through these tactics, organizers were able to win a substantial severance package of one and one-half to two weeks' pay for each year of employment. Since many Loeser's workers were long-time employees who had been with the store for several decades, the settlement totaled approximately $600,000 to be divided among the 1500 workers at Loeser's. Still, the union was able to find new jobs within the district for only around a hundred of the workers at Loeser's, and a substantial severance package still amounted to a bitter defeat for the workers at Loeser's and the union. The workers, despite their union, were now unemployed.[53]

The closing was a lesson to other department store workers in many respects. Store managers, if pushed too hard, would close their stores. If before

1952 managers had been on the defensive, backing down every time workers threatened to strike, after 1952 the situation was reversed. Managers now had the more powerful threat: that the stores might close. In 1952 and 1953 union organizers repeatedly capitulated to store management on a number of relatively minor issues. In April 1952, only a few weeks after the Loeser's store closed, Hearn's workers voted "to permit the store to be open on Monday nights" due to the company's "serious financial conditions." Similarly, in 1953 managers of the Norton's store asked Local 1250 to waive a dollar-a-week increase which the union had won for a year so that the managers could increase their advertising and thereby compete with Ohrbach's. Union members voted and agreed by 82 to 1 to give up the dollar a week.[54]

The closing of Loeser's also allowed more-conservative workers to renew their attacks on the union leaders. Disgruntled union members charged that the store closing was the result of all the time union leaders wasted on political causes, specifically radical political causes. In February 1952 Carnes was forced to devote the majority of at least one membership meeting to a defense of the union's actions during the closing of Loeser's. Cornered and outnumbered, Carnes resorted to surprisingly undemocratic tactics, including calling any criticism of union policy "slanders. . . . He pointed out how the Union made efforts to have the store purchased . . . He [also] pointed out the wonderful severance pay settlement achieved by the Union."[55]

Carnes was not alone in his new willingness to resort to authoritarian tactics to try to stem the rising tide of criticism. With the CIO's own retail unions floundering, by early 1952 some RWDSU leaders were talking about remerging with District 65. Department store union leaders, having already signed the Taft-Hartley petitions, seemed open to it, but when they raised the issue with union members, the fury was so great that even a leader as popular as Bill Michelson was forced to resort to authoritarian attacks on his opponents. Like Carnes only a few days earlier, Michelson first "deplored the 'noise' that was made over the issue," complaining that "members have abandoned the Union to a few leaders," and then argued that the union members should therefore trust those leaders. If before the closing of Loeser's, union democracy had been a key concept within the union, after the store closed, these democratic leaders sounded far more authoritarian than at any other time in the unions' history.[56]

As radical leaders began to talk about a merger with the CIO and adopt more authoritarian tactics in the aftermath of the closing of Loeser's, the federal government renewed its attacks. In the summer of 1952, a federal grand jury assembled to investigate the possibility that union leaders had contributed

District 65 funds to the Civil Rights Congress (CRC), an organization which—among other things—provided bail funds for Communist party leaders. Unsuccessful in efforts to get CRC leaders to testify about the source of funds, the grand jury charged that William Michelson and Nicholas Carnes had embezzled $80,000 from the union to send to the CRC. Subpoenaed to testify, both Michelson and Carnes vehemently denied the charges, which were dropped for lack of evidence. The grand jury investigation formally ended in the fall of 1952, but not before the CIO rescinded its offer of a merger.[57]

With the closing of Loeser's and the grand jury investigation resulting in increased criticism from workers, union leaders increasingly adopted anti-Communist positions in order to satisfy at least some of their critics. When the time came to endorse a candidate for the 1952 presidential election, union organizers first talked about not choosing a candidate at all, since both Democrat Adlai Stevenson and Republican Dwight Eisenhower endorsed such anti-Communist policies as the Korean War, the Taft-Hartley Act, and the Smith Act. In October 1952, when it came time for the union to choose a candidate, the organizers of District 65 had to choose between the liberal anti-Communist Stevenson or no candidate whatsoever. At a district-wide shop stewards' meeting on October 8, the stewards chose to endorse Adlai Stevenson. Union leaders, still desperately needing members' support against the mounting state attacks on the union, followed suit, and quickly set out to publicize their endorsement, which they viewed as an "example of union democracy," as one headline in the *Union Voice* called it. "The average working folk of America," the reporter covering the event reminded the union members, "don't usually have the place, the means or the opportunity to sound off on national political affairs . . . But in trade unions like District 65, it's different. The average working man and woman gets [*sic*] a chance to be heard . . . talking over the serious issues of public affairs—and most important, registering their sentiments and conclusions in public."[58]

Their endorsement of Stevenson was only one of many signs in 1952 that the union leaders were moving towards an anti-Communist line. By November of that year, the death of CIO leader Philip Murray appeared in the *Union Voice* with the announcement that "officers and members of DPO joined millions of American workers and their leaders . . . in expressing sorrow" at Murray's death. Rather than a critical assessment of Murray's achievements and short-comings, the *Union Voice* article focused exclusively on Murray's wonderful accomplishments, including an unusually vacuous quotation from Arthur Osman stating that Murray's "contribution . . . was inestimable. He served his fellow workers during his entire lifetime and finally gave his life in their service." If in the late 1940s Murray had been an open critic of the unions and had authorized CIO raids on these unions, by 1952 District 65 uncritically celebrated Murray and other CIO leaders who had once been dismissed as top-down and authoritarian figures.[59]

As the unions moved closer towards the anti-Communist CIO, some individual organizers adopted more and more anti-Communist rhetoric. Peter Stein announced to a Local 1250 Membership Meeting in May of that year a slew of charges against communism and Communists. Communists, Stein told the workers, "work to undermine the democratic processes of our union . . . They spread the story that . . . our leaders were preparing to abandon the struggle for Negro rights" by discussing rejoining the CIO.[60]

As the union increasingly became a site for anti-Communist rhetoric in late 1952, a second grand jury investigation began. This time, federal prosecutors charged District 65 leader David Livingston with perjury by claiming not to be a Communist in the affidavit he had signed to satisfy the Taft-Hartley Act. The grand jury subpoenaed Livingston, but Livingston refused to answer any questions, on the grounds that doing so would deprive him of the right to refuse to answer questions about the political or personal activities of other District 65 members.[61]

The second investigation became far more serious than the first. Following Livingston's refusal to answer questions, the grand jury issued a subpoena "ordering [the organizers] to produce every single book and record in their possession" relating to District 65. Union organizers adamantly refused, claiming that had they complied they "would be unable to operate. . . . We would have no contracts—we would be unable to collect dues or process claims in the Security Plan Office." In addition, they pointed out that it would have meant releasing "the names and addresses of hundreds of workers in unorganized shops . . . which would be made public and place their jobs in jeopardy." In the fall of 1952, a judge sentenced Livingston and fellow District 65 leader Jack Paley to three months in jail each for their refusal to provide the requested documents. In addition, after Livingston refused to answer these questions before the grand jury, the NLRB called Livingston to the stand. Before the NLRB, however, Livingston answered questions, assuring the board under oath "that he was not a member of the Communist Party, nor did he believe in overthrow of the government by force or any illegal means."[62]

With members and organizers demanding that their leaders stop supporting Communist policies, and the government sending District 65 leaders to jail for their suspected roles in the Communist party, union leaders found themselves again in freefall. Throughout 1952, in self-defense, they moved closer to an anti-Communist position. Union organizers withdrew from front organizations like the CP-backed National Negro Labor Congress (NNLC) in November 1952 when the NNLC began criticizing the DPOWU's unwillingness to devote more energy to organizing in the south. By April 1953, after the split with the NNLC, the DPOWU came out with an official statement condemning communism at their convention. Communists were, as Arthur Osman now declared, "sinister, disruptive, and incompatible with the spirit, aims and objectives of a free and democratic trade union movement."[63]

Communist party activists answered the DPOWU leaders' attacks on communism. By the summer of 1953, CP publications like the magazine *Political Affairs* openly attacked the DPOWU as revisionist and racist. As Alex Kendreck and Jerome Golden wrote in the June 1953 issue of the magazine, by trying to adhere to a liberal rather than a Communist line, District 65 leaders were adopting "third-force demagogy . . . to camouflage their roles as lackeys of Wall Street." The article also referred to David Livingston, who was singled out with particular ire, as a "foul-mouthed renegade," whose "path of renegacy was paved by the whole process of corruption and softening-up."[64]

Between members' increasing support for anti-communism, and the state's willingness to persecute Communists in the union, organizers had no choice but to separate themselves from their former allies in the Communist party. By early 1953, whether through the vocal attacks on Communists, the endorsement of Stevenson, or the union leaders' newfound admiration of Philip Murray, District 65 had become an avowedly anti-Communist organization. Radicalism had fallen, and the union leaders no longer needed to worry about workers' complaints that there was "too much politics" in the union.

Defeat

Throughout their history, department store union leaders had learned the value of a common enemy. Shared hatred for corrupt union leaders, wealthy women, and fascism had all been the foundation for alliances at various points in the unions' history. Now Communists joined that pantheon of villains, as District 65 leaders sought to reunite with the CIO around their shared anti-communism. Just weeks after the DPOWU's official resolution against communism, talks about a merger between the CIO and District 65 resumed, and this time the talks ended in a merger in early May 1953. As CIO leader Walter Reuther anointed the DPOWU conversion to anticommunism:

[T]he National Executive Board of the DPO has implemented its anti-totalitarian position by a statement of policy which pledges that the DPO "both by word and deed, has and will manifest an aggressive, affirmative support for democracy and democratic institutions, and at the same time vigorously oppose and distrust all forms of outside interference in the conduct of Union affairs."

Reuther's statement is a crucial one, both because it demonstrated his approval of the merger and because it indicated the reasons for the merger. To Reuther, and to many other CIO leaders, one qualification for CIO leadership had become a willingness to take a stand against communism. The department store union leaders, in their decision to become anti-Communists, had once again found a powerful set of allies.[65]

In late May 1953, just days after the merger, workers went on strike at Hearn's, the 14th Street store which had long been Local 1250's main base of operations. As already noted, after the opening of Stuyvesant Town, Hearn's managers attempted to restructure the store, to offer residents of these exclusive complexes a more upscale shopping experience than the other bargain stores on 14th Street. From now on, managers proudly announced, "only first quality goods" would be carried in the store, and customers would have only indirect access to goods.[66]

Within two years, Hearn's managers learned what other store managers had already known: that such a process was not cost-effective. This was especially true after the 1951 opening of the Lane's store at 14th Street and Fifth Avenue, another self-service, downscale store. Launched with tremendous fanfare, including an hour-and-a-half television show and massive charity donations to a fund drive to fight cerebral palsy, the opening of Lane's was one of the most important signs of the expansion of self-service retailing in New York City. It was an immediate and tremendous success. At least 50,000 customers attended the store's opening day, and the store did an estimated $175,000 worth of business that day. "By midday," *Women's Wear Daily* reporter Fred Eichelbaum wrote, "the crowds became so dense on the street floor that the management decided to close the doors and admit new waves of shoppers only in safe intervals. At times the 'human sea' of shoppers caused a complete paralysis of movement."[67]

Combined with Klein's and Ohrbach's, the opening of Lane's emphasized even more strongly the role of 14th Street as a center of downscale, self-service retailing. In 1952, therefore, Hearn's managers again decided to change the way in which the store was run, rapidly cutting both prices and services, to once again create "a 14th Street Store with 14th Street prices," one which could successfully compete with other, cheaper 14th Street stores. Managers quickly began cutting jobs, and the cuts were more severe than anyone had expected. Though Local 1250 organizer Peter Montanaro estimated when the job cuts were first announced that only 125 workers would lose their jobs, Hearn's managers had other plans. In July 1952, when the cuts began, Hearn's employed nearly 2000 workers at two stores (the main 14th Street store as well as a small branch store in the Bronx). By May 1953 the company employed only 800 workers. In addition to this mass firing, managers demanded severe concessions from workers who remained on the job, requiring Hearn's workers to put in extra hours on Monday nights in order to compete more effectively with the other stores on 14th Street.[68]

Throughout this transformation, union members and leaders alike willingly negotiated away both the jobs of many members and the rights of the workers who still had jobs. They did so in part because of the recent closing of Loeser's and the constant if unspoken threat that the same fate might befall Hearn's if they did not make concessions. In addition, store managers, particularly owner/manager Albert Greenfield, promised the union that the job cuts would be temporary, at least according to union organizers. As Montanaro described it to a Local 1250 membership meeting when one round of job cuts began in July 1952, they had managers' assurance that "in a short time, all [workers] will be back on the job, plus more."[69]

Whatever they may have promised, managers did not rehire workers. Instead, they continued cutting jobs. Some departments were closed down altogether and reopened as leased concessions, which were not covered by the union's contract. Hundreds of other workers were simply laid off. In the spring of 1953, when the union's contract expired, union organizers discovered that they had greatly underestimated managers' ruthlessness. For several weeks, managers at Hearn's stalled negotiations, and then on May 9, when Hearn's shop steward Max Klarer demanded that managers cease stalling and begin negotiating immediately, store managers promptly fired Klarer.[70]

On Thursday, May 14, workers at the two Hearn's stores began what *Women's Wear Daily* described as a "sit-down strike." Cashiers sat at their jobs, but refused to wait on customers. One customer "selected a spool of ribbon and asked a salesgirl to put it in a bag," but the worker refused. A reporter for *Women's Wear Daily* attempted to get change, but the cashiers would not even do that. The telephone operators went even further to disrupt store activity, informing all customers that "the store was not open for business and that there was labor trouble." Hearn's managers called the police and for the remainder of the day store managers themselves manned the telephones.[71]

Hearn's president Clement Conole responded by going down to the silent selling floor, where all the workers were standing around informing customers that the store was on strike. Conole made a prepared announcement informing workers that they must either get to work or leave; workers ignored him. At 4:30 P.M., accompanied by police officers and store executives, Conole went down to the selling floor again. "At 10:10," Conole announced, "I spoke to you to perform your regular duties or leave the store. Since you have not done so, management has no other alternative then [sic] to advise you that you are herewith discharged for the illegal seizure and retention of our premises. We again ask that you leave the premises." The strikers had now lost their jobs.[72]

Hearn's managers, united with other managers as part of the Retail Labor Standards Association, drew on the methods other association members had used to fight the unions, especially those employed during the Oppenheim Collins strike. First, Hearn's managers took out large advertisements in the city's major newspapers, calling the public's attention to the union leaders' radical politics. In a *New York Times* advertisement, Hearn's managers claimed that

> Arthur Osman . . . has for 16 long years spoken again and again for Soviet causes and Soviet ideas . . . David Livingston . . . was sentenced to 3 months in jail for refusing to show . . . union records to a Federal Grand Jury investigating subversive activities and espionage. . . . William Michelson . . . was identified by former FBI agent T.C. Kirkpatrick 'as a member of the Communist Party who has sat in at secret conferences and caucuses of the various officers of the Communist Party.'[73]

Also in a rehash of managers' successful tactics at Oppenheim Collins, Hearn's managers sought to take advantage of the divisions between the different retail workers' unions, inviting the RCIPA into the store to organize the scabs. The RCIPA agreed, at least initially, notifying the NLRB that they were prepared for a union election of the Hearn's scabs. (As the national CIO became more involved in the strike, the RCIPA would withdraw their request for a union election at Hearn's.) In addition, Hearn's managers immediately applied for and received an injunction against mass picketing. The injunction limited the number of picketers to 200 at the 14th Street store and 50 at the smaller Bronx store. Finally, store managers threatened to close down if the unions' remaining picketers did not desist. In a slightly veiled reference to the Loeser's closing a few months earlier, managers at Hearn's warned that "if this store were put out of business it would not be the first one they have succeeded in undermining." In fact, Albert Greenfield argued at a stockholder's meeting that the "undermining" was purposeful, making the far-fetched claim that the Communists who ran the unions "want to destroy all business," and were using the strike to do so. Store managers also came up with new tactics, such as offering a "strike price" discount for any customers willing to cross the picket lines.[74]

If store managers drew on their history to win the strike, workers attempted to follow suit. In particular, strikers returned to their 1930s tactics by making extensive use of pageantry and publicity stunts. On the day of the highly publicized coronation of Queen Elizabeth II of England, for example, Hearn's workers held a mock coronation of a queen of their own. Eleanor Cerro, a telephone operator at Hearn's, dressed up in a fancy gown, mounted a horse-drawn carriage (decorated with a banner reading "Royal Blessings to 800 Workers on Strike at Hearns Dept. Stores"), and accepted a crown from Carl Andren, the former leader of Bloomingdale's Local 3 who had since become vice-president of District 65.[75]

From the beginning, Hearn's strikers demonstrated that their message of choice was a demonstration of their support for anti-communism. Strikers carried picket signs calling potential shoppers' attention to managers' "Un-American Store," where managers had "fired Veterans and Gold Star Mothers." Other picket signs called on the public: "Let's not be 20% Americans—Make Hearn's negotiate 100% American way!" By calling attention to their own patriotism, as mothers of soldiers and as veterans, and their opposition to the "Un-American" activities of store managers, strikers attempted to use anti-communism against Hearn's managers.[76]

The strikers won at least some public support through these anti-Communist messages. Unlike the Gimbel's and Oppenheim Collins strikes of the 1940s and even the less-controversial five-and-dime sit-down strikes of 1937, some mainstream newspapers enthusiastically supported the Hearn's strike. The *New York Post,* for example, ran a lengthy editorial supporting the strike, condemning the "large-scale advertising campaign which Hearns has directed against the leadership of the union in an effort to create the impression that the strike is Communist-led and Communist-inspired." (Hearn's managers briefly pulled all their advertising from the *Post* in protest.) In addition to the *Post*'s editorial, television news programs aired frequent stories on the strike, including one on the crowning of the Hearn's strike queen. In addition, WABC broadcast a special 15-minute program, "The Story Behind the Hearn's Strike," in which union leaders (Arthur Osman and William

Figure 4

The disastrous strike at Hearn's, 1953. After a court injunction limited the strikers to three picketers, this is all that was left of the picket lines: three people with signs in front of the entrance to the store. (Courtesy of Robert F. Wagner Labor Archives, New York University, United Automobile Workers of America, District 65 Photographs Collection)

Michelson, most prominently) and five strikers spoke directly to the audience about the cause and goals of the strike.[77]

Like the local media, national union leaders strongly endorsed the Hearn's strike. Both AFL and CIO leaders voiced their support for the Hearn's strike, writing letters to the NLRB demanding that the board bring a suit against Hearn's over the company's unfair labor practices, such as the firing of union members without adequate notice. Even former enemies of the union, like Mike Quill, who had only two years earlier threatened to picket those stores which retained contracts with the department store unions, now called on the public to boycott Hearn's. In addition, the Teamsters voted to support the strike, meaning that no union truck drivers crossed the picket line. (Store managers were able to continue deliveries by using nonunion truck drivers.)[78]

CIO leaders also attempted to counteract managers' claim that the strike was inspired by communism. Walter Reuther called store managers' claims "selfish and unrealistic," and assured the public that the strike at Hearn's was "a legitimate strike over important economic issues," and he drew his readers' attention to the "continual use of deceitful propaganda" by Hearn's managers as a particularly despicable practice.[79]

The most important role CIO leaders played in supporting the strike was in their extensive fundraising for the strike fund, which grew rapidly. By mid-June, with the help of the CIO leaders, the union had raised $350,000 for the strike fund, by far the largest strike fund the union had ever had at its disposal. The New York City CIO Council also agreed to pay for newspaper advertisements to counter Hearn's anti-Communist advertising campaign.[80]

Perhaps due to the active roles played by so many national union leaders, the strikers also got strong support from local politicians during the Hearn's strike. Like the CIO and AFL union leaders, New York Senator Herbert Lehman called upon the NLRB to make sure that "the present law be fairly and reasonably applied, and that an unfair labor practices complaint be issued." Similarly, mayoral candidate Robert Wagner promised the union that if he became mayor, he would use his "power and influence to create a speedy settlement of the Hearn's strike."[81]

National citizens' groups also took strong pro-union stands. In particular, the liberal anti-Communist Americans for Democratic Action (ADA) and the National Association for the Advancement of Colored People (NAACP) both endorsed the strike. The ADA created a fact-finding committee to gather evidence to further disprove managers' claims that the strike was a Communist conspiracy. The NAACP's role was even more important, especially after Hearn's managers attempted to recruit African American workers as strikebreakers by offering them opportunities for sales jobs. The NAACP not only condemned this act publicly (spreading its message to a number of different New York City African American newspapers), but the Executive Board of the New York City chapter of the NAACP also released a statement that "the strike at the Hearn stores merits the support of all fair-minded people in our city."[82]

It was an impressive strike in many ways, many of them attributable to strikers' successful manipulation of anti-communism. Through adopting anti-communism as a defining concept for the strike, union organizers had recruited more powerful and more numerous allies than in any other strike they had conducted. And with hundreds of thousands of dollars at their disposal (in large part due to these supporters), the strikers were able to mount a public relations campaign to rival managers' own.

Despite all these supporters, far more prestigious and arguably far more numerous than in earlier strikes, the Hearn's strike ended in disaster and defeat. There were several reasons for the defeat. First, and most important, liberal alliances were not the same thing as radical ones. The supporters in the Hearn's strike, despite their prominence, were supportive in a very different way than earlier coalitions. If during earlier strikes allies had challenged managers' control over public space and stores alike, the unions' allies during the Hearn's strike showed no interest in presenting similar challenges. Here the support consisted of funds and public statements, a far cry from the illegal disruption that had been such a powerful part of the unions' activities in earlier years.

In addition to the very different nature of the allies, the federal government played a far more direct role in the Hearn's strike than it had in the unions' successful prewar strikes. Despite the public outcry around the strike and the demands of many different labor leaders and liberal politicians, the NLRB dismissed all of the union's claims of unfair labor practices, sanctioning the firing of Klarer and the other Hearn's workers. Even worse for the union, that summer, a federal appellate court issued a second injunction. This injunction forbade any further mass picketing at Hearn's, limiting the strikers to three pickets at each entrance. A third injunction in October banned "all picketing" at Hearn's, charging that the sit-down strike was an "illegal act calculated to deliver a knockout blow at the very outset at the strike," as well as finding the unions guilty of "undue noise, shouting, booing, catcalling, chanting in unison, and unlawful interference with persons desiring to patronize plaintiff's stores." But the final defeat came not because of the government's decision, but out of the union's obedience to the government's decision. No one—neither union leaders, nor workers, nor their allies—suggested that violating the injunction would be an acceptable tactic. With the court willing to act and the NLRB refusing to do so, and with all parties involved determined to prove their support for the government (and therefore their anti-communism) by following the law, by November 1953 the end had come. As Local 3 organizer Murray Silverstein sadly admitted at a General Membership Meeting, "The Hearn strike for all intents and purposes is over. We [have] suffered a severe blow."[83]

With anti-communism as a central tenet of the union's political platform, the workers were once again able to assemble an extremely powerful set of allies during the Hearn's strike. But this same practice limited their ability to challenge the government's decisions, whether in the NLRB's refusal to intervene or in the judge's anti-picketing injunction. With the federal government standing behind managers' right to restructure the department stores, anti-Communist unions could not resist restructuring. It was in many respects the ultimate defeat for the radical unions that had once represented the possibility of unionized retail workers in America.

Conclusion

In the five years following their split from the RWDSU, union leaders desperately sought a way to expand retail workers' unions. They never found it. Union democracy, while it gained them the support of some workers, proved unable to win much support after the closing of Loeser's. Once the union could not protect members' jobs, members demanded that union leaders spend more time trying to fight layoffs and less time taking part in radical political activity. The result was that the union democracy practiced within these unions led directly to the union leaders' eventual adoption of anti-Communist politics.

Union democracy had other limits as well, most of them relating to the union's stance on gender issues. Between 1948 and 1953, as they ostensibly made the union more democratic, Communist union leaders put cheesecake photographs in the union newspaper, appointed increasing numbers of men to union leadership, and declared their determination to support the rights of breadwinners and heads of families within the union. This opposition to women's equality represents in part Communists' always contradictory attitude that women's equality was an important cause that was still far less important than both working-class interests and racial equality. Other explanations exist, however. First, union leaders were not immune from larger historical forces; the country as a whole shifted towards a more conservative gender system in the late 1940s and early 1950s, and union leaders may have simply been caught up in this larger change. Additionally, union leaders' determination to not alienate union members in these years made union leaders even more susceptible to shifting mainstream views, especially on issues they viewed as secondary.

Like union democracy, the anti-communism adopted by the department store unions was a more limiting tactic than it might have seemed at the time. It did keep union leaders from going to jail after Livingston's and Paley's brief sentences. It also kept workers satisfied that union leaders were not pursuing any hidden political agendas. At the same time, it could not allow workers the ability to challenge managerial restructuring, largely because it did not allow for any strident criticism of the government's actions. Adopting anti-communism as a central tenet meant that workers and union leaders alike had to either go along with the government's decisions or face doubts as to whether their anti-communism was genuine. At a moment when the government supported managers' right to make profits, even if those profits came at the expense of workers' control over their jobs, anti-communism was not a viable strategy to fight for workers' interests.

As a result of the Hearn's strike, the members and leaders of New York City's department store unions brought an end to any chance they might once have had of creating a powerful retail workers' union in America. The unions continued to represent the workers at most of the stores where they had signed contracts, and continued to play an important role in the city's labor movement as part of District 65. But they would expand no further. And even where they remained, the changes were quite evident. By 1953 store managers increasingly employed casual, part-time, and unskilled labor, an extremely difficult group of workers to organize. If there was a moment when New York City's department store unions seemed to be the first step towards a national union of retail workers, by 1953 that moment was largely over. The unions, and the workers they represented, had indeed suffered a severe blow in their failure to prevent managerial restructuring during the Hearn's strike, a blow from which the American labor movement still has not recovered.

Where Labor Lost,
and Why

Over the past ten years, store managers have been experimenting with even less labor-intensive forms of retailing. Beginning in the 1990s, managers at several stores, including large downscale chain stores like Wal-Mart, K-Mart, and Home Depot, began installing automated checkout counters in addition to the more traditional staffed checkout counters. Customers at these stores can now take their goods to the automated counters, scan their goods, either swipe a credit card or feed bills into the machine, place their goods in a plastic bag, and leave the store. If all goes well, it is now possible to go shopping without having any contact at all with any store workers, except perhaps for the security guards at the door. Luckily for store workers, to date these experiments have been generally unsuccessful. Frequent breakdowns and customer inexperience make the machines so inefficient that managers at a few stores have given up automated checkout counters as a complete loss. So far, according to one source, store managers have been unable to use the automated checkout machines to replace any workers, since workers must be on hand to replace the machines at a moment's notice. Despite that, the number of machines is increasing, going from present in 6 percent of all stores in 1999 to present in 19 percent by 2002.[1]

The labor movement's response has been relatively muted. In September of 2002, a reporter asked John Sweeney, president of the AFL-CIO, about the emergence of automated checkout machines. Sweeney's response was telling:

> Sweeney . . . chuckled as he recounted the frantic phone message he received from a concerned neighbor. "Have you seen those self-checkout machines in our grocery store?" she asked the labor leader, whose federation represents 13 million union workers. . . . Sweeney's eyes widened for effect as he quoted the caller: "What's going to happen to all those workers?" Sweeney—who said he has not used the self-scan giz-

mos that popped up in his store last month—put his neighbor's mind at ease. "The union is very much aware of this," Sweeney said, and there is a general understanding "that no workers will be displaced as a result."

In his confidence, Sweeney left out a few points, including the fact that many stores using the automated checkout machines are not unionized, making it difficult to imagine how he could guarantee that no workers would be displaced. He also forgot his history, not remembering that CIO leaders had made similar assurances when self-service emerged fifty years ago. With such a lack of attention and concern, it is difficult to imagine that the labor movement will reemerge in the retail sector in the near future.[2]

The American labor movement, it should be noted, continues to be relatively strong in certain sectors, even some white-collar sectors such as government jobs (where many workers are forbidden to strike, making these unions rather ineffective). But for white-collar workers in the private sector, retailing included, the American labor movement is virtually nonexistent, with only a tiny fraction of these employees organized into unions. For a moment during the Great Depression, it looked as though the American labor movement could have been a far more powerful and representative movement, one that had unions that represented large numbers of retail workers. For blue-collar workers in the factories, the sit-down strikes led to permanent and relatively powerful unions. But in retailing, the parallel sit-down strikes led to no such result.

This study has examined both why retail workers' unions succeeded initially and why these unions failed in the long run. Their successes were remarkable. New York City's department store workers formed unions at the largest retail stores in the world; they won the eight-hour day, significant pay raises, and public acclaim; and they forced the CIO, dominated though it was by notions of male blue-collar workers storming the factories, to set up a retail workers' union.

The successes of these unions were inherently related to communism. Communists recognized that department store workers were, after all, part of the working class, that these men and women deserved support in their efforts to form unions. The Communists who organized these unions also deserve credit for their recognition that labor struggles had to be carried on in imaginative and nontraditional ways. A strike had to be dynamic and inventive; it had to take advantage of the surrounding environment, to challenge managerial control wherever possible, inside the store as well as outside. The men and women who organized New York City's department store unions took full advantage of these tactics. Whether at Union Square or on 34th Street, the Communists were remarkably successful at taking advantage of struggles going on around the stores. Finally, the Communists were both willing and able to create broad-based coalitions, especially in their use of cultural activities to create the Popular Front. These were important achievements for which they deserve credit.

It is important to note that Communists were responsible for these achievements, not the Communist party. In many respects, in fact, the Communist party almost limited the unions' successes. Gussie Reed's letter to Michelson, for instance, and the narrow interpretation of Communist policy that it represented, could have had major effects on the unions' future had Michelson not chosen to ignore Reed's instructions. In addition, and perhaps even more important, at the height of the attacks on the union in the early 1950s, the Communist leaders of the unions decided to follow Party policy and engage workers in a debate about American foreign policy and the Korean War, rather than focusing on the rise of self-service retailing and the massive numbers of layoffs. It should be noted, however, that there is little evidence that they lost department store workers' support due to their following of Russian policy in the 1940s and early 1950s, as other historians have claimed happened with Communists in other sectors of the labor movement. In fact, the moment it seemed possible that union leaders would wholly lose workers' support by following such policies, Communist union leaders split with the CP and adopted an anti-Communist line.

The Communist party was hardly the most important factor limiting the successes of Communists. There were other issues that the unions never successfully confronted, most important among them race and gender. The alliances the unions formed had extremely surprising racial limits. Had the unions been willing to ally with the "Don't Buy Where You Can't Work" campaigns, for instance, they might have found themselves part of an even more powerful movement, one that challenged understandings not only of class, but of the racial divide that continues to plague the labor movement in many industries. Instead, they ignored these movements, for the most part adopting a relatively conservative understanding of the importance of a labor union, which held that the union was designed to protect workers already employed, not to worry about who was being employed. As a result, racial segregation—whether in the city or in the stores—faced only a few fleeting challenges from the department store unions.

An equally serious limit of Communist leadership was the Communists' fleeting commitment to women's equality within the unions. While certainly the leaders of the department store unions gave lip service to women's rights and recognized that women workers could and should form unions, the fact remains that little effort was made to encourage women workers to take leadership roles in these unions, and women's response to the cheesecake photographs in the union paper in the late 1940s indicates that they felt their roles within the union were limited in the extreme.

The ultimate failure of retail workers' unions in America, however, was the result not of these limits of the unions' leadership, important though those limits are, but rather of three interlocking historical developments. The first was the rise of anti-communism. Anti-communism led to the destruction of the coalitions that had served the unions so well in their early struggles. Just as important, it meant the destruction of the CIO's retail workers' union, the RWDSU. Anti-communism also gave employers a valuable weapon during strikes. It would severely weaken the unions, leaving them isolated and vulnerable. Closely linked to anti-communism, the rise of the middle class meant that the white-collar workers who had once played so important a role in the unions' struggles had now disappeared into the suburbs or into developments like Parkchester and Stuyvesant Town, ceasing to accept that they had anything to do with unions or, indeed, with workers. The third of these developments was the transformation of American consumption, particularly the rise of self-service retailing. Once self-service retailing was introduced, stores could function with casual and easily replaceable labor, a difficult group of workers to organize. With stores that relied on this sort of labor, the collapse of the national union, and the disappearance of their allies, further union organizing in retail stores was nearly impossible.

It was the combination of these factors during the Hearn's strike that meant the final blow against New York City's department store unions. The government stepped in and declared that managers had a right to make profits through instituting self-service, and that unions had no right to interfere in that process through picket lines. This decision was momentous not only in its content, but also in its context. Certainly it was not unique; judges had issued similar injunctions during the unions' very first strikes at Klein's and Ohrbach's. But with union leaders and members clinging to the hope that the coalition formed around liberal anti-communism would adequately replace the coalitions once formed around communism, the injunction during the Hearn's strike took on a different meaning entirely. To violate the government's order would have meant adopting a radical, not a liberal, response. And to do so while attempting to fend off accusations that their liberal anti-communism was a sham was nearly impossible. To the leaders of the union as well as to their allies, anti-communism meant respect for the government's rulings, even when those rulings were against workers' interests. The strike ended in defeat, and with that defeat ended any chance of preventing the transformation of retail work.

The history of these retail workers' unions must be integrated into our larger understandings of the history of the labor movement during the CIO era. Historians who use male blue-collar workers to represent the history of the CIO allow the roles of communism and anti-communism in American history to remain underanalyzed. Male blue-collar workers were critical both to the CIO's success and to its representation throughout the union's history, but historians have all too frequently allowed them to stand in for the entire CIO workforce, including the CIO's advances in retailing only as a minor and peripheral anecdote. But the peripheral nature of unions in the retail field was itself a result of specific historical events. Without understanding these events, we fall far too easily into thinking that retail workers are fundamentally more difficult to organize than are workers in manufacturing or construction, or—even more tragically—we forget about the existence of retail workers' unions altogether. To do so represents a dangerous historical fallacy. Retail workers could and did form powerful and lasting unions given the correct historical circumstances. For a moment in the 1930s those circumstances existed: workers found leaders with diverse political and tactical approaches, and with strong connections to other social movements. Managerial restructuring and the concurrent rise of anti-communism in the late 1940s and early 1950s brought this historical moment to an end, crippling the American labor movement in the process.

Now, at the turn of the twenty-first century, there are few hopeful signs for the future of the American labor movement in the retail industry. Certainly John Sweeney's reported chuckle was not really warranted under the circumstances. In their 2003–4 strikes, the United Food and Commercial Workers took on the grocery industry in Southern California, and lost, as store managers used the threat of Wal-Mart openings and store closings to justify cutting benefits to a hesitant public. The UFCW's defeat in the Southern California strike, the largest retail workers' strike in American history, does not bode well for the future of the American labor movement. Until and unless union organizers figure out a way to recapture some of the dynamic radicalism and solidarity that characterized the 1930s labor movement, unions in American retailing—and indeed, in America as a whole—will remain ineffective, little more than fading shadows of the mass organizations they once were.

NOTES

Introduction

1. Bureau of Labor Statistics, "Union Members in 2004," News Release (January 27, 2005), 1. For unionization rates being at their lowest levels since the 1920s, see George Lipsitz, *Rainbow at Midnight: Labor and Culture in the 1940s* (Urbana: University of Illinois Press, 1994), 8.

2. "Union Members in 2004," 1.

3. For one historian's interpretation of labor's failure to organize more retail workers, see Tami J. Friedman, "The Workers Aren't Nontraditional—But The Strategy Should Be," *Dollars and Sense* (September/October 2002), 8.

4. There is a vast literature on department stores, beginning in the 1940s with histories written largely from the perspective of the managers; see R. M. Hower, *History of Macy's of New York, 1858–1919: Chapters in the Evolution of the Department Store* (Cambridge, MA: Harvard University Press, 1943) and Hans Pasdermadjian, *The Department Store: Its Origins, Evolution and Economics* (London: Newman Books, 1954). By the 1970s and 1980s, however, this literature was being challenged, most importantly by Theresa McBride, "A Woman's World: Department Stores and the Evolution of Women's Employment, 1870–1920," *French Historical Studies* 10 (Fall 1978), 664–83, Richard Sennett, *The Fall of Public Man* (New York: Knopf, 1976), and Rosalind Williams, *Dream Worlds: Mass Consumption in Late Nineteenth Century France* (Berkeley: University of California Press, 1981). By the late 1980s and early 1990s, Benson was one among many historians looking at department stores anew. See, for example, William Leach, *Land of Desire: Merchants, Power, and the Rise of a New American Culture* (New York: Pantheon Books, 1993), Michael B. Miller, *The Bon Marché: Bourgeois Culture and the Department Store, 1869–1920* (Princeton, NJ: Princeton University Press, 1994), Gail Reekie, *Temptations: Sex, Selling, and the Department Store* (St. Leonards, Australia: Allen & Unwin, 1993), Lisa Tiersten, *Marianne in the Market: Envisioning Consumer Culture in Fin-de-Siècle France* (Berkeley: University of California Press, 2001), and the various essays in Geoffrey Crossick and Serge Jaumain, eds., *Cathedrals of Consumption: The European Department Store, 1850–1939* (Aldershot, England: Ashgate Press, 1999).

5. For Benson's claim that shared womanhood united customers and workers, see Susan Porter Benson, *Counter Cultures: Saleswomen, Managers, and Customers in American Department Stores, 1890–1940* (Urbana: University of Illinois Press, 1988), 3–4.

6. Leo Troy, "Distribution of Union Membership among the States, 1939 and 1953," Occasional Paper 56 (New York: National Bureau of Economic Research, Inc., 1957), 24.

7. For a good summary of the new labor history argument, see James Green,

"Working-Class Militancy in the Depression," *Radical America* 6:6 (1972), 24. For Aronowitz and Lynd's studies, see Staughton Lynd, "The Possibility of Radicalism in the Early 1930s: The Case of Steel," *Radical America* 6:6 (1972), 36–65, and Stanley Aronowitz, "'Which Side Are You On?': Trade Unions in America," *Liberation* 16:7 (1971), 20–41. For other works that make a similar argument in the 1970s, see both Stanley Aronowitz, *False Promises: The Shaping of American Working Class Consciousness* (New York: McGraw-Hill, 1973), 214–63, and Jeremy Brecher, *Strike!* (Boston, MA: South End Press, 1977).

8. For the new historians of communism, see especially Roger Keeran, *The Communist Party and the Auto Workers Unions* (Bloomington: Indiana University Press, 1980), Mark Naison, *Communists in Harlem During the Depression* (New York: Grove Press, 1983), Ron Schatz, *The Electrical Workers: A History of Labor at General Electric and Westinghouse, 1923–1960* (Urbana: University of Illinois Press, 1983), and Robin Kelley, *Hammer and Hoe: Alabama Communists During the Great Depression* (Chapel Hill: University of North Carolina Press, 1990). For Cochran's consensus-style history of the Communists' role in the labor movement, see Bert Cochran, *Labor and Communism: The Conflict That Shaped American Unions* (Princeton, NJ: Princeton University Press, 1977). For the important debate between this school of historians and Theodore Draper, one of the founders of the consensus school of the history of communism, see Theodore Draper, "American Communism Revisited," *The New York Review of Books* (May 9, 1985), 32–37, and Draper, "The Popular Front Revisited," *The New York Review of Books* (May 30, 1985), 44–50; for the responses to Draper, see "Revisiting American Communism: An Exchange," *The New York Review of Books* (August 15, 1985), 40–44.

9. Even in the early 1970s, Stanley Aronowitz had argued for the generally conservative role played by Communist union leaders; see Aronowitz, "'Which Side Are You On?'," 35. For the more recent studies, see Nelson Lichtenstein, *Labor's War at Home: The CIO In World War II* (Cambridge: Cambridge University Press, 1982), 127, 145–46, and George Lipsitz, *Rainbow at Midnight; Labor and Culture in the 1940s* (Urbana: University of Illinois Press, 1994), 196–97.

10. See Elsa Jane Dixler, *The Women Question: Women and the American Communist Party, 1929–1941* (Doctoral Thesis, Yale University, 1974), Elizabeth Faue, *Community of Suffering and Struggle: Women, Men, and the Labor Movement in Minneapolis, 1915–1945* (Chapel Hill, NC: University of North Carolina Press, 1991), and especially Van Gosse, "'To Organize In Every Neighborhood, In Every Home': The Gender Politics of American Communists Between the Wars," *Radical History Review* 50 (1991), 108–41. Most recently, Kate Weigand has argued that these efforts eventually bore fruit in the women's movement of the 1960s; see Weigand, *Red Feminism: American Communism and the Making of Women's Liberation* (Baltimore: Johns Hopkins University Press. 2001).

Chapter 1.

1. Ruth Papa, telephone interview with author, January 14, 2001 (hereafter Papa interview).

2. Karl Monroe, quoted in Milton Meltzer, *Brother, Can You Spare A Dime?: The Great Depression, 1929–39* (New York: Knopf, 1969), 35–36. For homeless people sleeping in Union Square Park, see Nicolai Likovsky, "Union Square, executed for the Public Works of Art Project," New York Public Library Picture Collection.

3. Matthew Josephson, *Infidel In The Temple: A Memoir of the Nineteen-Thirties* (New York: Knopf, 1967), 126–27. Jacob Stein, interviewed by B. Hathaway [Library of Congress, Manuscript Division, WPA Federal Writers' Project Collection (hereafter FWP Collection)], December 27, 1938. See also Wayne Walden, "Conversations In A Park" (FWP Collection), October 24, 1938, and Arnold Eagle, "Man With Newspaper at Political Discussion Meeting, Union Square," undated photograph, "Union Square—Park And General 2/2 (Photos)" folder, Museum of the City of New York Archives (hereafter MCNY). While all of these sources indicate (it seems accurately) that most of the participants in these discussions were working-class men, women participated as well; see both Gertrude Reiss, interviewed by author, Brooklyn, NY, November 30, 2000 (hereafter Gertrude Reiss interview), and Arnold Eagle, "Men and Women in Discussion, Union Square," "Union Square—Park And General 2/2 (Photos)" folder, MCNY.

4. Reiss interview.

5. Albert Halper, *Good-bye, Union Square: A Writer's Memoir of the Thirties* (Chicago: Quadrangle Press, 1970), 79. For the history of Union Square, see Tamara Thompson, "Patriotism and Protest: The First Hundred Years of Union Square Park," *Columbia Journal of American Studies 5:1* (2002), 136–64.

6. For the street peddlers, see Halper, *Good-bye, Union Square*, 79, and Arnold Eagle, "Female Street Vendor At Union Square," Undated Photograph, "Union Square—Park and General 2/2 (Photos)" folder, MCNY. For the importance of Klein's and Ohrbach's, see Robert Hendrickson, *The Grand Emporiums: The Illustrated History of America's Great Department Stores* (New York: Stein And Day, 1979), 443–45. See also Herman Kirschbaum, interviewed by B. Hathaway (FWP Collection), September 1938–January 1939. For the quotation, see Reiss interview. For the effects of the Depression on Klein's in particular, see "S. Klein: On-The-Square Store Plays Santa to Its Employees," *Newsweek* (December 29, 1934), 29.

7. Photograph of S. Klein's, 1928; United States History, Local History and Genealogy Division, New York Public Library; reprinted in Ellen Wiley Todd, *The "New Woman" Revisited: Painting and Gender Politics on Fourteenth Street* (Berkeley: University of California Press, 1993), 100. Photograph of CP Headquarters on Union Square, Manhattan, 1930, reprinted in Michael Brown et al., *New Studies in the Politics and Culture of U.S. Communism* (New York: Monthly Review Press, 1993), 14.

8. "110,000 Demonstrate In New York For Jobless Demands; Defy Police" *Daily Worker* (March 7, 1930), 1, 3. See also "Workers' Newsreel, Unemployment Special, 1931" newsreel footage (New York: The Museum of Modern Art, 198–), and Harvey Klehr, *The Heyday of American Communism: The Depression Years* (New York: Basic Books, Inc., 1984), 33–38.

9. Alfred E. Smith, quoted in "Union Square Marks Its Centenary Gayly," *New York Times* (April 24, 1932), 17.

10. "Union Square is Ready for its Centennial," *New York Times* (April 22, 1932), 20; "Union Square Marks Its Centenary Gayly," *New York Times* (April 24, 1932), 17.

11. For the May Day march, see "Workers Line Both Sides Of Streets Despite Heavy Downpour in New York," *Daily Worker* (May 2, 1932), 1. For the formation of the Union Square Association, see "Form Union Square Group," *New York Times* (May 13, 1932), 35. There is no record of any activity conducted by the Union Square Association after its founding.

12. Anne Haicken, interviewed by author, Belleair Bluffs, FL, August 4, 2000 (hereafter Haicken interview); Josephson, *Infidel in the Temple*, 126–27.

13. "'Frontier' On Union Square! (But Not For Us: We Put It In Shops)," *Daily Worker* (June 20, 1930), 1. For more details on the Veterans of Foreign Wars parade, see Thompson, "Patriotism and Protest," 155–56.

14. Jeremy Brecher, *Strike!* (Cambridge, MA: South End Press, 1997 [Revised and Updated Edition]), 159–60.

15. Most, but not all, scholars of the Depression have agreed that these years are best characterized as years of social and economic upheaval, resulting in the New Deal. The most important dissenter is Melvyn Dubofsky, "Not So 'Turbulent Years': Another Look at the American 1930s," *Amerikastudien/American Studies,* 24 (1979), 5–20. Scholars who have, more or less, agreed that the Depression represented a time of upheaval which was met by the New Deal include Lizabeth Cohen, *Making a New Deal: Industrial Workers in Chicago, 1919–1939* (Cambridge: Cambridge University Press, 1990), and Frances Fox Piven and Richard Cloward, *Poor People's Movements: Why They Succeed, How They Fail* (New York: Vintage Books, 1979 [Paperback Edition]), 41–180.

16. "S. Klein: On-The-Square Store Plays Santa," 29.

17. For the shoppers in Union Square, see Haicken interview, Papa interview, and Reiss interview. Reiss, who lived in Brooklyn at the time, never worked in the stores but did support work during the strike, and remembered shopping at Klein's and Ohrbach's frequently. Papa, who lived in the Bronx, also remembered shopping at the two stores, particularly Ohrbach's, which she said had even nicer clothes, but remembered these shopping trips as special occasions rather than weekly or even monthly occurrences. For Klein's profits, see "S. Klein: On-The-Square Store Plays Santa," 29. For the high quality of the merchandise available at Klein's, see Elmer Rice, *Minority Report: An Autobiography* (New York: Simon and Schuster, 1963), 257

18. Halper, *Good-bye, Union Square*, 100.

19. "S. Klein: On-The-Square Store Plays Santa," 29. Haicken interview.

20. For the close supervision and the responsibility to catch shoplifters, see Leane Zugsmith, *A Time to Remember* (New York: Random House, 1936), 60; further discussion of Zugsmith's relationship to the unions will be provided in later chapters. For the ethnic ties between customers and workers, see Haicken interview. For the number of store workers at Klein's and Ohrbach's (there were 1200 at Klein's, and 1400 at Ohrbach's), see "S. Klein: On-The-Square Store Plays Santa," 28, and "Girl Striker Heckles LaGuardia; Chained to Box, Foils Ejection, *New York Times* (January 21, 1935), "Clippings" File, DSSO Papers.

21. "S. Klein: On-The-Square Store Plays Santa," 29; Stella Ormsby, "The Other Side of the Profile," *The New Republic* (August 17, 1932), 21.

22. Letter from Ben Davis on *The Negro Liberator* stationery, dated April 27, 1935 to the Committee of Unemployed Office, Store and Professional Workers, Clarina Michelson Papers, Box 3, Folder 2.

23. Nathan Ohrbach, *Getting Ahead in Retailing* (New York: McGraw-Hill, 1935), 174; for the lack of newspaper advertisements, "S. Klein: On-The-Square Store Plays Santa." For Klein on shop windows, see "S. Klein Plans 'No Fancy Stuff,' But He'll Be Ready for Fair Crowds,'" *Women's Wear Daily* (March 31, 1939), 7.

24. Ohrbach, *Getting Ahead In Retailing*, 62–65, 101–2. For Julia Jacobs, see "S. Klein: On-The-Square Store Plays Santa," 29. For the ethnicity of the workers, and for women as the overwhelmingly majority of Klein's and Ohrbach's employees (as well as the majority of the strikers), see Ormsby, "The Other Side of the Profile," and Haicken interview.

25. For store managers' determination to regulate workers' appearance, see "Stores Shy At Fat Clerks As Taking Too Much Space," *New York Times* (May 13, 1930), 31. For workers' dress codes, see Gertrude Sykes, "Dress Regulations in New York Metropolitan Stores," *Journal of Retailing* (January 1929), 28–29; during summer months, managers allowed workers to wear tan and gray clothing at some stores.

26. Nathan M. Ohrbach, *Getting Ahead in Retailing*, 37–38. On supervision, see also Elaine Abelson, *When Ladies Go A-Thieving: Middle-Class Shoplifters in the Victorian Department Store* (Oxford: Oxford University Press, 1989), 99–111, 133–35.

27. Susan Porter Benson, *Counter Cultures: Saleswomen, Managers, and Customers in American Department Stores, 1890–1940* (Urbana, Illinois: University of Illinois Press, 1988), 182–84, 196. For the announcement of shorter hours at Hearn's, see Julia Cameron, "Shorter Working Hours," *Journal of Retailing* (October 1927), 21.

28. Ormsby, "The Other Side of the Profile," 21; Todd, *The "New Woman" Revisited*, 257.

29. Benson, *Counter Cultures*, 187–89; 196; Ormsby, "The Other Side of the Profile," 21; for slightly later opening hours at Ohrbach's, see "Ohrbach Employees To Share In Profits," *New York Times* (June 17, 1930), 52; for the forty-hour week as a crucial strike demand, see "Department Store Strike Front," *Working Woman* (February 1935), 3.

30. Ormsby, "The Other Side of the Profile," 21. See also Office of War Information, Untitled Photograph [S. Klein's, trying on dresses], Museum of the City of New York, gift of the Department of Local Government, Public Record Office of South Australia.

31. The change may not have been as dramatic as these figures suggest; this second study, it should be noted, did not include temporary workers in calculating the turnover numbers, while approximately one-fourth of the store managers who participated in the first study did include temporary and seasonal employees in reporting their numbers. Nonetheless, O. Preston Robinson, a specialist in department store per-

sonnel relations and Associate Professor of Retailing at New York University's School of Retailing, did claim that "economic conditions" during the Depression tended to reduce labor turnover. For the first study, see O. Preston Robinson, "Labor Turnover In New York Metropolitan Stores," *Journal of Retailing* (October 1930), 88; for the 1936 statistics, as well as Robinson's interpretation of the change, see Robinson, *Retail Personnel Relations* (New York: Prentice-Hall, 1940), 361–63.

32. For a worker who left retailing altogether after a brief stint in Ohrbach's, see Anne Haicken interview. For one who moved from these stores into a career within the upscale stores, see Irving Fajans, interviewed by May Swenson (February 1, 1939), FWP Collection (hereafter Fajans interview).

33. "S. Klein: On-The-Square Store Plays Santa," 28–29; Benson, *Counter Cultures,* 194–95; "Ohrbach Employes To Share In Profits," *New York Times* (June 17, 1930), 48; Ann Barton, "Home Life," *Daily Worker* (January 28, 1935), "Clippings," folder, Department Store Strikes and Organizing in the 1930s Collection, Tamiment Library, New York University (hereafter "Clippings," DSSO Collection).

34. Ann Barton, "Home Life," "Clippings," DSSO Collection.

35. Irving Bernstein, *Turbulent Years: A History of the American Worker, 1933–41* (Boston: Houghton-Mifflin, 1970), 34.

36. "NIRA Hurdles: Auditing The New Deal," *Business Week* (August 18, 1934), 19.

37. Melvyn Dubofsky, *The State and Labor in Modern America* (Chapel Hill: University of North Carolina Press, 1994), 115.

38. Alice Kessler-Harris, *Out To Work: A History of Wage-Earning Women in the United States* (Oxford: Oxford University Press, 1982), 151–71; the quotation is from p. 156. For the family wage, see Martha May, "Bread Before Roses: American Workingmen, Labor Unions and the Family Wage," in Ruth Milkman, *Women, Work & Protest: A Century of U.S. Women's Labor History* (London: Routledge, 1985), 1–21. There were, of course, notable exceptions to the sexism that dominated the labor movement, most important among them in the garment trades, where women played fundamental roles in leading the unions. However, these unions, despite the attention they have received (and deserved) from historians, were nonetheless exceptional in this regard. For gender and the garment workers' unions, see especially Nan Enstad, *Ladies of Labor, Girls of Adventure: Working Women, Popular Culture and Labor Politics* (Columbia University Press, June, 1999), Elizabeth Ewen, *Immigrant Women in the Land of Dollars: Life and Culture on the Lower East Side* (New York: Monthly Review Press, 1985), Susan Glenn, *Daughters of the Shtetl: Life and Labor in the Immigrant Generation* (Ithaca, NY: Cornell University Press, 1991), and Annelise Orleck, *Common Sense and a Little Fire: Women and Working-Class Politics in the United States, 1900–1965* (Chapel Hill: The University of North Carolina Press, 1995).

39. Ruth Pinkson, interviewed by author, Garret Park, Maryland, March 10, 2000 (hereafter Pinkson interview)

40. "Fight! Don't Starve: Demands For Unemployment Insurance Made Upon the United States Congress" (TUUL pamphlet, 1931), "Publications Relating to the Trade Union Unity League," Vertical File, Tamiment Library, New York University. Elizabeth Faue, *Community of Suffering and Struggle* (Chapel Hill: University of

North Carolina Press, 1991), 65–99. For a more historicized understanding of gender and American Communism, see Van Gosse, "'To Organize In Every Neighborhood, In Every Home': The Gender Politics of American Communists Between the Wars," *Radical History Review* 50 (1991), 108–41.

41. "What Would You Do?" The *Working Woman* Contest, *Working Woman* (December 1934), 5. Women's union auxiliaries will be discussed further in chapter 2. On the issue of birth control see Grace Hutchins, "Birth Control," *Working Woman* (August 1935), 26; Dr. Margaret Lamont, "What Women Should Know," *Working Woman* (February 1934), 15. For an example of the articles on consumer struggles which appeared in *Working Woman* see Dora Rich, "Organize—Fight Against High Cost Of Living," *Working Woman* (November 1933), 10. For the history of consumer-based protest, see both Dana Frank, *Purchasing Power: Consumer Organizing, Gender, and the Seattle Labor Movement, 1919–29* (Cambridge: Cambridge University Press, 1994), Annelise Orleck, *Common Sense and a Little Fire* (Chapel Hill, NC: University of North Carolina Press, 1995), and Susan Levine, "Workers' Wives: Gender, Class, and Consumerism in the 1920's US," *Gender and History* 3, no. 11 (1991), 45–64. "Effects of Unemployment on Workers' Wives," *Working Woman* (February 1930), 3.

42. For one discussion of women in unions and strikes, see "Department Store Strike Front," *Working Woman* (February 1935), 3.

43. "Trade Union Unity League: Its Program, Structure, Methods, and History," undated pamphlet, pp. 43–44, "Publications Relating to the Trade Union Unity League," Vertical File.

44. See "Editorials," *Office Worker* (February 1935), 2; for the age of OWU members and strikers in particular, see also Arnold Honig, "The Klein-Ohrbach Strikes," *Office Worker* (February 1935), 3, "Clippings," DSSO Collection. Much of the information on gender and the OWU is taken from or confirmed by Pinkson interview. While Pinkson did suggest that men tended to be "macho" even within the OWU, she also observed that it was to a lesser extent than in the United Office and Professional Workers of America, where she worked as a West Coast organizer a few years later.

45. Pinkson interview; "Gigantic Demonstration in Union Square," *Office Worker* (May 1933), 1; see also Charles Rivers, "May Day March, New York, 1935," Photograph, "Union Square—Park And General 2/2 (Photos)" folder, MCNY.

46. Clarina Michelson, interviewed by Debra Bernhardt, New York, October 20, 1979 (hereafter Clarina Michelson interview). For her participation in the LSNR, which was not covered in her interview, see LSNR stationery and "Fight Discrimination Against Negro Workers!" flyer, both in Clarina Michelson Papers, Box 2, Folder 10, and "To All Store and Office Workers on 125th Street, Negro and White!" flyer, Clarina Michelson Papers, Box 3, Folder 2.

47. "S. Klein: On-The-Square Store Plays Santa," 29.

48. Arnold Honig (A Klein Striker), "The Klein-Ohrbach Strikes," *Office Worker* (February 1935), 3.

49. For the economic pressures faced by strikers and scabs alike, see Ann Barton, "Home Life;" Pinkson interview confirms this, as does Zugsmith's description of Aline. For the anti-picketing writ, see "125 Pickets Seized At Ohrbach Store,"

The New York Times (February 17, 1935), "Clippings," DSSO Collection. For the numbers of strikers and workers, see also "S. Klein: On-The-Square Store Plays Santa," 28, and "Girl Striker Heckles LaGuardia; Chained to Box, Foils Ejection" *New York Times* (January 21, 1935), "Clippings," DSSO Collection.

50. Leane Zugsmith, *A Time to Remember,* 211–13. It is possible that Zugsmith decided to use a theatrical scene after seeing a play about the strike; there was, at least according to one source, a play about the Klein's-Ohrbach's strikes being produced off-Broadway by the Theatre Collective. So far, neither copies nor detailed descriptions of the play have been found. For the single citation referring to the play, see Irving Bernstein, *A Caring Society: The New Deal, the Worker, and the Great Depression: A History of the American Worker, 1933–1941* (Boston: Houghton Mifflin, 1985), 219.

51. For the term "monkey business," see Clarina Michelson interview and Ruth Pinkson interview. Anne Haicken, somewhat curiously, did not remember the term, although she remembered participating in some of the actions which Michelson and Pinkson referred to as "monkey business."

52. Ruth Pinkson, "Life and Times of an Elderly Red Diaper Baby," in Judy Kaplan and Linn Shapiro, eds., *Red Diapers: Growing Up In The Communist Left* (Urbana: University of Illinois Press, 1998), 233. Zugsmith, *A Time to Remember,* 251; Honig, "The Klein-Ohrbach Strikes," *Office Worker* (February 1935), 3.

53. Edward Dahlberg, "Authors Declare Solidarity With Our Strikes," *Office Worker* (February 1935), 4. On the subject of the Depression's effects on middle-class identity, see also Daniel Walkowitz, *Working With Class: Social Workers and the Politics of Middle Class Identity* (Chapel Hill: University of North Carolina Press, 1999), 113–76.

54. Undated paper, "Early Strikes" file, DSSO Collection; Pinkson interview.

55. Pinkson interview. For the FAECT, see "Editorials," *Office Worker* (February 1935), 2; for the mice, see "Ohrbach Asks New Writ To Bar All Picketing By Striking Employees," *Daily Worker* (February 1, 1935), "Clippings," DSSO Papers.

56. Clarina Michelson interview

57. Pinkson interview.

58. "125 Pickets Seized at Ohrbach Store," *The New York Times* (February 17, 1935), and "10 to Face Court Today For Mass Picket Line Before Ohrbach Store," *Daily Worker* (January 28, 1935), "Clippings," DSSO Collection; see also Jay Martin, *Nathanael West: The Art of His Life* (New York: Farrar, Straus and Giroux, 1970), 255–57.

59. Pinkson interview; see also "Ohrbach and Klein Strikers To Greet Birthday of 'Daily,' *Daily Worker* (December 31, 1934), "Clippings," DSSO Collection.

60. Leane Zugsmith, *A Time To Remember,* 288–89. For the arrests, see also Reiss interview.

61. Clarina Michelson interview

62. Reginald Marsh, *End of the Fourteenth Street Crosstown Line,* 1936 (The Pennsylvania Academy of the Fine Arts, Philadelphia), rpt. in Todd, *The "New Woman" Revisited,* 261.

63. "125 Pickets Seized At Ohrbach Store;" Clarina Michelson interview. For the

arrest, but not the applause, see "9 'Sailors of Cattaro' Give Matinee in Police Station," *New York World-Telegram* (February 9, 1935), 1.

64. For Gypsy Rose Lee and Lillian Hellman at the meeting, the only source—surprisingly—is Pinkson interview, but both women had links to the left, and therefore might have come to speak in support of the strikers. Hellman, a committed radical, was involved with the League of Women Shoppers, a consumer support group which will be discussed further in chapter 2; for Hellman's involvement, see Clarina Michelson interview. Though less prominent in radical circles, Gypsy Rose Lee did support other left-wing causes; for this, see Sam Sills, "Abraham Lincoln Brigade," in Mari Jo Buhle, Paul Buhle, and Dan Georgakas, eds., *Encyclopedia of the American Left* (Urbana: University of Illinois Press, 1992), 3.

65. Arnold Honig, "The Klein-Ohrbach Strikes," *Office Worker* (February 1935), 3; Zugsmith, *A Time To Remember,* 266.

66. Pinkson interview; for the source of the tickets, see also "Ohrbach Feast Spoiled By Two Comely Pickets Voicing Strike Demands," *Daily Worker* (January 22, 1935), "Clippings," DSSO Collection.

67. This quotation is given in "Girl Striker Heckles La Guardia; Chained to Box, Foils Ejection," *New York Times* (January 21, 1935), "Clippings," DSSO Collection, and "Ohrbach Feast Spoiled By Two Comely Pickets Voicing Strike Demands."

68. Pinkson interview, Haicken interview. Anne Haicken was one of the two workers chained to the balcony.

69. "Girl Striker Heckles La Guardia; Chained to Box, Foils Ejection."

70. "Ohrbach Feast Spoiled By Two Comely Pickets Voicing Strike Demands;" Pinkson interview.

71. "Girl Striker Heckles La Guardia; Chained to Box, Foils Ejection;" "Ohrbach Feast Spoiled By Two Comely Pickets Voicing Strike Demands."

72. Zugsmith, *A Time To Remember,* 347–48.

73. Labor Research Association, "Some White Collar and Professional Workers' Strikes, 1934 to date" (March 19, 1936), 4, DSSO Collection.

74. "Hands Off!" *Office Worker* (April 1935), 6. For the layoffs, see also Pinkson interview. The second Ohrbach's strike and the controversy surrounding its settlement will be discussed further in chapter 2.

75. For corruption in the RCIPA, see Clarina Michelson interview, as well as chapter 2 of this study.

76. Frederick Woltman (*World-Telegram* Staff Writer), "Retail Clerks Remove Denise, East Organizer," *World Telegram* [?], Undated, "Clippings" folder, DSSO Papers. Denise was removed as East Coast organizer late in 1935; see Kirstein, *Stores and Unions,* 59.

77. Clarina Michelson interview.

Chapter 2

1. "32 ERA Pickets Arrested," *New York Times* (June 7, 1936), 2; "Four Girl Pickets Fined," *New York Times* (April 17, 1935), 18.

2. *The WPA Guide to New York City* (Random House, 1982 [first published 1939]), 448–49; "Urges Elevated Removal," *New York Times* (January 15, 1928), 154.

3. For the history of May's see "Over 12 Million in 22 Years Is Story Of Mays, Brooklyn," *Women's Wear Daily* (July 10, 1946), 63.

4. For May's as a working-class store, see "Over 12 Million in 22 Years," as well as Ken Thompson, "Ruminances & Smiles No. 1," Brooklyn Memories (October 13, 2003). http://www.brooklynmemories.com/ (accessed June 25, 2005). Also see Miriam Rivers, "The Law Was Aimed at Gangsters, But It Is The Shopgirls of May's That The Law Hits," *Daily Worker* (December 11, 1935), 5. For shoplifting at May's, see Sidney Street, "Plenty to Laugh About On Picket Line at May's," *Daily Worker* (December 18, 1935), 9; Street describes one May's striker who, when arrested for walking the picket line, met a May's shoplifter in jail. For Weinstein's method of dealing with workers, see Affidavit of Pearl Edison and Affidavit of Evelyn Cohen, both taken October 29, 1935, "May's Department Store Strike," Fiorello LaGuardia Papers, New York City Municipal Archives, Microfilm Reel 230 (hereafter La Guardia Papers, Reel 230). These two affidavits are identical in content.

5. See Affidavit of Pearl Edison (October 29, 1935), 1 and Affidavit of Evelyn Cohen (October 29, 1935), 1.

6. "Report of Findings of the Mayor's Committee Appointed to Investigate the Strike at the May's Department Store, 510 Fulton Street, Brooklyn, New York," (March 12, 1936), LaGuardia Papers, Reel 230 (hereafter "May's Strike Report"), 2; both Rivers, "The Law Was Aimed At Gangsters," 5; and Miriam Birge Wise and Jess P. Lacklen, Jr., *Unionization in the Retail Field* (New York: New York University School of Retailing, 1940), 7, confirm this sequence of events.

7. "May's Strike Pickets Beaten By The Police," *Daily Worker* (February 24, 1936), 3; see also Fajans interview.

8. "Memo From Borough Headquarters (Brooklyn and Richmond) To Police Commissioner, February 14, 1936," 1–2; La Guardia Papers, Reel 230. For the Artists' League and other rallies, see Testimony of Thomas A. Swift (rep., Downtown Brooklyn Association), Joint Legislative Committee on Industrial and Labor Conditions, *Public Hearing on Cross-Picketing* (New York, NY; December 5, 1941) [hereafter *Cross-Picketing Hearing*], 104.

9. For the LWS's founding, see Clarina Michelson interview. For the members of the LWS, see for example, League of Women Shoppers, Letter to Fiorello LaGuardia, dated February 14, 1936), 1, LaGuardia Papers, Reel 230. Many of these women chose to use their husbands' names on the LWS stationery; I have allowed these names to stand unaltered.

10. The strongest piece of propaganda portraying retail workers as white-collar workers was Leane Zugsmith's *A Time to Remember,* which was published during the May's strike. For the LWS's claim that they had no class affiliations, see "Use Your Buying Power For Justice," undated leaflet, "Publications Relating to the League of Women Shoppers," Vertical File, Tamiment Library, New York University.

11. Letter from Gussie Reed, dated August 21, 1935, in Michelson Papers, Box 3, Folder 20.

12. For police beatings during the strike, see Petition to Mayor LaGuardia

(December 14, 1935), 1. Michelson remembered Thomas's arrest, but erroneously claimed that it occurred during the Klein's-Ohrbach's strikes; see Clarina Michelson interview. For Thomas's arrest during the May's strike, see League of Women Shoppers, Letter to Fiorello LaGuardia (February 14, 1936), 1, LaGuardia Papers, Reel 230. For May's gifts to the Democratic Party, see "May's Store Accused; It and Restaurant Made Illegal Party Gifts, Blanchard Says," *New York Times* (May 21, 1936), 18. For the listening device, see "Pickets Cases Cause Dispute In Court," *New York Times* (December 24, 1935), 21.

13. For the singling out of individual picketers for arrest, see "May's Strike Report," 14. For the captain's statement, see LWS, Report On The May's Strike From Observers Miriam Rivers and Josephine Wertheim, LaGuardia Papers, Reel 230; May's Strike Report, 15–16.

14. "May's Strike Pickets Beaten By The Police," *Daily Worker* (February 24, 1936), 3; May's Strike Report, 26; for store managers' response, see "Response to May's Strike Committee Report" (March 20, 1936), LaGuardia Papers, Reel 230.

15. For the truck drivers, see Ruth Prince Mack, Ph.D., *Controlling Retailers: A Study of Cooperation and Control in the Retail Trade With Special Reference to the NRA* (New York: Columbia University Press, 1936), 482–83 (n. 101).

16. For Goodman's background, see "Trial Board Minutes," Meeting of October 12, 1936, 6, "Department Store Employees Union, Local 1250 (RCIPA)—Ohrbach's— Ben Goodman Case, 1936" folder, DSSO Papers.

17. Clarina Michelson interview; see also Charles E. Boyd, "Early Years of Local 1-S," "History (1939–1949) By Boyd, C. E." Folder, Local 1-S Papers, Box 1. See also "Retail Clerks' Union Heads Defend Methods," *Women's Wear Daily* (October 4, 1935), 1, 19.

18. "Trial Board Minutes," 6.

19. For the transfer of the strike, see "Union Support Is Now Denied May's Strikers," *Telegram* (July 2, 1936), "Local 1250—Newspaper Clippings" Folder, DSSO Papers, and "Trial Board Minutes," 6. Elsie Monokian, the May's worker whose firing led to the strike, was present at the trial documented in these minutes, suggesting that at least some workers at May's were unwilling to sever their ties with Local 1250. For Local 1125's support for the national RCIPA leaders, see "Rioting Marks Retail Clerks' 'New Era' Parley," *Women's Wear Daily* (February 19, 1937), 1, 20.

20. "Union Support is Now Denied May's Strikers," *Telegram* (July 2, 1936), in "Clippings," DSSO Papers.

21. For Carnes' participation in the 1936 Ohrbach's strike, see Eleanor Tillson, "United Storeworkers and RWDSU" (unpublished manuscript, 1982), "RWDSU— Local 3," Vertical File, Tamiment Library; Tillson interviewed Carnes about the union's history. Carnes was also present at Benjamin Goodman's trial, discussed further below. See "Trial Board Minutes," 1.

22. Michelson provides a chronology of these events during Goodman's trial; see "Trial Board Minutes," 8. See also the petition by Ohrbach's strikers in this same folder in protest to Goodman's actions, and "Picketing is Ended at Ohrbach Store," *Women's Wear Daily* (October 5, 1936), 14.

23. See again "Trial Board Minutes," 8. Goodman also sent a copy of his com-

plaints to LaGuardia; see Letter from Goodman to Fiorello LaGuardia (October 5, 1936), La Guardia Papers, Reel 115.

24. While the trial board was strongly predisposed against Goodman, the fact that every striker signed a petition supporting the board's findings suggests that workers did not feel that they had been "sold out," as Goodman claimed. Considering Michelson's close connection with these workers, and Goodman's lack of participation in the strike, this is not surprising. It is perhaps a mark of that closeness that the workers—without Michelson present—voted to spend part of the money from the settlement on a watch for Michelson. The full distribution of the settlement money was as follows: $230 for every worker who had walked the picket line (and two-thirds of that for those who had honored the picket line but had left the picketing to others), $560 to the lawyers; $25 to the union's bail fund, $75 for a banquet for the strikers, $2 for the union funds, and the remainder for a watch, which they gave as a present to Michelson; see "Trial Board Minutes," 4.

25. See Letter from Ben Davis on *The Negro Liberator* stationery, dated April 27, 1935 to the Committee of Unemployed Office, Store and Professional Workers, Clarina Michelson Papers, Box 3, Folder 2.

26. Wise and Lacklen, *Unionization in the Retail Field,* 8.

27. "Rioting Marks Retail Clerks' 'New Era' Parley," *Women's Wear Daily* (February 19, 1937), 1, 20.

28. For Wolchok's claim, see George Meisler, interviewed by Debra Bernhardt (New York, December 12, 1979 and December 21, 1979), hereafter Meisler interview. Irving Simon, a longtime ally of Wolchok's (which Meisler was not), said in 1939 that Wolchok had received his scars to wrest control of the union from the "underworld," rather than from Communists. Unfortunately, more research would need to be done on Wolchok and on the union struggles in the grocery industry before any definitive account of where Wolchok got his scars can be provided. For Simon's statement, see *Proceedings—Second Biennial Convention, URWEA* (December 11–14, 1939 [hereafter *Second Convention Proceedings*]), 109.

29. For the various fronts that the CP called for, see Klehr, *The Heyday of American Communism: The Depression Decade.*

30. See Meisler interview.

31. Samuel Wolchok, "Our Tasks . . ." *Retail Wholesale and Department Store Employee* (September 1940), 5. See also Helen Baker and Robert R. France, *Personnel Administration and Labor Relations In Department Stores: An Analysis of Developments and Practices,* Princeton Industrial Relations Series, No. 81 (Princeton, New Jersey, 1950), 102.

32. John W. Wingate and O. Preston Robinson, "Unionization in Retailing," *Journal of Retailing* (Vol. XIII, No. 2; "Special Personnel Issue," April 1937), 37.

33. "70% of Wealth Declared Held By 23 Women," *The Washington Post* (October 26, 1936), p. X3.

34. "Barbara Buys Historic Gems for $1,200,000," *LA Times* (June 17, 1936), 1.

35. Michael Gold, *Jews Without Money* (New York: Carroll & Graf, 1996), 217. Hammett, of course, would also join the Communist party later in the 1930s, but there is no indication that he did so before 1936; at the time of the writing of *The*

Thin Man, he remained politically independent and generally inactive. See also Paula E. Hyman, *Gender and Assimilation in Modern Jewish History: The Roles and Representation of Women* (Seattle: University of Washington Press, 1995), 129–30.

36. Godfrey M. Lebhar, *Chain Stores in America, 1859–1962* (New York: Chain Store Publishing Company, 1963), 178–79.

37. House Resolution 203, quoted in Charles Daughters, *Wells of Discontent* (Daughters, 1937), 71.

38. Daughters, *Wells of Discontent,* 64. For the Robinson-Patman Act, see *The Robinson-Patman Act: Its History and Probable Meaning* (Washington, D.C.: The Washington Post, 1936), 6–8.

39. Daughters, 274–76.

40. Ruth Gikow, "As A Woolworth Worker and Artist Views Her Job," *Daily Worker* (March 31, 1937), 5; Harry Raymond, "Girl Clerks Sit Tight in 4 'Five and Tens' on 2nd Day of Tieup," *Daily Worker* (March 15, 1937), 1, 4; and Papa interview.

41. Gikow, "As A Woolworth Worker and Artist Views Her Job," 5; "Woolworth Girl Sitdowners Win Demands In Detroit Stores," *Daily Worker* (March 6, 1937), 4.

42. "Woolworth To Shut Its Detroit Stores," *New York Times* (March 1, 1937), 5; "Seek Woolworth Boycott," *New York Times* (March 3, 1937), 15. For an excellent and detailed look at the Woolworth sit-downs in Detroit see Dana Frank, "Girl Strikers Occupy Chain Store, Win Big: The Detroit Woolworth's Strike of 1937," in Howard Zinn, Dana Frank, and Robin D.G. Kelley, *Three Strikes: Miners, Musicians, Salesgirls, and the Fighting Spirit of Labor's Last Century* (Boston: Beacon Press, 2001), 57–118.

43. "Woolworth Strike Spreads In Detroit," *New York Times* (March 2, 1937), 13; Local 1250 statement, quoted in "Seek Woolworth Boycott," *New York Times* (March 3, 1937), 15.

44. "Woolworth Girl Sitdowners Win Demands in Detroit Stores," *Daily Worker* (March 6, 1937), 4. See also Frank, "Girl Strikers."

45. Louise Mitchell, "You Bet The Five-and-Dime Girls Are Watching Sisters in Detroit," *Daily Worker* (March 4, 1937), 3. "What To Do In Case of a Sit-Down," (March 1937), "Sit-Down Strikes—Papers" Folder, DSSO Papers.

46. Harry Raymond, "Girl Clerks Sit Tight In 4 'Five and Tens' On 2nd Day of Tieup," *Daily Worker* (March 15, 1937), 1.

47. For Green's support, see "Green Letter Shelved In NY AFL Council," *Daily Worker* (March 19, 1937), 1. For the early days of the strikes and the numbers of supporters, see Clarina Michelson, "Five-and-Dime," *Woman Today* (May 1937), 9–10, as well as Clarina Michelson interview and Meisler interview.

48. "Store Union Meets Head of 5 and 10," *Daily Worker* (March 17, 1937), 1; "All Grand Stores Face Strike Call," *New York Times* (March 25, 1937), 13. See also Elizabeth Gurley Flynn, "We Point With Pride," *Woman Today* (May 1937), 10.

49. "Woolworth Girls Strike in 2 Stores," *New York Times* (March 18, 1937), 1; "Woolworth Girls On Hunger Strike," *Daily Worker* (March 18, 1937), 1. For the editorial, see "Editorial," *Dry Goods Economist* (March 16, 1937), cited in "Our Business Papers Condemn the Sit-Down," 1, "Sit-Down Strikes—Papers" Folder, DSSO Papers.

50. "Woolworth Girls on Hunger Strike," 1, and Clarina Michelson interview.

51. Clarina Michelson interview.

52. Clarina Michelson, "Five-and-Dime," 9–10. See also "Hidden Force of 70 Police Evict 59 Woolworth Strikers," *Daily Worker* (March 19, 1937), 1, 5; "Mayor Acts to End Store Sit-Downs," *New York Times* (March 20, 1937), 5.

53. "Mayor Acts To End Store Sit-Downs," *New York Times* (March 20, 1937), 5.

54. Wingate and Robinson, "Unionization In Retailing," 40–41.

55. "F & W Girls Celebrate," *Daily Worker* (March 18, 1937), 1, 4.

56. "'We Shall Not Be Moved,' Sing Girl Sit-In Strikers," *Daily Worker* (March 16, 1937), 3. For the demand of a boycott of German-made goods, see "Woolworth Union Asks Nazi Boycott," *New York Post* (March 18, 1937), 15.

57. "Woolworth Girls Strike In 2 Stores," *New York Times* (March 18, 1937), 1, 6; "Mayor Acts To End Store Sit-Downs," *New York Times* (March 20, 1937), 5.

58. Harry Raymond, "Girl Clerks Sit Down In 4 'Five And Tens' on 2nd Day Of Tieup," *Daily Worker* (March 15, 1937), 1; Esther Cantor, "Brooklyn Girls Bar Executives," *Daily Worker* (March 15, 1937), 1.

59. Raymond, "Girl Clerks Sit Tight In 4 'Five And Tens' on 2nd Day of Tieup," 1. For the estimated ages of workers at five-and-dime stores, see Papa interview.

60. "Woolworth Girls Strike In 2 Stores," *New York Times* (March 18, 1937), 1, 6; see also Clarina Michelson interview.

61. The lyrics to the song are reprinted in "They Sing While They Sit," *Daily Worker* (March 4, 1937), 3. Michelson remembered the chant; see Clarina Michelson interview.

62. Al Richmond, "Counter Girls vs. The Countess," *Sunday Worker* [*Daily Worker*], Magazine Section (March 7, 1937), 1. For the other picture of Hutton in the *Worker*, see Louise Mitchell, "You Bet The Five-and-Dime Girls Are Watching Sisters in Detroit," *Daily Worker* (March 4, 1937), 3; "Grand Strikers Win Recognition," *Daily Worker* (March 23, 1937), 1, 4.

63. "Babs Sits Down Also—After Swim, Sun Bath," *New York Post* (March 19, 1937), 19.

64. See Karen Plunkett-Powell, *Remembering Woolworth's: A Nostalgic History of the World's Most Famous Five-and-Dime* (New York: St. Martin's Press, 1999), 222–23. Though Plunkett-Powell claims that Hutton sold off all of her Woolworth's stock, this may be an exaggeration on her part. After a massive stock sale in 1926, when her guardians sold off nearly half her stock in one fell swoop, Hutton still retained almost 100,000 shares of Woolworth's common stock, and there are no records of additional stock sales after 1926. Whether Hutton retained those 100,000 shares or not, however, Hutton held only a small percentage of the total Woolworth's stock after 1926. For the sale of Hutton's stock, see "Stock Sale Brings $10,000,000 To Girl," *New York Times* (January 9, 1926), 1, and "Private Sale of 50,000 Woolworth," *Wall Street Journal* (January 9, 1926), 1.

65. "Editorial," *Dry Goods Economist* (March 16, 1937), cited in "Our Business Papers Condemn the Sit-Down," 1, "Sit-Down Strikes—Papers" Folder, DSSO Papers.

66. John W. Wingate and O. Preston Robinson, "Unionization in Retailing," *Journal of Retailing* (Volume XIII, No. 2: Special Personnel Issue, April 1937), 35–36.

67. Harold Rome, "Chain-Store Daisy," from *Pins And Needles,* Columbia Records, OS 2210, produced by Elizabeth Lauer and Charles Burr, recorded 1972.

68. New Era Committee, Letter to John L. Lewis (May 15, 1937), 1–2, CIO Collection, Box 9, Folder 12, Catholic University of America Archives, Washington, D.C. (hereafter CUAA).

69. John L. Lewis, Letter to Samuel Walckor [*sic*], (May 19, 1937), CIO Collection, Box 9, Folder 12, CUAA. Somewhat surprisingly, Steven Fraser's often excellent *Labor Will Rule: Sidney Hillman and the Rise of American Labor* (Ithaca: Cornell University Press, 1991), 345–46, offers a misleading chronology of these events, suggesting that the department store union's merger with the CIO led to the five-and-dime sit-down strikes.

70. Elizabeth Gurley Flynn, "We Point With Pride," *Woman Today* (May 1937), 10.

Chapter 3

1. "Police Push Carts As Peddlers Flee," *New York Times* (July 14, 1938), 10.

2. For the boundaries of the garment district (really multiple districts, with separate but overlapping areas for men's clothing and women's clothing, see "Job Rush Held Bar To Building Strike," *New York Times* (November 18, 1934), 26. For the guards' protest, see "400 Strike Guards Clamor For Wages," *New York Times* (November 6, 1934), 35. For other incidents, see "Bystander Shot In Strike Clash," *New York Times* (August 29, 1935), 13, "Service Strike Set for 20,000 Workers," *New York Times* (January 28, 1936), 2, and "Service Workers Quit," *New York Times* (May 20, 1937), 12.

3. "Forty Women Felled By Fumes In Factory," *New York Times* (February 18, 1941), 19.

4. Barbara Blumberg, *The New Deal and the Unemployed: The View From New York City* (Lewisburg: Bucknell University Press, 1979), 88–89.

5. Ibid., 107.

6. For managers' failed attempts to control May Day, see "May Day Parades Arouse Retailers," *New York Times* (April 25, 1935), 23; "May Day Parades Arouse 11 Groups," *New York Times* (April 26, 1935), 21.

7. Though not about department stores, Elizabeth Blackmar and Roy Rosenzweig, *The Park and the People: A History of Central Park* (Ithaca, New York: Cornell University Press, 1992) provides an excellent discussion of upper-class space in nineteenth-century New York City. For Stewart and the marble palace, see Stephen N. Elias, *Alexander T. Stewart: The Forgotten Merchant Prince* (Westport, CT: Praeger, 1992). For later architectural developments, see Leach, *Land of Desire,* 73–77.

8. "Windows Have Become News," *Women's Wear Daily* (March 8, 1939), 43.

9. Benson, *Counter Cultures*, 85.

10. For the Macy's advertisements, see "Latest Retail Selling Slants," *Women's Wear Daily* (September 18, 1936), 2.

11. Leach, *Land of Desire*, 335. During the Depression, managers organized store-sponsored parades in other cities across the country; see Alvin Rosensweet, "Parading into Prosperity," *Dry Goods Economist* (June 1935), 22.

12. Charles E. Boyd, "Early Years of Local 1-S," "History (1939–49), By Boyd, C. E." Folder, Local 1-S Papers, Box 1 (hereafter Boyd, "Early Years"). For African American women as matrons, see the fictionalized account of an upscale department store in Erle Stanley Gardner [1938], *The Case of the Shoplifter's Shoe* (Pocket Books, 1965), 4.

13. Kenneth Collins, "The Trend Toward Self-Service," *Journal of Retailing* (December 1940), 98. For another good description of the indirect access to goods, see "It Depends Which Store You Shop: What Happens in New York Stores When You 'Want To Buy A Dress,'" *Women's Wear Daily* (May 5, 1939), 20, 46.

14. Collins, "The Trend Toward Self-Service," 98–99. For customer shoplifting in upscale stores, see Elaine Abelson, *When Ladies Go A-Thieving* (Oxford: Oxford University Press, 1989).

15. For managers' attempts to regulate workers' appearances, a factor in both upscale and downscale stores, see chapter 1, note 25.

16. For the variety of workers in an upscale department store, see Agreement Between Gimbel Brothers, Inc. and CIO, URWDSEA, and Gimbel Local 2, Dated November 24, 1941 (effective as of September 12, 1941), Appendix A and Appendix B, Folder 18, Box 9, CIO Papers, Catholic University of America Archives (hereafter CUAA).

17. Benson, *Counter Cultures*, 115–16.

18. For the stores' customers, see Benson, *Counter Cultures*, 76–77. For store workers, see note 20.

19. Fajans interview. Betty Mindling, "A Shopgirl's Saga," from unnamed union publication, given to WPA interviewer by Michelson. This motive for joining the union is confirmed by Annette Rubinstein, interviewed by author, New York, NY, November 13, 2000 (hereafter Rubinstein interview). Rubinstein knew a number of department store workers quite well and later became active in the department store unions during the Gimbel's strike.

20. "Maintaining the Working Force On Jewish Holidays," *Journal of Retailing* (October 1932), 92. See also Jane Spadavecchio, interviewed by author New York, NY, January 13, 2000 (hereafter Spadavecchio interview); and Blanche Mendelssohn, interviewed by author, New York, NY, January 13, 2000.

21. Boyd, "Early Years", and William Atkinson, interviewed by Debra Bernhardt, New York, NY, June 26, 1981, Tamiment Library, New York University (hereafter Atkinson interview). As already mentioned, Boyd slightly overstated the case; as in the downscale stores, there is evidence that African American women acted as matrons in the upscale stores.

22. "The Long and Short Of It," *Macy Unionizer* ([misdated] 1936), 2, "Macy Unionizer—1936" Folder, DSSO Papers. (The date, written in pencil on this printed

newsletter, is almost certainly wrong, since one article mentions the CIO and the name of John Cooney, a UREA official; neither Cooney nor the CIO was involved with Macy's until 1937, a more probable date for this issue.)For lunch and working hours, see also Boyd, "Early Years," 5. The rushed schedule was confirmed by Spadavecchio interview. For the bureaucracy, see Shirley Jackson, "My Life with R.H. Macy," in *The Lottery and Other Stories* (New York: The Modern Library, 2000), 57.

23. The average salary of $15 a week is from Beth McHenry, "Worker Tires, Macy's Fires," *Daily Worker* (March 6, 1937), 7. For the vacation house, see Spadavecchio interview; and "Macy's Buys New Employee Camp Site," *Women's Wear Daily* (July 3, 1944), 15. While he does not mention the upstate vacation house, Boyd confirms the Thanksgiving turkey; see Boyd, "Early Years," 2. For the Greater New York Department Store Baseball League, see "President of O. And P. League Dead," *New York Times* (May 30, 1910), 13. For the dramatic clubs, see "'Retail Follies of 1939' A Lively Opening Bill," *Women's Wear Daily* (January 17, 1939), 12.

24. "We Made Macy's Answer," *Main Floor News* (December 1934), 2; Beth McHenry, "Worker Tires, Macy's Fires;" "Macy's Public Enemy #1—MMAA," *Main Floor News* [Undated], 1; see also May Swenson, "Lore of Department Store Workers," FWP Collection; for the specific complaints about how money was being spent, see "Unadvertised Specials: Hospital Malady," *Macy Unionizer* (misdated; see note 22), 2–3, "Macy Unionizer—CIO" Folder, DSSO Papers.

25. For the searches, see "Macy's Frisks Its Employees," *Main Floor News* [Undated], 1, "OWU—Department Store Section—Macy Local—Leaflets" Folder, DSSO Papers; for the money spent on security versus the money lost to shoplifting, see "1250 Organizer," [First Issue—Undated], 1, "DSEU (CIO)—Local 1250—1250 Organizer" Folder, DSSO Papers. Spadavecchio also remembered having to leave her belongings in lockers throughout the day.

26. "Macy's Frisks Its Employees," *Main Floor News* [Undated], 1.

27. Alfred Gerrity, "Undercover Man," *Readers' Digest* (July 1939), 20–24.

28. May Swenson, "Lore of Department Store Workers," FWP Collection.

29. "A Slap In The Face To Labor And Our Religious Rights" Flyer, Dated April 15, 1935, "OWU—Department Store Section—Macy Local—Leaflets," DSSO Papers.

30. Samuel Kovenetsky, interviewed by Deborah Bernhardt, November 6, 1979, December 19, 1979 (hereafter Kovenetsky interview).

31. May Swenson, "Lore of Department Store Workers," FWP Collection.

32. For the numbers in May 1937, see Letter from New Era Retail Sales Clerks Unions of America to John L. Lewis (dated May 15, 1937), 2; for the union's status in December, see "First Convention of Retail Workers Plans Vast Drive," *Retail Employee* (December 18, 1937), 1. *Retail Employee* was the UREA's official newspaper; during these early years, every issue of the eight-page *Retail Employee* contained at least one full page entitled "New York City," which covered some of the news of the New York City locals; other locations where the union grew—such as West Virginia, Philadelphia, and Michigan—generally received half or a quarter of a page.

33. For the history of Local 65, see Lisa Phillips, *The Labor Movement and Black Economic Equality in New York City: District 65, 1934–1954,* Doctoral Thesis (Rutgers, 2002).

34. Samuel Wolchok, Letter to John L. Lewis (dated September 1, 1937), 1–2; Box 9, Folder 13, CIO Collection, CUAA.

35. Lewis, Memorandum For [Walter] Smethurst (dated July 30 1937), Box 9, Folder 12, CIO Collection, CUAA.

36. For Lewis's strong support of Wolchok, see John V. Cooney, "Acceptance Speech," *First Convention Minutes,* 3; for Lewis's telegram to Wolchok, see "Lewis Congratulates Wolchok On New Gimbel's Contract," *Retail Employee* (March 1938), 1.

37. Samuel Wolchok, Memorandum to CIO (dated 1 October 1937), 3–4, Box 9, Folder 13, CIO Collection, CUAA.

38. Samuel Wolchok, Letter to Philip Murray (dated November 10, 1937), Box 9, Folder 13, CIO Collection, CUAA; see also *Second Convention Proceedings,* 56.

39. *Minutes of the First National Convention of the UREA held at the Webster Hall Hotel in the City of Pittsburgh* (hereafter *First Convention Minutes*), 4.

40. For references to the various accolades Wolchok received, see "Elect Wolchok Official of New York CIO," *CIO News—Retail Wholesale Edition* (October 8, 1938), 1; "Samuel Wolchok Invited to International Labor Congress," *Retail Employee* (April 15, 1938), 1.

41. For Broido's insistence upon negotiating with Wolchok, see William Michelson, interviewed by Debra Bernhardt, New York, NY, January 15, 1981, Tamiment Library, New York University (hereafter William Michelson interview). Broido, during his 1948 testimony before the House Un-American Activities Committee, denied being a friend of Wolchok's, but the two had at least gotten along fairly well, since Broido had appeared at a banquet in Wolchok's honor. See "Wolchok Honored With Histadrut Dinner," *Retail Wholesale and Department Store Employee* (May 1947), 3; for *Business Week*'s praise of Wolchok, see "Rise of Store Employees' Union," *Business Week* (January 1, 1938), 16–17.

42. *First Convention Minutes,* 4.

43. *First Convention Minutes,* page g. The delegate is not named.

44. M.D. Mosessohn and A. Furman Greene, "Collective Bargaining in Retailing," *Journal of Retailing* (February 1938), 2–5.

45. Clarina Michelson interview.

46. Like most department store union leaders, Loring never publicly admitted party membership. William Michelson later recalled that the department store local leaders, of whom Loring had certainly been one, had all been united by radical politics, except for Kovenetsky; see William Michelson interview. For Kovenetsky's emergence as a leader, see Boyd, "Early Years," 48, 71.

47. For William Michelson's involvement in radical politics, see especially William Michelson interview. Though some accounts suggest that the two were not related, in this interview William Michelson said that he was a distant cousin of Clarina Michelson's. At other times, however, he denied such a relationship; see particularly his testimony before the United States House of Representatives, *Investigation of Communism in New York Distributive Trades,* Special Subcommittee of the Committee on Education and Labor, House of Representatives, 80th Congress, Second Session, Pursuant to House Resolution 1111, U.S. Government Printing

Office, Washington, D.C. (hereafter *Investigation of Communism*), 454–55.

48. "Employees Negotiate At Bloomingdale Department Store," *Retail Employee* (November 5, 1938), 1, 9; "Bloomingdale Department Store Signs Contract," *Retail Employee* (December 12, 1938), 1. Bloomingdale's is a little difficult to pinpoint as far as the question of whether it was upscale or downscale. Certainly, considering its less than ideal location, it was not as prestigious a store as Gimbel's and Macy's; at the same time, managers there practiced full-service retailing, denying customers access to goods, and charging higher prices than one might have paid at the 14th Street stores. For Bloomingdale's history, see Marvin Traub, *Like No Other Store . . . : The Bloomingdale's Legend and the Revolution in American Marketing* (New York: Crown, 1993).

49. For the Wagner Act, see Melvyn Dubofsky, *The State and Labor in Modern America* (Chapel Hill: The University of North Carolina Press, 1994), 123–28.

50. Very little is known about Morris, since he died only a few years after becoming the business manager of Local 3; his connections with the CP are mostly an inference, based on later developments in the union's history and the high regard in which other radical leaders seemed to hold him . For Morris's work in the cafeteria and his left-wing politics, see Kirstein, *Stores and Unions*, 79. There is more evidence of Brown's Communist politics, which will be presented in later chapters.

51. Clarina Michelson interview; William Michelson interview; Bea Schwartz, interviewed by Debra Bernhardt, New York, May 14, 1980 and May 17, 1980 (hereafter Schwartz interview); Maxwell Schneider, "I Met Bill Michelson When He Said: Let's Organize!" *Department Store Employee* (March 9, 1946), 1.

52. See Boyd, "Early Years," 44. For local leaders' interpretations of these events, see Marcella Loring Michelson, interviewed by Debra Bernhardt, New York, NY, June 18, 1980, Tamiment Library, New York University (hereafter Loring interview), Meisler interview. Since having separate locals gave the radicals more votes, there was a minor contradiction here, but organizers nonetheless strongly argued that both the one-vote-per-local policy and breaking up the unions into separate locals weakened the union, both creating divisions between them while still giving them less representation than they felt they deserved considering that their unions were far larger than any of the other locals.

53. Meisler interview.

54. Atkinson interview.

55. See Clarina Michelson interview. She believed Alexander's to be one of the union's most serious defeats, because, as she pointed out, their failure to organize the store in the 1930s meant that the store would never be unionized.

56. William Michelson interview; Loring interview; Kovenetsky interview. No information is available on whether Sadka Brown or Lowell Morris viewed sales as a career. See also Pinkson interview; Haicken interview; Fajans interview; Spadavecchio interview. For turnover as a somewhat minor factor in the upscale stores, see "Job Stability Held to Create Store Problem," *Women's Wear Daily* (May 25, 1939), 1, 35.

57. "Bloomingdale Girls' Team Breaks Jinx," and "Upsets Mark Hoop League," *The CIO News, Retail Edition* (February 29, 1940), 9. For the swimming programs, see

"Gala Opening—Swim-Gym" Flyer, Dated October 11 (no year given), "Department Store Employees' Union (CIO)—Local 1250" Folder, DSSO Papers.

58. See "Gimbel Union's New Library Proves Popular" and "Forum Discusses Marriage," *CIO News—Retail Edition* (February 29, 1940), 9; for the parties and choral group see "Organizing On A Spree," *1250 Organizer* (First Issue, Undated), 1, Department Store Employees Union (CIO) Local 1250—1250 Organizer Folder," DSSO Papers. Both quotes are taken from "Organizing on a Spree."

59. "Sing And Be Happy" Booklet, printed by Local 1250 Song Shop, Undated, "Department Store Employees Union—Local 1250 (no indication AFL or CIO)" folder, DSSO Papers; though undated, the address of Local 1250's offices make it clear that this booklet was printed during the CIO years.

60. For Vallee's performance, see "Come To Our Grand Victory Ball" Flyer (dated Saturday, May 8 [1937?]), "Department Store Employees Union (no affiliation indicated)" Folder, DSSO Papers.

61. "Meet the Girls Behind the Counter at the Counter Carnival," flyer, "DSEU-Local 1250 (no indication AFL or CIO)" folder, DSSO Papers.

62. For the importance of *A Time to Remember,* see Rubinstein interview. For favorable reviews of Zugsmith's work, see B. E. Bettinger, review of *A Time To Remember,* by Leane Zugsmith, *The New Republic* (September 16, 1936), 165; Alfred Kazin, review of *A Time To Remember, The New York Times Book Review* (September 13, 1936), 5; and Fanny Butcher, review of *A Time To Remember, Chicago Daily Tribune* (September 12, 1936), 14. For biographical information on McKenney, see Mari Jo Buhle, "Ruth McKenney," in Mari Jo Buhle, Paul Buhle, and Dan Georgakas, *Encyclopedia of the American Left* (Urbana, Illinois: University of Illinois Press, 1992), 461–62. For Quill, see Joe Doyle, "Mike Quill," in Buhle, Buhle, and Georgakas, *Encyclopedia of the American Left,* 619–20.

63. For Macy's role in the World's Fair, see "Macy's Subscribes For $468,000 Fair Bonds," *Women's Wear Daily* (January 11, 1937), 19.

64. "Big Stores at the World's Fair," *Women's Wear Daily* (May 4, 1939), 8; J.W. Cohn, "Work Is Begun on Fair's N.Y. Dept. Store Exhibit," *Women's Wear Daily* (May 4, 1939), 8.

65. "Progress, Movement Key Windows of Herald Square to Fair's Tempo," *Women's Wear Daily* (May 1, 1939), 2; Donald L. Pratt, "S. Klein Plans 'No Fancy Stuff,' But He'll Be Ready for Fair Crowds," *Women's Wear Daily* (March 31, 1939), 7.

66. Larry Zim, Mel Lerner, Herbert Rolfes, *The World of Tomorrow: The 1939 World's Fair* (New York: Harper and Row, 1988), 39, 54.

67. For the planning of Parkchester, see Minutes of Special Housing Meeting Held at Offices of Mr. Gove, Thursday, March 31, 1938, in *Parkchester: Minutes of Meetings—Board of Design,* 3–4, Avery Library, Columbia University, New York, NY. See also "Low Cost Housing Without U.S. Aid Shown By Ecker," *Wall Street Journal* (July 7, 1939), 1; "Model of Housing Displayed At Fair," *New York Times* (May 5, 1939), 47; and Zim, Lerner, and Rolfes, *The World of Tomorrow,* 66.

68. For Met Life's control over public space at Parkchester, see Hank De Cillia, "Parkchester: The Grand Old Neighborhood," *Back in the Bronx* (Vol. III, Issue 10), 10–11, and James B. Fay, "Parkchester," *Back in the Bronx* (Volume II, Issue 8), 8.

69. John Stanton, "Town Within the City," *New York Times* (May 11, 1941), SM12; De Cillia, "Parkchester: The Grand Old Neighborhood," and Fay, "Parkchester."

70. "Macy Branch To Open," *New York Times* (October 12, 1941), 54.

71. For the history of Macy's in this era, see Robert Hendrickson, *The Grand Emporiums: The Illustrated History of America's Great Department Stores* (New York: Stein and Day, 1979), 61–71. For the opening of the Syracuse branch, see "Macy's Chain," *Business Week* (November 16, 1940), 54–56; see also "Retail Revolution," *Business Week* (December 21, 1940), 30–31. For the store as a laboratory, see "R.H. Macy to Close Store In Syracuse," *New York Times* (December 27, 1941), 29.

72. For the closing of Macy's Syracuse branch, see "R.H. Macy To Close Store In Syracuse," *New York Times* (December 27, 1941), 29, and "Macy's to Close Store in Syracuse Tomorrow," *Women's Wear Daily* (December 26, 1941), 1.

73. See Boyd, "Early Years," 41; "Renew Macy Union Pact For A Week," *Women's Wear Daily* (March 30, 1939), 1; "Tentative Pact At R.H. Macy Is Reached," *Women's Wear Daily* (April 4, 1939), 2.

74. "Refuses Union Plea for Higher Pay at Hearn's," *Women's Wear Daily* (April 14, 1939), 40.

75. Melvyn Dubofsky, *The State and Labor in Modern America,* 154–57.

76. At least two different explanations exist for Michelson's departure. Ruth Pinkson claims that Michelson's husband, Andrew Overgaard, was deported in that year, and that Michelson went abroad with him; see Pinkson interview. Pinkson's memory appears to be faulty, however, since Overgaard himself indicated that he was not deported until the late 1940s; see Andrew Overgaard, Autobiographical Transcript, Tamiment Library, New York University. In addition, the Smith Act, under which Overgaard was eventually deported, had not yet been passed. Journalist George Kirstein, citing an earlier article in *Women's Wear Daily,* claimed that Michelson resigned for "reasons of health"; see George Kirstein, *Stores and Unions,* 58–59. Though asked in a later interview, Michelson herself immediately changed the subject; see Clarina Michelson interview.

77. Unfortunately, no prewar editions of the *Department Store Employee* still exist; this suggestion of the paper's content is derived from Boyd, "Early Years," 50, as well as issues from the early 1940s.

78. Letter From Wolchok To John Brophy (dated July 13, 1939), 1–2, Collection 1, Box 9, Folder 15, CUAA.

79. *Second Convention Proceedings,* 10, 57.

80. *Second Convention Proceedings,* 31–35.

81. *Second Convention Proceedings,* 38.

82. Letter from Wolchok to James Carey (dated November 25, 1940), Folder 17, Box 9, CIO Papers, CUAA.

83. Schwartz interview. William Michelson interview. "Wolchok Honored With Histadrut Dinner," *Retail Wholesale and Department Store Employee* (May 1947), 3.

84. "Staff Report to the Subcommittee on Labor of the Committee on Labor and Public Welfare (United States Senate) on Retail Establishments and the Fair Labor Standards Act," (Washington, D.C.: U.S. Government Printing Office, 1956), 17. For

the importance of the forty-hour week, see Rubinstein interview. For Wolchok on the eight-hour day, see "CIO Store Drive," *Business Week* (July 26, 1941), 42.

85. For the beginning of the strike, see "Lewis Is Facing New C.I.O. Revolt," *The New York Times* (August 24, 1941), 19, and "Gimbel's Unions Begin Strike" *Daily Worker* (August 26, 1941), 4.

86. For Broido's view of the strike as a failure on Wolchok's part and a double cross by the local leaders, see *Investigation on Communism,* Testimony of Louis Broido, 43.

87. For the numbers of strikers, see both "Gimbel's Strike Continues," *New York Times* (August 22, 1941), 6, and "Gimbel's Unions Begin Strike," *Daily Worker* (August 26, 1941), 4.

88. Rubinstein interview.

89. Letters from Miss M. Dun, Mrs. E.T. Newell, and Miss R.T. Harnie (September 9, 1941) to Mayor Fiorello LaGuardia, LaGuardia Papers, New York City Municipal Archives, Microfilm Roll 113.

90. For Helen Jacobson's actions, see Letter from United Department Store Employees Union of Greater New York to Mayor LaGuardia, LaGuardia Papers, Microfilm Reel 113, September 5, 1941. See *Investigation On Communism,* Testimony of Louis Broido, 37, 41; and see "Involved In Strike, Bees Do Boomerang" *The New York Times* (September 7, 1941), 41. One curious note which indicates the possibility that the bees were the act of an *agent provocateur* is that during his testimony before the House of Representatives, Broido never mentioned the bees' release into the store. Every aspect of the story, however, is suspicious: the man who released the bees claimed that the union had hired him, but was unable to identify any individuals; he also failed to explain why he had not simply followed earlier examples and left the bees in a box inside the store instead of releasing them while he was still present and, as a result, getting himself stung and caught.

91. Rubinstein interview; Schwartz interview; Abe Rosen, interviewed by Debra Bernhardt, New York, NY, April 21, 1980.

92. *Public hearing on Cross-Picketing Before the New York State Joint Legislative Committee on Industrial and Labor Conditions,* New York, NY, December 5, 1941 (New York: Marshall & Berry, 1941), 46–49 (hereafter *Cross-Picketing Hearings*).

93. Agreement Between Gimbel Brothers, Inc. and CIO, URWDSEA, and Gimbel Local 2, Dated 24 November 1941 (effective as of September 12, 1941), 15–17, 21–22, Appendix A, Folder 18, Box 9, CIO Papers, CUAA. This minimum wage of $17 a week included the generally lower-paid workers in the employees' lunchroom, but excluded the low-paid elevator operators. It is not known if elevator operators at Gimbel's, like those at Macy's, were African American.

94. "A&S Staff to Get 5-Day Week Oct. 6," *Women's Wear Daily* (September 17, 1941), 1; "New Work Week and Store Hours in N.Y. Area By '42," *Women's Wear Daily* (October 10, 1941), 1, 2.

95. "Ninth Board Session Records Big Strides," *Retail Wholesale and Department Store Employee* (October 31, 1941), 1, 5. See also William Michelson interview.

96. Minutes, Executive Board Meetings of Local 1-S (October 8, 1941 and October 22, 1941), 4–6, Box 1, Folder 15, Local 1-S Papers, Tamiment Library.

97. Testimony of Louis Broido, *Cross-Picketing Hearings,* 26.

98. Statement of Chairman Irving Ives, *Cross-Picketing Hearings,* 59–60.

99. William Michelson interview.

100. For the film, see Michael Rogin, "How the Working Class Saved Capitalism: The New Labor History and *The Devil and Miss Jones," The Journal of American History* (June 2002), 87–114.

101. For racism in American unions in the 1930s, see especially Bruce Nelson, *Divided We Stand: American Workers and the Struggle for Black Equality* (Princeton, NJ: Princeton University Press, 2001).

Chapter 4

1. Jan Morris, *Manhattan '45* (New York: Oxford University Press, 1986), 11.

2. For the dimout, see Andreas Feininger [text by John von Hartz], *New York in the Forties* (New York: Dover, 1978), 76; Morris, *Manhattan '45,* 164; "'Brownout' Begins Tonight!" *Women's Wear Daily* (January 31, 1945), 1; "Lights Go Out in Store Windows," *Women's Wear Daily* (February 2, 1945), 1, 18.

3. For the Socialist party, see Bernard Johnpoll, *Pacifist's Progress: Norman Thomas and the Decline of American Socialism* (Chicago: Quadrangle, 1970), 232–34.

4. "State Labor Praised By Dewey," *New York Times* (September 2, 1945), 26.

5. "N.Y. Stores Note Rush For Blackout Materials," *Women's Wear Daily* (December 10, 1941), 1, 35.

6. For the professor's statement, see Bernice G. Chambers, "Fashions and the War," *Journal of Retailing* (December 1939), 98–102. For workers' opinion as a factor in retailers' support for the war, see "Dig Far Deeper in War Effort to Earn Permanence, Stores Told at Convention," *Women's Wear Daily* (January 14, 1942), 1, 44; and "Does Your Staff Envy Susan On The War Production Line?" *Women's Wear Daily* (March 11, 1943), 35. On the war as a time when business leaders revamped their public image, see Lizabeth Cohen, *A Consumer's Republic: The Politics of Mass Consumption in Postwar America (New York: Vintage, 2003).*

7. For government interference as a concern, see "Stores Eager to Prove by Actions Apparel Rationing Can Be Avoided," *Women's Wear Daily* (July 19, 1943), 1. For R. R. Guthrie's statement, see "Tells Retailers: Guide Consumption Into Channels That Lead to Victory," *Women's Wear Daily* (January 13, 1942), 34–35.

8. "Home Debut Made By Bomber Cloth," *New York Times* (September 8, 1942), 20. "Cholly Knickerbocker Presents Defense Fashions for Gimbels" [display advertisement for Gimbel's], *New York Times* (January 18, 1942), 46. For the *Times* fashion show, see "Mayor To Attend New Fashion Show," *New York Times* (October 5, 1942), 10.

9. For the flags, see "Fly Your Flag *Every* Day" [display advertisement for Gimbel's], *New York Times* (June 7, 1942), 23; for the films, see "Own Your Own Home Movie Actually Filmed While the Japs Bombed Pearl Harbor" [display advertisement for Macy's], *New York Times* (January 6, 1942), 8. "'MacArthur: America's

First Soldier' and 'Manila Bombed'" [display advertisement for Macy's], *New York Times* (April 28, 1942), 10.

10. "Macy's Has Been Selling Food Boxes For Men In Service" [display advertisement for Macy's], *New York Times* (April 1, 1942), 9. "Gimbels Patriotic Envelopes" [display advertisement for Gimbel's], *New York Times* (January 18, 1942), 24; "Sock and Sweater Yarn" [display advertisement for Gimbel's], *New York Times* (January 25, 1942), 23;

11. "The Best New Year's Resolution You Can Make—Buy War Stamps!" [display advertisement for Macy's], *New York Times* (January 1, 1942), 29. "Since December 7, 1941" [display advertisement for Macy's], *New York Times* (December 6, 1942), 53. For the war bonds and stamps sales, see also "All-Out For Victory," *Women's Wear Daily* (May 5, 1942), 29; "Rising to the Occasion," *Women's Wear Daily* (May 19, 1942), 27; "'Beat the Attack' Poster," *Women's Wear Daily* (August 17, 1943), 25; and "'Buy Bonds' and 'Sell Bonds' is Employee Goal," *Women's Wear Daily* (May 9, 1945), 1, 8.

12. "Repeated Sales of White Shirts," [display advertisement for Macy's], *New York Times* (February 17, 1942), 13; "Macy's Midwinter Furniture Sale" [display advertisement for Macy's], *New York Times* (February 18, 1942), 7; "Macy's Mammoth Month of Fur And Coat Sales" [display advertisement for Macy's], *New York Times* (January 1, 1942), 8. "Red Cross Stockings of Sheer Service Nylon" [display advertisement for Gimbel's], *New York Times* (March 8, 1942), 46; "All Wool Slacks" [display advertisement for Stern's], *New York Times* (March 15, 1942), 23; "Macy's Annual Event! Office Supplies" [display advertisement for Macy's], *New York Times* (January 4, 1942), 37. For the encouragement of sales during the war, see Lizabeth Cohen, *A Consumer's Republic, 73–75.*

13. For the anti-hoarding campaign, see "Publicity Guns of 12 N.Y. Stores Trained on Hoarder," *Women's Wear Daily* (February 12, 1942), 1. For the suggestions on how to consume less, see "Waste Not-Want Not," *Women's Wear Daily* (March 27, 1942), 34; "Macy's Week of Spring Sales" [display advertisement for Macy's], *New York Times* (April 5, 1942), 11; "Your Government Wants You To Buy Only What You Need—Take Care of What You Own!" (display advertisement for Macy's), *New York Times* (May 3, 1942), 31; "To Save Is To Serve" [display advertisement for Gimbel's], *New York Times* (May 31, 1942), 46; "It's Easy To Get To Gimbels Without A Spoonful of Gas" [display advertisement for Gimbel's], *New York Times* (May 31, 1942), 23; "The Voice Of The People" [display advertisement for Macy's], *Wall Street Journal* (January 20, 1942), 2; "The Great Piggybank Robbery" [display advertisement for Macy's], *Wall Street Journal* (April 10, 1942), 3.

14. "Macy's Famous Housewares Sale" [display advertisement for Macy's], *New York Times* (February 22, 1942), 16; "The Home Front News" [display advertisement for Macy's], *New York Times* (April 26, 1942), 18; "The Home Front News" [display advertisement for Macy's], *New York Times* (July 5, 1942), 14.

15. "N.Y. Stores aid in Book Collection for Servicemen," *Women's Wear Daily* (January 7, 1943), 1. "Red Cross Booth Opened," *New York Times* (January 26, 1943), 16; "Today is Kids' Day In Macy's War Bond Centre" [display advertisement for Macy's], *New York Times* (September 11, 1943), 5; "Binocular Booth Set Up," *New*

York Times (April 28, 1942), 7; "Store Shows A Garden," *New York Times* (February 21, 1943), 32; "Win-The-War Show To Be Opened Today," *New York Times* (August 17, 1942), 13. For Macy's mimicking Hearn's, see "Macy's To Stage Vast Show On New Way of Living," *Women's Wear Daily* (August 27, 1942), 1, 27.

16. "To the People of the Metropolitan Area," *New York Times* (September 4, 1942), 8. If this notice was a paid advertisement—and it is laid out as a display advertisement, complete with a drawing of a man in colonial dress holding up a scroll with the text on it—there is nothing in the piece itself to tell who paid for it.

17. "Stores to Portray Work of Red Cross," *New York Times* (February 4, 1943), 20. This practice apparently continued throughout the war; see "Apparel, Retail Red Cross Fund Drive Advances," *Women's Wear Daily* (March 6, 1944), 1, 15.

18. "Rallies, Parades, Open Retail Bond Drive Tomorrow," *Women's Wear Daily* (September 8, 1943), 1, 4. "Yes, Madam . . . We Sell Guns, Tanks Planes," [display advertisement for Hearn's], *New York Times* (January 1, 1942), 28. See also "All Out For Defense Savings," *Department Store Economist* (January 10, 1942), 14. For the USO hostesses, see "Sailors Excel At Dance," *New York Times* (June 24, 1942), 16. Jane Spadavecchio was a hostess in Macy's USO branch; see Spadavecchio interview.

19. "Stores Are Facing Worker Shortage," *New York Times* (January 17, 1942), 21, 26; "Retail Personnel Problem Grows As Industry Calls More Women," *Women's Wear Daily* (September 14, 1942), 1, 16; "New York Stores Find Personnel In Unusual Places," *Women's Wear Daily* (January 31, 1945), 27; for the hiring of high school students and older workers during the war, see "High School Boys and Girls More Needed by Stores," *Women's Wear Daily* (May 27, 1942), 23; "To Expand Use of Students In Stores in Christmas Rush," *Women's Wear Daily* (October 5, 1943), 1; William Michelson interview; Meisler interview; and John O'Neill, interviewed by Debra Bernhardt, New York, NY, July 23, 1980.

20. "Find Women Workers In Stock Rooms Are Satisfactory," *Women's Wear Daily* (October 27, 1942), 31; "The Delivery Man Is Now A Woman," *New York Times* (May 18, 1943), 20; for furniture sales as a high-paying job reserved for white men, see Atkinson interview. For lower pay for women, see "Squelch Prejudice Against New Employee, Is Advice," *Women's Wear Daily* (June 17, 1942), 27.

21. For African American women workers gaining some office and sales positions, see Spadavecchio interview; "Won't Take Jim Crow Lying Down," *Department Store Employee* (October 6, 1945), 4; "New York Stores Find Personnel In Unusual Places," *Women's Wear Daily* (January 31, 1945), 27; and J. W. Cohn, "Few Negro Workers in Selling Jobs," *Women's Wear Daily* (March 14, 1946), 54. For the lower pay of African American workers, see Minutes of Local 1-S General Membership Meeting (dated 11 October 1942), 62, in Local 1-S Papers, Box 1, Folder 15. It should be noted that, although the offices at Macy's and the sales force at Gimbel's were somewhat integrated at this time, the sales force at Macy's was strictly restricted for white workers until after the war; see Atkinson interview.

22. For the NRDGA talk, see "Self-Selection Held Way To Give Better Service," *Women's Wear Daily* (January 14, 1943), 36. For the effects of the failure of Macy's on retailers in the area, see Frederic Hillegas, "Syracuse Merchants Hesitate About

Wholesale Use of Self-Service," *Women's Wear* Daily (April 1, 1943), 39. For other discussions of self-service, see Viola Sylbert, "Self-Service Experiments in Department Stores," *Journal of Retailing* (October 1942), 74–81; Earl Elhart, "Personal Comment," *Women's Wear* Daily (May 27, 1942), 31; "Self-Service Offers Aid From Personnel Pinch," *Women's Wear Daily* (August 7, 1942), 37; "Self-Service—Is It Due To Grow In Department Stores?" *Women's Wear Daily* (October 28, 1942), 27; Edwin Hahn, "Self-Service Is Super-Service From Customer's Viewpoint," *Women's Wear Daily* (November 27, 1942), 43; "Self-Service After the War?" *Women's Wear Daily* (August 4, 1943), 27.

23. Sylbert, "Self-Service Experiments In Department Stores," 77. See also Jane Steagall, Viola Sylbert, and Shirley Victor, "Customer Services Under War Conditions," *Journal of Retailing* (April 1942), 50.

24. Sylbert, "Self-Service Experiments," 77–79.

25. Art Shields, "Spirit of Past May Days Breathes in the Shops in 1942," *Daily Worker* (April 26, 1942), 2. For the history of Communist party policy during the war, see Maurice Isserman, *Which Side Were You On?: The American Communist Party During the Second World War* (Urbana: University of Illinois Press, 1993).

26. For the parade, see "Drum to be Leader in March of 500,000," *New York Times* (June 10, 1942), 12.

27. "Thousands Jam 7th Ave. in Huge Bond Rally," *Women's Wear Daily* (June 21, 1944), 27; "Joy Permeates N.Y. Garmentown," *Women's Wear Daily* (May 8, 1945), 3; "Garment Center and Retailers Greet 'Ike," *Women's Wear Daily* (June 20, 1945), 1, 27. V-J Day and its aftermath will be discussed in the next chapter.

28. For the beginnings of the Stuyvesant Town development, see Lee E. Cooper, "Uprooted Thousands Starting Trek From Site for Stuyvesant Town," *New York Times* (March 3, 1945), 13, and Joel Schwartz, *The New York Approach: Robert Moses, Urban Liberals, and the Redevelopment of the Inner City* (Columbus, OH: The Ohio State University Press, 1993), 84–107.

29. For workers' and unions' support of management's pro-war efforts, see Loring interview.

30. William Michelson interview and Schwartz interview. For Morris's entrance into the war, see Eli Halpern, "In Memory of Lowell Morris," *Department Store Employee* (October 6, 1945), 3.

31. Atkinson interview and Schwartz interview. See also "New York Local Dept. Store Heads Inducted," *Retail Wholesale and Department Store Employee* (February 28, 1942), 6. Atkinson, like Kovenetsky and many other Macy's leaders, was not a Communist; less evidence exists about Blanck's political affiliations, but she remained in various leadership positions in Local 2 long after the 1948 split with the CIO.

32. Minutes, Local 1-S General Membership Meeting (dated October 11, 1942), 62, in Local 1-S Papers, Box 1, Folder 15. For unions' efforts to fight racial discrimination in the stores, see also Donald Pratt, "Store Unions Plan Pay Rise Requests," *Women's Wear Daily* (December 27, 1944), 24.

33. Minutes, Executive Board Meeting (dated June 2, 1942), 46, in Local 1-S Papers, Box 1, Folder 15. "Won't Take Jim Crow Lying Down," *Department Store*

Employee (October 6, 1945), 4; "Poll Tax," *Department Store Employee* (December 3, 1943), 2; "Anti-Bias Group Sets To Work," *Department Store Employee* (October 13, 1945), 4.

34. "House Votes Price Increase; Membership Action Urged," *Department Store Employee* (December 3, 1943), 1. Since only one wartime issue of the *Department Store Employee* mentions this campaign, and neither the Local 1-S Papers nor any oral histories mention the anti-inflation campaign, it is possible that little time was spent organizing around this issue. For one Second Front resolution, see Minutes, Executive Board Meeting (dated 29 April 1942), Local 1-S Papers, Box 1, Folder 15.

35. "The Water's Fine! Come On In, Boys And Girls!" *Department Store Employee* (October 13, 1945), 1; "Best Thing Union Has Done," *Department Store Employee* (October 6, 1945), 1, 4.

36. This summary is taken from Nicholas Carnes, "How It All Began—Where We Are Going," *Department Store Employee* (November 10, 1945), 3. Carnes had published an earlier article on the union's history; see Nicholas Carnes, "Our Unions Have a History," *Department Store Employee* (July 1943), 4; this issue of the newspaper, unfortunately, has been lost, and apparently no copies have survived. It is cited in Boyd, "Early Years of Local 1-S."

37. "Convention Resolutions: Women's Auxiliary," *Retail Wholesale Department Store Employee* (June 1942), 18.

38. "Women Still Underpaid in New York Service Trades," *Retail Wholesale Department Store Employee* (December 1943), 8.

39. *Proceedings of the Third Biennial Convention, United Retail, Wholesale, and Department Store Employees of America, CIO, May 18-24, 1942, Chicago, Illinois* (hereafter *Third Convention Proceedings*), 20; "FEPC—A Challenge To America," *Retail Wholesale Department Store Employee* (July 1945), 5.

40. For the RWDSU during the war, see cartoon accompanying "To NLRB Polls February 12," *Retail Wholesale and Department Store Employee* (January 31, 1942), 9, and cartoon accompanying "Convention Outlook," *Retail Wholesale and Department Store Employee* (April 30, 1942), 4. For the sole depiction of women as union representatives during the war, see "Doors Open May 18," *Retail Wholesale and Department Store Employee* (March 31, 1942), 4.

41. "A Record of Achievement and Progress," *Retail Wholesale Department Store Employee* (June 22, 1942), 3, 5, 11.

42. *Third Convention Proceedings,* 190. Wolchok probably mentioned Local 1250 organizer Eli Halpern instead of Carnes or Clarina Michelson because of Halpern's presence at the convention when these remarks were made rather than out of any greater animosity towards Halpern than towards the other department store union leaders or organizers.

43. *Third Convention Proceedings,* 194.

44. "President's Speech of Welcome to Convention," *Retail Wholesale Department Store Employee* (June 1942), 5.

45. *Investigation of Seizure of Montgomery Ward & Co.: Hearings Before the Select Committee to Investigate Seizure of Montgomery Ward & Co., House of Representatives, 78th Congress, Second Session, Pursuant To H. Res. 521* (May 22–25,

1944 and June 6–8, 1944). (U.S. Govt. Print Office; Washington, 1944) [Hereafter *Montgomery Ward Hearings*], Testimony of Samuel Wolchok, 481.

46. *Montgomery Ward Hearings,* Testimony of William H. Davis, 11. For these early struggles between Montgomery Ward and the federal government during the war, see also J. M. Baskin, "Ward's Charges Discrimination Anew By OPA," *Women's Wear Daily* (November 18, 1942), 1, 5; "Duress Charge Rekindles Ward Row With WLB," *Women's Wear Daily* (December 2, 1942), 1, 24; "To All Montgomery Ward People" [display advertisement], *Women's Wear Daily* (January 12, 1943), 52.

47. *Montgomery Ward Hearings,* Testimony of William H. Davis, 28–30.

48. Ibid., 30.

49. For the sympathy strikes, see "More on Job at Chicago Unit, Ward's States," *Women's Wear Daily* (April 17, 1944), 2. For Roosevelt's order, see "President Orders Dispute at Ward's to End Tomorrow," *Women's Wear Daily* (April 24, 1944), 1, 12; for the arrival of the military, see *Montgomery Ward Hearings,* Testimony of Sewell Avery, 331–32; "Ward, Chicago, Run By Commerce Dept.," *Women's Wear Daily* (April 27, 1944), 1, 6; and "Biddle Backs Legality of Ward Seizure," *Women's Wear Daily* (April 27, 1944), 1, 7.

50. Raymond Gibney, "Await Court Rule on Ward Seizure: Cannot Allow Employer or Union to Interfere," *Women's Wear Daily* (December 29, 1944), 1, 5; J.M. Baskin, "Army in Nominal Charge of Company Operations in 7 Cities," *Women's Wear Daily* (December 29, 1944), 1, 6; "Supreme Court Rules Thumbs Down on Ward," *Retail Wholesale Department Store Employee* (December 1944), 3; "Army Lays Down Law At Montgomery Ward," *Retail Wholesale Department Store Employee* (January 1945), 3, 7, 16; "Judge Sullivan Upholds Property Rights In Face of War Emergency; U.S. Appeals to Supreme Court," *Retail Wholesale Department Store Employee* (February 1945), 3; "Sweeping Redress for Chicago Ward Workers Ruled By Judge Knous," *Retail Wholesale Department Store Employee* (February 1945), 2; "Ward's 'Closed Shop' Ends as Army Leaves," *Women's Wear Daily* (October 19, 1945), 1, 22.

51. Quoted in Samuel Wolchok, "Treachery in Our Ranks," *Retail Wholesale Department Store Employee* (January 1945), 4.

52. Ibid., 3, 4, 8, 15.

53. "Condemn '65' Leadership," *Retail Wholesale Department Store Employee* (February 1945), 9; "Osman's True Allegiance? Shown By Turnabout Face," *Retail Wholesale Department Store Employee* (February 1945), 27; "Nails Foes of URWDSEA's War On Montgomery Ward," *Retail Wholesale Department Store Employee* (February 1945), 27; "Flays Local 65 Head for Union Treachery," *Retail Wholesale Department Store Employee* (February 1945), 26; "Points Out Flaws In 'Sudden Switch,'" *Retail Wholesale Department Store Employee* (February 1945), 26; "Osman Aligns Union With 'Worst Enemy,'" *Retail Wholesale Department Store Employee* (February 1945), 25; "Local 1102 Demands Board Nail Osman," *Retail Wholesale Department Store Employee* (March 1945), 24.

54. Samuel Wolchok, "A Message from Pres. Samuel Wolchok," *Retail Wholesale Department Store Employee* (August 1, 1943), 5.

55. For an insightful defense of the no-strike pledge, see Joshua Freeman,

"Delivering the Goods: Industrial Unionism During World War II," *Labor History* 19 (1978), 570–93.

56. If the department store union leaders did release any statements on the Montgomery Ward strike, these statements have been both lost and entirely ignored by Wolchok and the other national leaders, a combination of events which seems unlikely.

Chapter 5

1. For the garment district, see Frank Engle, "Joyful Throngs Greet War's End in Garment Area," *Women's Wear Daily* (August 15, 1943), p. C; for the store windows, see Earl A. Dash, "V-J Displays Are Patriotic and Solemn," *Women's Wear Daily* (August 15, 1943), p. C.

2. "Seven Apartments Tied Up By Strike," *New York Times* (September 7, 1945), 25; Frank S. Adams, "11,000 Are Idle," *New York Times* (September 25, 1945), 1. For the dock workers, see George Lipsitz, *Rainbow At Midnight: Labor and Culture in the 1940s* (Urbana: University of Illinois Press, 1994), 104–7.

3. For suburbanization and New York City, see Joshua B. Freeman, *Working-Class New York: Life and Labor Since World War II* (New York: The New Press, 2000), 171–74, and Kenneth T. Jackson, *Crabgrass Frontier: The Suburbanization of the United States* (Oxford: Oxford University Press, 1985), 238–39. For the figures on suburbanization, see "Growth In Queens Outdoes Services," *New York Times* (December 9, 1947), 31; "Suburbs Outstrip City in Population Growth," *New York Times* (November 12, 1948), 4; "18 Branches Set Up By City's Big Shops," *New York Times* (June 11, 1949), 15; and Dero A. Saunders, "Department Stores: Race For The Suburbs," *Fortune* (December 1951), 98–104, 166–70, 173.

4. "Bloomingdale's Calendar of Special Events," *Department Store Economist* (June 1947), 104–5. See also "18 Branches Set Up By City's Big Shops," 15; "Growing Trend to Suburban Branches Near N.Y. in Last Five Years Cited," *Women's Wear Daily* (January 2, 1952), 4; and "62 Branches of 28 Stores Signify Suburban Growth," *Women's Wear Daily* (May 7, 1952), 66.

5. Guernsey, "Suburban Branches: Part One In A Series," *Department Store Economist* (June 1951), 120; Guernsey, "Good Practices in Operation of Branch Stores," *Department Store Economist* (September 1952), 154.

6. Ibid, 154. More discussion of branch stores will be provided in chapter 6.

7. For Parkchester, see "Macy's Parkchester (org 1945) 1945 Agreement," in Local 1-S Papers, Box 7, Folder 2. For the Jamaica store, see *Jamaica Jottings* (February 2, 1948). For the opening of the Jamaica store, see Glenn Fowler, "Macy's Jamaica on First Day Draws Shelf-Clearing Crowd," *Women's Wear Daily* (September 8, 1947), 1, 41.

8. William B. Gorman, Secretary-Treasurer, Controllers' Congress of the NRDGA and Controller, Gimbel Brothers, NY, "Looking Through the Figures— 1945," *Department Store Economist* (July 1946), 18. Much of this data is reprinted in table 5.1. For similar statements about the lack of increased productivity, see Herman

Radolf, "McNair Links Store Pay Rise to Increase in Productivity," *Women's Wear Daily* (August 1, 1952), 1, 39.

9. Maurice Sagoff, "Stores Cite Lower Markups, Urge Price Cuts by Producers," *Women's Wear Daily* (September 18, 1947), 1, 64.

10. J. Howard Pew, "Labor's Stake in Freedom" *Department Store Economist* (July 1946), 23.

11. For price controls, see Andrew H. Bartels, "The Office of Price Administration and the Legacy of the New Deal, 1939–1946," *Public Historian* 5:3 (Summer 1983), 5–29; Meg Jacobs, "How About Some Meat?": The Office of Price Administration, Consumption Politics, and State Building from the Bottom Up, 1941–1946" *Journal of American History* 84:3 (December 1997), 910–41; and Lizabeth Cohen, *Consumer's Republic,* 64–70. For the efforts of store managers to end the OPA, see "Exhibit in Anti-Inflation Campaign," *Women's Wear Daily* (March 25, 1946), 32, and "Exhibit OPA 'Inequalities' in Capital Tomorrow," *Women's Wear Daily* (November 12, 1945), 19.

12. For the RLSA, see Marcella Loring, "Macy's Cracks the Whip," *Department Store Employee* (December 29, 1945), 1, "'We Fight Fire With Fire' In Forming Joint Board," *Department Store Employee* (October 5, 1946), 3; Donald L. Pratt, "N.Y. Stores Pick Labor Relations Spokesman," *Women's Wear Daily* (November 21, 1945), 1, 30; "N.Y. Stores Labor Relations Group Holds Organization Meeting Today," *Women's Wear Daily* (November 29, 1945), 6; "Report to Membership" (February 5, 1947), 9, in District 65 Papers, Box 60, Folder 23.

13. "Exhibits Stress Ways to Speed Store Functions," *Women's Wear Daily* (January 13, 1948), 86; Earl Dash, "Managers Seek Ways to Cut Operating Costs," *Women's Wear Daily* (January 14, 1948), 119.

14. This description of work simplification is taken from Herman Radolf, "Job Simplification Should Never Stop," *Women's Wear Daily* (May 16, 1947), 45 and "Work Simplification Program Started at Saks Stores," *Women's Wear Daily* (February 3, 1947), 50; the industrial consultant quote is from Radolf; the notion of breaking down jobs is from "Work Simplification Program Started at Saks Stores." For the focus on the simplification of nonsales jobs, see also "Stores Urged to Cut Corners, Increase Output Per Employee," *Women's Wear Daily* (June 12, 1947), 1, 47. For the layoffs, see Donald L. Pratt, "Dept. Store Union Locals Here Worried Over Rising Layoffs," *Women's Wear Daily* (March 20, 1947), 1, 4; "Hearn Workers Hit By Huge Layoffs," *Union Voice* (January 1, 1950), 9; and "Macy Workers Charge Speedup Takes Heavy Toll in N.Y. Stores," *Union Voice* (March 30, 1947), 3–4. For the union's inability to prevent layoffs, see "Union Softens B'dale Layoff Impact," *Union Voice* (January 1, 1950), 4. For the speedups, see especially Pratt, "Dept. Store Union Locals" and "Macys Denies Speedup, Stewards Map Action," *Union Voice* (June 22, 1947), 7.

15. "Prewar Services to be Restored," *Women's Wear Daily* (August 26, 1946), 37. For the Thanksgiving parade, see "Macy Thanksgiving Parade Revives Prewar Pageantry," *Women's Wear Daily* (November 29, 1946), 7.

16. "Strike Cripples Macy's; HCL Wage Talk Asked," *Department Store Employee* (July 1946), 1. For the Parkchester store, see "Sales off 30% At Parkchester in Macy

Strike," *Women's Wear Daily* (July 17, 1946), 1, 10. For strike violence, see "2 Hurt As Violence Marks Macy Strike," *New York Times* (July 13, 1946), 1, 3; "500 Macy Pickets Clash With Police," *New York Times* (July 18, 1946), 1, 12.

17. For the triple-pay policy, see Jack I. Straus, Letter to All Macy's Employees (July 22, 1946) in Local 1-S Papers, Box 5, Folder 29.

18. Bernie Morley, "Highlights of the Strike," *Department Store Employee* (July 1946), 1.

19. Letter from Ann Limitone to Sadka Brown (dated April 30, 1947), in District 65 Papers, Box 60, Folder 10.

20. Letter from Miss E. Goldstein to Sadka Brown (dated January 11, 1950), in District 65 Papers, Box 59, Folder 8.

21. For inflation, including subway fares, and department store wages, see William Michelson, "Dept. Store $$ and Sense," *Union Voice* (April 13, 1947), 16.

22. For the attacks on Wolchok, see Donald Pratt, "Retail Union Fight Here May Get Into Court," *Women's Wear Daily* (January 9, 1946), 1, 49; and "N.Y. Locals' Rift With Wolchok Grows," *Women's Wear Daily* (January 23, 1946), 1, 10

23. Proceedings of the Fourth Convention of the Retail Wholesale and Department Store Union, CIO (May 14–18, 1946), 6–12 (hereafter *Fourth Convention Proceedings*). For a discussion of international issues and the liberal agenda, especially the issue of world government, see Paul Boyer, *By The Bomb's Early Light: American Thought and Culture at the Dawn of the Atomic Age* (Chapel Hill: University of North Carolina Press, 1994), 29–45.

24. *Fourth Convention Proceedings*, 28–29, 38.

25. *Fourth Convention Proceedings*, 138–46; 427.

26. *Fourth Convention Proceedings*, 179–80, 223–41, 272.

27. Milton Zatinsky, Educational Director, St. Louis Joint Council, URWDSEA, CIO, "Let's Look At Our Union: Its Aims, Activities, and Accomplishments," pamphlet (October 1945), 22–25. Pamphlet in possession of author.

28. For Wolchok's earlier position, see Local 1-S Executive Board Meeting of April 24, 1946, Box 1, Folder 18, Local 1-S Papers. For his reversal and support for the Joint Board, see "Department Store Joint Board To Get Going In January," *Retail Wholesale Department Store Employee* (January 1947), 14. For the new hands-off policy, see Jack Altman, "On Department Stores," *Retail Wholesale Department Store Employee* (February 1947), 6.

29. "Left-Wing Parade To Salute May Day," *New York Times* (May 1, 1946), 27; A.H. Raskin, "Veterans in Uniform Head Red Unit in May Day Parade," *New York Times* (May 2, 1946), 1; "'We Want Peace!' May Day Call," *Department Store Employee* (May 11, 1946), 1, 3.

30. Donald I. Pratt, "5th Ave. Drive By CIO Retail Union Forecast," *Women's Wear Daily* (May 15, 1946), 1, 6; "CIO Store Union Maps Local Drive," *Women's Wear Daily* (November 4, 1946), 2; George Kirstein, "Labor and Management," *Women's Wear Daily* (July 5, 1946), 39, 42.

31. "Vets and Dept. Store Workers Join To Fight 'Daily News' Hate Policy," *Department Store Employee* (January 12, 1946), 3.

32. For the *Union Voice*, see "Employee, Union Voice Join After This Issue,"

Department Store Employee (January 11, 1947), 1. "The 1-S Glee Club In Action," *Department Store Employee* (November 24, 1945), 1; "Fun High on Agenda at Card Party," *Department Store Employee* (December 8, 1945), 1; "There Goes That Dance Again!" *Department Store Employee* (December 8, 1945), 1.

33. *Thursdays Till Nine,* Act I, 23, 32; Act II, 5–6.

34. *Thursdays Till Nine,* Act I, 16–17.

35. *Thursdays Till Nine,* Act I, 31; Arthur Adler, "Miracle on 34th Street is Delightful Whimsy—Should Happen in Macys," *Union Voice* (June 22, 1947), 21.

36. On the Taft-Hartley Act, see George Lipsitz, *Rainbow At Midnight: Labor and Culture in the 1940s* (Urbana: University of Illinois Press, 1994), 169–79.

37. Even those union members who worked in the stores for many years could be entirely unaware of the political issues surrounding the union; though she vividly remembered many of her experiences at Macy's, union member Jane Spadavecchio did not remember any political conflict within the union at this time. See Spadavecchio interview. The union leaders themselves stated that most workers were not particularly aware of "the extent of the problems" which Taft-Hartley presented for the union leaders; see Report on Structural Changes, delivered by Sadka Brown, Local 5 Leadership Conference (May 7, 1948), 3, 4, 6, in District 65 Papers, Box 60, Folder 23.

38. Minutes, Local 5 Executive Board Meeting (September 2, 1947), in Folder 23, Box 60, District 65 Papers. The Hearn's managers' statement is quoted in Joint Department Store Board, *Negotiations Bulletin* 6 (June 7, 1948), in District 65 Papers, Box 60, Folder 23.

39. "Administration Slate Wins in Local 1-S Record Vote; Red-Baiters Snowed Under," *Union Voice* (February 2, 1947), 2. Testimony of Bertha Kronthal, *Investigation On Communism In New York City Distributive Trade,* 649.

40. "Red Rule Charged in Tobacco Union," *New York Times* (July 24, 1947), 4; see also Ellen Schrecker, *Many Are the Crimes: McCarthyism in America* (Princeton: Princeton University Press, 1998).

41. "Clark Sees Nation Aware of Danger," *New York Times* (May 2, 1948), 5. Some Communist leaders claimed the parade had as many as 100,000 people in attendance, but this claim is in serious dispute; most observers were inclined to agree that the police estimate of just over 20,000 was closer to the actual number of people marching in the parade. For this dispute see "Left Outnumbered on May Day Here; Europe is Orderly," *New York Times* (May 2, 1948), 1, 3.

42. "NLRB Accepts Affidavits," *Retail Wholesale Department Store Employee* (March 1948), 1. John V. Cooney Letter "To All Locals . . ." (dated February 17, 1948) in Local 1-S Papers, Box 4, Folder 20.

43. Glenn Fowler, "CIO Store Locals Seek Pact Extension as Deadline Nears," *Women's Wear Daily* (August 21, 1947), 2; "CIO Contracts Extended by 9 Stores in N.Y.," *Women's Wear Daily* (August 25, 1947), 1, 32; and *Investigation on Communism,* Testimony of Louis Broido, 88.

44. For Kovenetsky as a non-Communist, see, for example, William Michelson interview. Kovenetsky himself was the only member of the New York coalition who denied being a Communist under oath; see *Investigation,* Testimony of Samuel

Kovenetsky, 584. Kovenetsky's refusal to sign the petition against the will of the members was stated in Kovenetsky interview, 31. He made substantially the same statement about his affidavit relying on the members' willingness to have him sign at the 1948 congressional hearings on the subject; see *Investigation,* Testimony of Samuel Kovenetsky, 565.

45. For the expulsions, see "Probe Ordered On Expulsions by Store Union," *Women's Wear Daily* (June 4, 1948), 1, 45; George G. Kirstein, "Labor and Management," *Women's Wear Daily* (June 11, 1948), 55; and also *Investigation,* Testimony of Alice Bartoli, Shop-Steward, Local 1-S, 658. For the *Daily News* articles, see "The Stores Had Better Fight," *Daily News* (June 3, 1948), 39, and "Shall Reds Boss The Stores?" *Daily News* (June 18, 1948), 35; as well as the editorial cartoon, "Invite," *Daily News* (June 18, 1948), 35. For the reversal of the expulsions, see Glenn Fowler, "Reversal Set on Expulsions By Store Union," *Women's Wear Daily* (June 18, 1948), 1, 7.

46. For the initial contract between Oppenheim Collins and Local 1250, see "Oppenheim Collins, Union Agree on Pact," *Women's Wear Daily* (August 27, 1946), 4. For the contract renewal, see "The Oppenheim Collins Strikers Thank The Public," undated flyer, issued by Local 1250, in Folder 12, Box 60, District 65 Papers; see also "GEB Orders T-H Compliance; Four Non-Complying Locals Suspended," *Retail Wholesale Department Store Employee* (September 1948), 3. A good summary of the various manipulations at Oppenheim Collins is available in *Women's Wear Daily;* see especially Fred Eichelbaum, "Election Won By AFL Union At Oppenheim's," *Women's Wear Daily* (August 3, 1948), 1, 12; and "Court Restrains Mass Picketing at Oppenheim's," *Women's Wear Daily* (August 16, 1948), 1.

47. For the union stance, see "Put Yourself In Our Place," sample leaflet, undated, issued by Local 1250, undated, in Folder 12, Box 60, District 65 Papers. For Oppenheim Collins' stance, see "Union Defeat in Oppenheim Poll Claimed," *Women's Wear Daily* (June 16, 1948), 5.

48. "Mass Picketing Ban Continued At Oppenheim's," *Women's Wear Daily* (August 10, 1948), 2; "Live Models Used As Counter-Pickets," *Women's Wear Daily* (September 28, 1948), 50.

49. "Sidewalk Vendors," *Daily News* (August 3, 1948), 26–27. See also Dominick Unsino, "Store Picket Held in Attack on Salesman," *Daily News* (August 4, 1948), 6, and Unsino, "Store Workers Vote AFL, Lefties Sue," *Daily News* (August 3, 1948), 3.

50. "Denies Petition to Curb Pickets at Oppenheim's," *Women's Wear Daily* (August 9, 1948), 1, 23; "Mass Picketing Ban Continued At Oppenheim's," *Women's Wear Daily* (August 10, 1948), 2.

51. *Investigation,* Testimony of Louis Broido, 87. For the picket lines, see *Investigation,* Testimony of Samuel Kovenetsky, 561, and "Mass Picketing of Gimbels Has Little Effect on Traffic," *Women's Wear Daily* (July 16, 1948), 6.

52. *Investigation,* Testimony of Samuel Wolchok, 502–4.

53. *Investigation,* Testimony of Jack Altman, 515.

54. *Investigation,* Testimony of John McCauley, 638; Testimony of Alice Bartoli, 652–53, 668–69.

55. Atkinson interview; Kovenetsky interview, 39.

56. "GEB Orders T-H Compliance; Four Non-Complying Locals Suspended." *Retail Wholesale Department Store Employee* (September 1948), 3. Letter from Samuel Wolchok to Samuel Kovenetsky (dated August 12, 1948), in Local 1-S Papers, Box 4, Folder 20.

57. Report To Executive Board Meeting (August 17, 1948), delivered by Sadka Brown, in District 65 Papers, Box 60, Folder 12; Report To Divisional Meetings (August 1948), delivered by Sadka Brown, in District 65 Papers, Box 60, Folder 12.

58. "Resolution on Disaffiliation, Adopted by Membership of Local 5, RWDSU, CIO, at Meeting Held September 21, 1948," District 65 Papers, Box 60, Folder 12. As we will see, contrary to the workers' supporting the RWDSU, it was union leaders who would soon become the strongest supporters of reaffiliation.

59. Samuel Wolchok, Letter to Membership (Undated), 2–3, in District 65 Papers, Box 60, Folder 12.

60. This event is recounted in Atkinson interview. Atkinson claimed that this event took place just before the war. The minutes from the executive board meetings in 1941, however, have no record of any such conflict. Also, no evidence indicates that Jack Altman was involved with the department store unions until the end of the war, when he became the new administrator of Local 1-S. It seems likely, therefore, that Atkinson's memory was inaccurate on the date of this incident. For the administrators, see "Administrators Named to Run Retail Locals," *Women's Wear Daily* (August 26, 1948), 1, 8.

61. "Retail Organizing Drive," *Business Week* (December 25, 1948), 62–66; "The Sin of Sloth," *Newsweek* (December 27, 1948), 50; George G. Kirstein, "Labor and Management," *Women's Wear Daily* (October 15, 1948), 47; "The Penalty of Failure," *Time* (December 27, 1948), 17. The CIO official is quoted in "Retail Organizing Drive," 66. For the ACWA's entrance into the field, see "Murray Asks Reorganization To Bolster CIO Store Union," *Women's Wear Daily* (November 23, 1948), 10, and Lloyd Schwartz, "ACW Gets Powers in Retail Fields," *Women's Wear Daily* (December 16, 1948), 1, 58.

62. Glenn Fowler, "Grant Wolchok Leave From Retail Union," *Women's Wear Daily* (December 21, 1948), 1, 37.

Chapter 6

1. There is a growing body of work on the decline of manufacturing in America. See especially the essays in Jefferson Cowie and Joseph Heathcott, eds., *Beyond the Ruins: The Meanings of Deindustrialization in America* (Ithaca: Cornell University Press, 2003).

2. For the failure of the drive, see "N.Y. Locals Concede Failure in Store Organizing Drive," *Women's Wear Daily* (April 13, 1953), 1, 34.

3. "7 St. East Near Stuyvesant Town," classified advertisement, *New York Times* (June 27, 1948), R18. For the description of Stuyvesant Town as suburbia, see "'Projects' Become Home, Sweet Home," *New York Times* (June 21, 1949), 27. For Stuyvesant Town as a project for "the middle-income group," see Robert M. Hallett,

"Slums Out, Homes In," *Christian Science Monitor* (January 11, 1947), WM2. For the unique nature of the project, see "Housing Squeeze Held Threat To N.Y. Department Stores," *Women's Wear Daily* (June 20, 1952), 2.

4. "Negroes To Stay In Banned 'Town,'" *New York Times* (September 12, 1949), 40. See also Arthur Simon, *Stuyvesant Town, U.S.A.: Pattern For Two Americas* (New York: New York University Press, 1970), 77–82. The quotation is taken from Simon, p. 78.

5. Simon, *Stuyvesant Town, U.S.A.,* 90–91.

6. For the evictions at Stuyvesant Town, see Simon, *Stuyvesant Town, U.S.A.,* 99–100. For the Levitt quote, see Dolores Hayden, *Redesigning the American Dream: The Future of Housing, Work, and Family Life* (New York: W.W. Norton, 1984), 8. For a good discussion of whiteness and the middle class in postwar New York, see Jerald Podair, *The Strike That Changed New York: Blacks, Whites, and the Ocean Hill-Brownsville Crisis* (New Haven, CT: Yale University Press, 2002), 206–14. For other aspects of the postwar middle class, see Andrew Hurley, *Diners, Bowling Alleys, and Trailer Parks: Chasing the American Dream in Postwar Consumer Culture* (New York: Basic Books, 2001).

7. For the expansion of branch stores in this era, see John Guernsey, "Suburban Branches: Part Two in a Series," *Department Store Economist* (July 1951), 111. See also "18 Branches Set Up By City's Big Shops," *New York Times* (June 11, 1949), 15; Glenn Fowler, "Stores Expected to Continue Pace of Branch Expansions," *Women's Wear Daily* (December 6, 1950), 5; Ed Stanton, "Suburban Stores Have Good Labor Pool," *Women's Wear Daily* (December 29, 1952), Section 2, p. 20. For the quote as well as a good discussion of suburbanization, see Minna Pearl Ziskind, "Citizenship, Consumerism, and Gender: A Study of District 65, 1945–1960," doctoral dissertation (University of Pennsylvania, 2001), 241.

8. For the quote on the new era of retailing, see Richard Neumaier, "A New Era In Unit Control Has Arrived," *Department Store Economist* (September 1953), 40–41. Others seconded Neumaier's opinion of the early 1950s as a new era in retailing; see especially Wade G. McCargo, "1953—A Year of Challenge and Opportunity," *Department Store Economist* (February 1953), 35. For her memories of Klein's, see Corrine Demas, *Eleven Stories High: Growing Up In Stuyvesant Town, 1948–1968* (Albany: State University of New York Press, 2000), 85, 88. Although they are not explicit about why customers disliked full-service, managers insisted that customer preference was a major reason for instituting self-service retailing. See, for instance, Abe Hackman, "Stores Should Explore All Ways to Raise Productivity," *Women's Wear Daily* (May 5, 1952), 42; the *Women's Wear Daily* survey summarized in "Self-Service Hailed As 100% Success," *Women's Wear Daily* (September 5, 1952), 9, also indicates that 89 percent of store managers believed self-service departments were more popular than full-service.

9. Mary Roche, "Model Apartment Adopts New Dress," *New York Times* (November 18, 1947), 35. See also Pete Montanaro, Untitled Report to Local 1250 Membership Meeting (August 19, 1952), 1–3, in District 65 Papers, Box 15, Folder 16. For Hearn's expansion into higher-priced goods (although Stuyvesant Town is not specifically mentioned), see "Store's New 'Look' Sells New Merchandising

Policy," *Women's Wear Daily* (May 9, 1944), 27; "Hearn's Policy to Expand Specialty, Suburban Shops," *Women's Wear Daily* (August 31, 1948).

10. "Filene's Coin Vending Center Draws Throngs," *Women's Wear Daily* (May 17, 1950), 1, 51; Ivor Boggiss, "How 'Vis-O-Matic' Shopping Works," *Women's Wear Daily* (June 15, 1950), 78; Herman Radolf, "What's Ahead for Automatic Selling?" *Women's Wear Daily* (June 28, 1950), 57; "Sales Machines Need Traffic," *Women's Wear Daily* (December 29, 1952), Section 2, p. 8.

11. For the elimination of the gift-wrapping unit and wage and cost-cutting at Gimbel's, see Minutes, Executive Board Meeting of Local 2, United Department Store Workers of New York (May 9, 1950), 1–2, in Folder 33, Box 14, District 65 Papers. For the quotations from buyers and the trend towards self-service, see "Transformation of Main Floor at Gimbels," *Department Store Economist* (January 1951), 33–34, 52. See also Herman Radolf, "Plain Old Gimbels Bows Out With New Main Floor," *Women's Wear Daily* (November 8, 1950), 94, and Fred Eichelbaum, "Need For Better Efficiency in Customer Services Emphasized," *Women's Wear Daily* (January 10, 1951), 106.

12. "All Eyes on Notions at Bloomingdale's," *Department Store Economist* (July 1952), 90, and "Bloomingdale's Housewares Put On Supermarket Basis," *Women's Wear Daily* (August 13, 1952), 1. For self-service at Macy's, see "Designed For Impulse Sales," *Women's Wear Daily* (February 7, 1952), 53; "One-Day Self-Service Dress Sale Reaches $30,000 Mark At Macy's," *Women's Wear Daily* (October 29, 1952), 4; and Ed Stanton, "Self-Service Toy Section A Lively Retail Subject," *Women's Wear Daily* (May 14, 1953), 64.

13. Julian H. Handler, "Survey of Supermarkets Reveals Rise In Non-Food Merchandising," *Women's Wear Daily;* "Self-Service Growing as Vital Merchandising Method," *Women's Wear Daily* (December 26, 1951), 5; "$2–$4 Billion Supermarket Soft Lines Potential Seen," *Women's Wear Daily* (May 15, 1952), 1, 13; Samuel Feinberg, "From Where I Sit," *Women's Wear Daily* (November 5, 1952), 86. For good summaries of the rise of self-service, see Robert F. Elder, "Consumer Markets Have Changed," *Women's Wear Daily* (February 25, 1952), 53; and Harry Berlfein, "40% of Retailers in Survey Plan to Expand Self-Service," *Women's Wear Daily* (December 3, 1952), 1, 59.

14. "Branded Lines Called Good Investment for the Future," *Women's Wear Daily* (July 21, 1944), 31; "Brands Make Selling Easier, Get Nod From Most Stores," *Women's Wear Daily* (October 15, 1953), Special Fashion Brands section, p. 4; "Many Customers Buy Merchandise By Brand Name," *Women's Wear Daily* (October 15, 1953), Special Fashion Brands section, p. 4; Samuel Feinberg, "From Where I Sit," *Women's Wear Daily* (December 18, 1953), 39. Department stores were unusually hesitant when dealing with television. While a few stores—A&S among them—launched major television campaigns, most store managers viewed television as expensive and ultimately useless, especially considering how poor early television sets were for conveying the styles and colors of the stores' clothing lines. For a good summary of the early history, see Ed Gold, "Fear of TV Traced to Early Flops," *Women's Wear Daily* (March 13, 1952), 65. For A&S's television efforts, see Alvin Dann, "Abraham & Strauss Launches Video Series With a New Slant," *Women's Wear Daily* (October 3, 1950), 59.

15. For the doubts about the greater efficiency of self-service, see "Greater Productivity's The Riddle," *Women's Wear Daily*, Section 2 (December 27, 1948), 4, 50, 52. For the ultimate decision that self-service was practical, see "Super Market Selling Methods Held Cost-Savers," *Women's Wear Daily* (January 10, 1952), 66.

16. For the television cameras in stores, see "TV Eye Helps Stores To Foil Shoplifters," *Women's Wear Daily* (December 11, 1953), 44; "This Customer May Not Know It . . . But She's On Television," *Women's Wear Daily* (November 19, 1953), 50; and "Effect of Self-Service On Protection Staff Cited," *Women's Wear Daily* (September 3, 1953), 47. For the electronic price tag, see Richard Neumaier, "A New Era In Unit Control Has Arrived," *Department Store Economist* (September 1953), 40–41, 68; Bob Johnston, "Punched Card Unit Control Safeguards Stock Investment," *Women's Wear Daily* (February 11, 1952), 41; and Herman Radolf, "Bloomingdale's to Get First Rem Rand Tag Reader Setup," *Women's Wear Daily* (April 1, 1953), 63. Neumaier's enthusiasm notwithstanding, in the early 1950s most store managers still hesitated to adopt these measures; see "Electronics Still Too Costly For Use in Department Stores," *Women's Wear Daily* (December 15, 1952), 38.

17. "Modern Merchandising Through Efficient Store Facilities," *Department Store Economist* (August 1948), 65.

18. Letter from Louis Broido to David Livingston, President DPOWA, dated August 1952, in Gimbels and Saks Collection (Volume 3), Baker Library, Harvard University.

19. Minutes, Local 1250 Executive Board Meeting (October 1, 1952), 1, in District 65 Papers, Box 15, Folder 16. For the CIO's stance, see "Self-Service Held Necessary Move at CIO Convention," *Women's Wear Daily* (November 23, 1953), 1, 29.

20. Post-1948 layoffs and restructuring will be discussed further later in this chapter. For anti-union announcements at training programs, see Minutes, Local 2 Executive Board Meeting (May 9, 1950), 1, District 65 Papers, Box 14, Folder 33. For the Macy's *Star,* see "Stress Employees' Role in Guiding Store Union Policy," *Women's Wear Daily* (July 2, 1948), 33.

21. For Quill's threat, see Bernard Tolkow, Report of 1250 Membership-Wage Drive (September 24, 1951), in District 65 Papers, Box 15, Folder 15. For the "iron curtain" quote, see "CIO Shaping 2-Prong Drive At N.Y. Stores," *Women's Wear Daily* (October 22, 1951), 1, 51.

22. Memorandum ("Sparklet") To Macy's Employees from Frederick G. Atkinson, Vice-President of Personnel at Macy's (September 7, 1948); managers' joint statement is discussed in Bernard Tolkow, "Collective Bargaining," Report Delivered at Local 1250 Membership Meeting (November 20, 1950), in District 65 Papers, Box 15, Folder 4. See also "Bloomingdale's Weighs Stand," *Women's Wear Daily* (September 15, 1948), 4; "International Officer Barred From Stern Wage Arbitration," *Women's Wear Daily* (September 17, 1948), 7; and, for a good summary of the position of managers on these struggles, George Kirstein, "Labor and Management," *Women's Wear Daily* (September 17, 1948), 59.

23. For the local leaders' decision to sign, see Report to Local 5 Membership Meeting, delivered by Sadka Brown, (dated October 25, 1948), 6, in District 65

Papers, Folder 12, Box 60. For Michelson's delay in signing, see "Remarks Made by Arthur Osman on Bill Michelson's Report at the UDSW General Council Meeting on May 24, 1950," 6, in District 65 Papers, Box 15, Folder 49.

24. "Remarks Made by Arthur Osman on Bill Michelson's Report at the UDSW General Council Meeting on May 24, 1950," 1, in District 65 Papers, Box 15, Folder 49.

25. Ibid., 2.

26. "Ykstenevok . . . Spelled Backwards is Kovenetsky," Undated RWDSU Flyer, and "A Letter to Sam Kovenetsky from Sam Meyers," Undated RCIA Flyer, both in Local 1-S Papers, Box 4, Folder 21.

27. "District 65—Largest N.Y. Union!" *Union Voice* (September 10, 1950), 3.

28. For the social calendar, see Minutes of Local 3 Membership Meeting (June 1951), 5, in District 65 Papers, Box 15, Folder 7. For the union leaders' determination to revive the union's cultural programs and its relation to union members' dedication to the union, see Irving Baldinger, "Report on Union Voice," Local 65 General Council (June 27, 1949), 2. For the boat trip, see Simon, *Stuyvesant Town, U.S.A.*, 78.

29. Glenn Fowler, "Retail Union Buying Service Activity Grows," *Women's Wear Daily* (May 26, 1950), 1, 41; for the pensions, see Fowler, "Retail Union in Pension Drive at N.Y. Stores," *Women's Wear Daily* (December 3, 1951), 1, 43;

30. For the Rosenberg vigil, see especially Laura Helton, "'It never became the same,': Memories of Union Square as a Center of Radicalism," Panel on "Site of Memory and Contestation: Union Square and Social Movements in the Twentieth Century," History Matters Conference (2003), New School University, New York.

31. Marty Solow, "Independents Sweep Stern, Bloomingdale; Crush AFL," *Union Voice* (April 10, 1949), 3.

32. "Carnes Cites DWU Constitution as Guarantee of Union Democracy," *Union Voice* (February 10, 1950), 4. David Livingston, "Democracy—65's Main Asset," *Union Voice* (September 10, 1950), M1.

33. "Gimbel Workers Halt Move to Cut Earnings," *Union Voice* (July 31, 1949), 7. See also Sadka Brown, "Short Analysis and Recommendations to Executive Board, Shop Stewards, Negotiations Committee" (February 2, 1949), 1, in District 65 Papers, Box 60, Folder 13.

34. See, for instance, "Gimbel Workers Halt Move to Cut Earnings," *Union Voice* (July 31, 1949), 7; "Hearn Units Speed Strike Preparations," *Union Voice* (November 6, 1949), 2; and "Flashbacks of 1949," *Union Voice* (January 15, 1950), M4–M5.

35. "Macyites Squelch Anti-Negro Display," *Union Voice* (March 27, 1949), 13.

36. Belle Johnson, "Negro History Report," to Local 2 General Membership Meeting, District 65 Papers, Box 15, Folder 19. For the sales jobs in Bloomingdale's, see Murray Silverstein, "Negro Worker Wins B'dale Selling Job," *Union Voice* (October 7, 1951), 6.

37. "Case #137, Accounts Payable Dept. (Gimbels) vs. Local 2 Executive Board, Hearing Held May 31st, 1951," in District 65 General Council Meeting Minutes (June 6, 1951), 1–2.

38. "Negroes Being Upgraded at Gimbels, Saks," *Union Voice* (December 18,

1949), 12. For the Stern's negotiations, see "Report and Proposals to Executive Board and Shop Stewards Meeting," (February 8, 1949), in District 65 Papers, Box 60, Folder 13. "Report to Membership Meeting" (January 26, 1949), 9, in District 65 Papers, Box 60, Folder 13.

39. Harold Pearlman, "Opposes 'Cheesecake' Pictures in Union Voice," *Union Voice* (July 31, 1949), 10. Leo Wolf, "He Says Let 'Cheesecake' Reign in UV Forever," *Union Voice* (August 14, 1949), 10.

40. Elizabeth Fallone, "Dept. Store Gal Avers She Likes Cheesecake Straight," *Union Voice* (August 28, 1949), 11; A. L. Schneeweis, "A Militant 'Cheese-Cake' Defender Speaks Up," *Union Voice* (September 11, 1949), 11; Joan A. Schenck, "Save The Cheesecake!" *Union Voice* (September 25, 1949), 11.

41. Norman Goldman, "Says Cheese-cake and Democracy Do Not Mix," *Union Voice* (September 25, 1949), 11.

42. For the pictures printed during the debate, see "Taking Sides," *Union Voice* (August 28, 1949), 11, and "Center of the Storm," *Union Voice* (September 11, 1949), 11. For the decision and the photograph which accompanied it, see "On Cheesecake," *Union Voice* (October 9, 1949), 8.

43. Florence Holt, "Report on Special Problems of Women Members" (April 23–25, 1951), delivered before Divisional Membership Meetings, Local 3, in District 65 Papers, Box 15, Folder 7. Divisional Membership Meetings were meetings where the membership met in separate divisions; at Bloomingdale's, these divisions consisted of office workers, sales workers, and nonsales workers.

44. Bernie Tolkow, "Report to Membership Meeting, Local 1250" (dated January 29, 1951), 1, in District 65 Papers, Box 15, Folder 10. Tolkow was quoting Local 65 leader David Livingston in this passage.

45. Minutes of June Membership Meeting (1951), Local 3, 1–2, in District 65 Papers, Box 15, Folder 7.

46. Murray Silverstein, "Report on Communications" (1951?), 1, in District 65 Papers, Box 15, Folder 7.

47. For Michelson's statements, see Minutes of Local 2 Executive Board Meeting (May 15, 1951), in District 65 Papers, Box 15, Folder 6. For Carnes' statement, see Minutes, Local 1250 Executive Board Meeting (February 5, 1951), 1, in District 65 Papers, Box 15, Folder 10.

48. "NY Locals Concede Failure in Store Organizing Drive," *Women's Wear Daily* (April 13, 1953), 1, 34.

49. "Brooklyn Store Makes Big Noise in New York Market," *Business Week* (December 1, 1951), 48–52; "Loeser Branch in Garden City Leased by A&S," *Women's Wear Daily* (September 20, 1950), 1, 40; "A&S TV Show Begins Oct. 2; Bloomingdale May Follow," *Women's Wear Daily* (September 21, 1950), 43, and "Abraham & Straus Launches Video Series With a New Slant," *Women's Wear Daily* (October 3, 1950), 59. For A&S managers' dedication to the branch stores, see "Advises Stores Tap Suburban Sales Potential," *Women's Wear Daily* (October 4, 1950), 6 and "A&S To Build Large Store in Hempstead," *Women's Wear Daily* (October 13, 1950), 2.

50. For the fair trade laws and the nullification of these laws, see "Individualism Held Returning to Retail Field," *Women's Wear Daily* (May 31, 1951), 1, 64. On the

1951 price war, see "Nation's Stores Plan To Meet Price Cuts; Action Widens in N.Y.," *Women's Wear Daily* (May 31, 1951), 1; Glenn Fowler, "New York Stores Jammed As Price Cuts Continue," *Women's Wear Daily* (June 1, 1951), 1; and "Price Cuts Spreading To Other Sections; Broaden in New York," *Women's Wear Daily* (June 4, 1951), 1; and Glenn Fowler, "A&S Taking Initiative In Price Battle," *Women's Wear Daily* (June 14, 1951), 1, 60.

51. "Loeser Jobs Threatened," *Union Voice* (January 13, 1952), 1, 4. See also "Died: Aged 92," *Business Week* (February 16, 1952), 24.

52. Minutes, District 65 General Council Meeting, Department Store Division (January 9, 1952). See especially Michelson, "Report to General Council on the Wage Drive," District 65 General Council Meeting, Department Store Division (January 9, 1952), 11. For Carnes's comments, see "Loeser Jobs Threatened," *Union Voice* (January 13, 1952), 1, 4.

53. "Severance Pay Upped As Loeser Liquidates," *Union Voice* (February 24, 1952), 3; Samuel Feinberg, "From Where I Sit," *Women's Wear Daily* (March 20, 1953), 51.

54. For the Hearn's concession on Monday nights, see Peter Stein, "report to Local 1250 Membership Meeting" (February 29, 1952), District 65 Papers, Box 15, Folder 16. For the Norton's concession, see Minutes, Norton Membership Meeting (November 20, 1953), in District 65 Papers, Box 15, Folder 22.

55. Minutes of Norton's Chapter Meeting (February 25, 1952), 1, in District 65 Papers, Box 15, Folder 16.

56. Minutes, Local 2 Executive Board Meeting (February 19, 1952), 1–2, in District 65 Papers, Box 15, Folder 13; "Distributive Union May Return to CIO," *Women's Wear Daily* (January 30, 1952), 2; and Glenn Fowler, "Retail Union Takes Stand On DPOWA," *Women's Wear Daily* (February 1, 1952), 51.

57. "Senate Group Charges Reds Hold DPOWA," *Women's Wear Daily* (September 4, 1952), 2, and Carl Andren, "Grand Jury Report," to District 65 General Council, Department Store Section (December 3, 1952), 2. For the CIO's withdrawal of the merger offer, see Murray Silverstein, "Report on Convention," Local 3 Membership Meeting (June 3, 1952), 5, in District 65 Papers, Box 15, Folder 14.

58. For the discussion of not endorsing a candidate in the 1952 election, see "65ers Say: Adlai! Debate on Stevenson Endorsement An Example of Union Democracy," *Union Voice* (October 19, 1952), Section 2, 1. For the final endorsement, see "Livingston Sees Endorsement of Stevenson Aiding '65' Unity," *Union Voice* (October 19, 1952), 5.

59. Catherine Parker, "DPOers Join All Labor in Mourning Death of Phil Murray," *Union Voice* (November 16, 1952), 2.

60. Pete Stein, "Report on Convention," Local 1250 Membership Meeting (May 27, 1952), 6, in District 65 Papers, Box 15, Folder 16.

61. Andren, "Grand Jury Report," 2–7; see also "Livingston Explains Stand at Grand Jury," *Union Voice* (November 30, 1952), 3.

62. Murray Silverstein, "Grand Jury Report" to Local 3 Membership Meeting (April 28, 1952), 1–2, in Box 15, Folder 14, District 65 Papers. "Livingston Answers NLRB Questions," *Union Voice* (December 28, 1952), 4.

63. "Convention Affirms DPOers' Patriotism, Desire for Peace," *Union Voice* (April 19, 1953), 4. "DPO Board's Reply to CIO Pres. Reuther," *Union Voice* (May 17, 1953), 4.

64. Alex H. Kendreck and Jerome Golden, "Lessons of the Struggle Against Opportunism in District 65, I," *Political Affairs* (June 1953), 26, 28, 36–37. This was to be the first of a two-part series; the second article, for reasons which are unclear, was never printed.

65. "Reuther Welcomes DPO," *Union Voice* (May 17, 1953), 3. For the merger, see also "New CIO Move Seeks United Retail Union," *Women's Wear Daily* (April 1, 1953), 1, 58; Hortense Huber, "2 Store Unions Agree to Unify as CIO Group," *Women's Wear Daily* (May 11, 1953), 2.

66. Pete Montanaro, Untitled Report to Local 1250 Membership Meeting (August 19, 1952), 1–3, in District 65 Papers, Box 15, Folder 16. For Hearn's efforts at restructuring, see "Details Given On Shift in Hearns Setup," *Women's Wear Daily* (September 17, 1952), 5; "Hearn's Operations Changing To Nearly 100% Supermarket," *Women's Wear Daily* (September 16, 1952), 1, 47; "Completion of Change-Over at Hearns Cited," *Women's Wear Daily* (July 11, 1950), 1, 42

67. "'Supermarket' Type Operation in Apparel Planned By Lerner's," *Women's Wear Daily* (March 16, 1951), 1, 47; Fred Eichelbaum, "'Highly Satisfactory' Results Reported on Lanes First Day," *Women's Wear Daily* (September 7, 1951), 1, 47.

68. Pete Montanaro, Untitled Report to Local 1250 Membership Meeting (August 19, 1952), 2. See also "Hearn's Operations Changing To Nearly 100% Supermarket," *Women's Wear Daily* (September 16, 1952), 1, 47; "Details Given On Shift in Hearn's Setup," *Women's Wear Daily* (September 17, 1952), 5; and "800 Hearns Store Strikers Solid in 3d Week of Walkout," *Union Voice* (May 31, 1953), 3. For the extra hours, see Pete Stein, Report to Local 1250 Membership Meeting (dated April 29, 1952), 2, District 65 Papers, Box 15, Folder 16.

69. Pete Stein, Report to Local 1250 Membership Meeting (dated April 29, 1952), 2, District 65 Papers, Box 15, Folder 16.

70. "Strike at Hearns 'Imminent,'" *Union Voice* (May 17, 1953), 2.

71. Harry Berlfein, "Sitdown Strike at Hearns Cuts Heavily Into Volume," *Women's Wear Daily* (May 14, 1953), 1, 13.

72. Berlfein, "Sitdown Strike at Hearns Cuts Heavily Into Volume," 1, 13.

73. "All New York Supports Hearn Department Stores," advertisement for Hearn's, *New York Times* (June 5, 1953), 8.

74. For the initial injunction at Hearn's, see "800 Hearns Store Strikers Solid in 3d Week of Walkout," (May 31, 1953), 3. For the reference to Loeser's and store closings, see Berlfein, "Hearns Threatens To Close if Union Action Continues," *Women's Wear Daily* (May 15, 1953), 1, 47 and "Warns Hearns May Fold If Program Fails," *Women's Wear Daily* (July 14, 1953), 1, 16. For the RCIPA's involvement, see "AFL Retail Union Acts to Represent Hearn Workers," *Women's Wear Daily* (June 9, 1953), 4, and "RCIA Withdrawal From Hearns Held Aid to Bargaining," *Women's Wear Daily* (August 31, 1953), 2. For the strike discount, see "'Strike' Price Discount Will End at Hearns," *Women's Wear Daily* (July 10, 1953), 2.

75. "Hearn Strikers Crown Their Queen," *Union Voice* (June 14, 1953), M 2.

76. Lynn Bortnick, untitled photograph of Hearn's strikers, *Union Voice* (June 14, 1953), 5.

77. "The Strike at Hearns," *New York Post* editorial, reprinted in Irving Baldinger, "Hearns vs. the People," *Union Voice* (June 14, 1953), 4; Max Diamond, "Praises N.Y. Post for Stand on Hearn Strike," Letter to *Union Voice* (July 12, 1953), M 3. "Hearns Strike Story on TV!" *Union Voice* (May 31, 1953), M1, and "TV Address by Osman on Hearn Strike," *Union Voice* (May 31, 1953), 4.

78. See Local 3 Executive Board Meeting Minutes (August 10, 1953), District 65 Papers, Box 15, Folder 20, District 65 Papers; "Hearn Strikers Get Support of National CIO," *Women's Wear Daily* (August 21, 1953), 1, 46; and "'65' Set For Summer-Long Strike," *Union Voice* (June 28, 1953), 3.

79. Walter Reuther, "Reuther on Hearns," *Union Voice* (June 28, 1953), 1.

80. "NYC CIO Council Aids Hearn Strike," *Union Voice* (May 31, 1953), 4; "Hearn Strikers Get All-Out CIO Aid," *Union Voice* (June 14, 1953), 2; "Strike Pace Stepped Up; $350,000 Appropriated," *Union Voice* (June 14, 1953), 5.

81. "Lehman Asks Fair Play at Hearns," *Union Voice* (August 23, 1953), 3; John Meegan, "Collective Bargaining and Hearn Strike Report," to Local 2 General Membership Meeting (dated September 29, 1953), 3, District 65 Papers, Box 15, Folder 19.

82. "NAACP Raps Hearn Company; ADA Group Acts," *Union Voice* (June 14, 1953), 5; "Civic Groups Blast Hearn Co. Stand," *Union Voice* (June 28, 1953), 4.

83. For the NLRB's dismissal, see "Union Charges Against Hearns Are Dismissed," *Women's Wear Daily* (July 8, 1953), 1, 69. For the injunction, see "Court Limits Pickets At Hearns; Restrains Violence, Intimidation," *Women's Wear* Daily (July 1, 1953), 6; "Appellate Court Restricts Pickets at Hearns to Three," *Women's Wear Daily* (July 9, 1953), 10; and "All Picketing At Hearns Is Barred By Writ," *Women's Wear Daily* (October 7, 1953), 1, 78. For the defeat at Hearn's, including the injunctions, see Murray Silverstein, "Collective Bargaining Report" to Membership Meeting, Local 3 (November 10, 1953), 1, District 65 Papers, Box 15, Folder 20.

Conclusion

1. Bruce Mohl, "Some May Wonder Who Self-Checkout Serves," *Boston Globe* (March 16, 2003), p. H3; Joseph T. Desmond, "Editorial: Supermarkets' Self-Service Checkout Lanes," *Patriot Ledger* [Quincy, Massachusetts] (May 7, 2003), 20; Julie Hirschfeld Davis, "Self-Scanners Move To Head of Grocery Line," *Baltimore Sun* (September 3, 2002), 1A.

2. Julie Hirschfeld Davis, "Self-Scanners Move To Head of Grocery Line," *Baltimore Sun* (September 3, 2002), 1A.

Bibliography

Archival Collections

Baker Library, Harvard Business School. Cambridge, Massachusetts. Gimbels and Saks. Collection.

Catholic University of America. Washington, D.C. CIO Papers.

Avery Library. Columbia University. New York, NY. Parkchester: Minutes of Meetings—Board of Design.

Library of Congress. Washington, D.C. Manuscript Division, WPA Federal Writers' Project Collection.

Municipal Archives. New York, NY. Fiorello LaGuardia Papers.

Museum of the City of New York. New York, NY. Union Square Vertical Files.

New York Public Library. New York, NY. Picture Collection.

Tamiment Library. New York University. New York, NY. Department Store Strikes and Organizing in the 1930s Collection. District 65 Collection. Local 1-S Collection.

Interviews

Atkinson, William, interviewed by Debra Bernhardt, New York, NY, June 26, 1981. Tape recording. Tamiment Library, New York University.

Fajans, Irving, interviewed by May Swenson, February 1, 1939. Transcript. Federal Writers' Project Collection, Library of Congress.

Haicken, Anne, interviewed by author, Belleair Bluffs, FL, August 4, 2000. Tape recording.

Kirschbaum, Herman, interviewed by B. Hathaway, September 1938–January 1939. Transcript. Federal Writers' Project Collection, Library of Congress.

Kovenetsky, Samuel, interviewed by Deborah Bernhardt, November 6, 1979, December 19, 1979. Transcript. Tamiment Library, New York University.

Meisler, George, interviewed by Debra Bernhardt, New York, NY, December 12, 1979 and December 21, 1979. Transcript. Tamiment Library, New York University.

Mendelssohn, Blanche, interviewed by author, New York, NY, January 13, 2000. Tape recording.

Michelson, Clarina, interviewed by Debra Bernhardt, New York, NY, October 20, 1979.

Michelson, Marcella Loring, interviewed by Debra Bernhardt, New York, NY, June 18, 1980. Transcript. Tamiment Library, New York University.

Michelson, William, interviewed by Debra Bernhardt, New York, NY, January 15, 1981. Tape recording. Tamiment Library, New York University.

O'Neill, John, interviewed by Debra Bernhardt, New York, NY, July 23, 1980. Tape recording. Tamiment Library, New York University.

Papa, Ruth, interviewed by author, January 14, 2001. Notes.

Pinkson, Ruth, interviewed by author, Garret Park, Maryland, March 10, 2000 Tape recording.

Reiss, Gertrude, interviewed by author, Brooklyn, NY, November 30, 2000. Tape recording.

Rosen, Abe, interviewed by Debra Bernhardt, New York, NY, April 21, 1980. Tape recording. Tamiment Library, New York University.

Rubinstein, Annette, interviewed by author, New York, NY, November 13, 2000. Tape recording.

Schwartz, Bea, interviewed by Debra Bernhardt, New York, NY, May 14, 1980 and May 17, 1980. Tape recording. Tamiment Library, New York University.

Spadavecchio, Jane, interviewed by author New York, NY, January 13, 2000. Tape recording.

Stein, Jacob, interviewed by B. Hathaway, December 27, 1938. Transcript. Federal Writers' Project Collection, Library of Congress.

Periodicals

Baltimore Sun

Boston Globe

Business Week

CIO News, Retail Edition

Daily News

Daily Worker

Department Store Economist

Department Store Employee

Dollars & Sense

Dry Goods Economist

Journal of Retailing

Macy Unionizer

Main Floor News

New York Times

New York Review of Books

New York World-Telegram

Newsweek

Office Worker

Patriot Ledger

Readers' Digest

Retail Employee

Retail Wholesale and Department Store Employee

The Nation
The New Republic
Time
Union Voice
Woman Today
Women's Wear Daily
Working Woman

Books and Publications

Abelson, Elaine. *When Ladies Go A-Thieving: Middle-Class Shoplifters in the Victorian Department Store.* Oxford: Oxford University Press, 1989.

Aronowitz, Stanley. "'Which Side Are You On?': Trade Unions in America." *Liberation* 16:7 (1971), 20–41.

———. *False Promises: The Shaping of American Working Class Consciousness.* New York: McGraw-Hill, 1973.

Baker, Helen, and Robert France. *Personnel Administration and Labor Relations in Department Stores: An Analysis of Developments and Practices.* Princeton Industrial Relations Series, No. 81. Princeton, New Jersey, 1950.

Bartels, Andrew H. "The Office of Price Administration and the Legacy of the New Deal, 1939–1946." *Public Historian* 5:3 (Summer 1983), 5–29.

Benson, Susan Porter. *Counter Cultures: Saleswomen, Managers, and Customers in American Department Stores, 1890–1940.* Urbana: University of Illinois Press, 1988.

Bernstein, Irving. *A Caring Society: The New Deal, the Worker, and the Great Depression: A History of the American Worker, 1933–1941.* Boston: Houghton Mifflin, 1985.

———. *Turbulent Years: A History of the American Worker, 1933–41.* Boston: Houghton-Mifflin, 1970.

Blackmar, Elizabeth, and Roy Rosenzweig. *The Park and the People: A History of Central Park.* Ithaca: Cornell University Press, 1992.

Blumberg, Barbara. *The New Deal and the Unemployed: The View from New York City.* Lewisburg: Bucknell University Press, 1979.

Boyer, Paul. *By The Bomb's Early Light: American Thought and Culture at the Dawn of the Atomic Age.* Chapel Hill: University of North Carolina Press, 1994.

Brecher, Jeremy. *Strike!* [Revised and Updated Edition]. Cambridge, MA: South End Press, 1997.

Brown, Michael et al. *New Studies in the Politics and Culture of U.S. Communism.* New York: Monthly Review Press, 1993.

Buhle, Mari Jo, Paul Buhle, and Dan Georgakas, eds. *Encyclopedia of the American Left.* Urbana: University of Illinois Press, 1992.

Cohen, Lizabeth. *A Consumer's Republic: The Politics of Mass Consumption in Postwar America.* New York: Vintage, 2003.

———. *Making a New Deal: Industrial Workers in Chicago, 1919–1939.* Cambridge:

Cambridge University Press, 1990.

Daughters, Charles. *Wells of Discontent.* Daughters, 1937.

Dubofsky, Melvyn. "Not So 'Turbulent Years': Another Look at the American 1930s." *Amerikastudien/American Studies,* 24 (1979), 5–20.

———. *The State and Labor in Modern America.* Chapel Hill: University of North Carolina Press, 1994.

Elias, Stephen N. *Alexander T. Stewart: The Forgotten Merchant Prince.* Westport, CT: Praeger, 1992.

Faue, Elizabeth. *Community of Suffering and Struggle.* Chapel Hill: University of North Carolina Press, 1991.

Feininger, Andreas [text by John von Hartz]. *New York in the Forties.* New York: Dover, 1978.

Fine, Sidney. *Sit-Down: The General Motors Strike of 1936–7.* Ann Arbor: University of Michigan Press, 1969.

Frank, Dana. *Purchasing Power: Consumer Organizing, Gender, and the Seattle Labor Movement, 1919–29.* Cambridge: Cambridge University Press, 1994.

———. "Girl Strikers Occupy Chain Store, Win Big: The Detroit Woolworth's Strike of 1937," in Howard Zinn, Dana Frank, and Robin D. G. Kelley, eds., *Three Strikes: Miners, Musicians, Salesgirls, and the Fighting Spirit of Labor's Last Century* (Boston: Beacon Press, 2001), 57–118.

Fraser, Steven. *Labor Will Rule: Sidney Hillman and the Rise of American Labor.* Ithaca: Cornell University Press, 1991.

Freeman, Joshua. "Delivering the Goods: Industrial Unionism During World War II," *Labor History* 19 (1978), 570–93.

Freeman, Joshua B. *Working-Class New York: Life and Labor since World War II.* New York: The New Press, 2000.

Friedman, Tami J. "The Workers Aren't Nontraditional—But the Strategy Should Be." *Dollars and Sense* (September/October 2002): 8.

Gardner, Erle Stanley [1938]. *The Case of the Shoplifter's Shoe.* Pocket Books, 1965.

Glenn, Susan. *Daughters of the Shtetl: Life and Labor in the Immigrant Generation.* Ithaca, NY: Cornell University Press, 1991.

Gosse, Van. "'To Organize In Every Neighborhood, In Every Home': The Gender Politics of American Communists Between the Wars." *Radical History Review* 50 (1991), 108–41.

Green, James. "Working-Class Militancy in the Depression." *Radical America* 6:6 (1972).

Halper, Albert. *Good-bye, Union Square: A Writer's Memoir of the Thirties.* Chicago: Quadrangle Press, 1970.

Hayden, Dolores. *Redesigning the American Dream: The Future of Housing, Work, and Family Life.* New York: W.W. Norton, 1984.

Hendrickson, Robert. *The Grand Emporiums: The Illustrated History of America's Great Department Stores.* New York: Stein and Day, 1979.

Hower, R. M. *History of Macy's of New York, 1858–1919: Chapters in the Evolution of the Department Store.* Cambridge, MA: Harvard University Press, 1943.

Hurley, Andrew. *Diners, Bowling Alleys, and Trailer Parks: Chasing the American Dream in Postwar Consumer Culture.* New York: Basic Books, 2001.

Hyman, Paula E. *Gender and Assimilation in Modern Jewish History: The Roles and Representation of Women.* Seattle: University of Washington Press, 1995.

Investigation of Communism in New York Distributive Trades, Special Subcommittee of the Committee on Education and Labor, House of Representatives, 80th Congress, Second Session, Pursuant to House Resolution 1111, U.S. Government Printing Office, Washington, D.C., 1948.

Investigation of Seizure of Montgomery Ward & Co.: Hearings Before the Select Committee to Investigate Seizure of Montgomery Ward & Co., House of Representatives, 78th Congress, Second Session, Pursuant To H. Res. 521 (May 22–25, 1944 and June 6–8, 1944). U.S. Government Printing Office, Washington, D.C., 1944.

Isserman, Maurice. *Which Side Were You On?: The American Communist Party during the Second World War.* Urbana: University of Illinois Press, 1993.

Jackson, Kenneth T. *Crabgrass Frontier: The Suburbanization of the United States.* Oxford: Oxford University Press, 1985.

Jackson, Shirley. *The Lottery and Other Stories.* New York: The Modern Library, 2000.

Jacobs, Meg. "How about Some Meat?": The Office of Price Administration, Consumption Politics, and State Building from the Bottom Up, 1941–1946." *Journal of American History* 84:3 (December 1997), 910–41.

Johnpoll, Bernard. *Pacifist's Progress: Norman Thomas and the Decline of American Socialism.* Chicago: Quadrangle, 1970.

Josephson, Matthew. *Infidel in the Temple: A Memoir of the Nineteen-Thirties.* New York: Knopf, 1967.

Kaplan, Judy, and Linn Shapiro, eds. *Red Diapers: Growing Up in the Communist Left.* Urbana: University of Illinois Press, 1998.

Keeran, Roger. *The Communist Party and the Auto Workers Unions.* Bloomington: Indiana University Press, 1980.

Kelley, Robin D. G. *Hammer and Hoe: Alabama Communists during the Great Depression.* Chapel Hill: University of North Carolina Press, 1990.

Kessler-Harris, Alice. *Out To Work: A History of Wage-Earning Women in the United States.* Oxford: Oxford University Press, 1982.

Klehr, Harvey. *The Heyday of American Communism: The Depression Years.* New York: Basic Books, Inc., 1984.

Kraus, Henry. *The Many and the Few.* Los Angeles: Plantin, 1947.

Leach, William. *Land of Desire: Merchants, Power and the Rise of a New American Culture.* New York: Pantheon Books, 1993.

Lebhar, Godfrey M. *Chain Stores in America, 1859–1962.* New York: Chain Store Publishing Company, 1963.

Levine, Susan. "Workers' Wives: Gender, Class, and Consumerism in the 1920's US." *Gender and History* 3, 11 (1991), 45–64.

Lichtenstein, Nelson. *Labor's War at Home: The CIO in World War II.* Cambridge: Cambridge University Press, 1982.

Lipsitz, George. *Rainbow at Midnight: Labor and Culture in the 1940s.* Urbana: University of Illinois Press, 1994.

Lynd, Staughton. "The Possibility of Radicalism in the Early 1930s: The Case of

Steel." *Radical America* 6:6 (1972), 36–65.

Mack, Ruth Prince. *Controlling Retailers: A Study of Cooperation and Control in the Retail Trade with Special Reference to the NRA.* New York: Columbia University Press, 1936.

Martin, Jay. *Nathanael West: The Art of His Life.* New York: Farrar, Straus and Giroux, 1970.

May, Elaine Tyler. *Homeward Bound: American Families in the Cold War Era.* New York: Basic Books, 1988.

May, Martha. "Bread Before Roses: American Workingmen, Labor Unions and the Family Wage," in Ruth Milkman, *Women, Work & Protest: A Century of U.S. Women's Labor History* (London: Routledge, 1985), 1–21.

McBride, Theresa. "A Woman's World: Department Stores and the Evolution of Women's Employment, 1870–1920," *French Historical Studies* 10 (Fall 1978), 664–83.

Meltzer, Milton. *Brother, Can You Spare A Dime?: The Great Depression, 1929–39.* New York: Knopf, 1969.

Milkman, Ruth. *Women, Work & Protest: A Century of U.S. Women's Labor History.* London: Routledge, 1985.

Miller, Michael B. *The Bon Marché: Bourgeois Culture and the Department Store, 1869–1920.* Princeton, NJ: Princeton University Press, 1994.

Minutes of the First National Convention of the UREA held at the Webster Hall Hotel in the City of Pittsburgh.

Morris, Jan. *Manhattan '45.* New York: Oxford University Press, 1986.

Nelson, Bruce. *Divided We Stand: American Workers and the Struggle for Black Equality.* Princeton, NJ: Princeton University Press, 2001.

Ohrbach, Nathan. *Getting Ahead in Retailing.* New York: McGraw-Hill, 1935.

Orleck, Annelise. *Common Sense and a Little Fire.* Chapel Hill, NC: University of North Carolina Press, 1995.

Pasdermadjian, Hans. *The Department Store: Its Origins, Evolution and Economics.* London: Newman Books, 1954.

Piven, Frances Fox, and Richard Cloward. *Poor People's Movements: Why They Succeed, How They Fail* [Paperback Edition]. New York: Vintage Books, 1979.

Plunkett-Powell, Karen. *Remembering Woolworth's: A Nostalgic History of the World's Most Famous Five-and-Dime.* New York: St. Martin's Press, 1999.

Podair, Jerald. *The Strike That Changed New York: Blacks, Whites, and the Ocean Hill-Brownsville Crisis.* New Haven, CT: Yale University Press, 2002.

Proceedings of the Fourth Convention of the Retail Wholesale and Department Store Union, CIO. May 14–18, 1946.

Proceedings—Second Biennial Convention, URWEA. December 11–14, 1939.

Proceedings of the Third Biennial Convention, United Retail, Wholesale, and Department Store Employees of America, CIO, May 18–24, 1942; Chicago, Illinois, 20.

Public Hearing on Cross-Picketing Before the New York State Joint Legislative Committee on Industrial and Labor Conditions. New York: Marshall & Berry, 1941.

Reekie, Gail. *Temptations: Sex, Selling, and the Department Store.* St. Leonards, Australia: Allen & Unwin, 1993.

Rice, Elmer. *Minority Report: An Autobiography.* New York: Simon and Schuster, 1963.

Robinson, O. Preston. *Retail Personnel Relations.* New York: Prentice-Hall, 1940.

The Robinson-Patman Act: Its History and Probable Meaning. Washington, D.C.: The Washington Post, 1936.

Rogin, Michael. "How the Working Class Saved Capitalism: The New Labor History and *The Devil and Miss Jones.*" *The Journal of American History* (June 2002), 87–114.

Schatz, Ron. *The Electrical Workers: A History of Labor at General Electric and Westinghouse, 1923–1960.* Urbana: University of Illinois Press, 1983.

Schrecker, Ellen. *Many Are the Crimes: McCarthyism in America.* Princeton: Princeton University Press, 1998.

Schwartz, Joel. *The New York Approach: Robert Moses, Urban Liberals, and the Redevelopment of the Inner City.* Columbus, OH: The Ohio State University Press, 1993.

Sellars, Nigel Anthony. *Oil, Wheat and Wobblies: The Industrial Workers of the World in Oklahoma, 1905–1930.* Norman: University of Oklahoma Press, 1998.

Sennett, Richard. *The Fall of Public Man.* New York: Knopf, 1976.

Simon, Arthur. *Stuyvesant Town, U.S.A.: Pattern for Two Americas.* New York: New York University Press, 1970.

Staff Report to the Subcommittee on Labor of the Committee on Labor and Public Welfare (United States Senate) on Retail Establishments and the Fair Labor Standards Act. Washington, D.C.: U.S. Government Printing Office, 1956.

Thompson, Tamara. "Patriotism and Protest: The First Hundred Years of Union Square Park." *Columbia Journal of American Studies* 5:1 (2002), 136–64.

Tiersten, Lisa. *Marianne in the Market: Envisioning Consumer Culture in* Fin-de-Siècle *France.* Berkeley: University of California Press, 2001.

Todd, Ellen Wiley. *The "New Woman" Revisited: Painting and Gender Politics on Fourteenth Street.* Berkeley: University of California Press, 1993.

Traub, Marvin. *Like No Other Store . . . : The Bloomingdale's Legend and the Revolution in American Marketing.* New York: Crown, 1993.

Troy, Leo. "Distribution of Union Membership among the States, 1939 and 1953." Occasional Paper 56. New York: National Bureau of Economic Research, Inc., 1957.

Vorse, Mary Heaton. *Labor's New Millions.* New York: Modern Age Books, 1938.

Walkowitz, Daniel. *Working with Class: Social Workers and the Politics of Middle Class Identity.* Chapel Hill: University of North Carolina Press, 1999.

Weigand, Kate. *Red Feminism: American Communism and the Making of Women's Liberation.* Baltimore: Johns Hopkins University Press, 2001.

Wise, Miriam Birge, and Jess P. Lacklen. *Unionization in the Retail Field.* New York: New York University School of Retailing, 1940.

Williams, Rosalind. *Dream Worlds: Mass Consumption in Late Nineteenth Century France.* Berkeley: University of California Press, 1981.

Zim, Larry, Mel Lerner, and Herbert Rolfes. *The World of Tomorrow: The 1939 World's Fair.* New York: Harper and Row, 1988.

Zinn, Howard, Dana Frank, and Robin D. G. Kelley. *Three Strikes: Miners, Musicians, Salesgirls, and the Fighting Spirit of Labor's Last Century.* Boston: Beacon Press, 2001.

Zugsmith, Leane. *A Time to Remember.* New York: Random House, 1936.

Dissertations and Unpublished Manuscripts

Boyd, Charles E. "Early Years of Local 1-S." Undated manuscript in Local 1-S Papers.

Dixler, Elsa Jane. *The Woman Question: Women and the American Communist Party, 1929–1941.* Doctoral Dissertation. Yale University, 1974.

Foner, Henry, and Norman Franklin. *Thursdays Till Nine.* Unpublished manuscript in District 65 Papers.

Overgaard, Andrew. Autobiographical Transcript. Tamiment Library, New York University.

Phillips, Lisa. *The Labor Movement and Black Economic Equality in New York City: District 65, 1934–1954.* Doctoral Dissertation. Rutgers, 2002.

Tillson, Eleanor. "United Storeworkers and RWDSU." Unpublished manuscript, 1982. "RWDSU—Local 3." Vertical File, Tamiment Library.

Ziskind, Minna Pearl. *Citizenship, Consumerism, and Gender: A Study of District 65, 1945–1960.* Doctoral dissertation. University of Pennsylvania, 2001.

Zatinsky, Milton. "Let's Look at Our Union: Its Aims, Activities, and Accomplishments." Pamphlet, October 1945.

Miscellaneous Sources

Rome, Harold. "Chain-Store Daisy," from *Pins And Needles,* Columbia Records, OS 2210.

Thompson, Ken. "Ruminances & Smiles No. 1," *Brooklyn Memories* (October 13, 2003). http://www.brooklynmemories.com/ (accessed June 25, 2005).

"Workers' Newsreel, Unemployment Special, 1931," newsreel footage (New York: The Museum of Modern Art, 198–).

INDEX